A Shakespeare Reader:
Sources and Criticism

Related titles:

Shakespeare: Texts and Contexts   *Edited by Kiernan Ryan*
Shakespeare 1609: *Cymbeline*   *Richard Danson Brown & David Johnson*
   and the *Sonnets*

Shakespeare: Text and Performance

A SHAKESPEARE READER: SOURCES AND CRITICISM

Edited by
Richard Danson Brown
and David Johnson

in association with

This publication forms part of an Open University course: AA306, *Shakespeare: Text and Performance*. Details of this and other Open University courses can be obtained from the Course Reservations Centre, PO Box 724, The Open University, Milton Keynes MK7 6ZS, United Kingdom: tel. +44 (0)1908 653231, e-mail ces-gen@open.ac.uk

Alternatively, you may visit the Open University website at http:// www.open.ac.uk where you can learn more about the wide range of courses and packs offered at all levels by the Open University.

To purchase this publication or other components of Open University courses, contact Open University Worldwide Ltd, The Berrill Building, Walton Hall, Milton Keynes MK7 6AA, United Kingdom: tel. +44 (0)1908 858785; fax +44 (0)1908 858787; e-mail ouwenq@open.ac.uk; website http:// www.ouw.co.uk

 First published in Great Britain 2000 by
Macmillan Press Ltd in association with The Open University

MACMILLAN PRESS LTD
Houndmills, Basingstoke, Hampshire RG21 6XS and London
Companies and representatives throughout the world

The Open University
Walton Hall, Milton Keynes
MK 7 6AA

A catalogue record for this book is available from the British Library.

ISBN 0-333-91314-0 hardcover
ISBN 0-333-91315-9 paperback

First published in the United States of America 2000 by
ST. MARTIN'S PRESS, INC.,
Scholarly and Reference Division,
175 Fifth Avenue, New York, N.Y. 10010

ISBN 0-312-23039-7 (cloth)
ISBN 0-312-23040-0 (paper)
Library of Congress Cataloging-in-Publication Data
A Shakespeare reader: Sources and criticism / edited by Richard Danson Brown and David Johnson.
      p. cm.
   Includes bibliographical references and index.
   ISBN 0-312-23039-7–ISBN 0-312-23040-0 (pbk.)
      1. Shakespeare, William, 1564-1616–Criticism and Interpretation.
   2. Shakespeare, William, 1564-1616–Sources. I. Brown, Richard Danson, 1967 July 23.
   II. Johnson, David, 1962 May 20.
   PR 2976. S3382 2000
   822.3'3–dc21   99-048799

This book is printed on paper suitable for recycling and made from fully managed and sustained forest sources.

10 9 8 7 6 5 4 3 2 1
09 08 07 06 05 04 03 02 01 00

Printed in Great Britain

CONTENTS

Contents

PREFACE

A Shakespeare Reader: Sources and Criticism is the third book in a three-volume series which is designed for the third-level Open University course *Shakespeare: Text and Performance*. *A Shakespeare Reader: Sources and Criticism* is a collection of secondary reading selected to inform critical engagement with nine of Shakespeare's major plays: *A Midsummer Night's Dream, Richard II, Macbeth, Antony and Cleopatra, Hamlet, Twelfth Night, Measure for Measure, King Lear*, and *The Tempest*.

The material in *A Shakespeare Reader: Sources and Criticism* is divided into three parts:

- Part One reprints sources and analogues for the nine plays.
- Part Two reprints competing critical readings of the nine plays, as well as extracts discussing their original theatrical contexts, and the difficulties of editing different textual versions of the plays.
- Part Three reprints critical interventions reflecting on the contested meanings of the key terms in the title of the course: 'Shakespeare', 'Text', and 'Performance'.

A Shakespeare Reader: Sources and Criticism is best read in conjunction with the first two books for the course *Shakespeare: Text and Performance*. The first book in the series, *Shakespeare: Texts and Contexts*, provides detailed critical commentaries on the same nine plays that are the focus of *A Shakespeare Reader: Sources and Criticism*. The second book, *Shakespeare 1609: 'Cymbeline' and 'The Sonnets'*, looks at two texts in the Shakespeare canon that have endured a controversial reception, namely the neglected play, *Cymbeline*, and Shakespeare's *Sonnets*. As such, it throws the Shakespeare canon into clear relief, and suggests important points of comparison for the nine plays studied in the first and third books.

In *A Shakespeare Reader: Sources and Criticism*, we have provided brief introductions to the reprinted extracts, trying in particular to set out the contexts in which they were first published. As *The Norton Shakespeare* (1997) edited by Stephen Greenblatt et al. is the set text for the *Shakespeare: Text and Performance* course, and reprints the widely accepted 1986 Oxford version of *The Collected Works*, we have changed or added act/scene/line references from Shakespeare's plays in all the extracts to coincide with *The Norton Shakespeare*, though we have retained the spelling and punctuation of the original. Finally, we have taken the difficult decision to suppress footnotes and references in the extracts. Faced with the choice of either reprinting the footnotes, or being able to include several more critical voices, we opted for the latter in the belief that our primary audience, undergraduate students, would thus be better served.

Open University courses undergo many stages of drafting and review, and thanks are accordingly due to a number of people for their invaluable contributions to the final product: Lizbeth Goodman and Stephen Regan, who chaired the course for much of its development, and edited the first draft of this Reader; Robert Doubleday and Roberta Wood, who were the course managers; Julie Bennett and Gill Marshall, who were the course editors; Tony Coulson, who was the picture researcher; Pat Phelps, who was the course secretary; and Stephanie Griffin, who provided clerical support.

Richard Danson Brown and David Johnson

Acknowledgements

The editor and publishers wish to thank the following for permission to use copyright material:

C. L. Barber, for material from *Shakespeare's Festive Comedy* (1959), pp. 240–57. Copyright © 1959, renewed © 1985 by Princeton University Press, by permission of Princeton University Press;

Jonathan Bate, for material from *The Genius of Shakespeare* (1997), pp. 187–94, 197–204, 209, by permission of David Godwin Associates on behalf of the author;

Susan Bennett, for material from *Performing Nostagia: Shifting Shakespeare and the Contemporary Past*, Routledge (1996), pp. 12–13, 17–21, 25–6, 18–35, 37, by permission of Taylor & Francis;

G. Bullough, translator, for material from G. B. Giraldi Cinthio, *Hecatommithi* (1583 edition) from G. Bullough (ed.), *Narrative and Dramatic Sources of Shakespeare*, Vol. II, *The Comedies 1597–1603*, Routledge and Kegan Paul (1963), pp. 420–7, 430, by permission of Taylor & Francis;

Neville Davies, for material from 'Jacobean *Antony and Cleopatra*', *Shakespeare Studies*, 17 (1985), pp. 123–58, by permission of the author;

Juliet Dusinberre, for material from 'Squeaking Cleopatras: Gender and Performance in *Antony and Cleopatra*' in James C. Bulman (ed.), *Shakespeare, Theory and Performance*, Routledge (1996), pp. 46, 53–5, 57–62, 64, by permission of Taylor & Francis;

Jay L. Halio, for material from 'The Staging of *A Midsummer Night's Dream*, 1595–1895' in J. M. Mucciola et al. (eds), *Shakespeare's Universe: Renaissance Ideas and Conventions: Essays in Honour of W. R. Elton*, Scolar Press (1996), pp. 158–71, by permission of the author;

Terence Hawkes, for material from *That Shakespeherian Rag: Essays on Critical Process*, Methuen (1986), pp. 92–6, 100–7, 109–12, 114–17, by permission of Taylor & Francis;

Acknowledgements

Jean E. Howard and Phyllis Rackin, for material from *Engendering a Nation: A feminist account of Shakespeare's English histories*, Routledge (1997), pp. 137–52, 155, 157–9, by permission of Taylor & Francis;

Coppélia Kahn, for material from 'The Absent Mother in *King Lear*' in Margaret W. Ferguson et al. (eds), *Rewriting the Renaissance: The Discourses of Sexual Difference in Early Modern Europe*, (1986), pp. 35–45, by permission of University of Chicago Press;

Arnold Kettle, for material from 'From *Hamlet* to *Lear*' from Arnold Kettle (ed.), *Shakespeare in a Changing World* (1964) by permission of Lawrence & Wishart;

L. C. Knights, for material from 'How Many Children had Lady Macbeth?' in *'Hamlet' and Other Shakespearean Essays* (1979), pp. 270, 272–5, 285–91, 293–5, 298–306, by permission of Cambridge University Press;

F. R. Leavis, for material from *The Common Pursuit*, Chatto & Windus (1952), pp. 160–72, by permission of Random House UK and New York University Press;

Alexander Leggatt, for material from 'Grigori Kozintsev's *King Lear*' in *King Lear: Shakespeare in Performance*, Manchester University Press (1991), pp. 79–85, 89, 91–3, by permission of the author;

Ania Loomba, for material from *Gender, Race, Renaissance Drama*, Oxford University Press, India (1992), pp. 124–30, by permission of the author;

Leah S. Marcus, for material from *Puzzling Shakespeare: Local Reading and its Discontents*, University of California Press (1988), pp. 171–82, by permission of the author;

Louis Montrose, for material from *The Purpose of Playing: Shakespeare and the Cultural Politics of the Elizabethan Theatre* (1996), pp. 151–4, 158–61, 167–78, by permission of University of Chicago Press;

Joseph Pequigney, for material from 'The Two Antonios and Same-sex love in *Twelfth Night* and *The Merchant of Venice*', *English Literary Renaissance*, 22 (1992), pp. 201–21, by permission of English Literary Renaissance;

Rob Nixon, for material from 'African and Caribbean Appropriations of *The Tempest*', *Critical Inquiry*, 13 (1987), pp. 557–67, 570–4, 576–8, by permission of University of Chicago Press;

David Norbrook, for material from ' "What Cares These Roarers for the Name of the King?": Language and Utopia in *The Tempest*' in K. Ryan (ed.), *Shakespeare: The Last Plays*, Longman (1999), pp. 246–52, 258–62, by permission of Pearson Education Ltd;

Stephen Orgel, for 'What is an Editor?', *Shakespeare Studies*, 24 (1996), pp. 23–9, by permission of Associated University Presses;

E. Pearlman, for material from '*Macbeth* on Film: Politics', in S. Wells (ed.), *Shakespeare Survey*, 39 (1987), pp. 67–74, by permission of Cambridge University Press;

Jacqueline Rose, for material from 'Hamlet – the *Mona Lisa* of Literature' in D. B. Barker and I. Kamps (eds), *Shakespeare and Gender: A History*, Verso (1995), pp. 104–14, 116–17, by permission of the author;

Alan Sinfield, for material from *Faultlines: Cultural Materialism and the Politics of Dissident Reading* (1992), pp. 95–108. Copyright © 1992 The Regents of the University of California, by permission of Oxford University Press and University of California Press;

Gary Taylor, for material from *Reinventing Shakespeare: A Cultural History from the Restoration to the Present*, Hogarth Press (1989), pp. 311–18, by permission of the author;

Robert Weimann, for material from 'The Elizabethan Drama' in R. Schwartz (ed.), *Shakespeare and the Popular Tradition in the Theater: Studies in the Social Dimension of Dramatic Form and Function* (1978), pp. 161–3, 165–6, 168–74, by permission of The Johns Hopkins University Press.

Every effort has been made to trace the copyright holders but if any have been inadvertently overlooked the publishers will be pleased to make the necessary arrangement at the first opportunity.

ILLUSTRATIONS

Part 1

SOURCES AND ANALOGUES

Introduction and Headnotes

Introduction

In Part One we reprint some of the source materials and literary analogues Shakespeare drew on in writing these plays. These are intended both to give a sense of the literary culture Shakespeare was working in during the 1590s and 1600s, and to facilitate comparisons between Shakespeare's reading and the play scripts he wrote. In selecting these extracts, rather than going for the most obvious sources for every play, we have tried to include writings from a wide range of genres that Shakespeare might have used. Don't worry if you come across unfamiliar words or spellings of words; you should not try to read these extracts in the same way that you would a Shakespeare play. Rather, you should try to get a sense of the narrative excitement Shakespeare found in these texts.

1 *A Midsummer Night's Dream*

1.1 *From Reginald Scot,* The Discoverie of Witchcraft *(1584)*

Source: G. Bullough (ed.), *Narrative and Dramatic Sources of Shakespeare*, Volume I: *Early Comedies, Poems, Romeo and Juliet* (London: Routledge and Kegan Paul, 1964), pp. 395–7.

Scot's (*c.* 1538–99) work is a long and detailed rejection of the beliefs of contemporaneous demonologists, who asserted the reality of such things as witchcraft and fairies. In the course of attempting to demolish these ideas, Scot gives much invaluable information about early modern ideas of magic and witchcraft. In these extracts, Scot ridicules the popular belief in Robin Goodfellow and a whole range of other fantastical creatures. It is interesting to compare Scot's attitude to fairies with that exhibited in *A Midsummer Night's Dream*.

Book VII. Chapter II

[Robin Goodfellow is not now much believed in.]

And know you this by the waie, that heretofore Robin goodfellow, and Hob gobblin were as terrible, and also as credible to the people, as hags and witches be now: and in time to come, a witch will be as much derided and contemned, and as plainlie perceived, as the illusion and knaverie of Robin goodfellow. And in truth, they that mainteine walking spirits, with their transformation, &c: have no reason to denie Robin goodfellow, upon whom there hath gone as manie and as credible tales, as upon witches; saving that it hath not pleased the translators of the Bible, to call spirits by the name of Robin goodfellow, as they have termed divinors, soothsaiers, poisoners, and couseners by the name of witches.

Booke VII. Chapter XV

Of vaine apparitions, how people have beene brought to feare bugges, which is partlie reformed by preaching of the gospell, the true effect of Christes miracles

But certeinlie, some one knave in a white sheete hath cousened and abused manie thousands that waie; speciallie when Robin good-fellow kept such a coile in the countrie. But you shall understand, that these bugs speciallie are spied and feared of sicke folke, children, women, and cowards, which through weaknesse of mind and bodie, are shaken with vaine dreames and continuall feare. The *Scythians*, being a stout and a warlike nation (as divers writers report) never see anie vaine sights or spirits. It is a common saieng; A lion feareth no bugs. But in our childhood our mothers maids have so terrified us with an ouglie divell having hornes on his head, fier in his mouth, and a taile in his breech, eies like a bason, fanges like a dog, clawes like a beare, a skin like a Niger, and a voice roring like a lion, whereby we start and are afraid when we heare one crie Bough: and they have so fraied us with bull beggers, spirits, witches, urchens, elves, hags, fairies, satyrs, pans, faunes, sylens, kit with the cansticke, tritons, centaurs, dwarfes, giants, imps, calcars, conjurors, nymphes, changlings, *Incubus*, Robin good-fellowe, the spoorne, the mare, the man in the oke, the hell waine, the fierdrake, the puckle, Tom thombe, hob gobblin, Tom tumbler, boneles, and such other bugs, that we are afraid of our owne shadowes: in so much as some never feare the divell, but in a darke night; and then a polled sheepe is a perillous beast, and manie times is taken for our fathers soule, speciallie in a churchyard, where a right hardie man heretofore scant durst passe by night, but his haire would stand upright. For right grave writers report, that spirits most often and speciallie take the shape of women appearing to monks, &c: and of beasts, dogs, swine, horsses, gotes, cats, hairs; of fowles, as crowes, night owles, and shreeke owles; but they delight most in the likenes of snakes and dragons. Well, thanks be to God, this wretched and cowardlie infidelitie, since the preaching of the gospell, is in part forgotten: and doubtles, the rest of those illusions will in short time (by Gods grace) be detected and vanish awaie.

1.2 From Ovid, Metamorphoses, *translated by* Arthur Golding *(1567), Book IV, pp. 67–201*

Source: G. Bullough (ed.), *Narrative and Dramatic Sources of Shakespeare*, Volume I: *Early Comedies, Poems, Romeo and Juliet* (London: Routledge and Kegan Paul, 1964), pp. 405–9.

Ovid's (43 BCE–c. 17 CE) long Roman poem was one of Shakespeare's favourite books; it was a source he frequently drew on in both drama and poetry (see for example the 1593 narrative poem *Venus and Adonis*). The *Metamorphoses* is a witty and digressive redaction of a great range of classical myths, unified by its concern with stories in which people change from one state or body to another. Though he would have been able to read the Latin original, Shakespeare also drew on Arthur Golding's accurate translation of 1567. This example is the source for the Pyramus and Thisbe narrative staged by Bottom and his friends in *A Midsummer Night's Dream*.

PYRAMUS AND THISBE

Within the towne [. . .]
Dwelt hard together two young folke in houses joynde so nere
That under all one roofe well nie both twaine conveyed were.
The name of him was *Pyramus*, and *Thisbe* calde was she.
So faire a man in all the East was none alive as he,
Nor nere a woman maide nor wife in beautie like to hir.
This neighbrod bred acquaintance first, this neyghbrod first did stirre
The secret sparkes, this neighbrod first an entrance in did showe,
For love to come to that to which it afterward did growe.
And if that right had taken place, they had bene man and wife,
But still their Parents went about to let which (for their life)
They could not let. For both their heartes with equall flame did burne.
No man was privie to their thoughts. And for to serve their turne

In steade of talke they used signes: the closelier they supprest
The fire of love, the fiercer still it raged in their brest.
The wall that parted house from house had riven therein a crany
Which shronke at making of the wall. This fault not markt of any
Of many hundred yeares before (what doth not love espie?)
These lovers first of all found out, and made a way whereby
To talke togither secretly, and through the same did goe
Their loving whisprings verie light and safely to and fro.
Now as at oneside *Pyramus* and *Thisbe* on the tother
Stoode often drawing one of them the pleasant breath from other,
O thou envious wall (they sayd), why letst thou lovers thus?
What matter were it if that thou permitted both of us
In armes eche other to embrace? Or if thou thinke that this
Were overmuch, yet mightest thou at least make roume to kisse.
And yet thou shalt not finde us churles: we thinke our selves in det
For the same piece of courtesie, in vouching safe to let
Our sayings to our friendly eares thus freely come and goe.
Thus having where they stoode in vaine complayned of their woe,
When night drew nere, they bade adew and eche gave kisses sweete
Unto the parget on their side, the which did never meete.
Next morning with hir cherefull light had driven the starres aside
And *Phebus* with his burning beames the dewie grasse had dride.
These lovers at their wonted place by foreappointment met.
Where after much complaint and mone they covenanted to get
Away from such as watched them, and in the Evening late
To steale out of their fathers house and eke the Citie gate.
And to thentent that in the feeldes they strayde not up and downe,
They did agree at *Ninus* Tumb to meete without the towne,
And tarie underneath a tree that by the same did grow
Which was a faire high Mulberie with fruite as white as snow,
Hard by a coole and trickling spring. This bargaine pleasde them both,
And so daylight (which to their thought away but slowly goth)
Did in the Ocean fall to rest: and night from thence doth rise.
Assoone as darkenesse once was come, straight *Thisbe* did devise
A shift to wind hir out of doores, that none that were within
Perceyved hir: And muffling hir with clothes about hir chin,
That no man might discerne hir face, to *Ninus* Tumb she came
Unto the tree, and sat hir downe there underneath the same.
Love made hir bold. But see the chaunce, there comes besmerde with blood
About the chappes a Lionesse all foming from the wood,
From slaughter lately made of kine, to staunch hir bloudie thurst
With water of the foresaid spring. Whome *Thisbe* spying furst
Afarre by moonelight, thereupon with fearfull steppes gan flie,
And in a darke and yrksome cave did hide hirselfe thereby.
And as she fled away for hast she let hir mantle fall
The whych for feare she left behind not looking backe at all.
Now when the cruell Lionesse hir thurst had stanched well,
In going to the Wood she found the slender weede that fell
From *Thisbe*, which with bloudie teeth in pieces she did teare.
The night was somewhat further spent ere *Pyramus* came there:

Who seeing in this suttle sande the print of Lions paw,
Waxt pale for feare, But when also the bloudie cloke he saw
All rent and torne, one night (he sayd) shall lovers two confounde,
Of which long life deserved she of all that live on ground.
My soule deserves of this mischaunce the perill for to beare.
I wretch have bene the death of thee, which to this place of feare
Did cause thee in the night to come, and came not here before.
My wicked limmes and wretched guttes with cruell teeth therfore
Devour ye O ye Lions all that in this rocke doe dwell.
But Cowardes use to wish for death. The slender weede that fell
From *Thisbe* up he takes, and streight doth beare it to the tree,
Which was appointed erst the place of meeting for to bee.
And when he had bewept and kist the garment which he knew,
Receyve thou my bloud too (quoth he) and therewithall he drew,
His sworde, the which among his guttes he thrust, and by and by ⎫
Did draw it from the bleeding wound beginning for to die, ⎬
And caste himselfe upon his backe. The bloud did spin on hie ⎭
As when a Conduite pipe is crackt, the water bursting out
Doth shote itselfe a great way off and pierce the Ayre about.
The leaves that were upon the tree besprincled with his blood
Were dyed blacke. The roote also bestained as it stoode,
A deepe darke purple colour straight upon the Berries cast. ⎫
Anon scarce ridded of hir feare with which she was agast, ⎬
For doubt of disapointing him commes *Thisbe* forth in hast, ⎭
And for hir lover lookes about, rejoycing for to tell
How hardly she had scapt that night the daunger that befell.
And as she knew right well the place and facion of the tree
(As whych she saw so late before:) even so when she did see
The colour of the Berries turnde, shee was uncertaine whither
It were the tree at which they both agreed to meete togither.
While in this doubtfull stounde she stood, shee cast hir eye aside
And there beweltred in his bloud hir lover she espide
Lie sprawling with his dying limmes: at which she started backe,
And looked pale as any Box, a shuddring through hir stracke,
Even like the Sea which sodenly with whissing noyse doth move, ⎫
When with a little blast of winde it is but toucht above. ⎬
But when approching nearer him she knew it was hir love, ⎭
She beate hir brest, she shricked out, she tare hir golden heares,
And taking him betweene hir armes did wash his wounds with teares.
She meynt hir weeping with his bloud, and kissing all his face
(Which now became as colde as yse) she cride in wofull case
Alas what chaunce my *Pyramus* hath parted thee and mee?
Make aunswere O my *Pyramus*: It is thy *Thisb*, even shee
Whome thou doste love most heartely that speaketh unto thee.
Give eare and rayse thy heavie heade. He hearing *Thisbes* name,
Lift up his dying eyes, and having seene hir closde the same.
But when she knew hir mantle there and saw his scabberd lie

Without the swoorde: Unhappy man thy love hath made thee die:
Thy love (she said) hath made thee slea thy selfe. This hand of mine
Is strong inough to doe the like. My love no lesse than thine
Shall give me force to worke my wound. I will pursue the dead.
And wretched woman as I am, it shall of me be sed
That like as of thy death I was the only cause and blame,
So am I thy companion eke and partner in the same.
For death which only coulde alas a sunder part us twaine,
Shall never so dissever us but we will meete againe.
And you the Parentes of us both, most wretched folke alyve,
Let this request that I shall make in both our names bylive,
Entreate you to permit that we whome chaste and stedfast love
And whome even death hath joynde in one, may as it doth behove
In one grave be together layd. And thou unhappie tree
Which shroudest now the corse of one, and shalt anon through mee
Shroude two, of this same slaughter holde the sicker signes for ay. ⎫
Blacke be the colour of thy fruite and mourninglike alway,   ⎬
Such as the murder of us twaine may evermore bewray.   ⎭
This said, she tooke the sword yet warme with slaughter of hir love
And setting it beneath hir brest, did too hir heart it shove.
Hir prayer with the Gods and with their Parentes tooke effect.
For when the frute is throughly ripe, the Berrie is bespect
With colour tending to a blacke. And that which after fire
Remained, rested in one Tumbe as *Thisbe* did desire.

2 *Richard II*

From *A Myrroure for Magistrates* (1559)

'How kyng Richarde the seconde was for his evyll governaunce deposed from his seat, and miserably murdred in prison'

Source: G. Bullough (ed.), *Narrative and Dramatic Sources of Shakespeare*, Volume III: *Earlier English History Plays: Henry VI, Richard III, Richard II* (London: Routledge and Kegan Paul, 1960), pp. 419–22.

A Myrroure for Magistrates was an extremely influential collection of political and moral counsels addressed to governors and monarchs ('Magistrates') which aimed to provide them with a 'Mirror' of behaviours and practices they should avoid. A *Myrroure* was the product of a coterie of literary figures centring around the editor, William Baldwin. Written in the form of poetic monologues by dead kings and notable figures from history, these texts were widely read and helped to inform Shakespeare's history plays. In this poem, Richard II gives a moralizing account of his fall from power. Compare it with Shakespeare's dramatic treatment of the same events.

I would (quoth one of the cumpany) gladly say sumwhat for king Richard [...] I will in the kinges behalfe recount such part of his story as I thinke most necessary. And therfore imagine *Baldwin* that you see him al to be mangled, with blew woundes, lying pale and wanne al naked upon the cold stones in Paules church, the people standing round about him, and making his mone in this sort.

> Howe kyng Richarde the seconde
> was for his evyll governaunce
> deposed from his seat, and
> miserably murdred
> in prison.

Happy is the prince that hath in welth the grace
To folowe vertue, keping vices under,
But wo to him whose will hath wisedomes place:
For who so renteth ryght and law a sunder
On him at length loe, al the world shall wunder,
Hygh byrth, choyse fortune, force, nor Princely mace
Can warrant King or Keysar fro the case,
Shame sueth sinne, as rayne drops do the thunder.
Let Princes therfore vertuous life embrace
That wilfull pleasures cause them not to blunder.   10

   Beholde my hap, see how the sely route
Do gase upon me, and eche to other saye:
Se where he lieth for whome none late might route,
Loe howe the power, the pride, and riche aray
Of myghty rulers lightly fade away.
The Kyng whych erst kept all the realme in doute,
The veryest rascall now dare checke and lowte:
What moulde be Kynges made of, but carayn clay?
Beholde his woundes, howe blew they be about,
Whych whyle he lived, thought never to decay.   20

   Me thinke I heare the people thus devise:
And therfore Baldwin sith thou wilt declare
How princes fell, to make the living wise,
My vicious story in no poynt see thou spare,
But paynt it out, that rulers may beware
Good counsayle, lawe, or vertue to despyse.
For realmes have rules, and rulers have a syse,
Which if they kepe not, doubtless say I dare
That eythers gryefes the other shall agrise
Till the one be lost, the other brought to care.   30

I am a Kyng that ruled all by lust,
That forced not of vertue, ryght, or lawe,
But always put false Flatterers most in trust,
Ensuing such as could my vices clawe:
By faythful counsayle passing not a strawe.
What pleasure pryckt, that thought I to be just.
I set my minde, to feede, to spoyle, to just,
Three meales a day could skarce content my mawe,
And all to augment my lecherous minde that must
To Venus pleasures alway be in awe.   40

For mayntenaunce wherof, my realme I polde
Through Subsidies, sore fines, loanes, many a prest,
Blanke charters, othes, & shiftes not knowen of olde,
For whych my Subjectes did me sore detest.
I also made away the towne of Brest,
My fault wherin because mine uncle tolde
(For Prynces vyces may not be controlde)
I found the meanes his bowels to unbrest.
The Piers and Lordes that did his cause uphold,
With death, exile, or grevous fines opprest.   50

Neyther lakt I ayde in any wicked dede,
For gaping Gulles whom I promoted had
Woulde furder all in hope of higher mede.
A king can never imagine ought so bad
But most about him will perfourme it glad
For sickenes seldeme doth so swiftely brede
As vicious humors growe the griefe to feede.
Thus kinges estates of all be wurst bastad,
Abusde in welth, abandoned at nede,
And nerest harme whan they be least adrad.   60

My life and death the truth of this can trye:
For while I fought in Ireland with my foes,
Mine uncle Edmunde whom I left to gide
My realme at home, right traytrously arose
To helpe the Percies plying my depose,
And cald fro Fraunce Erle Bolenbroke, whom I
Condemned ten yeres in exyle to lye:
Who cruelly did put to death all those
That in myne ayde durst looke but once awry,
Whose number was but slender I suppose.   70

For whan I was cum back this stur to stay,
The Erle of Worcester whom I trusted moste
(Whiles we in Wales at Flint our castell lay
Both to refresh and multiply mine oste)
Did in my hall in sight of least and moste
Bebreake his staffe, my houshold office stay,

Bad eche man shifte, and rode him selfe away.
See princes, see the power whereof we boste,
Whome most we trust, at nede do us betray,
Through whose false faith my land and life I lost.　　　　　80

　For whan my trayterous Stuard thus was goen,
My servauntes shranke away on every side,
That caught I was, and caryed to my foen:
Who for theyr prince a prison dyd provide,
And therin kept me, til duke Henryes pride
Dyd cause me yeld him up my crowne and throne.
Whych shortly made my frendly foes to grone:
For Henry seing in me their falshode tryde
Abhorde them all, and would be rulde by none,
For whych they sought to stoppe him strayt a tyde.　　　　　90

　The chiefe conspirde by death to drive him down,
For which exployte, a solemne othe they swore
To render me my libertie and crown,
Wherof them selves deprived me before.
But salves helpe seeld an overlong suffred sore.
To stoppe the brech no boote to runne or rowne
When swelling fluds have overflowen the town:
Til sailes be spred the ship may kepe the shore.
The Ankers wayed, though al the frayte do frowne,
With streame and steere perforce it shalbe bore.　　　　　100

　For though the piers set Henry in his state,
Yet could they not displace him thence agayne:
And where they easily put me downe of late,
They could restore me by no maner payne:
Thinges hardly mende, but may be mard amayne.
And when a man is falne in froward fate
Still mischeves light one in anothers pate:
And wel meant meanes his mishaps to restraine
Waxe wretched mones, wherby his joyes abate.
Due proofe wherof in me appreth playne.　　　　　110

　For whan king Henry knew that for my cause
His lordes in maske would kil him if they might,
To dash all dowtes, he tooke no farther pause
But sent sir Pierce of Exton a traytrous knight
To Pomfret Castell, with other armed light,
Who causeles kild me there agaynst all lawes.
Thus lawles life, to lawles deth ey drawes.
Wherfore byd Kynges be rulde and rule by right,
Who wurketh his wil, & shunneth wisedomes sawes
In flateries clawes, & shames foule pawes shal light.　　　　　120

3 *Macbeth*

From Raphael Holinshed, Chronicles (1587 edn)

Source: G. Bullough (ed.), *Narrative and Dramatic Sources of Shakespeare*, Volume VII: *Major Tragedies: Hamlet, Othello, King Lear, Macbeth* (London: Routledge and Kegan Paul, 1973), pp. 494–506.

The major narrative source for *Macbeth* is Raphael Holinshed's *Chronicles of England, Scotland, and Ireland*. Holinshed's work was an important text for Shakespeare: he drew on it for the History plays, as well as later plays like *King Lear*. Holinshed died in about 1580, two years after the first two-volume edition of his work appeared; the three-volume 1587 edition is in fact, like *A Myrroure for Magistrates*, the work of a committee of writers who collected, edited and revised an enormous body of historical sources into a coherent narrative. We reprint most of Holinshed's account of Macbeth's reign to give a sense of how Shakespeare reworked his source text. You could compare Holinshed's balanced account of Macbeth's reign with Shakespeare's more schematic presentation in *Macbeth*, Acts 3 and 4.

It fortuned as Makbeth and Banquho journied towards Fores, where the king then laie, they went sporting by the waie togither without other companie, save onelie themselves, passing thorough the woods and fields, when suddenlie in the middest of a laund, there met them three

Figure 1 *Macbeth and Banquo accosted by the weird sisters*
Reproduced by permission of the Trustees of the National Library of Scotland

women in strange and wild apparell, resembling creatures of elder world, whome when they attentivelie beheld, woondering much at the sight, the first of them spake and said; All haile Makbeth, thane of Glammis (for he had latelie entered into that dignitie and office by the death of his father Sinell.) The second of them said; Haile Makbeth thane of Cawder. But the third said; All haile Makbeth that heereafter shalt be king of Scotland.

Then Banquho; What manner of women (saith he) are you, that seeme so little favourable unto me, whereas to my fellow heere, besides high offices, ye assigne also the kingdome, appointing foorth nothing for me at all? Yes (saith the first of them) we promise greater benefits untos thee, than unto him, for he shall reigne in deed, but with an unluckie end: neither shall he leave anie issue behind him to succeed in his place, where contrarilie thou in deed shalt not reigne at all, but of thee those shall be borne which shall govern the Scottish kingdome by long order of continuall descent. Herewith the foresaid women vanished immediatlie out of their sight. This was reputed at the first but some vaine fantasticall illusion by Mackbeth and Banquho, insomuch that Banquho would call Mackbeth in jest, king of Scotland; and Mackbeth againe would call him in sport likewise, the father of manie kings. But afterwards the common opinion was, that these women were either the weird sisters, that is [...] the goddesses of destinie, or else some nymphs or feiries, indued with knowledge of prophesie by their necromanticall science, bicause everie thing came to passe as they had spoken. For shortlie after, the thane of Cawder being condemned at Fores of treason against the king committed; his lands, livings, and offices were given of the kings liberalitie to Mackbeth.

The same night after, at supper, Banquho jested with him and said; Now Mackbeth thou hast obteined those things which the two former sisters prophesied, there remaineth onelie for thee to purchase that which the third said should come to passe. Whereupon Mackbeth revolving the thing in his mind, began even then to devise how he might atteine to the kingdome: but yet he thought with himselfe that he must tarie a time, which should advance him thereto (by the divine providence) as it had come to passe in his former preferment. But shortlie after it chanced that king Duncane, having two sonnes by his wife which was the daughter of Siward earle of Northumberland, he made the elder of them called Malcolme prince of Cumberland, as it were thereby to appoint him his successor in the kingdome, immediatlie after his deceasse. Mackbeth sore troubled herewith, for that he saw by this means his hope sore hindered (where, by the old lawes of the realme, the ordinance was, that if he that should succeed were not of able age to take the charge upon himselfe, he that was next of bloud unto him should be admitted) he began to take counsell how he might usurpe the kingdome by force, having a just quarell so to doo (as he tooke the matter) for that Duncane did what in him lay to defraud him of all maner of title and claime, which he might in time to come, pretend unto the crowne.

The woords of the three weird sisters also (of whom before ye have heard) greatlie incouraged him hereunto, but speciallie his wife lay sore upon him to attempt the thing, as she that was verie ambitious, burning in unquenchable desire to beare the name of a queene. At length therefore, communicating his purposed intent with his trustie friends, amongst whome Banquho was the chiefest, upon confidence of their promised aid, he slue the king at Enverns, or (as some say) at Botgosuane, in the sixt yeare of his reigne. Then having a companie about him of such as he had made privie to his enterprise, he caused himselfe to be proclaimed king, and foorthwith went unto Scone, where (by common consent) he received the investure of the kingdome according to the accustomed maner. The bodie of Duncane was first conveied unto Elgine, & there buried in kinglie wise; but afterwards it was removed and conveied unto Colmekill, and there laid in a sepulture amongst his predecessors, in the yeare after the birth of our Saviour, 1046.

Malcolme Cammore and Donald Bane the sons of king Duncane, for feare of their lives (which they might well know that Mackbeth would seeke to bring to end for his more sure confirmation in the estate) fled into Cumberland, where Malcolme remained, till time that saint Edward the sonne of Etheldred recovered the dominion of England from the Danish power, the which Edward received Malcolme by way of most friendlie enterteinment: but Donald passed over into Ireland, where he was tenderlie cherished by the king of that land. Mackbeth, after the departure thus of Duncanes sonnes, used great liberalitie towards the nobles of the

Figure 2 *Macbeth is crowned*
Reproduced by permission of the Trustees of the National Library of Scotland

realme, thereby to win their favour, and when he saw that no man went about to trouble him, he set his whole intention to mainteine justice, and to punish all enormities and abuses, which had chanced through the feeble and slouthfull administration of Duncane. [Macbeth punished murderers sternly] in such sort, that manie yeares after all theft and reiffings were little heard of, the people injoieng the blissefull benefit of good peace and tranquillitie. Mackbeth... was accounted the sure defense and buckler of innocent people; and hereto he also applied his whole indevor, to cause young men to exercise themselves in vertuous maners, and men of the church to attend their divine service according to their vocations ... He made manie holesome laws and statutes for the publike weale of his subjects. [...]

These and the like commendable lawes Makbeth caused to be put as then in use, governing the realme for the space of ten yeares in equall justice. But this was but a counterfet zeale of equitie shewed by him, partlie against his naturall inclination to purchase thereby the favour of the people. Shortlie after, he began to shew what he was, in stead of equitie practising crueltie. For the pricke of conscience (as it chanceth ever in tyrants, and such as atteine to anie estate by unrighteous means) caused him ever to feare, least he should be served of the same cup as he had ministred to his predecessor. The woords also of the three weird sisters, would not out of his mind, which as they promised him the kingdome, so likewise did they promise it at the same time unto the posteritie of Banquho. He willed therefore the same Banquho with his sonne named Fleance, to come to a supper that he had prepared for them, which was in deed, as he had devised, present death at the hands of certeine murderers, whom he hired to execute that deed, appointing them to meete with the same Banquho and his sonne without the palace, as they returned to their lodgings, and there to slea them, so that he would not have his house slandered, but that in time to come he might cleare himselfe, if anie thing were laid to his charge upon anie suspicion that might arise.

It chanced yet by the benefit of the darke night, that though the father were slaine, the sonne yet by the helpe of almightie God reserving him to better fortune, escaped that danger: and afterwards having some inkeling [...] how his life was sought no lesse than his fathers, who was slaine not by chancemedlie (as by the handling of the matter Makbeth woould have had it to appeare) but even upon a prepensed devise: whereupon to avoid further perill he fled into Wales. [...]

But to returne unto Makbeth, [...] ye shall understand that after the contrived slaughter of Banquho, nothing prospered with the foresaid Makbeth: for in maner everie man began to doubt his owne life, and durst unneth appeare in the kings presence; and even as there were manie that stood in feare of him, so likewise stood he in feare of manie, in such sort that he began to make those awaie by one surmised cavillation or other, whome he thought most able to worke him anie displeasure.

At length he found such sweetnesse by putting his nobles thus to death, that his earnest thirst after bloud in this behalfe might in no wise be satisfied: for ye must consider he wan double profite (as hee thought) hereby: for first they were rid out of the way whome he feared, and then againe his coffers were inriched by their goods which were forfeited to his use, whereby he might the better mainteine a gard of armed men about him to defend his person from injurie of them whom he had in anie suspicion. Further, to the end he might the more cruellie oppresse his subjects with all tyrant like wrongs, he builded a strong castell on the top of an hie hill called Dunsinane, situate in Gowrie, ten miles from Perth, on such a proud height, that standing there aloft, a man might behold well neere all the countries of Angus, Fife, Stermond, and Ernedale, as it were lieng underneath him. This castell then being founded on the top of that high hill, put the realme to great charges before it was finished, for all the stuffe necessarie to the building, could not be brought up without much toile and businesse. But Makbeth being once determined to have the worke go forward, caused the thanes of each shire within the realme, to come and helpe towards that building, each man his course about.

At the last, when the turne fell unto Makduffe thane of Fife to build his part, he sent workemen with all needfull provision, and commanded them to shew such diligence in everie behalfe, that no occasion might bee given for the king to find fault with him, in that he came not himselfe as other had doone, which he refused to doo, for doubt least the king bearing him (as he partlie understood) no great good will, would laie violent handes upon him, as he had doone upon diverse other. Shortly after, Makbeth comming to behold how the worke went forward, and bicause he found not Makduffe there, he was sore offended, and said; I perceive this man will never obeie my commandements, till he be ridden with a snaffle: but I shall provide well inough for him. Neither could he afterwards abide to looke upon the said Makduffe, either for that he thought his puissance over great; either else for that he had learned of certeine wizzards, in whose words he put great confidence (for that the prophesie had happened so right, which the three fairies or weird sisters had declared unto him) how that he ought to take heed of Makduffe, who in time to come should seeke to destroie him.

And suerlie hereupon had he put Makduffe to death, but that a certeine witch, whome hee had in great trust, had told that he should never be slaine with man borne of anie woman, nor vanquished till the wood or Bernane came to the castell of Dunsinane. By this prophesie Makbeth put all feare out of his heart, supposing he might doo what he would, without anie feare to be punished for the same, for by the one prophesie he beleeved it was unpossible for anie man to vanquish him, and by the other unpossible to slea him. This vaine hope caused him to doo manie outragious things, to the greevous oppression of his subjects. At length Makduffe, to avoid perill of life, purposed with himselfe to passe into England, to procure Malcolme Cammore to claime the crowne of Scotland. But this was not so secretlie devised by Makduffe, but that Makbeth had knowledge given him thereof: for kings (as is said) have sharpe sight like unto Lynx, and long ears like unto Midas. For Makbeth had in everie noble mans house one slie fellow or other in fee with him, to reveale all that was said or doone within the same, by which slight he oppressed the most part of the nobles of his realme.

Immediatlie then, being advertised whereabout Makduffe went, he came hastilie with a great power into Fife, and foorthwith besieged the castell where Makduffe dwelled, trusting to have found him therein. They that kept the house, without anie resistance opened the gates, and suffered him to enter, mistrusting none evill. But neverthelesse Makbeth most cruellie caused the wife and children of Makduffe, with all other whom he found in that castell, to be slaine. Also he confiscated the goods of Makduffe, proclaimed him traitor, and confined him out of all the parts of his realme; but Makduffe was alreadie escaped out of danger, and gotten into England unto Malcolme Cammore, to trie what purchase hee might make by means of his support to revenge the slaughter so cruellie executed on his wife, his children, and other friends. At his comming unto Malcolme, he declared into what great miserie the estate of Scotland was brought, by the detestable cruelties exercised by the tyrant Makbeth, having committed manie horrible slaughters and murders, both as well of the nobles as commons, for the which he was hated right mortallie of all his liege people, desiring nothing more than to be delivered of that intollerable and most heavie yoke of thraldome, which they susteined at such a caitifes hands.

Malcolme hearing Makduffes woords, which he uttered in verie lamentable sort, for meere compassion and verie ruth that pearsed his sorowfull hart, bewailing the miserable state of his countrie, he fetched a deepe sigh; which Makduffe perceiving, began to fall most earnestlie in hand with him, to enterprise the delivering of the Scotish people out of the hands of so cruell and bloudie a tyrant, as Makbeth by too manie plaine experiments did shew himselfe to be: which was an easie matter for him to bring to passe, considering not onelie the good title he had, but also the earnest desire of the people to have some occasion ministred, whereby they might be revenged of those notable injuries, which they dailie susteined by the outragious crueltie of Makbeths misgovernance. Though Malcolme was verie sorrowfull for the oppression of his countriemen the Scots, in maner as Makduffe had declared; yet doubting whether he were come as one that ment unfeinedlie as he spake, or else as sent from Makbeth to betraie him, he thought to have some further triall, and thereupon dissembling his mind at the first, he answered as followeth.

I am truelie verie sorie for the miserie chanced to my countrie of Scotland, but though I have never so great affection to relieve the same, yet by reason of certeine incurable vices, which reigne in me, I am nothing meet thereto. First, such immoderate lust and voluptuous sensualitie [...] followeth me, that if I were made king of Scots, I should seeke to defloure your maids and matrones, in such wise that mine intemperancie should be more importable unto you than the bloudie tyrannie of Makbeth now is. Heereunto Makduffe answered: this suerly is a verie evill fault, for manie noble princes and kings have lost both lives and kingdomes for the same; neverthelesse there are women enow in Scotland, and therefore follow my counsell, Make thy selfe king, and I shall conveie the matter so wiselie, that thou shalt be so satisfied at thy pleasure in such secret wise, that no man shall be aware thereof.

Then said Malcolme, I am also the most avaritious creature on the earth, so that if I were king, I should seeke so manie waies to get lands and goods, that I would slea the most part of all the nobles of Scotland by surmised accusations, to the end I might injoy their lands, goods, and possessions; [...] Therefore saith Malcolme, suffer me to remaine where I am, least if I atteine to the regiment of your realme, mine inequenchable avarice may proove such; that ye would thinke the displeasures which now grieve you, should seeme easie in respect of the unmeasurable outrage, which might insue through my comming amongst you.

Makduffe to this made answer, how it was a far woorse fault than the other: for avarice is the root of all mischiefe, and for that crime the most part of our kings have been slaine and brought to their finall end. Yet notwithstanding follow my counsell, and take upon thee the crowne, There is gold and riches inough in Scotland to satisfie thy greedie desire. Then said Malcolme againe, I am furthermore inclined to dissimulation, telling of leasings, and all other kinds of deceit, so that I naturallie rejoise in nothing so much, as to betraie & deceive such as put anie trust or confidence in my woords. Then sith there is nothing that more becommeth a prince than constancie, veritie, truth, and justice, with the other laudable fellowship of those faire and noble vertues which are comprehended onelie in soothfastnesse, and that lieng utterlie overthroweth the same; you see how unable I am to governe anie province or region: and therefore sith you have remedies to cloke and hide all the rest of my other vices, I praie you find shift to cloke this vice amongst the residue.

Then said Makduffe: This yet is the woorst of all, and there I leave thee, and therefore saie; Oh ye unhappie and miserable Scotishmen, which are thus scourged with so manie and sundrie calamities, ech one above other! Ye have one cursed and wicked tyrant that now reigneth over you, without anie right or title, oppressing you with his most bloudie crueltie.

This other that hath the right to the crowne, is so replet with the inconstant behaviour and manifest vices of Englishmen, that he is nothing woorthie to injoy it: for by his owne confession he is not onelie avaritious, and given to unsatiable lust, but so false a traitor withall, that no trust is to be had unto anie woord he speaketh. Adieu Scotland, for now I account my selfe a banished man for ever, without comfort or consolation: and with those woords the brackish teares trickled downe his cheekes verie abundantlie.

At the last, when he was readie to depart, Malcolme tooke him by the sleeve, and said: Be of good comfort Makduffe, for I have none of these vices before remembred, but have jested with thee in this manner, onelie to proove thy mind: for diverse times heeretofore hath Makbeth sought by this manner of meanes to bring me into his hands, but the more slow I have shewed my selfe to condescend to thy motion and request, the more diligence shall I use in accomplishing the same. Incontinentlie heereupon they imbraced ech other, and promising to be faithfull the one to the other, they fell in consultation how they might best provide for all their businesse, to bring the same to good effect. Soone after, Makduffe repairing to the borders of Scotland, addressed his letters with secret dispatch unto the nobles of the realme, declaring how Malcolme was confederat with him, to come hastilie into Scotland to claime the crowne, and therefore he required them, sith he was right inheritor thereto, to assist him with their powers to recover the same out of the hands of the wrongfull usurper.

In the meane time, Malcolme purchased such favor at king Edwards hands, that old Siward earle of Northumberland, was appointed with ten thousand men to go with him into Scotland, to support him in this enterprise, for recoverie of his right. After these newes were spread abroad in Scotland, the nobles drew into two severall factions, the one taking part with Makbeth, and the other with Malcolme. Heereupon insued oftentimes sundrie bickerings, & diverse light skirmishes: for those that were of Malcolmes side, would not jeopard to joine with their enimies in a pight field, till his comming out of England to their support. But after that Makbeth perceived his enimies power to increase, by such aid as came to them foorth of England with his adversarie Malcolme, he recoiled backe into Fife, there purposing to abide in campe fortified, at the castell of Dunsinane, and to fight with his enimies, if they ment to pursue him, howbeit some of his friends advised him, that it should be best for him, either to make some agreement with Malcolme, or else to flee with all speed into the Iles, and to take his treasure with him, to the end he might wage sundrie great princes of the realme to take his part, & reteine strangers, in whome he might better trust than in his owne subjects, which stale dailie from him: but he had such confidence in his prophesies, that he beleeved he should never be vanquished, till Birnane wood were brought to Dunsinane; nor yet to be slaine with anie man, that should be or was borne of anie woman.

Malcolme following hastilie after Makbeth, came the night before the battell unto Birnane wood, and when his armie had rested for a while there to refresh them, he commanded everie man to get a bough of some tree or other of that wood in his hand, as big as he might beare, and to march foorth therewith in such wise, that on the next morrow they might come closelie and without sight in this manner within viewe of his enimies. On the morrow when Makbeth beheld them comming in this sort, he first marvelled what the matter ment, but in the end remembred himselfe that the prophesie which he had heard long before that time, of the comming of Birnane wood to Dunsinane castell, was likelie to be now fulfilled. Neverthelesse, he brought his men in order of battell, and exhorted them to doo valiantlie, howbeit his enimies had scarsely cast from them their boughs, when Makbeth perceiving their numbers, betooke him streict to flight, whom Makduffe pursued with great hatred even till he came unto Lunfannaine, where Makbeth perceiving that Makduffe was hard at his backe, leapt beside his horsse, saieng; Thou traitor, what meaneth it that thou shouldest thus in vaine follow me that am not appointed to be slaine by anie creature that is borne of a woman, come on therefore, and receive thy reward which thou hast deserved for thy paines, and therwithall he lifted up his swoord thinking to have slaine him.

But Makduffe quicklie avoiding from his horsse, yer he came at him, answered (with his naked swoord in his hand) saieng: It is true Makbeth, and now shall thine insatiable crueltie have an end, for I am even he that thy wizzards have told thee of, who was never borne of my mother, but ripped out of her wombe: therwithall he stept unto him, and slue him in the place. Then cutting his head from his shoulders, he set it upon a pole, and brought it unto Malcolme. This was the end of Makbeth, after he had reigned 17 yeeres over the Scotishmen. In the beginning of his reigne he accomplished manie woorthie acts, verie profitable to the common wealth, (as ye have heard) but afterward by illusion of the divell, he defamed the same with most terrible crueltie. He was slaine in the yeere of the incarnation 1057, and in the 16 yeere of king Edwards reigne over the Englishmen.

Malcolme Cammore thus recovering the relme (as ye have heard) by support of king Edward, in the 16 yeere of the same Edwards reigne, he was crowned at Scone the 25 day of Aprill, in the yeere of our Lord 1057. Immediatlie after his coronation he called a parlement at Forfair, in the which he rewarded them with lands and livings that had assisted him against Makbeth, advancing them to fees and offices as he saw cause, & commanded that speciallie those that bare the surname of anie offices or lands, should have and injoy the same. He created manie earles, lords, barons, and knights. Manie of them that before were thanes, were at this time made earles, as Fife, Menteth, Atholl, Levenox, Murrey, Cathnes, Rosse, and Angus. These were the first earles that have beene heard of amongst the Scotishmen, (as their histories doo make mention.)

4 Antony and Cleopatra

From Plutarch's Lives of the Noble Grecians and Romanes (trans. Sir Thomas North, 1579)

Source: Michael Neill (ed.), *Antony and Cleopatra* (Oxford University Press, Oxford Classics, 1994), pp. 331–9.

Plutarch was a Greek historian (*c.*46–120 CE) who wrote a voluminous work of historical biography, the *Lives of the Greeks and Romans*, which also included the narrative sources for Shakespeare's *Julius Caesar* and *Coriolanus*. Plutarch's *Lives* were translated into French by Jacques Amyot in 1559; Sir Thomas North translated Amyot's work into English in 1579, which is the text Shakespeare used for these plays. Our extract from Plutarch's 'Life of Marcus Antonius' focuses mainly on events dramatized in the first two acts of *Antony and Cleopatra*. In particular, Plutarch's description of Cleopatra's appearance at Cydnus gives you the opportunity to make a detailed comparison with how Shakespeare verbalizes the same events through Enobarbus's famous description in Act 2, Scene 2.

... [Antonius] had a noble mind, as well to punish offenders as to reward well-doers; and yet he did exceed more in giving than in punishing. Now for his outrageous manner of railing he commonly used, mocking and flouting of every man, that was remedied by itself. For a man might as boldly exchange a mock with him, and he was as well contented to be mocked as to mock others. But yet it oftentimes marred all. For he thought that those which told him so plainly and truly in mirth would never flatter him in good earnest in any matter of weight. But thus he was easily abused by the praises they gave him, not finding how these flatter[er]s mingled their flattery, under this familiar and plain manner of speech unto him, as a fine device to make difference of meats with sharp and tart sauce, and also to keep him, by this frank jesting and bourding with him at the table, that their common flattery should not be troublesome unto him, as men do easily mislike to have too much of one thing; and that they handled him finely thereby, when they would give him place in any matter of weight and follow his counsel, that it might not appear to him they did it so much to please him, but because they were ignorant and understood not so much as he did.

Antonius being thus inclined, the last and extremest mischief of all other (to wit, the love of Cleopatra) lighted on him, who did waken and stir up many vices yet hidden in him, and were never seen to any; and, if any spark of goodness or hope of rising were left him, Cleopatra quenched it straight and made it worse than before.

The manner how he fell in love with her was this. Antonius, going to make war with the Parthians, sent to command Cleopatra to appear personally before him when he came into Cilicia, to answer unto such accusations as were laid against her – being this, that she had aided Cassius and Brutus in their war against him. . . . [Cleopatra,] guessing by the former access and credit she had with Julius Caesar and Gnaeus Pompey (the son of Pompey the Great) only for her beauty, she began to have good hope that she might more easily win Antonius. For Caesar and Pompey knew her when she was but a young thing, and knew not then what the world meant; but now she went to Antonius at the age when a woman's beauty is at the prime, and she also of best judgement. So she furnished herself with a world of gifts, store of gold and silver, and of riches and other sumptuous ornaments, as is credible enough she might bring from so great a house and from so wealthy and rich a realm as Egypt was. But yet she carried nothing with her wherein she trusted more than in herself and in the charms and enchantment of her passing beauty and grace.

Therefore when she was sent unto by divers letters, both from Antonius himself and also from his friends, she made so light of it and mocked Antonius so much that she disdained to set forward otherwise but to take her barge in the river of Cydnus, the poop whereof was of gold, the sails of purple, and the oars of silver, which kept stroke in rowing after the sound of the music of flutes, hautboys, citherns, viols, and such other instruments as they played upon in the barge. And now for the person of herself: she was laid under a pavilion of cloth-of-gold of tissue, apparelled and attired like the goddess Venus commonly drawn in picture; and hard by her, on either hand of her, pretty fair boys apparelled as painters do set forth god Cupid, with little fans in their hands, with the which they fanned wind upon her. Her ladies and gentlewomen also, the fairest of them were apparelled like the nymphs Nereides (which are the mermaids of the waters) and like the Graces, some steering the helm, others tending the tackle and ropes of the barge, out of the which there came a wonderful passing sweet savour of perfumes that perfumed the wharf's side, pestered with innumerable multitudes of people. Some of them followed the barge all alongst the river's side; others also ran out of the city to see her coming in; so that in the end there ran such multitudes of people one after another to see her that Antonius was left post-alone in the market-place in his imperial seat to give audience. And there went a rumour in the people's mouths that the goddess Venus was come to play with the god Bacchus for the general good of all Asia.

When Cleopatra landed, Antonius sent to invite her to supper to him. But she sent him word again, he should do better rather to come and sup with her. Antonius therefore, to show himself courteous unto her at her arrival, was contented to obey her, and went to supper to her, where he found such passing sumptuous fare, that no tongue can express it. But amongst all other things he most wondered at the infinite number of lights and torches hanged on the top of the house, giving light in every place, so artificially set and ordered by devices, some round, some square, that it was the rarest thing to behold that eye could discern, or that ever books could mention. The next night, Antonius feasting her contended to pass her in magnificence and fineness; but she overcame him in both. So that he himself began to scorn the gross service of his house, in respect of Cleopatra's sumptuousness and fineness. And, when Cleopatra found Antonius' jests and slents to be but gross and soldierlike in plain manner, she gave it him finely and without fear taunted him thoroughly.

Now her beauty, as it is reported, was not so passing as unmatchable of other women, nor yet such as upon present view did enamour men with her; but so sweet was her company and conversation that a man could not possibly but be taken. And, besides her beauty, the good grace she had to talk and discourse, her courteous nature that tempered her words and deeds was a spur that pricked to the quick. Furthermore, besides all these, her voice and words were marvellous pleasant; for her tongue was an instrument of music to divers sports and pastimes, the which she easily turned to any language that pleased her. She spake unto few barbarous people by interpreter, but made them answer herself, or at the least the most part of them – as, the Ethiopians, the Arabians, the Troglodytes, the Hebrews, the Syrians, the Medes, and the Parthians, and to many others also, whose languages she had learned. Whereas divers of her progenitors, the Kings of Egypt, could scarce learn the Egyptian tongue only, and many of them forgot to speak to Macedonian.

Now Antonius was so ravished with the love of Cleopatra that, though his wife Fulvia had great wars and much ado with Caesar for his affairs, and that the army of the Parthians (the which the king's lieutenants had given to the only leading of Labienus) was now assembled in Mesopotamia ready to invade Syria; yet, as though all this had nothing touched him, he yielded himself to go with Cleopatra into Alexandria, where he spent and lost in childish sports (as a man might say) and idle pastimes the most precious thing a man can spend, as Antiphon saith: and that is, time. For they made an order between them which they called *Amimeto-bion* (as much to say, 'no life comparable and matchable with it'), one feasting each other by turns, and in cost exceeding all measure and reason. And, for proof hereof, I have heard my grandfather Lampryas report that one Philotas a physician, born in the city of Amphissa, told him that he was at that present time in Alexandria and studied physic; and that, having acquaintance with one of Antonius' cooks, he took him with him to Antonius' house (being a young man desirous to see things), to show him the wonderful sumptuous charge and preparation of one only supper. When he was in the kitchen and saw a world of diversities of meats, and, amongst others, eight wild boars roasted whole, he began to wonder at it and said: 'Sure you have a great number of guests to supper.' The cook fell a-laughing, and answered him: 'No,' quoth he, 'not many guests, nor above twelve in all. But yet all that is boiled or roasted must be served in whole, or else it would be marred straight. For Antonius peradventure will sup presently; or it may be a pretty while hence; or likely enough he will defer it longer, for that he hath drunk well today or else hath had some other great matters in hand; and therefore we do not dress one supper only, but many suppers, because we are uncertain of the hour he will sup in.'

But now again to Cleopatra. Plato writeth that there are four kinds of flattery; but Cleopatra divided it into many kinds. For she, were it in sport or in matter of earnest, still devised sundry new delights to have Antonius at commandment, never leaving him night nor day, nor once letting him go out of her sight. For she would play at dice with him, drink with him, and hunt commonly with him, and also be with him when he went to any exercise or activity of body. And sometime also when he would go up and down the city disguised like a slave in the night, and would peer into poor men's windows and their shops, and scold and brawl with them within the house, Cleopatra would be also in a chambermaid's array, and amble up and down the streets with him, so that oftentimes Antonius bare away both mocks and blows. Now, though most men misliked this manner, yet the Alexandrians were commonly glad of this jollity and liked it well, saying very gallantly and widely that Antonius showed them a comical face – to wit, a merry countenance; and the Romans a tragical face – to say, a grim look. [...]

Now Antonius delighting in these fond and childish pastimes, very ill news were brought him from two places. The first from Rome, that his brother Lucius and Fulvia his wife fell out first between themselves, and afterwards fell to open war with Caesar, and had brought all to nought, that they were both driven to fly out of Italy. The second news, as bad as the first, that Labienus conquered all Asia with the army of the Parthians, from the river of Euphrates and from Syria unto the countries of Lydia and Ionia. Then began Antonius, with much ado, a little to rouse himself, as if he had been wakened out of a deep sleep and, as a man may say, coming out of a great drunkenness. So first of all he bent himself against the Parthians, and went as far as the country of Phoenicia. But there he received lamentable letters from his wife Fulvia. Whereupon he straight returned towards Italy with two hundred sail; and, as he went, took up his friends by the way that fled out of Italy to come to him. By them he was informed that his wife Fulvia was the only cause of this war; who, being of a peevish, crooked, and troublesome nature, had purposely raised this uproar in Italy, in hope thereby to withdraw him from Cleopatra.

But, by good fortune, his wife Fulvia, going to meet with Antonius, sickened by the way, and died in the city of Sicyon. And therefore Octavius Caesar and he were the easilier made friends together. For when Antonius landed in Italy, and that men saw Caesar asked nothing of him, and that Antonius on the other side laid all the fault and burden on his wife Fulvia, the friends of both parties would not suffer them to unrip any old matters, and to prove or defend who had the wrong or right, and who was the first procurer of this war, fearing to make matters worse between them; but they made them friends together, and divided the Empire of Rome between them, making the sea Ionium the bounds of their division. For they gave all the provinces eastward unto Antonius, and the countries westward unto Caesar, and left Afric unto Lepidus; and made a law that they three one after another should make their friends Consuls, when they would not be themselves.

This seemed to be a sound counsel, but yet it was to be confirmed with a straiter bond, which fortune offered thus: there was Octavia, the eldest sister of Caesar. [. . .] It is reported that he dearly loved his sister Octavia, for indeed she was a noble lady, and left the widow of her first husband Caius Marcellus, who had died not long before; and it seemed also that Antonius had been widower ever since the death of his wife Fulvia. For he denied not that he kept Cleopatra; but so did he not confess that he had her as his wife; and so with reason he did defend the love he bare unto this Egyptian Cleopatra. Thereupon every man did set forward this marriage, hoping thereby that this lady Octavia, having an excellent grace, wisdom, and honesty, joined unto so rare a beauty, that when she were with Antonius (he loving her as so worthy a lady deserveth) she should be a good mean to keep good love and amity betwixt her brother and him. ...

Sextus Pompeius at that time kept in Sicilia, and so made many an inroad into Italy with a great number of pinnaces and other pirates' ships, of the which were captains two notable pirates, Menas and Menecrates, who so scoured all the sea thereabouts that none durst peep out with a sail. Furthermore, Sextus Pompeius had dealt very friendly with Antonius, for he had courteously received his mother when she fled out of Italy with Fulvia; and therefore they thought good to make peace with him. So they met all three together by the mount of Misena, upon a hill that runneth far into the sea, Pompey having his ships riding hard by at anchor, and Antonius and Caesar their armies upon the shore side, directly over against him.

Now after they had agreed that Sextus Pompeius should have Sicilia and Sardinia, with this condition, that he should rid the sea of all thieves and pirates and make it safe for passengers, and withal that he should send a certain [sic] of wheat to Rome, one of them did feast another, and drew cuts who should begin. It was Pompeius' chance to invite them first; whereupon Antonius asked him: 'And where shall we sup?' 'There', said Pompey, and showed him his admiral galley which had six banks of oars. 'That', said he, 'is my father's house they have left me.' He spake it to taunt Antonius, because he had his father's house, that was Pompey the Great. So he cast anchors enow into the sea to make his galley fast, and then built a bridge of wood to convey them to his galley from the head of Mount Misena; and there he welcomed them, and made them great cheer.

Now in the midst of the feast, when they fell to be merry with Antonius' love unto Cleopatra, Menas the pirate came to Pompey and, whispering in his ear, said unto him:
'Shall I cut the cables of the anchors, and make thee lord not only of Sicilia and Sardinia, but of the whole Empire of Rome besides?' Pompey, having paused awhile upon it, at length answered him: 'Thou shouldst have done it, and never have told it me; but now we must content us with that we have. As for myself, I was never taught to break my faith nor to be counted as a traitor.' . . .

Antonius, after this agreement made, sent Ventidius before into Asia to stay the Parthians and to keep them they should come no further; and he himself in the meantime, to gratify Caesar, was contented to be chosen Julius Caesar's priest and sacrificer; and so they jointly together dispatched all great matters concerning the state of the Empire. But in all other manner of sports and exercises wherein they passed the time away the one with the other, Antonius was ever inferior unto Caesar, and alway lost, which grieved him much. With Antonius there was a soothsayer or astronomer of Egypt that could cast a figure and judge of men's nativities to tell them what should happen to them. He, either to please Cleopatra or else for that he found it so by his art, told Antonius plainly that his fortune, which of itself was excellent good and very great, was altogether blemished and obscured by Caesar's fortune; and therefore he counselled him utterly to leave his company and to get him as far from him as he could. 'For thy Demon,' said he, '(that is to say, the good angel and spirit that keepeth thee) is afraid of his; and, being courageous and high when he is alone, becometh fearful and timorous when he cometh near unto the other.' Howsoever it was, the events ensuing proved the Egyptian's words true. For it is said that as often as they two drew cuts for pastime who should have anything, or whether they played at dice, Antonius alway lost. Oftentimes when they were disposed to see cock-fight, or quails that were taught to fight one with another, Caesar's cocks or quails did ever overcome. The which spited Antonius in his mind – although he made no outward show of it; and therefore he believed the Egyptian the better.

In fine, he recommended the affairs of his house unto Caesar, and went out of Italy with Octavia his wife, whom he carried into Greece, after he had a daughter by her. [. . .]

. . . But Antonius, notwithstanding, grew to be marvellously offended with Caesar, upon certain reports that had been brought unto him, and so took sea to go towards Italy with three hundred sail. And, because those of Brundusium would not receive his army into their haven, he went farther unto Tarentum. There his wife Octavia, that came out of Greece with him, besought him to send her unto her brother; the which he did. Octavia at that time was great with child, and moreover had a second daughter by him; and yet she put herself in journey, and met with her brother Octavius Caesar by the way, who brought his two chief friends, Maecenas and Agrippa, with him. She took them aside and, with all the instance she could possible, entreated them they would not suffer her, that was the happiest woman of the world, to become now the most wretched and unfortunatest creature of all other. 'For now', said she, 'every man's eyes do gaze on me, that am the sister of one of the Emperors and wife of the other. And if the worst counsel take place (which the gods forbid!) and that they grow to wars, for yourselves, it is uncertain to which of them two the gods have assigned the victory or overthrow; but for me, on which side soever victory fall, my state can be but most miserable still'.

These words of Octavia so softened Caesar's heart that he went quickly unto Tarentum. But it was a noble sight for them that were present, to see so great an army by land not to stir, and so many ships afloat in the road, quietly and safe; and, furthermore, the meeting and kindness of friends, lovingly embracing one another. First, Antonius feasted Caesar, which he granted unto for his sister's sake. Afterwards they agreed together that Caesar should give Antonius two legions to go against the Parthians, and that Antonius should let Caesar have a hundred galleys armed with brazen spurs at the prows. Besides all this, Octavia obtained of her husband twenty brigantines for her brother, and of her brother for her husband a thousand armed men. After they had taken leave of each other, Caesar went immediately to make war with Sextus Pompeius, to get Sicilia into his hands. Antonius also, leaving his wife Octavia and little children begotten of her with Caesar, and his other children which he had by Fulvia, he went directly into Asia.

Then began this pestilent plague and mischief of Cleopatra's love – which had slept a long time, and seemed to have been utterly forgotten, and that Antonius had given place to better counsel – again to kindle and to be in force, so soon as Antonius came near unto Syria. And in the end, 'the horse of the mind', as Plato termeth it, that is so hard of rein (I mean the unreined lust of concupiscence), did put out of Antonius' head all honest and commendable thoughts. For he sent Fonteius Capito to bring Cleopatra into Syria – unto whom, to welcome her, he gave no trifling things, but unto that she had already he added the provinces of Phoeniciá, those of the nethermost Syria, the isle of Cyprus, and a great part of Cilicia, and that country of Jewry where the true balm is, and that part of Arabia where the Nabatheians do dwell, which stretcheth out towards the Ocean.

These great gifts much misliked the Romans. But now, though Antonius did easily give away great signiories, realms, and mighty nations unto some private men ... yet all this did not so much offend the Romans as the unmeasurable honours which he did unto Cleopatra. But yet he did much more aggravate their malice and ill will towards him, because that, Cleopatra having brought him two twins, a son and a daughter, he named his son Alexander and his daughter Cleopatra, and gave them to their surnames, 'the Sun' to the one and 'the Moon' to the other. This notwithstanding, he that could finely cloak his shameful deeds with fine words said that the greatness and magnificence of the Empire of Rome appeared most not where the Romans took, but where they gave much; and nobility was multiplied amongst men by the posterity of kings when they left of their seed in divers places; and that by this means his first ancestor was begotten of Hercules, who had not left the hope and continuance of his line and posterity in the womb of one only woman, fearing Solon's laws or regarding the ordinances of men touching the procreation of children; but that he gave it unto nature, and established the foundation of many noble races and families in divers places. [. . .]

5 *Hamlet*

5.1 *From Thomas Kyd,* The Spanish Tragedy *(c.1582–92)*

Source: J. R. Mulryne (ed.), *The Spanish Tragedy.* The New Mermaids (A. & C. Black, 1970), pp. 40–6, 53.

The Spanish Tragedy by Thomas Kyd (1558–94) is a document of prime importance both for the Elizabethan theatre and for the understanding of *Hamlet.* Though the date of its first performance is uncertain it was probably in the late 1580s or early 1590s. The play was a massive popular success, and was apparently still in demand by as late as 1614. Its popularity is chiefly due to its exciting and emotive plot, in which

Hieronimo, a Spanish court official, attempts to avenge the murder of his son Horatio by Lorenzo, the son of the Duke of Castile. In this sense, the plot of *Hamlet* (in which a son revenges the murder of his father) reverses that of *The Spanish Tragedy*. It has been thought that Kyd himself wrote the earlier, lost version of *Hamlet* which Shakespeare updated in his famous play. Our extracts show the murder of Horatio, and Hieronimo's reaction to it, followed by Hieronimo's anguished rhetorical soliloquy which articulates both his grief and the apparent impossibility of avenging Horatio's murder. Compare these scenes with the play-within-a-play (3.2) and Hamlet's soliloquies (1.2.129–59; 2.2.526–82).

Act II, Scene iv

Enter HORATIO, BEL-IMPERIA, *and* PEDRINGANO

HORATIO
Now that the night begins with sable wings
To overcloud the brightness of the sun,
And that in darkness pleasures may be done,
Come Bel-imperia, let us to the bower,
And there in safety pass a pleasant hour. 5
BEL-IMPERIA
I follow thee my love, and will not back,
Although my fainting heart controls my soul.
HORATIO
Why, make you doubt of Pedringano's faith?
BEL-IMPERIA
No, he is as trusty as my second self.
Go Pedringano, watch without the gate, 10
And let us know if any make approach.
PEDRINGANO
[*Aside*] Instead of watching, I'll deserve more gold
By fetching Don Lorenzo to this match.
Exit PEDRINGANO
HORATIO
What means my love?
BEL-IMPERIA   I know not what myself.
And yet my heart foretells me some mischance. 15
HORATIO
Sweet say not so, fair fortune is our friend,
And heavens have shut up day to pleasure us.
The stars thou see'st hold back their twinkling shine,
And Luna hides herself to pleasure us.
BEL-IMPERIA
Thou hast prevailed, I'll conquer my misdoubt, 20

27

And in thy love and counsel drown my fear.
I fear no more, love now is all my thoughts.
Why sit we not? for pleasure asketh ease.

HORATIO

The more thou sit'st within these leafy bowers,
The more will Flora deck it with her flowers.   25

BEL-IMPERIA

Ay, but if Flora spy Horatio here,
Her jealous eye will think I sit too near.

HORATIO

Hark, madam, how the birds record by night,
For joy that Bel-imperia sits in sight.

BEL-IMPERIA

No, Cupid counterfeits the nightingale,   30
To frame sweet music to Horatio's tale.

HORATIO

If Cupid sing, then Venus is not far:
Ay, thou art Venus or some fairer star.

BEL-IMPERIA

If I be Venus, thou must needs be Mars,
And where Mars reigneth, there must needs be wars.   35

HORATIO

Then thus begin our wars: put forth thy hand,
That it may combat with my ruder hand.

BEL-IMPERIA

Set forth thy foot to try the push of mine.

HORATIO

But first my looks shall combat against thine.

BEL-IMPERIA

Then ward thyself: I dart this kiss at thee.   40

HORATIO

Thus I retort the dart thou threw'st at me.

BEL-IMPERIA

Nay then, to gain the glory of the field,
My twining arms shall yoke and make thee yield.

HORATIO

Nay then, my arms are large and strong withal:
Thus elms by vines are compassed till they fall.   45

BEL-IMPERIA

O let me go, for in my troubled eyes
Now may'st thou read that life in passion dies.

HORATIO

O stay a while and I will die with thee,
So shalt thou yield and yet have conquered me.

BEL-IMPERIA
Who's there? Pedringano! We are betrayed!   50

Enter LORENZO, BALTHAZAR, SERBERINE, PEDRINGANO, *disguised*
LORENZO
My lord, away with her, take her aside.
O sir, forbear, your valour is already tried.
Quickly despatch, my masters.
                                  They hang him in the arbour
HORATIO
What, will you murder me?
LORENZO
Ay, thus, and thus; these are the fruits of love.   55
                                              They stab him
BEL-IMPERIA
O save his life and let me die for him!
O save him, brother, save him, Balthazar:
I loved Horatio, but he loved not me.
BALTHAZAR
But Balthazar loves Bel-imperia.
LORENZO
Although his life were still ambitious proud,   60
Yet is he at the highest now he is dead.
BEL-IMPERIA
Murder! murder! Help, Hieronimo, help!
LORENZO
Come, stop her mouth, away with her.
                          Exeunt, [leaving HORATIO'S *body]*

Act II, Scene v

Enter HIERONIMO *in his shirt, etc.*

HIERONIMO
What outcries pluck me from my naked bed,
And chill my throbbing heart with trembling fear,
Which never danger yet could daunt before?
Who calls Hieronimo? Speak, here I am.
I did not slumber, therefore 'twas no dream,   5
No, no, it was some woman cried for help,
And here within this garden did she cry,
And in this garden must I rescue her.
But stay, what murderous spectacle is this?
A man hanged up and all the murderers gone,   10
And in my bower to lay the guilt on me.

29

This place was made for pleasure not for death.

He cuts him down

Those garments that he wears I oft have seen –
Alas, it is Horatio, my sweet son!
Oh no, but he that whilom was my son.   15
O was it thou that calledst me from my bed?
O speak, if any spark of life remain:
I am thy father. Who hath slain my son?
What savage monster, not of human kind,
Hath here been glutted with thy harmless blood,   20
And left thy bloody corpse dishonoured here,
For me, amidst this dark and deathful shades,
To drown thee with an ocean of my tears?
O heavens, why made you night to cover sin?
By day this deed of darkness had not been.   25
O earth, why didst thou not in time devour
The vild profaner of this sacred bower?
O poor Horatio, what hadst thou misdone,
To leese thy life ere life was new begun?
O wicked butcher, whatsoe'er thou wert,   30
How could thou strangle virtue and desert?
Ay me most wretched, that have lost my joy,
In leesing my Horatio, my sweet boy!

Act III, Scene ii

Enter HIERONIMO

HIERONIMO
O eyes, no eyes, but fountains fraught with tears;
O life, no life, but lively form of death;
O world, no world, but mass of public wrongs,
Confused and filled with murder and misdeeds!
O sacred heavens! if this unhallowed deed,   5
If this inhuman and barbarous attempt,
If this incomparable murder thus
Of mine, but now no more my son,
Shall unrevealed and unrevengéd pass,
How should we term your dealings to be just,   10
If you unjustly deal with those that in your justice trust?
The night, sad secretary to my moans,
With direful visions wake my vexed soul,
And with the wounds of my distressful son
Solicit me for notice of his death.   15
The ugly fiends do sally forth of hell,

And frame my steps to unfrequented paths,
And fear my heart with fierce inflamed thoughts.
The cloudy day my discontents records,
Early begins to register my dreams   20
And drive me forth to seek the murderer. [...]

5.2 Sir Francis Bacon 'Of Revenge' (1625)

Source: from J. Pitcher (ed.), *The Essays* (Harmondsworth: Penguin, 1985), pp. 72–3.

Sir Francis Bacon (1561–1626) was one of the most important English writers of the early modern period. He was a powerful courtier and lawyer as well as a philosopher and natural scientist. Because of his literary abilities – as well as his aristocratic status – he used to be the prime candidate as the 'real' writer of Shakespeare's works for those who could not accept that the humbly born William Shakespeare could have written plays of the literary and political sophistication of *Hamlet*. While very few scholars now give such theories any credence at all, some people still try to prove that Shakespeare – 'the man from Stratford' – was a cover for some courtier. Bacon's *Essays* are characteristically short and pithy 'counsels' (pieces of advice) on moral and political issues. 'Of Revenge' valuably indicates the complex moral and legal debates about ethics of revenge in Shakespeare's England, fleshing out its generalizations with allusions to classical and Biblical examples, as well as to contemporaneous European politics. Compare it with Hamlet's soliloquies, especially 3.3.73–96.

Revenge is a kind of wild justice, which the more man's nature runs to, the more ought law to weed it out. For as for the first wrong, it doth but offend the law; but the revenge of that wrong putteth the law out of office. Certainly, in taking revenge a man is but even with his enemy, but in passing it over he is superior, for it is a prince's part to pardon. And Solomon, I am sure, saith, *It is the glory of a man to pass by an offence*. That which is past is gone and irrevocable, and wise men have enough to do with things present and to come: therefore they do but trifle with themselves that labour in past matters. There is no man doth a wrong for the wrong's sake, but thereby to purchase himself profit or pleasure or honour or the like. Therefore why should I be angry with a man for loving himself better than me? And if any man should do wrong merely out of ill nature, why, yet it is but like the thorn or briar, which prick and scratch, because they can do no other. The most tolerable sort of revenge is for those wrongs which there is no law to remedy: but then let a man take heed the revenge be such as there is no law to punish; else a man's enemy is still beforehand, and it is two for one. Some, when they take revenge, are desirous the party should know whence it cometh. This is the more generous, for the delight seemeth to be not so much in doing the hurt as in making the party repent. But base and crafty cowards are like the arrow that flieth in the dark. Cosmus, Duke of Florence, had a desperate saying against perfidious or neglecting friends, as if those wrongs were unpardonable: *You shall read* (saith he) *that we are commanded to forgive our enemies; but you never read that we are commanded to forgive our friends.* But yet the spirit of Job was in a better tune: *Shall we* (saith he) *take good at God's hands, and not be content to take evil also?* And so of friends in a proportion. This is certain, that a man that studieth revenge keeps his own wounds green, which otherwise would heal and do well. Public revenges are for the most part fortunate: as that for the death of Caesar, for the death of Pertinax, for the death of Henry the Third of France, and many more. But in private revenges it is not so. Nay rather, vindicative persons live the life of witches, who, as they are mischievous, so end they infortunate.

6 *Twelfth Night*

From Barnabe Riche, Riche his Farewell to Militarie Profession (1581)

Source: G. Bullough (ed.), *Narrative and Dramatic Sources of Shakespeare*, Volume II: *The Comedies, 1597–1603* (London: Routledge and Kegan Paul, 1963), pp. 345, 357–63.

Though Shakespeare was indebted in *Twelfth Night* to sixteenth-century Italian comedies like *l'Ingannati (The Deceived)*, he also drew on an English source for the main Viola–Orsino–Olivia–Sebastian love intrigue. Barnabe Riche's (*c.* 1540–1617) story 'Of Apolonius and Silla' provides many illuminating points of comparison with Shakespeare's play. The extract reprinted here takes up the plot at the point where the Duke has been told by the Ladie Julina (Shakespeare's Olivia) that she does not love him, but loves his page Silla/Silvio (Shakespeare's Viola/Cesario) instead; it roughly corresponds to the denouement of *Twelfth Night* in 5.1. In comparing *Twelfth Night* and 'Of Apolonius and Silla', you might look particularly at Silla's role as a go-between and *Twelfth Night* 1.5 and 2.2; and compare Julina and Silvio's relationship with that of Olivia and Sebastian in 4.1 and 4.3. Note particularly that in Riche's version, the Sebastian figure (also confusingly called Silvio!) gets Juliner pregnant and temporarily abandons her.

OF APOLONIUS AND SILLA

The Argument of the Second Historie

Apolonius Duke, havyng spent a yeres service in the warres against the Turke,
returning homward with his companie by sea, was driven by force of weather to
the Ile of Cypres, where he was well received by Pontus, gouvernour of the same
ile, with whom Silla, daughter to Pontus, fell so straungely in love, that after
Apolonius was departed to Constantinople, Silla, with one man, followed, and
commyng to Constantinople, she served Apolonius in the habite of a manne, and
after many prety accidentes falling out, she was knowne to Apolonius, who, in
requitall of her love, maried her.

[. . .]

The Duke, having heard this discourse, caused Silvio presently to be
sent for and to be brought before hym, to whom he saied: Had it not been
sufficient for thee, when I had reposed myself in thy fidelitie and the
trustinesse of thy service, that thou shouldest so traiterously deale with
me, but since that tyme hast not spared still to abuse me with so many
forgeries and perjured protestations, not onely hatefull unto me, whose
simplicitie thou thinkest to bee suche that by the plotte of thy pleasaunt
tongue thou wouldest make me beleeve a manifest untrothe; but moste
habominable bee thy doynges in the presence and sight of God, that hast
not spared to blaspheme his holy name by callyng hym to bee a witnesse
to maintaine thy leasynges, and so detestably wouldest forsweare thyself
in a matter that is so openly knowne.

Poore Silvio, whose innocencie was suche that he might lawfully
sweare, seing Julina to be there in place aunswered thus.

Moste noble Duke, well understandyng your conceived greefe, moste
humbly I beseche you paciently to heare my excuse, not mindyng therby
to aggravate or heape up youre wrathe and displeasure, protestyng before
God that there is nothyng in the worlde whiche I regarde so much or dooe
esteeme so deare, as your good grace and favour; but desirous that your
grace should know my innocencie, and to cleare my self of suche imposi-
tions, wherewith I knowe I am wrongfully accused, whiche as I understande should be in the practisyng of the Ladie Julina who standeth here
in place, whose acquitaunce for my better discharge now I moste humbly
crave, protestyng before the Almightie God that neither in thought,
worde, nor deede, I have not otherwise used my self then accordyng to
the bonde and duetie of a servante that is bothe willyng and desirous to
further his maister's sutes; which if I have otherwise saied then that is
true, you, Madame Julina, who can verie well deside the depthes of all
this doubte, I moste humbly beseche you to certifie a trothe, if I have in
any thyng missaied or have other wise spoken then is right and just.

Julina, havyng heard this discourse whiche Silvio had made,
perceivyng that he stoode in greate awe of the Duke's displeasure,

aunswered thus: Thinke not, my Silvio, that my commyng hither is to accuse you of any misdemeanour towardes your maister, so I dooe not denaie but in all suche imbassages wherein towardes me you have been imployed, you have used the office of a faithfull and trustie messenger; neither am I ashamed to confesse, that the first daie that mine eyes did beholde the singular behaviour, the notable curtesie, and other innumerable giftes wherewith my Silvio is endued, but that beyonde all measure my harte was so inflamed that impossible it was for me to quenche the fervente love or extinguishe the leaste parte of my conceived torment, before I had bewraied the same unto hym and of my owne motion craved his promised faithe and loialtie of marriage; and now is the tyme to manifest the same unto the worlde whiche hath been doen before God and betwene ourselves, knowyng that it is not needefull to keepe secret that whiche is neither evill doen nor hurtfull to any persone. Therefore (as I saied before) Silvio is my housbande by pli[gh]ted faithe, whom I hope to obtaine without offence or displeasure of any one, trustyng that there is no manne that will so farre forget hymself as to restraine that whiche God hath left at libertie for every wight, or that will seeke by crueltie to force ladies to marrie otherwise then accordyng to their owne likyng. Feare not then my Silvio, to keepe your faith and promise whiche you have made unto me; and as for the reste, I doubte not thynges will so fall out as you shall have no manner of cause to complaine.

Silvio, amased to heare these woordes, for that Julina by her speeche seemed to confirme that whiche he moste of all desired to bee quit of, saied: Who would have thought that a ladie of so great honour and reputation would her self bee the embassadour of a thyng so prejuditiall and uncomely for her estate! What plighted promises be these whiche bee spoken of? altogether ignoraunt unto me, whiche if it bee otherwise then I have saied, you sacred goddes consume me straight with flashyng flames of fire. But what woordes might I use to give credite to the truthe and innocencie of my cause? Ah, Madame Julina! I desire no other testimonie then your owne, I desire no other testimonie then your owne honestie and vertue, thinkyng that you will not so muche blemishe the brightnesse of your honour, knowyng that a woman is, or should be, the image of curtesie, continencie, and shamfastnesse, from the whiche so sone as she stoopeth, and leaveth the office of her duetie and modestie, besides the degraduation of her honour, she thrusteth her self into the pitte of perpetuall infamie. And as I can not thinke you would so farre forgette yourself, by the refusall of a noble Duke to dimme the light of your renowne and glorie, which hetherto you have maintained emongest the beste and noblest ladies, by suche a one as I knowe my self to bee, too farre unworthie your degree and callyng, so moste humbly I beseche you to confesse a trothe, whereto tendeth those vowes and promises you speake of, whiche speeches bee so obscure unto mee as I knowe not for my life how I might understande them.

Julina, somethyng nipped with these speeches, saied: And what is the matter, that now you make so little accompte of your Julina? that, beeyng my housband in deede, have the face to denaie me to whom thou art contracted by so many solemne othes? What! arte thou ashamed to have me to thy wife? How muche oughtest thou rather to be ashamed to breake thy promised faithe, and to have despised the holie and dreadfull name of God? but that tyme constraineth me to laye open that whiche shame rather willeth I should dissemble and keepe secret, behold me then here, Silvio, whom thou haste gotten with childe; who, if thou bee of suche honestie as I trust for all this I shall finde, then the thyng is doen without prejudice or any hurte to my conscience, consideryng that by the professed faithe thou diddest accoumpte me for thy wife, and I received thee for my spouse and loyall housbande, swearyng by the Almightie God that no other then you have made the conquest and triumphe of my chastitie, whereof I crave no other witnesse then yourself and mine owne conscience.

I praie you, gentilwomen, was not this a foule oversight of Julina, that would so precisely sweare so greate an othe that she was gotten with childe by one that was altogether unfurnishte with implementes for suche a tourne? For God's love take heede, and let this bee an example to you, when you be with childe, how you sweare who is the father before you have had good proofe and knowledge of the partie; for men be so subtill and full of sleight that, God knoweth, a woman may quickly be deceived.

But now to returne to our Silvio, who, hearyng an othe sworne so divinely that he had gotten a woman with childe, was like to beleeve that it had bin true in very deede; but remembryng his owne impediment, thought it impossible that he should committee suche an acte, and therefore, half in a chafe he saied. What lawe is able to restraine the foolishe indiscretion of a woman that yeeldeth herself to her owne desires? what shame is able to bridle or withdrawe her from her mynd and madnesse, or with what snaffell is it possible to holde her backe from the execution of her filthinesse? but what abhomination is this, that a ladie of suche a house should so forget the greatnesse of her estate, the aliaunce whereof she is descended, the nobilitie of her deceased housbande, and maketh no conscience to shame and slaunder her self with suche a one as I am, beyng so farre unfit and unseemely for her degree! but how horrible is it to heare the name of God so defaced, that wee make no more accompt but for the maintenaunce of our mischifes, we feare no whit at all to forsweare his holy name, as though he were not in all his dealinges mooste righteous, true, and juste, and will not onely laie open our leasinges to the worlde, but will likewise punishe the same with moste sharp and bitter scourges.

Julina, not able to indure hym to proceede any farther in his sermon, was alreadie surprised with a vehement greefe, began bitterly to crie out, utteryng these speeches followyng.

Alas! is it possible that the soveraigne justice of God can abide a mischiefe so greate and cursed? why maie I not now suffer death, rather than the infamie whiche I see to wander before myne eyes? Oh, happie, and more then right happie had I bin, if inconstant fortune had not devised this treason wherein I am surprised and caught! Am I thus become to be intangled with snares, and in the handes of hym who, injoiyng the spoyles of my honour, will openly deprive me of my fame by makyng me a common fable to al posteritie in tyme to come? Ah, traitour and discourtious wretche! is this the recompence of the honest and firme amitie which I have borne thee? wherein have I deserved this discourtesie? by loving thee more then thou art able to deserve? Is it I, arrant theefe! is it I, uppon whom thou thinkest to worke thy mischives? doest thou think me no better worth, but that thou maiest prodigally waste my honour at thy pleasure? didest thou dare to adventure uppon me, having thy conscience wounded with so deadly a treason? Ah, unhappie, and above all other most unhappie! that have so charely preserved myne honour, and now am made a praie to satisfie a yong man's lust that hath coveted nothyng but the spoyle of my chastitie and good name!

Here withall her teares so gushed doune her cheekes that she was not able to open her mouth to use any farther speeche.

The Duke, who stood by all this while and heard this whole discourse, was wonderfully moved with compassion towardes Julina, knowyng that from her infancie she had ever so honourably used herself, that there was no man able to detect her of any misdemeanour otherwise then beseemed a ladie of her estate: wherefore, beyng fully resolved that Silvio his man had committed this villanie against her, in a greate furie, drawyng his rapier, he saied unto Silvio:

How canst thou, arrant theefe, shewe thy self so cruell and carelesse to suche as doe thee honour? Hast thou so little regard of suche a noble ladie as humbleth herself to suche a villaine as thou art, who, without any respecte either of her renowne or noble estate, canst be content to seeke the wracke and utter ruine of her honour? But frame thyself to make such satisfaction as she requireth, although I knowe, unworthie wretche, that thou art not able to make her the least parte of amendes, or I sweare by God that thou shalt not escape the death which I will minister to thee with my owne handes, and therefore advise thee well what thou doest.

Silvio, havyng heard this sharpe sentence, fell doune on his knees before the Duke, cravyng for mercie, desiryng that he might be suffered to speake with the Ladie Julina aparte, promising to satisfie her accordyng to her owne contentation.

Well (quoth the Duke), I take thy worde; and therewithall I advise thee that thou performe thy promis, or otherwise I protest, before God, I will make thee suche an example to the worlde that all traitours shall tremble for feare how they doe seeke the dishonouryng of ladies.

But now Julina had conceived so greate greefe againste Silvio, that there was muche a dooe to perswade her to talke with hym; but remembryng her owne case, desirous to heare what excuse he could make, in the ende she agreed, and beyng brought into a place severally by themselves, Silvio beganne with a piteous voice to saie as followeth.

I knowe not, madame, of whom I might make complaint, whether of your or of my self, or rather of Fortune, whiche hath conducted and brought us both into so greate adversitie. I see that you receive greate wrong, and I am condemned againste all right; you in perill to abide the bru[i]te of spightfull tongues, and I in daunger to lose the thing that I moste desire; and although I could alledge many reasons to prove my saiynges true, yet I referre my self to the experience and bountie of your minde. And here with all loosing his garmentes doune to his stomacke, and shewed Julina his breastes and pretie teates, surmountyng farre the whitenesse of snowe itself, saying: Loe, Madame! behold here the partie whom you have chalenged to bee the father of your childe. See, I am a woman, the daughter of a noble Duke, who, only for the love of him whom you so lightly have shaken off, have forsaken my father, abandoned my countreie, and in maner as you see am become a servyng-man, satisfiying myself but with the onely sight of my Apolonius. And now Madame, if my passion were not vehement, and my tormentes without comparison, I would wish that my fained greefes might be laughed to scorne and my desembled paines to be rewarded with floutes; but my love beyng pure, my travaile continuall, and my greefes endlesse, I trust madame, you will not onely excuse me of crime but also pitie my distresse, the which, I protest, I would still have kept secrete if my fortune would so have permitted.

Julina did now thinke her self to be in a worse case then ever she was before, for now she knewe not whom to chalenge to be the father of her child; wherfore, when she had told the Duke the very certaintie of the discourse which Silvio had made unto her, she departed to her owne house with suche greefe and sorrowe, that she purposed never to come out of her owne doores againe alive, to be a wonder and mocking stocke to the worlde.

But the Duke, more amased to heare this straunge discourse of Silvio, came unto him, whom when he had vewed with better consideration, perceived indeede that it was Silla the daughter of Duke Pontus, and imbracing her in his armes he saied.

Oh, the braunche of all vertue and the flowre of curtesie it self! pardon me, I beseche you, of all suche discourtesies as I have ignorantlie committed towardes you, desiring you that without farther memorie of auncient greefes you will accept of me, who is more joyfull and better contented with your presence, then if the whole worlde were at my commaundement. Where hath there ever been founde such liberalitie in a lover, whiche havyng been trained up and nourished emongest the delicacies and banquettes of the courte, accompanied with traines of many faire and noble ladies, living in pleasure and in the middest of delightes, would so prodigallie adventure your self, neither fearing mishapps nor misliking to take suche paines as I knowe you have not been accustomed unto? O, liberalitie never heard of before! O, facte that can never bee sufficiently rewarded! O, true love moste pure and unfained! Here withall sendyng for the moste artificiall woorkmen, he provided for her sondrie sutes of sumpteous apparell, and the marriage daie appoincted, whiche was celebrated with greate triumphe through the whole citie of Constantinople, every one prasing the noblenesse of the Duke; but so many as did behold the excellent beautie of Silla gave her the praise above all the rest of the ladies in the troupe.

The matter seemed so wonderfull and straunge that the bru[i]te was spreade throughout all the partes of Grecia, in so muche that it came to the hearyng of Silvio, who, as you have heard, remained in those partes to enquire of his sister: he beyng the gladdest manne in the worlde, hasted to Constantinople, where comming to his sister he was joyfullie receved and moste lovynglie welcomed, and entertained of the Duke his brother in lawe. After he had remained there twoo or three daies the Duke revealed unto Silvio the whole discourse how it happened betweene his sister and the Ladie Julina, and how his sister was chalenged for gettyng a woman with childe.

Silvio, blushyng with these woordes, was striken with greate remorse to make Julina amendes, understanding her to bee a noble ladie and was lefte defamed to the worlde through his default: he therefore bewraied the whole circumstance to the Duke, whereof the Duke beyng verie joyfull, immediatelie repaired with Silvio to the house of Julina, whom they founde in her chamber in greate lamentation and mournyng. To whom the Duke saied: Take courage, madam, for beholde here a gentilman that will not sticke bothe to father your child and to take you for his wife; no inferiour persone, but the sonne and heire of a noble Duke, worthie of your estate and dignitie.

Julina, seyng Silvio in place, did know very well that he was the father of her childe, and was so ravished with joye that she knewe not whether she were awake or in some dreame. Silvio, imbracyng her in his armes, cravyng forgivenesse of all that was past, concluded with her the marriage daie, which was presently accomplished with greate joye and contentation to all parties. And thus, Silvio havyng attained a noble wife and Silla, his sister, her desired housband, they passed the residue of their daies with suche delight as those that have accomplished the perfection of their felicities.

7 *Measure for Measure*

From G. B. Giraldi Cinthio, Hecatommithi (1583 edn)

Source: G. Bullough (ed.), *Narrative and Dramatic Sources of Shakespeare*, Volume II: *The Comedies 1597–1603* (London: Routledge and Kegan Paul, 1963), pp. 420–7, 430.

Measure for Measure dramatizes an old and familiar story, in which a corrupt judge seduces a woman who pleads on behalf of her condemned brother, husband or father with the promise of a pardon. It has analogues in the work of writers as far removed as the fourth-century theologian St Augustine of Hippo (*The Lord's Sermon on the Mount*) and the 1960s singer Bob Dylan ('Seven Curses'). Shakespeare, however, probably chiefly relied on a short story by G. B. Giraldi Cinthio (1504–73), which he would have read either in the original Italian or a French translation. Compare especially Cinthio's handling of the sexual intrigue and of the system of justice in *Measure for Measure*, 2.4 and 5.1.

...While this great Lord, who was a rare example of courtesy, magnanimity and singular justice, reigned happily over the Roman Empire, he sent out his ministers to govern the states that flourished under his rule. And among them he sent to govern Innsbruck one of his intimates, a man very dear to him named Juriste. Before sending him he said: 'Juriste, the good opinion I have formed of you while you have been in my service makes me send you as Governor to this noble City of Innsbruck. I could instruct you about many things concerning your rule there but I shall limit myself to one thing only, which is: that you keep Justice inviolate, even if you have to give sentence against me who am your overlord. And I warn you that I could forgive you all other faults, whether you did them through ignorance or through negligence (though I wish you to guard against this as much as possible), but anything done against Justice could never obtain pardon from me. If therefore you do not feel it incumbent on you to behave in this way I urge you (since every man is not good for every thing) do not take up this charge, but rather remain here at Court, where I hold you dear, in your accustomed duties; for otherwise, once you are Governor of that City you might oblige me to do against you that which, if I had to do it on behalf of Justice, would give me the utmost unhappiness.' And hereupon he was silent.

Juriste was more pleased with the office to which the Emperor called him than sound in knowledge of his own nature. He thanked his master for the proof of his favour and said that he was always animated by the desire to serve Justice, but that he would preserve her the more ardently henceforth, since the Emperor's words were like a torch which had fired him to it all the more keenly; that he would bend his mind to succeed in his new charge so that his master could not but praise him. The Emperor rejoiced at Juriste's words and said to him. 'Truly you will give me cause only to praise you if your deeds prove as good as your words.' And having the letters patent given to him which were already made out, he sent him on his way.

Juriste began to rule over the City with great prudence and diligence, taking the utmost care and deliberation to ensure that the balance of Justice should be rightly poised not only in judgements but also in the bestowal of offices, in the reward of Virtue and the punishment of Vice. For a long time his moderation gained him great favour from his master and earned him the approval of all the people. And he would have been thus happily celebrated above all others if his government had continued in that fashion.

It happened that a young man of the region, called Vico, violated a virgin, a citizen of Innsbruck, and complaint was made to Juriste. He immediately had the young man arrested, and on his confessing that he had done violence to the maiden, condemned him to death in accordance with the law of that City by which such a criminal was to be beheaded even if he were willing to take his victim for his wife.

The young man had a sister, a virgin not more than eighteen years old, who besides being adorned with extreme beauty, had a very sweet way of speaking and a charming presence together with all feminine goodness. This lady, whose name was Epitia, was smitten with grief on hearing that her brother was condemned to die, and resolved to see whether she could, if not liberate him, at least soften the penalty; and having been, with her brother, under the tutelage of an old man whom their father had kept in the house to teach them both Philosophy (though her brother had followed its precepts but ill) she went to Juriste and prayed him to have compassion on her brother, because of his youth (he was no more than sixteen years old) which made him deserving of pardon, and because of his inexperience of life, and the violent impulse that Love had in his heart. She argued that many wise men held the opinion that adultery committed through the violence of Love, and not undertaken to do injury to a woman's husband, deserved a less penalty than if committed with injurious intent; that the same might be said in her brother's case, who had done the deed for which he was condemned not out of malice but spurred by ardent love; that he was ready and willing to marry the girl, and do whatever else the law might demand; and that although the law might declare that such a settlement did not apply to a man who violated virgins, yet Juriste, being the wise man he was, could mitigate the severity of his attitude, which was more rigorous than Justice demanded; for he was in that City through the authority he held from the Emperor, as the living law, and His Majesty in his equitable fairness showed himself rather merciful than savage in his judgements. She claimed that if the law might be alleviated in any case, it should be in offences done for love, especially where the honour of the injured lady remained unharmed, as it would in her brother's case, who was very willing to make her his wife. She believed that the law had been thus severely framed to strike terror rather than to be rigorously carried out, for it would be (she pleaded) cruel to punish with death a crime which could be honourably and religiously recompensed to the satisfaction of the injured party. Thus she sought, with many other reasons, to induce Juriste to pardon the poor youth.

Juriste, whose ears were no more delighted by Epitia's sweet way of talking than his eyes were charmed by her great beauty, was eager to hear and see more of her; so he asked her to repeat her plea. Taking this for a good augury the lady spoke again with even greater force, and now, overcome by Epitia's graceful speech and rare loveliness he was smitten with lustful desire, till it came into his mind to commit against her the same crime for which he had condemned Vico to death. He said: 'Your pleadings have so much helped your brother that whereas his head should have been cut off tomorrow, the execution will be deferred until I have considered the reasons you have given me. If I find that they enable me to give your brother his freedom, I shall give him to you the more willingly because I should have been grieved to see him led out to his death through the rigour of the hard law which has imposed it.'

At these words Epitia took good hope and thanked him for showing himself so courteous, telling him that she would be eternally obliged, believing that she would find him no less generous in liberating her brother than she had found him in prolonging his life. She added that she firmly hoped that if he considered the things she had said, he would complete her happiness by freeing Vico. Juriste repeated that he would give them every consideration, and that if at all possible without offending Justice he would not fail to fulfil her wishes.

So Epitia departed, full of hope, and went to her brother whom she informed of what she had done with Juriste and how much hope she had obtained from the first interview. In his desperate situation this was very welcome to Vico, and he prayed her to beg for his release. His sister promised to make every effort to that end.

Juriste meanwhile, in whose mind the form of Epitia had deeply impressed itself, turned all his thoughts – lascivious as they became – towards enjoying her, and he waited eagerly for her to come back and speak to him. After three days she returned and asked him courteously what he had decided. As soon as he saw her Juriste felt himself aflame. He said: 'Welcome, lovely maiden; I have not failed to examine diligently all that your arguments could do in your brother's cause, and I have myself searched for others so that you might rest content; but I find that every thing points to his death. For there is a universal law, that when a man sins, not through ignorance, but negligently, his crime cannot be excused, since he ought to know that all men without exception should live virtuously; he who sins in neglect of this principle deserves neither pardon nor pity. Your brother was in this position; he must have been fully aware that anybody who raped a virgin deserved to die; so he must die for it, nor can I reasonably accord him mercy. Nevertheless, for your sake, whom I long to please, if, in your great love for your brother, you are willing to let me enjoy your favours, I am disposed to allow him his life and change the death penalty to one less grave.'

At these words Epitia's cheeks blushed fiery red and she replied: 'My brother's life is very dear to me, but still dearer is my virtue, and I would much sooner try to save him by giving up my life than by losing my honour. Set aside this dishonourable suggestion of yours; but if by any other means of pleasing you I can win back my brother I shall do so very gladly.' 'There is no other way,' said Juriste, 'and you should not behave so coyly, for it might easily happen that our first coming-together would result in your becoming my wife.' 'I do not wish,' said Epitia 'to put my honour in danger.' 'But why in danger?' asked Juriste. 'You may well become my wife though now you cannot think it could ever be. Think well upon it, and I shall expect your answer tomorrow.' 'I can give you my answer at once,' she said, 'Unless you take me for your wife, if you really mean that my brother's release depends on that, you are throwing your words to the wind.' Again Juriste replied that she should think it over before returning with her answer, considering who he was, what power he had, and how useful he could be not only to her but to any of her friends, since he had in his hand both Reason and Authority.

Epitia left him, deeply disturbed, and went to her brother. She described to Vico all that had passed between her and Juriste, affirming that she did not want to lose her honour even to save his life, and tearfully she begged him to prepare himself patiently to endure the lot which either Fate or his own ill-fortune had brought upon him. At this Vico began to weep and entreat his sister not to consent to his death, since she could obtain his release in the manner proposed by Juriste. 'Can you wish, Epitia,' he said, 'to see me with the executioner's axe on my neck, and my head struck off; to see the head of him who came from the same womb, born of the same father, who grew up and was taught side by side with you, thrown on the ground by the executioner? Ah, sister! may the motions of Nature in our blood and the love we have always shared be so strong in you that, since it is in your power to do so, you will free me from so shameful and wretched an end. You can atone for my error; do not be miserly in your aid. Juriste has told you that he might make you his wife, and why should you disbelieve that it would be so? You are very beautiful and adorned with all the graces which Nature can give to a lady. You are noble and charming; you have an admirable gift of speech, virtues any one of which could endear you – I will not say to Juriste only – but to the Emperor of the whole world. You have no right to doubt that Juriste would want you as his wife. Thus you may save your honour, and at the same time save the life of your brother.'

Vico wept as he spoke, and Epitia wept with him. She embraced him and did not leave him until, overcome by his tears, she had been persuaded to promise that she would surrender herself to Juriste, provided that he were willing to save Vico's life and confirm her hope of becoming his wife.

Having come to this decision with her brother the maiden went back to Juriste and told him that the hope he had given her of marrying her after their first embraces, and her wish to free Vico not only from death but from any other punishment for his error, had induced her to place herself entirely at his disposal; for both these reasons she was willing to surrender herself, but above all she requested him to promise the safety and release of her brother.

This made Juriste think himself the happiest of men since he would be able to enjoy so lovely and charming a maiden. He told her that he would repeat the promise he had previously made her and that she would receive her brother free from prison the morning after he had been with her. So having dined together Juriste and Epitia went to bed and the false villain took his full pleasure of the lady. But before he went to lie with the virgin, instead of setting Vico free, he ordered him to be beheaded at once. The lady in her anxiety for her brother's release thought only of the hour of daybreak, and never did the sun seem so to delay bringing in the day as on that night.

When morning was come, Epitia, betaking herself from Juriste's embrace, prayed him in the sweetest way to fulfil the hope he had raised of making her his wife, and meanwhile to send Vico to her, freed from prison. He replied that it had been delightful for him to be with her, that he was pleased that she had entertained the hope he had given her, and that he would send her brother to her at home. So saying he called for the gaoler and said: 'Go to the prison, remove thence the lady's brother, and take him to her house.'

Hearing this Epitia went home full of joy, expecting her brother's liberation. The gaoler had Vico's body put on a bier, set the head at its feet, and covering it with a pall had it carried to Epitia, himself going before. Entering the house he called for the young lady, and 'This,' he said, 'is your brother whom my lord Governor sends you freed from

43

prison.' With these words he had the bier uncovered and offered her brother in the way you have heard.

I do not believe that tongue could tell or human mind could comprehend the nature and depth of Epitia's anguish on being thus offered her brother's corpse when she was so joyfully expecting to see him alive and released from all penalties. I think, ladies, that you will recognize that the wretched lady's pain surpassed any ordinary grief. But she shut it deep in her heart, and whereas any other lady would have begun to weep and cry aloud, she, whom Philosophy had taught how the human soul should bear itself in every kind of fortune, showed herself unmoved. She said to the gaoler: 'You will tell your lord – and mine – that I accept my brother in the way in which he has been pleased to send him to me; and although he has not wished to fulfil my desire, I remain content to have fulfilled his; and thus I make his will my own, assuming that what he has done he must have done justly. I send him my respects, offering myself as always ready to do his will.'

The gaoler took back Epitia's message to Juriste, telling him that she had shown no sign of discomposure at so horrible a spectacle. Juriste was happy at this, reflecting that he could have had his will of the maid no more satisfactorily even if she had been his wife and if he had sent her Vico alive.

But Epitia, when the gaoler had departed, fell upon the body of her dead brother, weeping bitterly, complaining long and grievously, cursing Juriste's cruelty and her own simplicity in giving herself to him before he had released her brother. Shutting herself up alone in her room, urged on by just anger she began to say to herself: 'Will you tolerate it, Epitia, that this ruffian has taken your honour and, after promising to restore your brother alive, has sent him to you dead and in so miserable a state? Will you suffer him to boast of having deceived your simplicity with two such tricks, without giving him condign punishment?' And inciting herself thus to revenge she thought: 'My simplicity opened the way for this scoundrel to achieve to the full his dishonest desires. I resolve that his lasciviousness shall give me a way of revenge; and although to seek vengeance will not restore my brother alive, yet it will be a way of removing my vexation of spirit.' And in such a turmoil of ideas her mind closed with the thought that Juriste would send for her again to lie with him; going whither she resolved to carry concealed about her a knife and to take the first opportunity she might find of killing him, whether he were awake or asleep; and if she found it possible to cut off his head she would carry it to her brother's tomb and consecrate it to him. But then, thinking it over more maturely she saw that even if she managed to kill the deceiver, it could easily be presumed that she, as a fallen woman and eager therefore for every kind of evil, had done it in an impulse of fury, not because he had failed to keep his word. Then because she had heard how great was the justice of the Emperor (who was then at Villaco) she determined to go and find him, and to complain to his Majesty of the ingratitude and injustice shown her by Juriste, for she felt sure that the best and most just of Emperors would wreak the heaviest of punishments on that false man for his injustice and ingratitude.

So clad in mourning weeds Epitia set out alone on the journey, reached Maximian, sought audience with him, and having obtained it threw herself at his feet, and, suiting her mourning garb with a sad voice she said: 'Most Sacred Emperor, I am impelled to appear thus before you by the tyrannous ingratitude and incredible injustice shown me by Juriste, your Imperial Majesty's Governor in Innsbruck, hoping that you will so exercise your Justice that no other wretch will have to suffer such pain as the infinite misery I have received from Juriste by the wrong he has done me – no greater wrong was ever heard – and that no arrogant man will do what he has done to me, that is, miserably assassinated me (if I may be allowed to use that word before your Majesty), so that, however bitterly he be punished for it, that cannot equal the cruel and unheard of shame done me by this wicked man, giving me proof at once of both his injustice and his ingratitude.'

And now, bitterly sobbing and sighing, she told his Majesty how Juriste (giving hope of becoming his wife and freeing her brother) had robbed her of her virginity, and then had sent her her brother dead on a bier with his head at his feet; and here she gave so great a cry, and so bedewed her eyes with tears, that she moved the Emperor and the Lords about him so that they stood like men cast down for very pity. [...]

So summoning Juriste before him at the very hour when he was expecting to be led out to die, he said to him: 'The generosity of Epitia, you evil man, has such power over my will that although your crime deserves to be punished with a double death, not with one alone, she has moved me to spare your life. Your life, I wish you to understand, comes from her; and since she is willing to live with you, joined in the marriage which I ordained, I am willing to let you live with her. But if I shall ever hear that you treat her as anything but a most loving and gracious wife, I shall make you realize what great displeasure that will give me.'

With these words the Emperor, taking Epitia by the hand, gave her to Juriste. Together she and Juriste gave thanks to his Majesty for his graciousness and favour towards them; and Juriste, realizing the extent of Epitia's generosity to him, held her ever dear; so that she lived happily with him for the rest of her days.

8 King Lear

8.1 From Edmund Spenser, The Faerie Queene (1590–6)

Source: G. Bullough (ed.), *Narrative and Dramatic Sources of Shakespeare*, Volume VII: *Major Tragedies: Hamlet, Othello, King Lear, Macbeth* (London: Routledge and Kegan Paul, 1973), pp. 332–5.

The story of Lear and his daughters was a folk tale from the mythic pre-history of Britain Shakespeare would have known from a variety of sources: there were versions of it in Holinshed's *Chronicles*, the 1574 edition of *A Myrroure for Magistrates,* and there was also an earlier anonymous play on the subject, *The True Chronicle History of King Leir* (*c.*1594). We reprint an extract from Book II, Canto X of *The Faerie Queene* of Edmund Spenser (*c.*1552–99) to enable you to compare the different treatment of the Lear story by two of the most celebrated writers of early modern England. Like Shakespeare, Spenser was also profoundly interested in British pre-history as a metaphoric embodiment of political concerns which were still relevant to England during the 1590s. Shakespeare seems to have derived the stimulus for his version of Cordelia's death from Spenser's account. But take special note of the fact that Spenser's version – like Shakespeare's other sources – actually restores Lear to power, and that he predeceases Cordelia. Also compare Spenser's handling of the division of the kingdom with *King Lear,* 1.1.

27

Next him king *Leyr* in happie peace long raind,
    But had no issue male him to succeed,
    But three faire daughters, which were well uptrained,
    In all that seemed fit for kingly seed:
    Mongst whom his realme he equally decreed
    To have divided. The when feeble age
    Night to his utmoste date he saw proceed,
    He cald his daughters; and with speeches sage
Inquyrd, which of them most did love her parentage.

28

The eldest *Gonorill* gan to protest,
    That she much more then her owne life him lov'd:
    And *Regan* greater love to him profest,

Then all the world, when ever it were proov'd;
But *Cordeill* said she lov'd him, as behoov'd:
Whose simple answere, wanting colours faire
To paint it forth, him to displeasance moov'd,
That in his crowne he counted her no heire,
But twixt the other twaine his kingdome whole did shaire.

29

So wedded th' one to *Maglan* king of Scots,
And th' other to the king of *Cambria*,
And twixt them shayrd his realme by equall lots:
But without dowre the wise *Cordelia*
Was sent to *Aganip* of *Celtica*.
Their aged Syre, thus eased of his crowne,
A private life led in *Albania*,
With *Gonorill*, long had in great renowne,
That nought him griev'd to bene from rule deposed downe.

30

But true it is, that when the oyle is spent,
The light goes out, and weeke is throwne away;
So when he had resigned his regiment,
His daughter gan despise his drouping day,
And wearie waxe of his continuall stay.
Tho to his daughter *Regan* he repayrd,
Who him at first well used every way;
But when of his departure she despayrd,
Her bountie she abated, and his cheare empayrd.

31

The wretched man gan then avise too late,
That love is not, where most it is profest,
Too truely tryde in his extreamest state;
At last resolv'd likewise to prove the rest,
He to *Cordelia* him selfe addrest,
Who with entire affection him receav'd,
As for her Syre and king her seemed best;
And after all an army strong she leav'd,
To war on those, which him had of his realme bereav'd.

32

So to his crowne she him restor'd againe,
In which he dyde, made ripe for death by eld,
And after wild, it should to her remaine:

> Who peaceably the same long time did weld:
> And all mens harts in dew obedience held:
> Till that her sisters children, woxen strong
> Through proud ambition, against her rebeld,
> And overcommen kept in prison long,
> Till wearie of that wretched life, her selfe she hong.

8.2 *From Sir Philip Sidney*, Arcadia *(1590)*

Source: G. Bullough (ed.), *Narrative and Dramatic Sources of Shakespeare*, Volume VII: *Major Tragedies: Hamlet, Othello, King Lear, Macbeth* (London: Routledge and Kegan Paul, 1973), pp. 402–6.

For the story of Gloucester and his two sons, Shakespeare turned to another classic Elizabethan text, the *Arcadia* of Sir Philip Sidney (1554–86). Sidney had been both a leading courtier and a significant writer. In this extract, Sidney's protagonists Pyrocles and Musidorus come upon – in a landscape reminiscent of the storm scene of *King Lear* (3.2, 3.4) – the blinded Paphlogonian king and his faithful son, Leonatus. Compare this narrative especially with *King Lear*, 4.1 and 4.6.

It was in the kingdome of *Galacia*, the season being (as in the depth of winter) very cold, and as then sodainely growne to so extreame and foule a storme, that never any winter (I thinke) brought foorth a fouler child: so that the Princes were even compelled by the haile, that the pride of the winde blew into their faces, to seeke some shrowding place within a certaine hollow rocke offering it unto them, they made it their shield against the tempests furie. And so staying there, till the violence thereof was passed, they heard the speach of a couple, who not perceiving them (being hidde within that rude canapy) helde a straunge and pitifull disputation which made them steppe out; yet in such sort, as they might see unseene. There they perceaved an aged man, and a young, scarcely come to the age of a man, both poorely arayed, extreamely weather-beaten; the olde man blinde, the young man leading him: and yet through all those miseries, in both these seemed to appeare a kind of noblenesse, not sutable to that affliction. But the first words they heard, were these of the old man. Well *Leonatus* (said he) since I cannot perswade thee to lead me to that which should end my griefe, & thy trouble, let me now entreat thee to leave me: feare not, my miserie cannot be greater then it is, & nothing doth become me but miserie; feare not the danger of my blind steps, I cannot fall worse then I am. And doo not I pray thee, doo not obstinately continue to infect thee with my wretchednes. But flie, flie from this region, only worthy of me. Deare father (answered he) doo not take away from me the onely remnant of my happinesse: while I have power to doo your service, I am not wholly miserable. Ah my sonne (said he, and with that he groned, as if sorrow strave to breake his harte,) how evill fits it me to have such a sonne, and how much doth thy kindnesse upbraide my wickednesse? These dolefull speeches, and some others to like purpose (well shewing they had not bene borne to the fortune they were in,) moved the Princes to goe out unto them, and aske the younger what they were? Sirs (answered he, with a good grace, and made the more agreable by a certaine noble kinde of pitiousnes) I see well you are straungers, that know not our miserie so well here knowne, that no man dare know, but that we must be miserable. In deede our state is such, as though nothing is so needfull unto us as pittie, yet nothing is more daungerous unto us, then to make our selves so knowne as may stirre pittie. But your presence promiseth, that cruelty shall not over-runne hate. And if it did, in truth our state is soncke below the degree of feare.

This old man (whom I leade) was lately rightfull Prince of this countrie of *Paphlagonia*, by the hard-harted ungratefulnes of a sonne of his, deprived, not onely of his kingdome (whereof no forraine forces were ever able to spoyle him) but of his sight, the riches which Nature graunts to the poorest creatures. Whereby, and by other his unnaturall dealings, he hath bin driven to such griefe, as even now he would have had me to have led him to the toppe of this rocke, thence to cast himselfe headlong to death: and so would have made me (who received my life of him) to be the worker of his destruction. But noble Gentlemen (said he) if either of you have a father, and feele what duetifull affection is engraffed in a sonnes hart, let me intreate you to convey this afflicted Prince to some place of rest and securitie. Amongst your worthie actes it shall be none of the least, that a King, of such might and fame, and so unjustly oppressed, is in any sort by you relieved.

But before they could make him answere, his father began to speake, Ah my sonne (said he) how evill an Historian are you, that leave out the chiefe knotte of all the discourse! my wickednes, my wickednes. And if thou doest it to spare my eares, (the onely sense nowe left me proper for knowledge) assure thy selfe thou dost mistake me. And I take witnesse of that Sunne which you see (with that he cast up his blinde eyes, as if he would hunt for light,) and wish my selfe in worse case then I do wish my selfe, which is as evill as may be, if I speake untruely; that nothing is so welcome to my thoughts, as the publishing of my shame. Therefore know you Gentlemen (to whom from my harte I wish that it may not prove ominous foretoken of misfortune to have mette with such a miser as I am) that whatsoever my sonne (O God, that trueth binds me to reproch him with the name of my sonne) hath said, is true. But besides those truthes, this also is true, that having had in lawful mariage, of a mother fitte to beare royall children, this sonne (such one as partly you see, and better shall knowe by my shorte declaration) and so enjoyed the expectations in the world of him, till he was growen to justifie their expectations (so as I needed envie no father for the chiefe comfort of mortalitie, to leave an other ones-selfe after me) I was caried by a bastarde sonne of mine (if at least I be bounde to beleeve the words of that base woman my concubine, his mother) first to mislike, then to hate, lastly to destroy, to doo my best to destroy, this sonne (I thinke you thinke) undeserving destruction. What waies he used to bring me to it, if I should tell you, I should tediously trouble you with as much poysonous hypocrisie, desperate fraude, smoothe malice, hidden ambition, and smiling envie, as in any living person could be harbored. But I list it not, no remembrance, (no, of naughtines) delights me, but mine own; and me thinks, the accusing his traines might in some manner excuse my fault, which certainly I loth to doo. But the conclusion is, that I gave order to some servants of mine, whom I thought as apte for such charities as my selfe, to leade him out into a forrest, and there to kill him.

But those theeves (better natured to my sonne then my selfe) spared his life, letting him goe, to learne to live poorely: which he did, giving himselfe to be a private souldier, in a countrie here by. But as he was redy to be greatly advaunced for some noble peeces of service which he did, he hearde newes of me: who (dronke in my affection to that unlawfull and unnaturall sonne of mine) suffered my self so to be governed by him, that all favors and punishments passed by him, all offices, and places of importance distributed to his favourites; so that ere I was aware, I had left my self nothing but the name of a King: which he shortly wearie of too, with many indignities (if any thing may be called an indignity, which was laid upon me) threw me out of my seat, and put out my eies; and then (proud in his tyrannie) let me goe, nether imprisoning, nor killing me: but rather delighting to make me feele my miserie; miserie indeed, if ever there were any; full of wretchednes, fuller of disgrace, and fullest of guiltines. And as he came to the crowne by so unjust meanes, as unjustlie he kept it, by force of stranger souldiers in *Cittadels*, the nestes of tyranny, & murderers of libertie; disarming all his own countrimen, that no man durst shew himself a welwisher of mine: to say the trueth (I think) few of them being so (considering my cruell follie to my good sonne, and foolish kindnes to my unkinde bastard:) but if there were any who fell to pitie of so great a fall, and had yet any sparkes of unstained duety lefte in them towardes me, yet durst they not shewe it, scarcely with giving me almes at their doores, which yet was the onelie sustenaunce of my distressed life, no bodie daring to shewe so much charitie, as to lende me a hande to guide my darke steppes. Till this sonne of mine (God knowes, woorthie of a more vertuous, and more fortunate father) forgetting my abhominable wrongs, not recking danger, and neglecting the present good way he was in doing himselfe good, came hether to doo this kind office you see him performe towards me, to my unspeakable griefe; not onely because his kindnes is a glasse even to my blind eyes, of my naughtines, but that above all griefes, it greeves me he should desperatly adventure the losse of his soul-deserving life for mine, that yet owe more to fortune for my deserts, as if he would cary mudde in a chest of christall. For well I know, he that now raigneth, how much soever (and with good reason) he despiseth me, of all men despised; yet he will not let slippe any advantage to make away him, whose just title (ennobled by courage and goodnes) may one day shake the seate of a never secure tyrannie. And for this cause I craved of him to leade me to the toppe of this rocke, indeede I must confesse, with meaning to free him from so Serpentine a companion as I am. But he finding what I purposed, onely therein since he was borne, shewed himselfe disobedient unto me. And now Gentlemen, you have the true storie, which I pray you publish to the world, that my mischievous proceedinges may be the glorie of his filiall pietie, the onely reward now left for so great a merite. And if it may be, let me obtaine that of you, which my sonne denies me: for never was there more pity in saving any, then in ending me; both because therein my agonies shall ende, and so shall you preserve this excellent young man, who els wilfully folowes his owne ruine. [. . .]

9 *The Tempest*

9.1 *From 'The Strachey Letter' (1610) from* Purchas his Pilgrimes *(1625)*

Source: S. Orgel (ed.), *The Tempest* (Oxford University Press: Oxford Classics, 1987), pp. 209–10, 213–14, 216–19.

William Strachey's Letter provides an analogue to *The Tempest* which many critics claim Shakespeare would have seen in manuscript in 1610 or 11. Strachey (*fl.* 1609–18) describes Sir William Somers's 1609 voyage to Virginia, in which Somers's ship was caught in a sea storm and eventually shipwrecked in Bermuda (see *The Tempest*, 1.2.230). Our three extracts focus firstly on the detailed account of the storm and Strachey's description of the island; then on the rebellion against Somers's authority in Bermuda; finally, we give a brief extract which concentrates on some of the problems the Virginian colonizers experienced with American Indians. Whether or not Shakespeare was thinking directly of the experience of the Virginian colony, Strachey's letter provides a vivid parallel for the tempest which opens the play, the experience of landing on a strange and unsettling island, and for the power relationships between Prospero and Caliban.

A true repertory of the wreck and redemption of Sir Thomas Gates, Knight, upon and from the islands of the Bermudas, his coming to Virginia, and the estate of the colony then and after under the government of the Lord La Warre. July 15, 1610, written by William Strachey, Esquire.

I

A most dreadful tempest (the manifold deaths whereof are here to the life described), their wreck on Bermuda, and the description of those islands.

...We were within seven or eight days at the most...of making Cape Henry upon the coast of Virginia when on St James his day, July 14, being Monday (preparing for no less all the black night before), the clouds gathering thick upon us, and the winds singing and whistling most unusually, which made us to cast off our pinnace (towing the same until then astern), a dreadful storm and hideous began to blow from out the north-east, which swelling and roaring as it were by fits, some hours with more violence than others, at length did beat all light from heaven, which like an hell of darkness turned black upon us, so much the more fuller of horror, as in such cases horror and fear use to overrun the troubled and overmastered senses of all, which, taken up with amazement, the ears lay so sensible to the terrible cries and murmurs of the winds and distraction of our company, as who was most armed and best prepared was not a little shaken. For surely...as death comes not so sudden nor apparent, so he comes not so elvish and painful (to men especially even then in health and perfect habitudes of body) as at sea; who comes at no time so welcome, but our frailty (so weak is the hold of hope in miserable demonstrations of danger) it makes guilty of many contrary changes and conflicts. For indeed, death is accompanied at no time nor place with circumstances everyway so uncapable of particularities of goodness and inward comforts as at sea....

For four and twenty hours the storm in a restless tumult had blown so exceedingly as we could not apprehend in our imaginations any possibility of greater violence; yet did we still find it not only more terrible but more constant, fury added to fury, and one storm urging a second more outrageous than the former, whether it so wrought upon our fears, or indeed met with new forces. Sometimes strikes in our ship amongst women and passengers, not used to such hurly and discomforts, made us look one upon the other with troubled hearts and panting bosoms, our clamours drowned in the winds, and the winds in thunder. Prayers might well be in the heart and lips, but drowned in the outcries of the officers; nothing heard that could give comfort, nothing seen that might encourage hope.... Our sails wound up lay without their use, and if at any time we bore but a hullock, or half forecourse, to guide her before the sea, six and sometimes eight men were not enough to hold the whipstaff in the steerage and the tiller below in the gunner room, by which may be imagined the strength of the storm, in which the sea swelled above the clouds and gave battle to the heaven. It could not be said to rain; the waters like whole rivers did flood in the air. And this I did still observe, that whereas upon the land, when a storm hath poured itself forth once in drifts of rain, the wind as beaten down and vanquished therewith not long after endureth, here the glut of water, as if throttling the wind erewhile, was no sooner a little emptied and qualified but instantly the winds, as having gotten their mouths now free and at liberty, spake more loud and grew more tumultuous and malignant. What shall I say? Winds and seas were as mad as fury and rage could make them. For mine own part, I had been in some storms before, ... yet all that I had ever suffered gathered together might not hold in comparison with this: there was not a moment in which the sudden splitting or instant oversetting of the ship was not expected. [...]

[On landing on the island] We found it to be the dangerous and dreaded island, or rather islands, of the Bermuda, whereof let me give a brief description before I proceed to my narration. And that the rather, because they be so terrible to all that ever touched on them, and such tempests, thunders, and other fearful objects are seen and heard about them that they may be called commonly the Devil's Islands, and are feared and avoided of all sea travellers alive, above any other place in the world. Yet it pleased our merciful God to make even this hideous and hated place both the place of our safety and means of our deliverance.

And hereby also I hope to deliver the world from a foul and general error, it being counted of most that they can be no habitation for men, but rather given over to devils and wicked spirits; whereas indeed we find them now by experience to be as habitable and commodious as most countries of the same climate and situation, insomuch as if the entrance into them were as easy as the place itself is contenting, it had long ere this been inhabited as well as other islands. Thus shall we make it appear that Truth is the daughter of Time, and that men ought not to deny everything which is not subject to their own sense. [...]

The soil of the whole island is one and the same, the mould dark, red, sandy, dry, and uncapable, I believe, of any of our commodities or fruits. Sir George Summers in the beginning of August squared out a garden ... and sowed musk melons, peas, onions, radish, lettuce, and many English seeds and kitchen herbs. All which in some ten days did appear above ground, but whether by the small birds, of which there were many kinds, or by flies (worms I never saw any, nor any venomous thing, as toad or snake or any creeping beast hurtful, only some spiders, which as many affirm are signs of great store of gold; but they were long and slender-leg spiders, and whether venomous or no I know not – I believe not, since we should still find them amongst our linen in our chests and drinking cans, but we never received any danger from them; a kind of melolontha, or black beetle, there was, which bruised, gave a savour like many sweet and strong gums pounded together) – whether, I say, hindered by these or by the condition or vice of the soil, they came to no proof, nor thrived. It is like enough that the commodities of the other western islands would prosper there, as vines, lemons, oranges, and sugar canes: our governor made trial of the latter and buried some two or three in the garden mould, which were reserved in the wreck amongst many which we carried to plant here in Virginia, and they began to grow; but the hogs breaking in both rooted them up and ate them. There is not through the whole islands either champaign ground, valleys, or fresh rivers. They are full of shaws of goodly cedar, fairer than ours here of Virginia, the berries whereof our men seething, straining, and letting stand some three or four days made a kind of pleasant drink. [...]

II

[The settlers fall into dissension. A conspiracy is discovered and aborted.]

In these dangers and devilish disquiets (whilst the almighty God wrought for us and sent us, miraculously delivered from the calamities of the sea, all blessings upon the shore to content and bind us to gratefulness) thus enraged amongst ourselves to the destruction of each other, into what a mischief and misery had we been given up had we not had a governor with his authority to have suppressed the same? Yet was there a worse practice, faction and conjuration afoot, deadly and bloody, in which the life of our governor, with many others, were threatened, and could not but miscarry in his fall. But such is ever the will of God (who in the execution of his judgements breaketh the firebrands upon the head of him who first kindleth them), there were who conceived that our governor indeed neither durst nor had authority to put in execution or pass the act of justice upon anyone, how treacherous or impious soever; their own opinions so much deceiving them for the unlawfulness of any act which they would execute, daring to justify among themselves that if they should be apprehended before the performance, they should happily suffer as martyrs. They persevered therefore not only to draw unto them such a number and associates as they could work in to the abandoning of our governor and to the inhabiting of this island. They had now purposed to have made a surprise of the storehouse and to have forced from thence what was therein, either of meal, cloth, cables, arms, sails, oars, or what else it pleased God that we had recovered from the wreck and was to serve our general necessity and use, either for the relief of us while we stayed here, or for the carrying of us from this place again when our pinnace should have been furnished.

But as all giddy and lawless attempts have always something of imperfection, and that as well by the property of the action, which holdeth of disobedience and rebellion (both full of fear), as through the ignorance of the devisers themselves, so in this, besides those defects, there were some of the association who, not strong enough fortified in their own conceits, broke from the plot itself, and before the time was ripe for the execution thereof discovered the whole order and every agent and actor thereof, who nevertheless were not suddenly apprehended, by reason the confederates were divided and separated in place, some with us, and the chief with Sir George Summers in his island (and indeed all his whole company); but good watch passed upon them, every man from thenceforth commanded to wear his weapon, without which, before, we freely walked from quarter to quarter and conversed among ourselves; and every man advised to stand upon his guard, his own life not being in safety, whilst his next neighbour was not to be trusted. The sentinels and nightwarders doubled, the passages of both the quarters were carefully observed, by which means nothing was further attempted until a gentleman amongst them, one Henry Paine, the thirteenth of March, full of mischief, and every hour preparing something or other, stealing swords, adzes, axes, hatchets, saws, augurs, planes, mallets, etc. to make good his own bad end, his watch night coming about, and being called by the captain of the same to be upon the guard, did not only give his said commander evil language, but struck at him, doubled his blows, and when he was not suffered to close with him, went off the guard, scoffing at the double diligence and attendance of the watch appointed by the governor for much purpose, as he said; upon which the watch telling him if the governor should understand of his insolency, it might turn him to much blame, and haply be as much as his life were worth. The said Paine replied with a settled and bitter violence and in such unreverent terms as I should offend the modest ear too much to express it in his own phrase, but the contents were how the governor had no authority of that quality to justify upon anyone how mean soever in the colony an action of that nature, and therefore let the governor (said he) kiss etc. Which words being with the omitted additions brought the next day unto every common and public discourse, at length they were delivered over to the governor, who, ... calling the said Paine before him, and the whole company, where (being soon convinced both by the witness of the commander and many which were upon the watch with him) our governor, who had now the eyes of the whole colony fixed upon him, condemned him to be instantly hanged; and the ladder being ready, after he had made many confessions, he earnestly desired, being a gentleman, that he might be shot to death; and towards the evening he had his desire, the sun and his life setting together.

But for the other which were with Sir George, upon the Sunday follow-ing... by a mutual consent forsook their labour and Sir George Summers, and like outlaws betook them to the wild woods. Whether mere rage, and greediness after some little pearl (as it was thought) wherewith they conceived they should forever enrich themselves, and saw how to obtain the same easily in this place, or whether the desire forever to inhabit here, or whatever other secret else moved them thereunto, true it is, they sent an audacious and formal petition to our governor subscribed with all their names and seals, not only entreating him that they might stay here, but with great art importuned him that he would perform other condi-tions with them, and not wave nor evade from some of his own promises, as namely to furnish each of them with two suits of apparel and con-tribute meal rateably for one whole year, so much among them as they had weekly now, which was one pound and an half a week, for such had been our proportion for nine months. Our governor answered this their petition, writing to Sir George Summers to this effect.

[The petition is granted, but only two of the malcontents choose to remain in Bermuda. The rest of the company set sail for Virginia.] [...]

IV

[In the course of describing the settlers' troubles with the Indians, Stra-chey recounts how one of Gates's men attempts to recover a longboat that has been stranded near a native encampment.]

...certain Indians, watching the occasion, seized the poor fellow and led him up into the woods and sacrificed him. It did not a little trouble the lieutenant-governor, who since his first landing in the country, how justly soever provoked, would not by any means be wrought to a violent proceeding against them for all the practices of villainy with which they daily endangered our men, thinking it possible by a more tractable course to win them to a better condition; but now, being startled by this, he well perceived how little a fair and noble entreaty works upon a barbarous disposition, and therefore in some measure purposed to be revenged.

9.2 *From Ovid,* Metamorphoses

Source: S. Orgel (ed.), *The Tempest* (Oxford University Press: Oxford Classics, 1987), pp. 240–1.

For Ovid, see the note on the extract from *Metamorphoses* above (1.2). Shakespeare drew on this extract for Prospero's abjuring of his magic in 5.1.33–57. But the literary contexts of these speeches are very different:

Ovid's speech is part of the witch Medea's incantation as she gathers herbs to rejuvenate her father-in-law Aeson. During the course of *Metamorphoses* VII, however, Medea will use her occult powers for the purposes of revenge and murder. The fact that Prospero's speech is so closely modelled on the words of a 'black' witch may lead you to question whether or not Prospero is simply the 'white' magician (who uses his magic to virtuous ends) which he claims to be in the bulk of the play.

Before the moon should circlewise close both her horns in one
Three nights were yet as then to come. As soon as that she shone
Most full of light, and did behold the earth with fulsome face,
Medea with her hair not trussed so much as in a lace,
But flaring on her shoulders twain, and barefoot, with her gown
Ungirded, got her out of doors and wandered up and down
Alone the dead time of the night. Both man and beast and bird
Were fast asleep; the serpents sly in trailing forward stirred
So softly as you would have thought they still asleep had been.
The moisting air was whist; no leaf ye could have moving seen.
The stars alonely fair and bright did in the welkin shine.
To which she lifting up her hands did thrice herself incline,
And thrice with water of the brook her hair besprinkled she,
And gasping thrice she oped her mouth, and bowing down her knee
Upon the bare, hard ground she said, 'O trusty time of night
Most faithful unto privities, O golden stars whose light
Doth jointly with the moon succeed the beams that blaze by day,
And thou three-headed Hecatè, who knowest best the way
To compass this our great attempt and art our chiefest stay;
Ye charms and witchcrafts, and thou earth, which both with herb and weed
Of mighty working furnishest the wizards at their need;
Ye airs and winds; ye elves of hills, of brooks, of woods alone,
Of standing lakes, and of the night, approach ye every one,
Through help of whom (the crooked banks much wond'ring at the thing)
I have compellèd streams to run clean backward to their spring.
By charms I make the calm seas rough and make the rough seas plain,
And cover all the sky with clouds and chase them thence again.
By charms I raise and lay the winds and burst the viper's jaw,
And from the bowels of the earth both stones and trees do draw.
Whole woods and forests I remove; I make the mountains shake,
And even the earth itself to groan and fearfully to quake.
I call up dead men from their graves; and thee, O lightsome moon,
I darken oft, though beaten brass abate thy peril soon;
Our sorcery dims the morning fair and darks the sun at noon.
The flaming breath of fiery bulls ye quenchèd for my sake,
And causèd their unwieldy necks the bended yoke to take.
Among the earth-bred brothers you a mortal war did set,
And brought asleep the dragon fell whose eyes were never shet,
By means whereof deceiving him that had the golden fleece

In charge to keep, you sent it thence by Jason into Greece.
Now have I need of herbs that can by virtue of their juice
To flowering prime of lusty youth old withered age reduce.
I am assured ye will it grant; for not in vain have shone
These twinkling stars, ne yet in vain this chariot all alone
By draught of dragons hither comes.' With that was from the sky
A chariot softly glancèd down, and stayèd hard thereby.

CRITICAL READINGS

Part 2

Introduction and Headnotes

Introduction

In Part Two, we reprint critical interpretations of the nine plays, as well as extracts on Shakespeare's theatre, and the editing of the Shakespeare text. For each of the plays, there are two or three extracts that focus on different aspects of the play, including its subsequent critical reception and production history. In selecting the critical extracts, we have been guided by the following (not always compatible) criteria.

- The first criterion is that the extracts complement and build on the commentaries on the plays in *Shakespeare: Texts and Contexts*.
- Secondly, as many as possible of the major schools of Shakespeare criticism of the last 60 years are represented at some length.
- Thirdly, Shakespeare critics from different generations and writing in different contexts are represented.
- Fourthly, read together, the extracts juxtapose very different interpretations of the same texts, provoking readers (we hope) to return to the texts themselves, and develop their own readings.
- Finally, given the particular interests of this course, we have favoured critical extracts that engage with performance issues, and with the relation between the Shakespeare text and its multiple contexts.

In the headnotes, in addition to describing the contexts of the extracts, and summarizing their main points of interest, we have cross-referenced to other related extracts reprinted here. Note finally, that the bibliographies and further reading sections in *Shakespeare: Texts and Contexts* and in *The Norton Shakespeare* provide a useful starting point for more extensive reading.

1   *A Midsummer Night's Dream*

1.1   *Louis Montrose, 'The Imperial Votaress'*

Source: L. Montrose, *The Purpose of Playing: Shakespeare and the Cultural Politics of the Elizabethan Theatre* (Chicago and London: University of Chicago Press, 1996), Chapter 10, pp. 151–4, 158–61, 167–78.

Published in 1996, this extract from Louis Montrose's chapter on *A Midsummer Night's Dream* examines the historical context of the play's original production. Part of the critical movement that arose in the United States in the 1980s designated 'new historicism', Montrose is concerned with how the theatre functioned in relation to the power structures of the Elizabethan state. The rich historical detail in the extract enables an informed assessment of *A Midsummer Night's Dream* at the moment of its first performance, while at the same time highlighting the limitations of formal, decontextualized interpretations of the play. In the particular case of *A Midsummer Night's Dream*, the concern with historical context is inflected to account for the complex gender politics of the period, with the presence of a female monarch complicating masculine hierarchies, both at the level of the state, and on the stage. New historicists have been criticized for reading Renaissance plays as enacting the state's capacity to contain all forms of dissent, but Montrose detects in *A Midsummer Night's Dream* a subversive dimension at odds with the conservative resolutions in the final act. As the extracts below by critics as diverse as John Dover Wilson and Alan Sinfield demonstrate, Shakespeare critics concerned with the historical context of Elizabethan England are far from unified. They bring the preoccupations of their own contexts to bear on how they read Shakespeare's plays and world, and Montrose writing in 1990s North America is no exception.

[A] counter-discourse is active in *A Midsummer Night's Dream*, and [...] this counter-discourse intermittently disrupts and destabilizes the normative discourse of patriarchy that dominates both Elizabethan culture and Shakespeare's play. Through its production of textual and performative ironies, dissonances, and contradictions, *A Midsummer Night's Dream* pinpoints some of the joints and stresses in the ideological structures that shaped the culture of which it is an instance; and it discloses – perhaps, in a sense, despite itself – that patriarchal norms are compensatory for men's perceptions that they are vulnerable to the powers of women. Such moments of textual disclosure also illuminate the interplay between gender politics in the Elizabethan household and gender politics in the Elizabethan state, for the woman to whom *all* Elizabethan men were subject and vulnerable was Queen Elizabeth herself. As summarized by Thomas Wilson in 1600, it was the exclusive privilege of the Queen to

> pardon and give lyfe to the condemned or to take away the life or member of any subject at her pleasure, and none other in all ye Kingdom hath power of life and member but onely the Prince, noe not so much as to imprison or otherwise to punish any other, unless it be his servant, without express commission from the Queen.

Within legal and fiscal limits, this female prince held the power of life and death over every Englishman; the power to advance or frustrate the worldly desires of all her subjects. I explore the modes in which that gendered royal power is figured and mediated in *A Midsummer Night's Dream*. Since the play's figures are complex reworkings of already existing representations, to study them is also to locate the play in the Elizabethan cultural intertext that constituted "the Queen."

I

At the beginning of her reign, Elizabeth formulated the strategy by which she turned the political liability of her gender to advantage for the next half century. She told her first parliament that she was content to have as her epitaph, "that a Queene, having raigned such a tyme, lived and dyed a virgin"; and she assured her second, "that though after my death yow may have many stepdames, yet shall yow never have any a more naturall mother then I meane to be unto you all." She appropriated not only the suppressed cult of the Blessed Virgin but also the Tudor conception of the Ages of Woman. Thus, the queen's self-mastery and mastery of others were enhanced by an elaboration of her maidenhood into a cult of eroticized virginity that "allows of amorous admiration but prohibits desire"; the displacement of her wifely duties from a household to a nation; and the sublimation of her temporal and ecclesiastical authority into a nurturing maternity. By fashioning herself into a singular combination of maiden, matron, and mother, the Queen transformed the normative domestic life-cycle of an Elizabethan woman into what was at once a social paradox and a quasi-religious mystery.

At the very beginning of her reign, Elizabeth's parliaments and counselors boldly but unsuccessfully urged her to marry and to produce an heir. In her delicately balanced response to her first parliament, she pointedly contrasted a petition "that is simple and conteineth no limytacion of place or person" to one that seeks to constrain the sovereign; of the latter sort, she declared, with obvious irritation and disdain,

> I muste nedes have myslyked it verie muche and thought it in yow a verie great presumption, being unfitting and altogether unmete for yow to

> require them that may commande, or those to appoynte whose partes are to
> desire, or such to bynde and lymite whose duties are to obaye, or to take
> upon yow to drawe my love to your lykinges or frame my will to your
> fantasies.
>
> (*Proceedings in the Parliaments of Elizabeth I*, 45)

Despite the royal warning, Elizabethan masculine subjects were to continue, by various and sometimes highly elaborate or subtle rhetorical and
performative means, to seek to draw the queen's love to their likings and
to frame her will to their fantasies. Throughout the reign, Queen Elizabeth's marital status and her sexual condition remained matters of state,
but ones more safely negotiated through the oblique strategies of fictive
forms and actions than through parliamentary petitions and printed
tracts.

There was a deeply felt and loudly voiced need to insure a legitimate
succession, upon which the welfare of the whole people depended. But
there may also have been another, more obscure motivation that amplified these requests. The political nation, which was wholly a nation of
men, seems at times to have found it frustrating or degrading to serve a
female prince – a woman who was herself unsubjected to any man. Late in
Elizabeth's reign, the French ambassador observed that "her government
is fairly pleasing to the people, who show that they love her, but it is little
pleasing to the great men and nobles; and if by chance she should die, it is
certain that the English would never again submit to the rule of a woman."
Elizabeth's rule was not intended to undermine the masculine hegemony
of her society. The emphasis upon her *difference* from other women seems
to have been designed, in part, to neutralize the appearance of such a
threat; it was a strategy for personal survival and political legitimation
within a social and political culture that was pervasively patriarchal. That
the threat nevertheless remained quite real is apparent from the evidence
that at least some of her masculine subjects worked very hard to contain
or contest it. This attitude was an affective consequence of a fundamental
cultural contradiction specific to Elizabethan society: namely, the expectation that English gentlemen would manifest loyalty and obedience to their
sovereign at the same time that they exercised masculine authority over
women. It would be naïvely reductive to suggest that either the person or
the cult of Queen Elizabeth provides an adequate causal explanation for
the heightened social perception of women's challenge to the patriarchal
order, the beginnings of which perception coincide with the beginning of
her reign. However, without going so far as to redefine history as the
biography of great women, I think it may reasonably be claimed that there
existed an indirect but nevertheless reciprocally influential relationship
between the widespread social perception that Elizabethan women were
more apt to be out of place than their predecessors and the contempora-

neous political and cultural reality that the throne was occupied by a woman of remarkable skills and accomplishments who was unmarried and thus not subjected to any man. [...]

Perhaps four or five years before the first production of *A Midsummer Night's Dream*, in a pastoral entertainment enacted before the Queen at Sudeley during the progress of 1591, the royal presence changed Ovid's metamorphosis of Daphne into an emblem of Constancy. Daphne, pursued by Apollo, was transformed into a tree; Apollo's ensuing song concluded that "neither men nor gods, can force affection." "The song ended, the tree rived, and DAPHNE issued out, APOLLO ranne after," himself apparently unregenerate. "DAPHNE running to her Majestie uttred this": "I stay, for whether should chastety fly for succour, but to the Queene of chastety." Daphne was then reprieved from the potential consequences of Apollo's lust and craft simply by the power of Elizabeth's presence, "that by vertue, there might be assurance in honor." As "the Queene of chastety," Elizabeth incarnated Diana, to whom Ovid's Daphne was votary. In Ovid's *Metamorphoses*, when Daphne cried for succour to her father Peneus, she was changed into the laurel. At Sudeley, Daphne's metamorphosis into a tree was less an escape than a demonic incarceration from which she had to be liberated. The queen's virtuous magic derived from a kind of matriarchal virginity; her powers transcended those of the lustful and paternal pagan gods. In Elizabethan royal iconography, the Queen was made responsible for the fate of only one victim of Ovidian metamorphosis: namely, Actaeon, the transgressing masculine devotee of a virgin goddess.

From early in the reign, Elizabeth had been directly addressed and engaged by such performances as the one at Sudeley. Distinctions were effaced between the spatio-temporal locus of the royal spectator/actor and that of the characters being enacted before her. Debates were referred directly to her arbitration; the magic of her presence civilized savage men, restored the blind to sight, released errant knights from enchantment, and rescued virgins from defilement. These social dramas of celebration and coercion played out the delicately balanced relationship between the monarch and those of her subjects who constituted the political nation – nobility, gentry, and urban elites. A significant collateral effect of these events must have been to evoke reverence and awe in the local common folk who assisted in and witnessed them. And because texts and descriptions of most of these processions, pageants, and shows were in print within a year – sometimes, within just a few days – of their performance, they may have had a cultural impact far more extensive and enduring than their occasional and ephemeral character might at first suggest. The scenarios of such royal pageantry as was presented at Kenilworth, Norwich, Elvetham, and Sudeley appropriated materials from popular late medieval romances, from Ovid, Petrarch, and other literary sources; and when late Elizabethan plays and poems such as *A Midsummer Night's Dream* and *The Faerie Queene* reappropriated those sources, they were now inscribed by the allegorical discourse of Elizabethan royal courtship, panegyric, and political negotiation. Thus, the deployment of Ovidian, Petrarchan, and allegorical romance modes by late Elizabethan writers must be read in terms of an intertextuality that includes both the discourse of European literary history and the discourse of Elizabethan state power.

II

As has long been recognized, *A Midsummer Night's Dream* has affinities with Elizabethan royal iconography and courtly entertainments. Harold Brooks cautiously endorses two familiar and frequently conflated hypotheses regarding the play's occasion: that it was "designed to grace a wedding in a noble household," and that "it seems likely that Queen Elizabeth was present when the *Dream* was first acted. . . . She delighted in homage paid to her as the Virgin Queen, and receives it in the myth-making about the imperial votaress." It should be noted that both of these hypotheses make originary claims for a royal or aristocratic occasion. Nevertheless, it seems to have been common practice for the professional players to perform at court or in noble houses plays that were already part of their repertory in the public playhouse, perhaps revising or cutting them for a special occasion and venue. Although attractive, the widely accepted general hypothesis of the play's occasion is without substantiation. Furthermore, scholars have advanced competing candidates for the specific occasion, the evidence in each case being entirely conjectural. My own perspective on the play's connection to the monarch and to the culture of the court construes their relationship as dialectical rather than causal, as structural rather than incidental. Whether or not Elizabeth was physically present at the first performance of *A Midsummer Night's Dream*, and whether or not the play was first (or ever) performed for an aristocratic wedding, the pervasive cultural presence of the Queen was a condition of the play's imaginative possibility. And, in the sense that the royal presence was itself represented within the play, the play appropriated and extended the imaginative possibilities of the queen. Thus, I construe Shakespeare's *A Midsummer Night's Dream* as calling attention to itself, not only as an end but also as a source of cultural production.

At Sudeley, it was in the power of the royal virgin to undo the metamorphosis, to release Daphne from her arboreal imprisonment and to protect her from the advances of Apollo. In *A Midsummer Night's Dream*, however, magical power is invested not in the Queen but in the King, her husband. Immediately after invoking the royal vestal and vowing to torment the Fairy Queen, Oberon encounters Helena in pursuit of Demetrius. In Shakespeare's metamorphosis of Ovid – and, perhaps, his metamorphosis of Sudeley – "the story shall be chang'd / Apollo flies, and Daphne holds the chase" [2.1.230–1]. Oberon's response is neither to extinguish desire nor to make it mutual but rather to restore the normal pattern of pursuit: "Fare thee well, nymph; ere he do leave this grove / Thou shalt fly him and he shall seek thy love" [2.1.245–6]. Unlike Elizabeth, Oberon uses his mastery over Nature to subdue others to their passions. The festive conclusion of *A Midsummer Night's Dream* depends upon the success of a process by which the feminine pride and power manifested in Amazon warriors, possessive mothers, unruly wives, and willful daughters are brought under the control of lords and husbands. When the contentious young lovers have been sorted into pairs by Oberon, then Theseus can invite them to share his own wedding day. If the Duke finally overbears Egeus' will [4.1.176], it is because the father's obstinate claim to "the ancient privilege of Athens" [1.1.41] threatens to obstruct the very process by which Athenian privilege and Athens itself are reproduced. The desires of Hermia and Helena are, of course, fulfilled; nevertheless, those apparently subjective individual choices have been shaped by a social imperative. Thus, neither for Oberon nor for Theseus does a contradiction exist between mastering the desires of a wife and patronizing the desires of a maiden. [...]

In their study of English state formation as cultural revolution, Philip Corrigan and Derek Sayer point out the significance of the inclusion of witchcraft among a number of other acts that became classified as felonies and thus as capital crimes during the Tudor period. The witches' compact with Satan and with each other constituted a conspiracy against the godly state. Noting that witchcraft in this period was perceived to be a crime overwhelmingly (although not exclusively) committed by women, they suggest that witchcraft prosecutions exemplify the "structuring by gender of society and its self-images through state routines." Beliefs that all women were potentially dangerous, and that "women not under patriarchal authority were particularly dangerous," are reflected in the datum that "the largest single category of convicted witches, who were ritually burned to death, were old, single women." As the Virgin Queen – and, by the 1590s, as an old, single woman – Elizabeth was, uniquely, a ruler whose political power, personal mythology, and physical condition bore a disquieting resemblance to those associated with Amazons, witches, and other unruly women. In *A Midsummer Night's Dream*, the conjuncture of the witch and the Virgin Queen is effected through a mythological displacement, and activated through the trope of "the triple Hecate" invoked by Puck. The multiform goddess was ubiquitous not only in Roman mythological poetry and drama but in the Renaissance mythography that pervaded the learned culture of Elizabethan England. As Abraham

Fraunce describes this triune goddess, "in heaven she is called *Luna*, in the woods *Diana*, under the earth *Hecate*, or *Proserpina*." [...] [At] the same time that Shakespeare's play evokes Queen Elizabeth through its allusions to Cynthia and Diana, by the same means it insinuates her malign and dangerous aspect. [...]

III

In the third scene of Shakespeare's play, after Titania has remembered her Indian votaress [2.1.123–37], Oberon remembers his "imperial votress." He has once beheld,

> Flying between the cold moon and the earth,
> Cupid all arm'd; a certain aim he took
> At a fair vestal, throned by the West,
> And loos'd his love-shaft smartly from his bow
> As it should pierce a hundred thousand hearts.
> But I might see young Cupid's fiery shaft
> Quench'd in the chaste beams of the watery moon;
> And the imperial votress passed on,
> In maiden meditation, fancy-free.
> Yet mark'd I where the bolt of Cupid fell:
> It fell upon a little western flower,
> Before milk-white, now purple with love's wound:
> And maidens call it 'love-in-idleness'.
> ...
> The juice of it, on sleeping eyelids laid,
> Will make or man or woman madly dote
> Upon the next live creature that it sees.
> [2.1.156–68, 170–2]

The evocative monologues of Titania and Oberon are carefully matched and contrasted: The Faery Queen speaks of a mortal mother from the east; the Faery King speaks of an invulnerable virgin from the west. Their memories express two myths of origin: Titania provides a genealogy for the changeling and an explanation of why she will not part with him; Oberon provides an aetiology of the metamorphosed flower that he will use to make her part with him.

Subsequently, the deluded Titania treats Bottom as if he were both her child and her lover – which seems entirely appropriate, since he is a substitute for the changeling boy, who is, in turn, Oberon's rival for Titania's attentions. Titania herself is ambivalently benign and sinister, imperious and enthralled. She dotes upon Bottom, and indulges in him all those desires to be fed, scratched, and coddled that render Bottom's dream recognizable to us as a parodic fantasy of infantile narcissism and dependency. But it is also, at the same time, a parodic fantasy of upward social mobility. Titania mingles her enticements with threats:

> Out of this wood do not desire to go:
> Thou shalt remain here, whether thou wilt or no.
> I am a spirit of no common rate;
> The summer still doth tend upon my state;
> And I do love thee: therefore go with me.
> I'll give thee fairies to attend on thee;
> And they shall fetch thee jewels from the deep,
> And sing, while thou on pressed flowers dost sleep:
> And I will purge thy mortal grossness so,
> That thou shalt like an airy spirit go.
> [3.1.134–43]

The sublimation of matter into spirit is identified with the social elevation of the base artisan into the gentry: Titania orders her attendants to "be kind and courteous to this gentleman" [3.1.146], to 'do him courtesies' [156], and to "wait upon him" [178]; she concludes the scene, however, with an order to enforce her minion's passivity, thus reducing him to the demeanor prescribed for women, children, and servants: "Tie up my love's tongue, bring him silently" [182]. This order is, perhaps, a sinister glance at the dangerously powerful feminine personages of Diana and Circe, with whom Titania shares her name. [. . .]

Unlike the inviolable vestal, or the already espoused Titania, Shakespeare's comic heroines are in transition between the conditions of maiden and wife, daughter and mother. These transitions are mediated by the wedding rite and the act of defloration, which are brought together at the end of *A Midsummer Night's Dream*: When the newlyweds have retired for the night, Oberon and Titania enter the court in order to bless the "bridebed" where the marriages are about to be consummated. By the act of defloration, the husband takes physical and symbolic possession of his bride. The sexual act in which the man draws blood from the woman is already implicit, at the beginning of the play, in Theseus's vaunt: "Hippolyta, I woo'd thee with my sword, / And won thy love doing thee injuries" [1.1.16–17]. In the play-within-the-play, which wears away the hours 'between our after-supper and bedtime' [5.1.34], the impending injury is evoked by malapropism and is thus dismissed with laughter: Pyramus finds Thisbe's mantle "stain'd with blood," and concludes that "lion vile hath here deflower'd [his] dear" [5.1.272, 281]. The image in which Oberon describes the flower's metamorphosis suggests the immanence of defloration in the very origin of desire: "The bolt of Cupid fell/ . . . Upon a little western flower,/Before milk-white, now purple with love's wound." Cupid's shaft violates the flower when it has been deflected from the vestal: Oberon's purple passion flower is procreated in a displaced and literalized defloration.

The change suffered by the flower – from the pristine whiteness of milk to the purple wound of love – juxtaposes maternal nurturance and erotic violence. For Elizabethan auditors and readers, the metamorphosis may have carried a suggestion not only of defloration but also of menstruation – and, perhaps, of the menarche, which was taken to be the sign of female sexual maturity, the advent of womanhood and potential motherhood. In Elizabethan popular gynecology, the observed relationship between lactation and amenorrhea was explained by the belief that mother's milk is a transubstantiation and refinement of menstrual blood: "Why have not women with childe the flowers?... Because that then the flowers turne into milke, and into the nourishment of the childe" (*Problemes of Aristotle*, E5r). An awareness that the commonest Elizabethan term for menses was "flowers" adds a peculiar resonance to certain occurrences of flower imagery in Renaissance texts. This is especially the case in *A Midsummer Night's Dream*, in which flowers are conspicuously associated with female sexuality and with the moon. Consider Titania's observation:

> The moon, methinks, looks with a watery eye,
> And when she weeps, weeps every little flower,
> Lamenting some enforced chastity.
> [3.1.179–81]

The answer to the question, "Why do the flowers receive their name *Menstrua*, of this word *Mensis* a moneth?" constitutes a gloss on Titania's speech:

> Bicause it is a space of time which doth measure the Moone. ...Now the Moone hath dominion over moist things, and bicause the flowers are an humiditie, they take their denomination of the moneth, and are called monethly termes: for moist things do increase as the Moone doth increase, and decrease as she doth decrease.
> (*Problemes of Aristotle*, E5r)

Such oblique menstrual symbolism suggests that a subliminal discourse on female sexuality pervades Shakespeare's text. The imagery of the text insinuates that, whatever its provenance in horticultural lore, Oberon's maddening love-juice is also a sublimation of vaginal blood. It conflates menstrual blood with the blood of defloration: The former is the ambivalent sign of women's generative power and of their sexual pollution, of the dangers they pose to men's potency, to their reason, and to their honor; the latter is the sign of men's assertion of control over women's bodies, the sign of masculine mastery over potentially dangerous feminine generative and erotic powers.

Unlike the feminine *dramatis personae* of *A Midsummer Night's Dream,* Oberon's vestal virgin is not subject to Cupid's shaft, to the frailties of the flesh and the fancy. Nor is she subject to the mastery of men. Isolated from the experiences of desire, marriage, and maternity, she is immune to the pains and pleasures of human mutability. But it is precisely her bodily and mental impermeability which make possible Oberon's pharmacopoeia. The floral symbolism of female sexuality that is begun in Oberon's description of "love-in-idleness" is completed when he names "Dian's bud" [4.1.70] as its antidote. With Cupid's flower, Oberon can make the Fairy Queen "full of hateful fantasies" [2.1.258]; and with Dian's bud, he can win her back to his will. In the very act of preserving "Dian's bud," the "fair vestal" is indirectly responsible for the creation of "love-in-idleness." Thus, her invulnerability to desire becomes doubly instrumental to Oberon in his reaffirmation of romantic, marital, and parental norms that have been inverted during the course of the play. Ironically, the vestal's very freedom from fancy guarantees the subjection of others. She is necessarily excluded from the erotic world of which her own chastity is the efficient cause. [. . .]

My point is not that the structure and ethos of *A Midsummer Night's Dream* are indifferent to the cultural resonance of the Queen but rather that the play's own cultural resonance may be said to depend precisely upon the dramaturgical exclusion of the queen, upon her *conspicuous* absence. It has been the norm for critics and editors of *A Midsummer Night's Dream* to identify the "imperial votress" as an allusion to Queen Elizabeth, and to interpret it as an incidental, topical compliment, rather than as an integral element of the play's dramaturgy and ideology. From the latter perspective, however, Shakespeare's ostensible royal compliment may be seen as a complex mediation of the charismatic royal presence that pervaded late Elizabethan culture and as an appropriation of the cult of the Virgin Queen. The poetic texts of Spenser often fragment the royal image, refracting aspects of the Queen "in mirrours more then one" (*FQ.*3.Proem.5). In a similar way, Shakespeare's play text splits the triune Elizabethan cult image between the fair vestal, who is an unattainable *virgin*, and the Fairy Queen, who is represented as both an intractable *wife* and a dominating *mother*. Oberon uses one against the other in order to reassert masculine prerogatives.

Within Elizabethan society, relationships of authority and dependency, of desire and fear were characteristic of both the public and the domestic domains. Domestic relations between husbands and wives, parents and children, masters and servants were habitually politicized: the household was a microcosm of the state; at the same time, socioeconomic and political relationships of patronage and clientage were habitually eroticized: the devoted suitor sought some loving return from his master-mistress. The collective and individual impact of Elizabethan symbolic forms frequently depended upon an interplay between these domains. Indeed, the political transactions of Elizabeth's reign were so fundamentally individual and interpersonal in character that it is perhaps anachronistic to distinguish any exclusively public domain of Elizabethan political life.

Within *A Midsummer Night's Dream*, the public and domestic domains of Elizabethan culture converge in the absent figure of the imperial votaress. Queen Elizabeth was a woman ruler officially represented, by herself and by others, as the virgin mother of her subjects. When those same Elizabethan subjects employed the themes of masculine procreative power, autogeny, and mastery of women in their own speech and writing, the familiar tropes of misogyny and patriarchy could acquire a seditious resonance, a resonance that was specific to the gendered discourse of Elizabethan state power. In this sense, the ruler and the ruled, the Queen and the playwright, are construable as subjects differentially shaped within a shared conjuncture of language and social relations, who jointly reshape that conjuncture in the very process of performing it.

All of Shakespeare's plays may have been written with the possibility in mind of courtly as well as commercial performances, and there is evidence that a number of them during both the Elizabethan and Jacobean reigns were performed in both venues. Some plays may have received their most lucrative performances at court or in aristocratic households, but there is no evidence that any of them was originally written for such a performance. Certainly, the potential for both courtly and public performances provides evidence for the shared tastes of Queen and commoner. And, needless to say, the advertisement that a play had been performed at court or before the Queen was intended to enhance the interest of Elizabeth's theatre-going or play-reading subjects, who might thereby vicariously share the source of her majesty's entertainment. Nevertheless, despite the very broad social appeal of Shakespearean and other plays, we should resist any consequent impulse to homogenize Elizabethan culture and society into an organic unity. Shakespeare's plays played to both courtly and popular audiences, and these audiences constituted frequently overlapping but nevertheless distinct and potentially contradictory sources of socioeconomic support and ideological constraint.

The writing of plays that would be playable in both the commercial playhouses and in the royal court points toward the transitional nature of the material and ideological conditions in which the Elizabethan theatre emerged and thrived. That *A Midsummer Night's Dream* was originally (or ever) performed as an aristocratic wedding entertainment, at which the Queen herself was present, is an attractive but unproven hypothesis.

What we know for certain is that the title page of the first quarto, printed in 1600, claims to present *A Midsummer Night's Dream* "As it hath been sundry times publickely acted, by the Right honourable the Lord Chamberlaine his servants." Shakespeare's play was not itself a product of the court but rather of a professional and commercial theatre that existed in an ambiguous and delicate relationship to the court. Despite the legal fiction that public performances served to keep the privileged players of the Lord Chamberlain's Men in readiness for performance at court, and despite whatever adaptions may have been made in repertory plays to suit them to the conditions of particular court performances, the dramaturgical and ideological matrix of the Shakespearean drama was located not in the royal court but in the professional playhouse.

1.2 Jay L. Halio, 'The Staging of A Midsummer Night's Dream, *1595–1895*'

Source: J. M. Mucciolo et al., *Shakespeare's Universe: Renaissance Ideas and Conventions: Essays in Honour of W. R. Elton* (London: Scolar Press, 1996), pp. 158–71.

Published in the same year as Montrose's book, Jay Halio's essay on the staging of *A Midsummer Night's Dream* is a performance history of the play from the sixteenth to the nineteenth century. Whereas Montrose directs substantial attention to the political and social pressures framing *A Midsummer Night's Dream* in the 1590s, Halio refers only incidentally to extra-literary and extra-dramatic material, and focuses instead upon the minutiae of different performances of the play over three centuries. Halio records the variety of innovations and changes introduced since the original production: the replacement of boy actors with actresses; the rewriting and editing of the Folio text; the addition of music; the utilization of new technological possibilities; and changes in stage design and dress. In the process, he shows clearly how in translating the play from text to performance, new interpretations of *A Midsummer Night's Dream* have been forged. While it might lack the kind of detailed contextualization provided by Montrose, and as a result give relatively superficial interpretations of the different productions, Halio's essay foregrounds the instability of the Shakespeare text, and offers an invaluable resource for theatre practitioners contemplating a production of *A Midsummer Night's Dream* now.

[. . .] While we have no concrete, first-hand reports of the play's reception in Shakespeare's time – or indeed any time before the Restoration in 1660 – we can infer that it was revived fairly often and was therefore quite popular. It was probably one of the first plays chosen for performance before King James I on New Year's Day, 1604, if the play 'of Robin goode-fellow' reported by Dudley Carlton refers in fact to *The Dream*. In the Folio text, which contains some revisions as well as new stage directions and was probably printed from a copy of the second quarto marked up from a theatrical manuscript (very likely the promptbook), an actor named Tawyer, who did not join the King's Men until later on, is mentioned by name in a stage direction at [5.1.125]: 'Tawyer with a Trumpet before them'. Other variants between the first edition (the Fisher quarto of 1600) and the Folio also suggest revision for stage revival. Chambers suspects that, curiously, an amateur performance in 1631 was held 'for the Sabbath delectation of Bishop Williams'.

The King's Men apparently revived the play for their patron again on 17 October 1630 at Hampton Court Palace, according to a document printed in G. E. Bentley's *Caroline and Jacobean Drama*. How often it had been revived between 1604 and 1630 for the sovereign's pleasure or others' is not known. Some parts of it remained popular even during the period when the theatres were officially closed (1642–60); the comic interludes involving Bottom and his friends tended to separate from the main body of the play and develop a life of their own under such titles as *The Comedy of Pyramus and Thisbe* and *The Merry Conceits of Bottom the Weaver*. A 'droll' called *Bottom the Weaver*, published in 1661, maintains on the title page that 'It hath been often publickely Acted by some of his Majesties Comedians, and lately, privately, presented, by several Apprentices for their harmless recreation, with Great Applause', but no details of these purported performances have come down to us.

Bottom the Weaver is the earliest published adaptation of the play after the Restoration and preserves all the episodes involving Quince, Bottom, and the rest taken from the text of the Second Folio. The young lovers are omitted, and the roles of Titania, Oberon and Puck severely cut. A few brief additions, based on Shakespeare's lines, are included to provide continuity. The printed list of actors indicates that a number of parts may be doubled, especially the roles of Theseus and Oberon. The doubling probably reflects earlier stage tradition – one that recent productions have revived with interesting effects. *Bottom the Weaver* was reprinted in 1673 in a collection of short plays (*The Wits*, Part II) and is the longest play in it.

Other adaptations indicate how the play caught the imagination, if not as Shakespeare wrote it, then as current taste dictated he might have or should have written it. By 1660, when the theatres reopened and productions were heavily influenced by French neo-classicism, a more 'refined' stage decorum prevailed. Shakespeare's plays were mined by other dramatists, such as Davenant and Dryden, who rewrote them to meet the tastes of their age. Samuel Pepys saw the *Dream* acted on 29 September 1662.

Although we don't know what version he saw or who performed in it, it was among Shakespeare's plays assigned to Thomas Killgrew and the King's Company after the Restoration. Probably the text was close to that of the Folio, for Pepys did not like what he saw. His remarks, often quoted, say more about the taste of his time than the actual production: 'Then to the King's Theatre, where we saw "Midsummer Night's Dream", which I had never seen before nor shall ever again, for it is the most insipid ridiculous play that I ever saw in my life. I saw, I confess, some good dancing and some handsome women, which was all my pleasure.'

Dancing indeed. By this time, of course, following the French lead, women had taken the female roles hitherto usually played by boys. Under Continental influences, too, Elkanah Settle transformed Shakespeare's *Dream* into an opera called *The Fairy Queen* with music by Henry Purcell. Thomas Betterton produced it in 1692 at Dorset Gardens Theatre. It was revived the next year with additional music and songs by Purcell. However, he did not set a single line of Shakespeare's to music. The Shakespearean parts in this severely mangled version are all spoken and acted. The lovers, the fairies, the rude mechanicals are there, but so are new characters: Coridon, Mopsa, nymphs, 'a Chorus of *Fawns*, and *Naids*, with *Woodmen*, and *Hay-makers* Dancers'. In addition, allegorical figures – Night, Mystery, Secrecy, Sleep – and their attendants appear, as well as Spring, Summer, Autumn and Winter with Phoebus for a 'Dance of the Four Seasons'. The opera has still more for the delight of the age: Juno, a chorus of Chinese men and women, a dance of six monkeys, and 'a Grand Dance of 24 *Chineses*' (as recorded in 'The Names of the Persons' in Jacob Tonson's edition of 1692).

Tonson's edition does not give Purcell's music, which is now available (in a form adapted for modern voices) among Edwin F. Kalmus's vocal scores that includes the augmentations of 1693. Therefore, to reconstruct the productions of 1692–3 one must consult both the Tonson edition and Kalmus's score. With origins in Italy and France, opera was a relatively recent art form in Britain that Sir William Davenant had introduced. The Preface to *The Fairy Queen* calls his *Siege of Rhodes* 'the first Opera we ever had in England' and bemoans the lack of financial support from the crown that would make English opera a true rival to the Continental. Perhaps the enormous expense in mounting such a production – £3000 – is the reason the complete opera was not revived after 1693, when the opera just barely broke even, despite its highly successful staging, which definitely catered to the taste of the times, debased though it may appear to us.

A good deal of cutting of Shakespeare's text was obviously necessary to make room for the songs, instrumental music, dancing, and spectacle that were now inserted. Some omissions were doubtless concessions to contemporary taste, for example, the deletion of Titania's description of the games she played with the pregnant Indian princess [2.1.124–35]. Diction was also altered for much the same reason: to satisfy the 'refinements' of the age. Hence, Lysander and Hermia's dialogue in Act 1.1 is not only abbreviated, but transformed in part as follows:

> *Ly.* O my true *Hermia*! I have never found
> By Observation, nor by History,
> That Lovers run a smooth, and even course:
> Either they are unequal in their Birth –
> *Her.* O cross too high to be impos'd on Love!
> *Ly.* Or if there be a Simpathy in choice,
> War, Sickness, or pale Death lay Siege to it,
> Making it momentary as a sound,
> Swift as the Lightning in the blackest night …

Such changes invariably flattened the poetic effect. But in an age that saw – and preferred – Nahum Tate's *King Lear* (1681) to Shakespeare's, that is hardly surprising.

Aided by advances in theatrical machinery and movable stage sets, spectacle became increasingly important on the Restoration stage (as it has done these days in Broadway and West End musicals), and *The Fairy Queen* was 'second to none for mechanical marvels'. At the end of Act 3, for example, Titania summons her elves to prepare 'a Fairy Mask' to entertain Bottom and orders her bower to become an 'Enchanted Lake'. At once '*The Scene changes to a great Wood; a long row of large Trees on each side: A River in the middle: Two rows of lesser Trees of different kind just on the side of the River, which meet in the middle, and make so many Arches: Two great Dragons make a Bridge over the River; their Bodies form two Arches, through which two Swans are seen in the River at a great distance*'. Then 'a Troop of Fawns, Dryads and Naides' enter, and a soprano and chorus sing a song of 12 lines, not Shakespeare's ('If Love's a Sweet Passion, why does it torment?'). '*While a Symphany's Playing, the two Swans come Swimming on through the Arches to the bank of the River, as if they would Land; there turn themselves into* Fairies *and Dance; at the same time the Bridge vanishes, and the Trees that were Arch'd, raise themselves upright*'; whereupon '*Four Savages Enter, fright the* Fairies *away, and Dance an Entry*'. In the 1693 version, a soprano sings another song, 'Ye Gentle Spirits of the Air', but both the early and the later versions then introduce the quite unShakespearean dialogue and duet by Coridon and his coy Mopsa. As if not satisfied by this intrusion of conventional pastoralism into Shakespeare's more interesting one, Settle and Purcell conclude the act with 'A Dance of Hay-Makers', another choral song, and (not until then) Titania's ardent wooing of Bottom with his ass's head.

But this is only a precursor to what followed. Making room for the spectacular ending of the opera, the playlet 'Pyramus and Thisbe' was transferred from the last act to the rehearsal in the forest – a transposition that some later versions of the *Dream* in the eighteenth and nineteenth centuries would also adopt. For the conclusion, Oberon and Titania appear before Theseus, Hippolyta and their assembled guests, and show them Juno *'in a Machine drawn by Peacocks'. 'While a Symphony Plays, the Machine moves forward, and the Peacocks spread their Tails, and fill the middle of the Theater'*; then Juno sings a song to the lovers. As Oberon and the others depart, the machine ascends, the scene darkens, a symphony plays, and the scene is suddenly illuminated, revealing a Chinese garden. Before the final curtain comes down, a Chinese man and woman sing, six monkeys come from between the trees and dance, and two sopranos sing 'in parts' a song summoning Hymen, who appears and responds with a song of his own. The Chinese man and woman dance, and then all the dancers join in after 'The Grand Chorus'. Finally, after Oberon and Titania briefly bless the newly-weds, they end the opera with satirical verses directed at 'Wits, and Criticks'; 'Sharpers, Beau's, the very Cits' – altogether different in both substance and style from Puck's epilogue in Shakespeare's original. [. . .]

Not ten years later, in 1763, Garrick (who was actually a staunch admirer of Shakespeare) attempted to stage something closer to the original text, something actually called *A Midsummer Night's Dream*. The eighteenth century, after all, was the first great age of Shakespeare editing, and complete texts of the plays became increasingly available after Nicholas Rowe's edition of the *Works* appeared in 1709. But Garrick's efforts to restore Shakespeare's original were in large measure stymied by his colleague, George Colman, and the result was a fiasco. Garrick was by then living abroad, having fallen temporarily into disfavour after the riots instigated by Thaddeus Fitzpatrick at Drury Lane. Colman therefore supervised rehearsals at the Lane; he also frequently and abundantly altered the playscript. Garrick's version shows much more of Shakespeare's verse retained than Colman's, which cut an additional 561 lines that Garrick had retained. Colman's largest excision was the omission of almost all of Act 5. But he also added lines; for example, 18 inserted at the end of Act 1.2 which turn the first meeting of Quince and his friends into what G. W. Stone calls 'a glee club rehearsal'. These are followed by four eight-line stanzas sung consecutively by Quince, Starveling, Bottom and Flute intended for an 'epilogue' before the Duke, although of course the playlet was never performed despite Garrick's intention to retain it.

Given the quality of performance by the leading actors, Garrick's longer version probably would not have been any more successful than Colman's, which closed after a single night, 23 November 1763. The *St. James*

Chronicle maintained that however 'admirable' the children's performance was, the acting of the adults was 'execrable'. The sleeping scene
particularly displeased, as reported in the *Diary* of William Hopkins (the
prompter): 'The Performers first Sung the Audience to sleep, & then went
to sleep themselves'. Three of the four vocal performers could not adequately deliver blank verse, except in recitative, and quite destroyed
whatever good effect the children playing the fairies produced. [...]

* * *

The nineteenth century saw a continuation of the depredations and
borrowings, or adaptations, of Shakespeare's *Dream*, as it did for many
other plays in the canon. In this great age of theatrical spectacle, text was
often sacrificed for historical or technological display, as in the extravan-
gazas of Charles Kean at the Princess's Theatre in mid-century. Scene
painting had surpassed anything ever seen before and was consequently
thoroughly utilized for productions. The advent of Mendelssohn's great
score for an overture and incidental music to *A Midsummer Night's Dream*
also had its impact on productions of that play as the century wore on.
Garrick's rather abortive attempts to restore Shakespeare's texts nevertheless began to gather momentum, and eventually redactions such as
Nahum Tate's *King Lear* disappeared from the stage. At the same time,
romantic criticism and theory proclaimed that many of Shakespeare's
plays could only be distorted or corrupted – certainly not properly realized – in performance. Granted, much of that criticism was grounded, in
part, on plays performed in mutilated versions as compared with
printed editions. But romantic critics held that the *Dream* was so highly
imaginative a work of art, that *any* representation was bound to fall far
short of what the language of the play itself could convey to an active
intelligence.

Typical is William Hazlitt's comment on the first performance of Reynolds's *Dream* at Covent Garden on 17 January 1816: 'All that is fine in the
play, was lost in the representation'. This view continued to dominate
much thinking about Shakespeare in performance during the Romantic
period in England.

What Hazlitt saw, however, was yet another adaptation of Shakespeare's play. Reynolds criticized Colman's 1763 version as 'inefficient'
and attributed its failure on the stage to two main causes: (1) the omission
of many of Shakespeare's 'poetical' passages, particularly those by the
fairies, and (2) the excision of all of 'Pyramus and Thisbe', though
the audience had been led to expect it. He claims to preserve more of
the original 'beauties', admitting nevertheless that Shakespeare's name
may be 'degraded', perhaps, insofar as his lines are 'interwoven with
those of a modern Dramatist'. The modern dramatist is of course

Reynolds, who confesses he was 'compelled to alter, transpose, introduce new Songs, and new Speeches' and even to compose a whole new scene and part of another. He insists, nevertheless, that he has made 'some atonement' for his own 'defects', by 'restoring to the Stage, the lost, but divine Drama, of *A Midsummer Night's Dream*' ('Advertisement' in the 1816 edition).

A careful collation of Reynolds's adaptation with any modern edition will show that his claims are overstated. As the promptbook in the Folger Shakespeare Library demonstrates, Kemble went still further in deleting more of the original script, as did Edmund Kean, who followed him, using the Reynolds text. Reynolds deleted or revised many lines, adding new ones along with songs, 'quartettos', choruses, and even a 'Bird Symphony' near the end of Act 2.1. Most of the lovers' dialogue [3.2.188–344] is omitted, and a new 'finale' ends the scene (although this is crossed out in pencil in the Folger promptcopy). A new 'Hunting Scene' appears at [4.1.100] and afterwards Reynolds transposed a good deal, so that 'Pyramus and Thisbe' occurs earlier, and the play ends with the discovery and awakening of the young couples in the forest, an air by Hermia, and a rousing recitative, 'Warriors! march on!'; whereupon, instead of Shakespeare's fairy masque or Puck's epilogue, '12 or 20 warriors enter in procession in their way to the Hall of State' in a Grand Pageant proclaiming Theseus's triumphs. Finally, Hermia sings 'Now pleasure's voice be heard around' to conclude the action. No wonder Hazlitt reacted as he did!

Spectacle and operatic adaptation thus continued to overwhelm Shakespeare's fairy play. Describing the set designs and scenery, Odell admits that they must have been 'very pretty pictures', alluring in their way, as the designs of *The Fairy Queen* once had been. Audiences of all periods seem to be attracted by spectacle; 'designer's theatre', bemoaned by some critics today, is not a new phenomenon. Reynolds adapted more of Shakespeare's plays, but by 1833 his version of the *Dream* had been reduced to an afterpiece of merely two acts, whose only distinction is that it was the first to use Mendelssohn's great 'Overture'. Not until the end of the nineteenth century, which witnessed the experiments of William Poel and Harley Granville-Barker, did reaction against extravagant display begin in earnest. Meanwhile, Madame Vestris's production at Covent Garden in 1840, Samuel Phelps's at Sadler's Wells in 1853, and Charles Kean's at the Princess Theatre in 1856 are major productions of the *Dream* at mid-century.

Although we can credit the Italian contralto and theatrical manager Madame Lucia Elizabeth Vestris with restoring Shakespeare's language to *A Midsummer Night's Dream*, it is also true that her production, staged at Covent Garden in 1840, continued the tradition of spectacle, song and dance that *The Fairy Queen* began a century and a half earlier. The promptbook used for the production is lost, but the edition published by James Pattie in 1840–1 was taken from it and gives a reasonably accurate picture of what it was like. To make room for musical interludes and dances, and to provide time for scene shifting, Vestris cut nearly 400 lines, or about 18 per cent, of Shakespeare's text, mostly from the lovers' dialogue in Act 3.2. Still, Vestris's production retained a good deal more of Shakespeare's language than theatre audiences had heard for over two centuries – and more than they would hear in Charles Kean's celebrated production 16 years later. Vestris, furthermore, tended to keep major passages, such as Titania's 'forgeries of Jealousy' [2. 1. 81–117] and Puck's epilogue, relatively intact. In this respect, she was ahead of her time, as later nineteenth-century productions did not quite follow her example. Mid-Victorian taste, moreover, soon dominated poetic decorum. Although Vestris's production omitted the metaphors of 'big-bellied' sails and 'wanton wind' [2.1.128–9, 131], Hermia still spoke of giving up her 'virgin patent' [1.1.80]; and at the end Theseus could say, 'Lovers, to bed'. In later Victorian productions Hermia refers to her 'maiden heart' and Theseus cries, 'Lovers, away'.

Madam Vestris's colleague, James Robinson Planché, deserves much of the credit for such integrity as the script retained. He was also the scenic and costume supervisor and devised the elegant staging of the last scene which, unlike earlier productions, such as Reynolds's, was developed from a reading of Shakespeare's lines rather than a disregard for them. It was none the less spectacular, with more than 50 fairies flying or dancing through architectural galleries, up and down palace stairs, carrying blue and yellow lanterns. Vestris also used music differently – to set off Shakespeare's words, not to replace them, and to develop a dramatic purpose. The 14 songs, all taken from Shakespeare's text, are sung by fairies to distinguish them further from the mortals. Mendelssohn's great overture raised the curtain, as it had for Tieck's production in Berlin 13 years earlier, but thereafter Vestris tended to stay with one composer, Thomas Simpson Cooke, instead of a hodgepodge of others, as her predecessors had done.

Costumes were 'classical' for the Athenians, sandals and tunics for the mechanicals, and variations on Greek themes for the wingéd fairies. Vestris herself played Oberon and sang nine of the songs, while a girl played Puck – traditions that originated earlier and continued throughout the nineteenth century; even today an actress sometimes assumes the role of Puck. A woman playing Oberon seemed in the nineteenth century to convey better than a man the 'ephemeral idea' of fairyland consistent with the taste of the age (recall that it was a woman who posed for the famous portrait of Sir Galahad). This consideration outweighed whatever 'impotence' or contradiction the casting of women for both Oberon and Titania might bring to the quarrel between the fairy king and queen.

Covent Garden required spectacle, and spectacle there was, as noted; but it was not quite so extravagant as before. Vestris employed Reynolds's excellent scene painters, and she took full advantage of their talent. The first scene, for example, disclosed a view of Athens from Theseus's palace – a long perspective of fanes overlooking the Acropolis towering in the distance. Of the forest scenes, one reviewer remarked: 'all is sylvan and visionary; the wood scenes change like the phases of a dream' (*The Spectator*, 21 November 1840). In Act 3 the lovers lose their way in 'a mist of descending gauzes', a device that influenced many later productions of the play. One delightful touch (used again by eight-year-old Ellen Terry in Charles Kean's production) was Puck's first appearance, not as Shakespeare introduces him – the text was altered slightly for the effect – but rising up centre stage sitting on a mushroom at [2.1.31].

Except for the difficulty conveying the subtleties of Shakespeare's poetry through the vast spaces of Covent Garden – a defect of the production many commentators remarked – Vestris's *Dream* was artistically successful, though not financially. With an enormous payroll to cover, Vestris and her husband, James Matthews, found (like Betterton in 1692–3) that receipts could not cover costs, and the production consistently lost money even as it made history. Others might enchant their audiences more completely, but Vestris's *Dream* set the pattern for the century.

Foremost among those who thoroughly enchanted their audiences was Samuel Phelps at Sadler's Wells a dozen years later. His production was a culmination of much Romantic theorizing, which maintained that Shakespeare's *Dream* had to be ethereal, truly dreamlike, to succeed in performance – if it could be actualized on stage at all. Thus Henry Morley begins his review in 1853 by stating: 'Every reader of Shakespeare is disposed to regard the *Midsummer Night's Dream* as the most essentially unactable of all his plays. It is a dramatic poem of the utmost grace and delicacy; its characters are creatures of the poet's fancy that no flesh and blood can properly present. ... The words they speak are so completely spiritual that they are best felt when they are not spoken'. No wonder, then, that Madame Vestris's 'spectacle...altogether wanted the Shakespearean spirit'.

But predisposed as Morley was, even he recognized Phelps's accomplishment. Both the acting and the set design conspired to realize in the theatre something closely approximating Shakespeare's ideal, because Phelps understood that he had to present 'merely shadows'. To persuade the audience, therefore, that they but slumbered on their seats, that what appeared before them were merely visions, Phelps subdued everything to this 'ruling idea'. 'There is no ordinary scene-shifting, but, as in dreams, one scene is made to glide insensibly into another.' To achieve this effect, Frederick Fenton, Phelps's scene designer, used a diorama and a piece of greenish-blue gauze let down in front of the stage for Acts 2 to 4.

The acting was something else again, and here Morley rather misses an important point in the play when he complains that the four lovers 'could not fancy themselves shadows'. Of course they could not – and should not have done. The 'arguing and quarrelling and blundering', which Morley says should be 'playful and dreamlike and poetical', are, if anything, harsh and discordant and nightmarish, as more recent critics have insisted. Morley's sympathies, typical of his time, favour Hermia in Act 3 as 'a gentle maid forlorn...not at all meant to excite mirth', but here again he misconstrues the action of the play and its point. He is closer to the mark in praising Phelps's Bottom, especially as he moved from the violently gesticulating clown of Act 1 to the quieter, accepting dream-figure in Act 4. But Morley goes too far in regarding Bottom 'as unsubstantial, as airy and refined as all the rest'.

If dreaminess is what the audience wanted, dreaminess is mainly what they got in Phelps's production. It was the greatest triumph of his career, and Bottom his most notable role. Gas lighting, which Fenton introduced for the first time at Sadler's Wells, along with the diorama and gauze curtain, helped produce the desired effect. Costumes also contributed and harmonized with the scenery. The fairies 'were none of your winged, white-muslin fairies with spangles and butterfly wands, but were real, intangible shadowy beings that...would infallibly at the first cockcrow melt into thin air'. In keeping with the 'ruling idea', quiet movement and, where appropriate, a bright, full moon also characterized the production. Music there was, and dancing, although which music has not as yet been discovered for either this production or its revival in 1855–6. For the 1861 revival, however, Mendelssohn's score (arranged by W. H. Montgomery) and new scenery were featured.

Whether Phelps used it or not, by mid-century Felix Mendelssohn's music was becoming a fixture in many stage productions. Williams records the use of nine pieces and the overture, with additional pieces 'by Beethoven, T. Cooke, Horn, Levey, &c.', at the Theatre Royal, Dublin, in November 1852; and in February 1854 two New York productions, one by William Evans Burton and the other by Thomas Barry and E. A. Marshall, advertised the whole of Mendelssohn's score, Burton claiming its use for the first time anywhere. If this was the first time Mendelssohn's music was used in America, it was not the first production of the play across the Atlantic. There had been an operatic version in 1826; and in 1841, possibly inspired by Vestris's success, Charlotte Cushman played Oberon in a non-operatic version.

The competing New York productions of 1854 were likewise probably inspired by a British success – Phelps's – although Burton insisted that, as he had never seen the *Dream* performed, all the stage business and spectacular effects were new and original. He also claimed that both scenery and costumes were historically correct. The warriors were attired, for example, as pictured by 'Willemin, in his Costumes des Peuples d'Antiquité', Hermia and Helena wore 'the long sleeveless tunic, the caladris or stole, with the rich and varied peplum over the bust, and the crepida sandal', etc. In Act 2, Oberon and Titania descended in aerial cars, and in Act 4 at sunrise, mists rose from the valleys and the sun rose in powerful splendour. This was, after all, an age that emphasized archae-ological verisimilitude, and for once, as Shattuck says, 'New York was served as fulsomely with erudition as Charles Kean served his audiences at the Princess's in London'. Burton scored a resounding triumph as Bottom and was led shortly afterwards to introduce another Shakespeare play, a spectacular *Tempest*. But Barry's production, if more spacious, was less successful and even occasioned negative comments on the play itself. Shakespeare in America was gradually coming of age, but for a long time would still follow British leads.

A watershed for nineteenth-century productions of the *Dream* was surely reached in Charles Kean's version, which opened on 15 October 1856. Kean heavily cut more than 800 of Shakespeare's lines to keep performances under three hours, despite a great deal of music, dance and spectacle. Not only Mendelssohn's music, but many other pieces were used – the promptbook is studded with music cues – although the orchestra at Kean's Princess Theatre did not do justice to them. Never-theless, the production was immensely successful, running for 150 per-formances. Once again, a woman, Fanny Ternan, played Oberon, but the fairies were all full-grown adults, not children. Morley generally admired the production but criticized some aspects, particularly the famous May-pole ballet that ended the third act. Complaining that 'we miss a portion of the poem most essential to its right effect – the quarrel between Hermia and Helena', he comments on its substitute: 'a ballet of fairies round a maypole that shoots up out of an aloe, after the way of a transformation in a pantomime, and rains down garlands. Fairies, not airy beings of the colour of the greenwood, or of the sky, or robed in misty white, but glittering in the most brilliant dresses, with a crust of bullion about their legs...' Evidencing the 'depraved taste' of the audience, in Morley's view, the ballet was encored.

Although Kean here eschewed historical authenticity, representing Athens in the Age of Pericles rather than of Theseus (explained in the Preface to his edition), his set designs were greatly admired. Even Morley remarked on 'the exquisite scenery' of the play, for which the original water-colour paintings are still extant. Then as now, however, set designs could – and in Morley's view did – detract from the poetry of the play. Instead of letting the verse provide the scenery, the designers foreclosed abruptly on the audience's imagination. Thus, instead of an unspecified room in Theseus's palace, an elaborate painted set filled the stage. The scene location in the edition (as in the playbill) hardly conveys what the audience actually saw: '*A terrace adjoining the Palace of Theseus, overlooking the City of Athens*'. Kean's biographer more fully describes the vista: 'We saw, on the hills of the Acropolis, the far-famed Parthenon, the Erichtheum, and the statue of the tutelary goddess Minerva, or Athena; by its side the theatre of Bacchus; in advance, the temple of Jupiter Olympus, partially hiding the hall of the Museum; and on the right the temple of Theseus.' Even the summit of Mars Hill appeared. The setting of course recalls Madame Vestris's production, but Kean outdid even hers, as did the final spectacle of 'some ninety fairies tripping up and down the stairs of Theseus's palace, waving bell-like lanterns while the fairy chorus sang Mendelssohn's "Through this house give glimmering light" '.

Just as Vestris's production had inspired Edmund Simpson's and Phelps's had inspired both Burton's and Barry's, so Kean's inspired Laura Keene's in New York in 1859 at the Olympic Theatre. She used both his text and the Maypole ballet with still greater dollops of Mendelssohn's music, and the opera singer Fanny Stockton as Oberon. On 8 October 1867 at the same theatre but under different management and with a different cast the play was revived, but its chief claim to fame was its scenic splendour. In 1873, Augustin Daly went further yet with spectacle and extended pantomimes using 'the famous Golden Quartette of California, in the dress of Satyrs' to sing the lullabye to Titania in Act 2. Daly again staged the play in 1888, with John Drew, Otis Skinner, and Ada Rehan; Isadora Duncan in papier-maché wings was one of the dancing fairies. But this time Weber's *Oberon* overture opened the performance and more of Bishop's 1816 score than Mendelssohn's was played.

Daly once again staged the play in 1895. On 9 July, George Bernard Shaw reviewed the performance at Daly's Theatre and remarked how Daly had fitted up all his fairies 'with portable batteries and incandescent lights, which they switch on and off from time to time, like children with a new toy'. He is especially harsh on Lillian Swain as Puck and on Daly's casting a woman as Oberon, although he has the highest praise for Ada Rehan's Helena. Above all, he criticizes Daly for his persistent illusionism, which destroys rather than complements the effect of Shakespeare's verse. The time was ripe, if not overripe, for reaction, and in Granville-Barker's productions early in the twentieth century, reaction indeed began.

Interval One: Shakespeare's Theatre

Robert Weimann, 'The Elizabethan Drama'

Source: Robert Weimann, *Shakespeare and the Popular Tradition in the Theater: Studies in the Social Dimension of Dramatic Form and Function*, ed. R. Schwartz (Baltimore, MD: Johns Hopkins University Press, 1978 [1967]), Chapter V, pp. 161–3, 165–6, 168–74.

While there have been a number of substantial contributions to our understanding of Shakespeare's theatre in recent years, Robert Weimann's study, first published in East Germany in 1967, remains an important milestone in the field. Building on a formidable tradition of Shakespeare scholarship in Germany going back to the late eighteenth century, Weimann's critical method derives from the Marxist assumption that 'material conditions determine consciousness'. As a consequence, this extract first sets out the changing 'material conditions' – the economic and political transformations – in Shakespeare's England, and then explores how these changes determined Shakespeare's theatre. However, although Marx's axiom provides the organizing principle of Weimann's study, he is at pains to avoid a crude determinism, emphasizing at all times the contradictions and complexities of the relationship between the broader context and Shakespeare's theatre. A second concern Weimann shares with Marx is the need to acknowledge the agency of the poorer classes of society. This concern is expressed here in his detailed exploration of how the popular culture of the period informed both the production and the reception of Shakespeare's plays.

1

Toward the Culture of a Nation

When the Elizabethan theater flowered in the 1580s, England was in the midst of an economic expansion and national awakening. The medieval structures of life, which still predominated in other European countries, with their rural agricultural systems based on payment in kind and their unwieldy guild organization in the towns, had been greatly weakened or even superseded in England. The growth of a market – first for goods, then for land and labor, and finally for money – as well as the development of an extensive cloth industry serving overseas export markets, the great influx of American gold and silver, and the sharp rise in prices dating from the midcentury all proved powerful dissolvents of the traditional economy. As productivity accelerated, so did building, shipping, and trade. The decline of feudal social organization and medieval habits of life ushered in a new era of prosperity for England – an age fundamentally of an economic revolution which nonetheless, despite the profound disruptions, was also an era of social compromise that achieved a temporary political stability and a cultural synthesis of old and new. Here was the basis of a modern national consciousness and of a newly found creative cultural potential that enriched and transformed the sixteenth-century theater.

The rise of what was at the time a small nation did not come unannounced, however. As early as the fourteenth century a monetary economy had to a considerable extent replaced the direct exchange of goods, and feudal villeinage had in many places given way to payments in tender. But the collapse of the feudal organization of the rural economy was a process greatly accelerated by many other circumstances. Disastrous plagues produced an acute labor shortage, so that farm laborers were often able to escape the patriarchal control of their landlords. The enclosures, which became increasingly common after 1470, also helped to weaken the old system in many parts of the country. English landowners, particularly in the south and east, turned their backs on the local market economy and began to produce wool for Flemish, and, soon after, for home manufacture.

The number of people dislocated by the conversion of arable land into pasture was further increased by the dispersal of feudal retainers under Henry VII and the extensive sale of church lands during the Reformation. Without work and without masters, those released by an outmoded economic structure sought new protection or sold their labor to the manufacturers and landowners who operated the new system. Stiff laws insured that the majority of those expropriated adapted to the new economy, especially as paid workers. Those who could not adapt were persecuted and punished as outlaws, vagabonds, or jugglers.

The uneven development of capitalism in the various parts of England was accompanied by what modern historians have noted as the gradual dissolution of the medieval estates in favor of a greater "mobility of social classes" (A. L. Rowse), and even a "babylonian confusion of classes" (J. B. Black) especially true in the earlier part of the century and still evident by the end at Court, in London, and in parts of the eastern and southern countryside where the majority of the population still lived. The Elizabethan chronicler William Harrison provided a vivid description of the changes under way in rural England when he noted that "the ground of the parish is gotten vp into a few mens hands, yea sometimes into the tenure of (one) two or three, whereby the rest are compelled, either to be hired seruants vnto the other, or else to beg their bread in miserie from doore to doore." These changes profoundly affected the ancient cultural traditions and customs which the shared land of the medieval village had immemorially fostered. Once the land was enclosed and made an object of speculation, traditions associated with it were, when not completely destroyed, severely threatened.

But economic conditions were not the only factors working to transform the old, collective elements in the feudal village culture. The new Puritan morality, with its sexual repression, thundered against the "Dionysian" freedoms characteristic of popular custom. Contemporary pamphleteers [...] were quick to adopt the new moral and ascetic viewpoint. [...]

[T]he pamphleteer's new social and ethical outlook was a perspective that challenged the communal elements in the traditional culture because it rejected its underlying assumptions. The Protestant individualism that abandoned inherited and collective religious authority (Pope, bishop, and confessional) manifested itself in the social sphere as an ethic of private choice as opposed to the traditions of an entire community ("yung men and maides, olde men and wiues"). [...] It is the individual who chooses to enjoy the festival, the wine, and the love, but at the risk of losing business, sobriety, and chastity. The associations between sensuality and sin are clear: "plesant pastimes" become "cursed pastimes," and involvement is condemnable, for "sweet nosegay" here turns abruptly into "stinking Ydol." [...]

In political life, as in the economy, the old and the new confronted each other. The hegemony of the barons was past, and their bankruptcy was military and political as well as economic. After the Wars of the Roses their ranks were thinned, their castles and strongholds had become too vulnerable, their housekeeping too expensive, and their retainers unlawful; after the last feudal rising, the Northern Rebellion of 1569, their decline was an irrevocable trend. But while the feudal aristocracy was no longer in a position to rule the country at large, those sections that a hundred years later succeeded in winning the Civil War were as yet too immature to achieve political supremacy. The bourgeoisie, together with the "improving" gentry and the lower middle classes that ultimately shared (or aspired to share) their modes of living, were not yet politically emancipated. They were more concerned about the settlement of the succession, the threat of foreign invasion, the maintenance of civil order, and their more immediate economic interests, than with challenging state power by advancing their own (as distinct from the national) policies and ideologies. Like the merchants, the moneyed landlords who owned most of the abbey lands, enclosed the commons, and introduced capitalist practices into agriculture, did not for a moment think of challenging the prerogative of the Tudor monarchs under whose peaceful rule they had obtained vast estates and had thrived so unprecedentedly. Policy-making was as yet the undisputed privilege of the crown.

It was the crown and the court, then, that became the focal point of the nation's political, religious, and cultural life. The immense prestige of the monarchy, the homage paid to it by men such as Ascham, Spenser, Hooker, and Bacon, cannot be dismissed as empty eulogium; for the Tudors – as Shakespeare viewed them in *Richard III* – had overthrown the warring factions of the nobility and thus made possible that "smooth-fac'd peace,/ With smiling plenty and fair prosperous days" (V, 5, 33–4) of which the Elizabethans were so gratefully conscious. Although themselves of the nobility, the Tudors were prepared (and indeed they had no other choice) to compromise with those forces which had opposed the disastrous rule of the barons and which still were suspicious of the rebelliousness of the over-mighty subject. By providing favorable conditions for trade and shipping the Tudor monarchs developed their customs revenues; by promoting a stable and more centralized administration, they reorganized their fiscal system and controlled their own landed revenues much more effectively; at the same time, they advanced the economic development of the country by welding together hitherto local communities of exchange into a larger national whole. In doing all this, the Tudors, without breaking with the more conservative aristocracy, promoted the interests of the newer gentry and the middle classes which, especially in the economically advanced south and east, were moving closer together. In Tudor England those who upheld the independence of the nation supported the sovereignty of the crown; its authority was accepted not only against the claims of the Roman church but also in the face of domestic unrest and foreign invasion. [...]

And yet, as the balance of power gradually changed, it became more and more difficult to contain the Puritans and to conceal the cracks in the Tudor alliance. Elizabeth, as late as 1601, still could fall back on compromise measures and the crown's long-standing prestige, which neither her subtle evasiveness nor her many studied ambiguities were quite able to undermine. As James Harrington sarcastically remarked, she succeeded in "converting her reign through the perpetuall Love-tricks that passed between her and her people into a kind of Romanze." Part of this "Romanze" may, in the words of a later historian, have consisted in "bribing her people with prosperity." But when the old queen died, prosperity – now that it was taken for granted – was no longer good enough at its traditional level; and what proved more important, there were indications that its growth was to be less secure than before. At the same time, the compromise in religion and the foundation for an all-inclusive national church had become increasingly tenuous, until James I discovered (in 1604, at the Hampton Court conference) that "Presbytery agreeth as well with monarchy as God and the devil." Now Hooker, in the seventh book of his great *Laws*, might well deplore "those extreme conflicts of the one part with the other, which continuing and increasing" were reminiscent of "those words of the Prophet Jeremiah, 'thy breach is great like the sea, who can heal thee?'" English absolutism ceased to be an absolutism by consent, and out of the national alliance emerged the gradual (although by no means straightforward) formation of two increasingly antagonistic class positions.

Facing these far reaching divisions (there were significant, if almost imperceptible, changes from at least 1588), how was the humanist scholar or poet to react? Was he still, like Gabriel Harvey, to consider the court as "the only mart of praeferment and honour?" Or could he honestly, as Stephen Gosson did, throw in his lot with the Puritans? As early as 1586 the death of Sidney, followed by that of Leicester, was a blow to poets and all those who might have continued to reconcile humanism with the principles of militant Protestantism; in affecting the national position of both movements, it was an event scarcely less significant than the execution of Essex (1601) to whom, in the 1590s, the leadership of Leicester's court party and the popular support of the citizenry had passed. But while the new aristocracy was losing valuable territory at Whitehall, the court – at least since the appointment of Archbishop Whitgift to the Privy Council – was drawing nearer to an Episcopalian church increasingly determined to oppose and suppress Puritan innovations. As the court grew, under James, to be part of a corrupt administration (in which preferment and a public career had for a long time become rare to underprivileged scholars), the more advanced sections of the bourgeoisie showed an increasing hostility to the arts and a growing impatience with the philological traditions of Christian humanism.

Thus, the foundations of the national compromise – so essential to Gascoigne, Sidney, or Spenser – were crumbling away, and neither side proved really acceptable to the humanist imagination. Classically trained poets, even before the end of the century, turned to satire, and their writing reflected an attitude toward experience more sardonic, somber, and savage than that of the earlier decade. The melancholy malcontent became a symbol of the disillusioned academic, and the Italianate courtier – his affected imitator, the fashionable "gull" – was held up to ridicule, while the covetous Puritan was attacked with equal scorn.

But in the theater, the growing antagonism between the realigned classes did not, at this stage, endanger the dramatic images and poetic transmutations of submerged conflicts and tensions. As long as important links remained between the traditional background of the popular culture and the new sense of nationalism embraced by both the middle classes and the aristocracy, the theater supported widely divergent viewpoints. More than any other social institution, the theater still resembled a "laboratory in which the various elements of society were...mixed and worked" on. Just as in education, religion, philosophy, social ethics, and other moral attitudes, the old confronted, and often held its own against, the new. Older conceptions of honor were confronted by the new pride of possession, hatred of usury by the fervor for gold, the idea of service by the idea of profit, deeply rooted community consciousness by passionate individualism. Feudal family pride mingled with the bourgeois sense of family, pomp with thrift, frivolity with chastity, pessimism with optimism. In the late sixteenth and early seventeenth centuries these heterogeneous ideas and attitudes jostled each other, and the resulting wealth and depth of conflict was reflected, more than anywhere else, in the Renaissance theater, where the popular tradition was free to develop relatively independent of, and yet in close touch with, the conflicting standards and attitudes of the dominant classes.

2

'Scene individable': Toward a Sociology of the Elizabethan Stage

The capacity of popular Renaissance drama to accommodate and synthesize differing cultural and ideological perspectives was the result of specific sociological conditions upon which the Elizabethan theater, its audiences and their tastes, were based. But although the playhouses themselves and the staging of plays in them have frequently been studied, their sociological foundations have received considerably less attention. It is true that facts about the social context of the founding of the first public theaters are few, but those that we have are fortunately reliable. They include, among others, the contract for the construction of the Fortune theater, Henslowe's diary, and the records of the law suits concerning the site rented for the Theatre. These documents not only tell us something about what the first theaters looked like, they also reveal some facts about the social status of their founders. The Theatre, the first permanent public playhouse, was built by James Burbage in 1576; the Curtain followed shortly after, and a few years later the Rose (1587), the Swan (1595), and the famous Globe (1599), which was built with materials from the dismantled Theatre.

None of these, of course, was a spontaneous product of popular culture. Burbage was originally a carpenter, his brother-in-law and partner, John Brayne, was a prosperous shopkeeper; Philip Henslowe was a busy merchant and speculator, and Francis Langley, who built the Swan, was a goldsmith. Their theaters were private commercial enterprises, erected only after projected profits had been carefully calculated. It is especially clear from the history of the Theatre that business and not communal spirit urged these particular theatrical ventures. Alleyn, the Theatre's owner, and Burbage and Brayne fought bitterly for the profits to be made in their playhouse.

But in spite of the postfeudal, postpatriarchal business ethics that made these theaters commercially viable, they were still dependent on large plebeian audiences – people who remained attached to the old miming and festival traditions and still removed from the new Puritan ethos. This is clear even from the sites on which the first theaters were built. It was no accident that they were built in Halliwell, to the north and outside the city walls (on the grounds of a former priory), and on the southeast edge of Finsbury Fields, on the big playing fields where Londoners went on Sundays to practice archery and engage in other timehonored amusements. Here they were outside the jurisdiction of the city authorities (controlled by the London bourgeoisie), but perfectly congruent with local traditions. Halliwell – "holy well" – was, like Clerkenwell and other local shrines, associated with legendary powers of healing, and probably still a meeting place for festivals – such as the May festival – in Shakespeare's day.

Bankside, on the south bank, where the later Rose, Swan, and Globe theaters were built, was also closely connected with the sports and pastimes of old London. Well before the theaters were built people congregated there to watch bear-baiting, bull fights, wrestling, and fencing, as well as juggling and other displays. In fact, there is some evidence that elements of the May games and Morris and Sword dances lived on in the growing city; and it is only in light of these still living traditions that the remarkable popularity of Tarlton and Kempe can be understood. If there was any place in London where the older popular miming culture, the lay drama, and the Robin Hood plays were vividly remembered it was in Finsbury Fields and Bankside. It was the common people who met there, who engaged in the pleasure and the games, and who brought with them an appreciation for traditional arts of acting. Like those who watched the mystery plays, the simple London public was well able to bring a surprising amount of intelligence and understanding to the theater. At any rate, they were prepared to spend their pennies to maintain several large playhouses in what was, by modern standards, still a small city. Thus, while growing capitalism and its related asceticism had *not yet* become a way of life for the masses, the new economy and corresponding social changes had *already* created conditions whereby a permanent public theater independent of the controlling influence of clergy and conservative guilds, could develop.

This illuminates not only the rise, but also the remarkable range of the new theatrical culture. London was a city of only about 160,000 inhabitants in 1600, but it supported more than half-a-dozen theaters, each with a varied program, in the years when *Hamlet*, *King Lear*, and *Volpone* were first performed. According to Alfred Harbage, during the 1605 theater season (when attendance was at its highest) nearly 21,000 Londoners probably went to the theater every week. This means that about thirteen percent of the population of London regularly went outside of the city to attend plays. At the same time, or soon after, bourgeois or Puritan opposition to the theater intensified. The theater, it was said, spread the plague, kept apprentices from their work, and, according to Puritan pamphleteers and numerous complaints by the city fathers to the Privy Council, constituted a pagan glorification of the devil, a form of idolatry. Although exaggerated, such complaints had some truth. Audiences, Phillip Stubbes wrote, "are alwaies eating, & neuer satisfied: euer seeing, & neuer contented; continualie hearing, & neuer wearied; they are greedie of wickednes, and wil let no time, nor spare for anie weather (so great is their deuotion to make their pilgrimage) to offer their penie to the Deuil." And it is that same word – devotion – perhaps suggesting more homage than a play warrants, that Stubbes used in his attack on the May festival. There may well have been more than moral prejudice behind the equation of "playes and bawdy enterluds' with 'hethenrie, paganrie, scurrilitie, and deuilrie it self," for such performances may indeed have harkened back to the late ritual heritage of those "doble dealing ambodexters" to whom the Puritans so deeply objected.

The fact that the Elizabethan theater was in constant and bitter conflict with both nascent Puritanism and the leading London bourgeoisie shows very clearly that despite its popularity, its social position was precarious. Yet puritanical attacks and municipal interference, at least until the second decade of the seventeenth century, were limited in their effects, especially in light of the protection that the theater received from court patronage. Such patronage was perfectly in keeping with the New Monarchy's interest in culture and the arts. It was officially justified by the argument that actors needed professional experience in order to provide suitable entertainments and diversions for the Queen during the Christmas season. So long as the bourgeoisie as well as the middle classes and the crown were allies in an "absolutism by consent," or even "a middle class despotism," so long as the great compromise was practicable, patronage represented not only royal protection, but cultural distinction as well.

The Queen not only protected actors, she also saw their performances, for, as some complained, the common players "present before her maiestie such plaies as haue ben before commonly played in open stages before all the basest assemblies in London and Middlesex. ..." Such points of contact between court art and plebeian drama were indeed remarkable. It was not unknown for the Queen to decline a play prepared for her in favor of a "company of base and common fellows." Often success on the common stages meant success at court, where performances by troupes popular in the city were frequent. Costumes used for court performances were lent to the actors, who wore them as they played "in the cytye or contre." The popular Renaissance theater enjoyed a truly royal reception, and as a national institution was, to be sure, "a theatre of the people and of the court."

Nor was the cultural function of the New Monarchy simply an external one. As early as Bale's *King Johan* it is "Imperial Majestie" that overthrows the enemy "Sedycyon" so as to make room for the triumph of "Cyvyle Order": this is a major motif taken up and varied from the humanist *Gorboduc* to the popular chronicles and history plays. Under the transitional conditions of Elizabeth's reign the crown would assume the role of arbiter pretending to what Hooker regarded as "the soundest... and most indifferent rule." It kept in check not only the feudal reaction of the Northern earls but also (in Crowley's words) those new "men that would be alone on the earth,... that would eate up menne, women and chyldren." It protected the stage against the chronic indignation of the city authorities and helped both the playwrights and their audiences in preventing the Puritans from "preaching awey theyr pastime." Most important of all, the crown stood for and upheld the conditions to which the theater owed so much. By deliberately promoting mercantile capital and blurring the lines of gentry and aristocracy, old and new, the Tudors helped to bring about that "mingle-mangle" which the theater in its organization and audience, the drama in its genres, structures, and speech conventions, reflected. This "gallimaufrey" was clearly perceived in the 1580s by John Lyly, a humanist in close contact with the court:

> At our exercises, Souldiers call for Tragedies, their obiect is bloud: Courtiers for Commedies, their subiect is love: Countriemen for Pastoralles, Shepheards are their Saintes. Trafficke and trauell hath wouen the nature of all Nations into ours, and made this land like Arras, full of deuise... Time hath confounded our mindes, our mindes the matter; but all commeth to this passe, that what heretofore hath been serued in serueral dishes for a feaste, is now minced in a charger for a Gallimaufrey. If wee present a minglemangle, our fault is to be excused, because the whole worlde is become an Hodge-podge.

Unlike Sidney's assault on "mongrell Tragicomedie," this statement is already confidently apologetic, but its classically trained author is still too bewildered to realize that the contradictions (which he points out) are about to yield a new and superior kind of unity. For Shakespeare it is the awareness of both the possibilities of, and the contradictions contained in, the social and theatrical "mingle-mangle" that can be shown to inform the range and richness of his dramatic language and structure. But Lyly stood at the very threshold of the new "gallimaufrey": it opened up a synthesis to be achieved by the great Elizabethan laboratory – so remarkably effective both in society and in the theater. Against the "hodge-podge" of a transitional age, the medieval estates of the realm were no less mixed and transformed than the various dramatic genres: the craft cycle tradition, the drama of the schools, the interlude of the hall, the masque and courtly revels were now no longer "serued in seueral dishes." Instead they were so "minced" that in the country's metropolis the result was a drama neither farcical nor learned nor courtly. It was a drama unlike any of the continental burgess or classical or pastoral genres, but one whose bewildering medley of kinds could indeed be defined as "tragedy, comedy, history, pastoral, pastoral-comical, historical-pastoral, tragical-historical, tragical-comical-historical-pastoral, scene individable, or poem unlimited." It was in truth a theater "individable" with a poetry "unlimited" in its social and aesthetic appeal; for it embraced many of the popular, humanist and some of the courtly elements, together with their theatrical equivalents such as rhetoric, allegory, singing, dancing, clowning, dumb-shows, disguisings, and corresponding modes of speech, presentation and acting. But by fusing these elements in the light of a unifying and exalting experience of nationhood, the Elizabethan theater brought forth something new which *nevertheless* appealed to all sections of its audience ("from potboy to prince," as a great authority on the subject writes). "This three years," says Hamlet [5.1.126–31], "I have took note of it: the age is grown so picked that the toe of the peasant comes so near the heel of the courtier, he galls his kibe." It is an observation that might have been made by a spectator in Shakespeare's theater. Its audience was made up of every rank and class of society; its greatest literature so written that (as a contemporary observed) "it should please all, like Prince *Hamlet*". Through underlying tensions and in the face of imminent divisions Shakespeare's theater achieved a "unity of taste." It was a multiple unity based on contradictions, and as such allowed the dramatist a flexible frame of reference that was more complex and more vital to the experience of living and feeling within the social organism than the achievement of any other theater before or since.

The integration, in the theater, of heterogeneous elements is a historical process, and as such it affects the history of the stage as a social institution; but it also – and more deeply – affects the quality of the plays themselves, their themes, forms, and structures. If it is a truism to say that Shakespeare's subject-matter is as rich in potentialities of experience as the world in which he lived, it perfectly corresponds to his own ideas of how the art of the theater was related to the contemporary world. Hamlet's words about "the purpose of playing" [3.2.18–19] illuminate a relationship, which, in an earlier scene [2.2.504], is summed up by a reference to the players as "the abstracts and brief chronicles of the time." The point that is worth making is of course not that Shakespeare's drama – in line with the Aristotelian concept of *mimesis* – reflected the issues of his time (in this he was not at all unique); but that he, more than any of his contemporaries, succeeded in the discovery of how the issues of his time, its "form and pressure," could most significantly be turned into material for great art. It was a discovery that involved the capacity for so absorbing and molding the varied themes and modes of drama that its latent tensions might be released into dramatic poetry. [...]

The vast range of conflicting values and standards within the Elizabethan situation retained its imaginative pregnancy just as long as the dramatist was in a position honestly to face and incorporate their tensions within his poetic vision of society. He could do this only as long as he possessed, as a touchstone to test any experience or concept, a standpoint involving more freedom, or "license," and imagination than the particular social attitude or moral concept in question. Shakespeare's superiority over his material was of course based on his incomparably deep feeling for reality and humanity; but it was so secure and remained essentially unshaken because he could still fall back on the techniques and the standards of a popular culture in a national theater which gave his vision – amidst the temporary "mingle-mangle" of social values – the strength to achieve contradictions within new areas of universality, conflicts within new levels of unity. This was a position only partly of genial detachment, amused tolerance, and dispassionate irony. For apart from the negative virtue of avoiding a facile identification with any of the emerging class concepts, this vision possessed (through its freedom and skepticism) the positive capacity for bringing to bear varied perspectives on the actions and morals of men, thus creating the experience rather than the ideologies of heroism, love, and tyranny. The universalizing pattern in Shakespeare and the "myriad-mindedness" of his art were never outside history, but they lived beyond the historical conditions that made them possible. The basis of Shakespeare's "negative capability" is itself sociohistorical, and it is unthinkable without the freedom, the detachment, and the imagination made available to him by the popular tradition in the theater.

2 *Richard II*

2.1 *John Dover Wilson, 'The Political Background of Shakespeare's* Richard II *and* Henry IV'

Source: *Shakespeare Jahrbuch*, 75 (1939), pp. 36–51.

John Dover Wilson, the long-standing professor of English at Edinburgh University, first delivered this paper as an address to the German

Shakespeare Society at Weimar on the eve of the Second World War. Deferring to the legacy of German Shakespeare scholarship, he claims disingenuously to be no more than an editor raising fresh questions for future study. Starting with the claim that 'political clouds can never obscure the light of Shakespeare', Dover Wilson then proceeds to display an acute sense of how 'our historical perspective changes from age to age'. In assembling his own understanding of the age of Shakespeare, he refers not only to Tudor texts like Sir Thomas Elyot's *Book of the Governour* (1531), but also to the work of contemporary historians like Sir George Trevelyan. The result is a version of English history that emphasizes a general fear of social chaos, and *Richard II* is accordingly interpreted as Shakespeare's expression of his own deep fears of a return to 'the abyss of chaos in England' during the Wars of the Roses. Writing at the end of the turbulent decade of the 1930s, Dover Wilson's own anxieties about political upheaval in Britain therefore colour his historical contextualization of *Richard II*. Further information on Dover Wilson is given in Extract 5.2, Terence Hawkes's 'Telmah'.

After the production of his text, probably the chief of a Shakespearian editor's tasks is to attempt to recreate the attitude of both the dramatist and his original audience to the topics with which the plays deal. There are three partners to the production of any play: author, performers (with whom I include the producer), and audience. All have their influence; the author most of all of course, the actors a good deal, and the spectators least. Yet the contribution of the last is a very real one, and it is the one most likely to be overlooked. [...]

[T]urn to Shakespeare himself and take *Hamlet*. To the modern reader or spectator who knows nothing of the intellectual climate of Elizabethan England, *Hamlet* is one thing; to the reader or spectator who has made some study of the contemporary political and religious notions which underlie the play from beginning to end, it is something quite different. *Hamlet* is a very great play. It remains a great play, even to those totally ignorant of the unspoken assumptions which Shakespeare shared with his audience at its first production. Yet if we desire to know *Shakespeare's Hamlet*, there is no doubt which of these two approaches to the play we must take. Now if study, the study of Elizabethan cosmology and politics, is essential to the full appreciation and understanding of *Hamlet*, study is even more needed for the apprehension of Shakespeare's history plays. And this study must concern, not what modern historians think took place in the epochs that Shakespeare writes of, or with the interpretation which modern historians place upon those events, but what the Elizabethans thought and taught about the epochs in question. Nor is there any doubt that the history plays have suffered severely with the passage of time in this respect. They have inevitably suffered, since the historical issues in the past which interest us would have been unintelligible to the original spectators, even to Shakespeare himself, while the issues that excited them appear either of minor importance or entirely unreal to us. [...]

It is, of course, a truism that every generation possesses the history it desires, refashions the past in its own image, reads into it its own pre-judices and looks at it from its own peculiar angle of vision. I speak nationally; for, despite our European history-books and the more preten-tious histories of civilization, what we mean by history is usually the account of our own, national development in a warring world. Employing the term history, then, in this sense, we say that our historical perspective changes from age to age. And this implies not merely that each age interprets the past in the light of its own preoccupations; it signifies something more definite. If you think of it, is it not generally true that the historical vision of most persons is more or less bounded by a parti-cular horizon, beyond which if we see at all we see but little, and which is defined by the main limits of our contemporary interests? I suspect, though it is a mere guess, that this watershed for the majority of Germans is constituted by the Thirty Years War, which led directly to the rise of Prussia under the Great Elector. In England our watershed also lies in the seventeenth century. There are to be found the origins of the epoch in which we still live. Then took place the changes, which beginning with the Puritan Rebellion and the execution of Charles I and culminating in the Revolution of 1688 gave us the constitutional, social and legal conditions which determine our lives to-day; and of which the great reforms of the nineteenth century are seen to be merely an extension and a fulfilment. There is a further point, moreover. Contemporary pre-judice is usually able to fix upon dates or events which represent the genesis and final triumph of the *principles* of which subsequent changes are only the inevitable outcome. And the period between these two is likely to attract the special attention of the historians of the age, who will be eager to detect and describe the causes of such – as we say – epoch-making events. Thus for nineteenth century and twentieth century Eng-lishmen, undoubtedly the most interesting field of historical study was that which began with the struggle between Charles I and his Long Parliament and ended with the Whig victory under William and Mary. Not, let us note, that this victory meant the triumph of one of the two contending parties or principles over the other. It represents a *compromise* which brings the quarrel to an end and ushers in a new age.

This is, I fear, a long preamble; but I can now at last pose the question up to which I have been leading all this while. It is this. If the Civil Wars of the seventeenth century and the constitutional settlement of 1688 form the watershed of history for modern Englishmen, what was the correspond-ing watershed for English people who lived before these events took

place? What, in a word, was the historical perspective of the Elizabethans? With superficial points of similarity it was profoundly different
from that of their successors to-day. They like us (or our fathers) looked
back to a great deliverance, a deliverance from a terrible national evil,
from a time of chaos, insecurity and bloodshed. They too rejoiced in
special institutions, constitutional, legal and social, which though mostly
swept away by the Puritan Revolution, were themselves the product of a
previous revolution, or rather of the compromise and national consolidation which followed that revolution. The time of trouble to which they
looked back was the Wars of the Roses, the English "thirty years war", in
which rival claimants to the throne ravaged the country from 1455 to 1485.
The agency of their deliverance, the saviour of England, was the House of
Tudor. And so the constitution in which they rejoiced was not a democ-
racy, with a party system and the paraphernalia of parliamentary government, but a monarchy, ruling through its own chosen bureaucracy, a
monarchy divinely ordained, strong, absolute, unchallenged, and entirely
popular. To them the blessings of the Tudor government were so patent,
so unquestionable that their only fear was lest something should arise to
threaten its permanence or supremacy.

The most sensitive political spot in the modern Englishman's soul is
personal liberty. Let the government, the executive, touch that and in a
few hours a storm may spring up which will shake the firmest ministry
from its seat. To the Elizabethans the most sensitive spot was Order,
together with its external aspect, national Security. The Tudor absolutism
made modern liberty possible; for order first, liberty afterwards, is the law
of political growth. But liberty was a notion hardly comprehensible to
Shakespeare, and only to some – very few – of his contemporaries in the
form of religious liberty. Read *Julius Caesar* through, the play which above
all others would seem to imply modern conceptions of liberty, and you
will not, I think, be able to discover anywhere in the play even a glance at
political liberty, as we now understand it. Order, or Degree, is the basis of
his political philosophy, as it is of all thinking Elizabethans. And the most
elaborate and deliberate expression of it, the famous speech of Ulysses in
the third scene of *Troilus and Cressida*, is itself little more than an expansion of ideas the opening words of which Shakespeare found in Sir
Thomas Elyot's *Book of the Governour*, the best known of Tudor political
treatises. The speech is familiar to you all. But its content is so germane to
the purport of this lecture, that perhaps you will allow me to quote a
portion of it to you, if only to remind you that then, as ever, political
theory was closely associated with cosmological conceptions.

> The heavens themselves, the planets and this centre
> Observe degree, priority and place,
> Insisture, course, proportion, season, form,

Office and custom, in all line of order;
And therefore is the glorious planet Sol
In noble eminence enthroned and sphered
Amid the other; whose medicinable eye
Corrects the ill aspects of planets evil,
And posts, like the commandment of a king,
Sans check to good and bad: but when the planets
In evil mixture to disorder wander,
What plagues and what portents! what mutiny!
What raging of the sea! shaking of earth!
Commotion in the winds! frights, changes, horrors,
Divert and crack, rend and deracinate
The unity and married calm of states
Quite from their fixture! O, when degree is shaked,
Which is the ladder to all high designs,
The enterprise is sick! How could communities,
Degrees in schools and brotherhoods in cities,
Peaceful commerce from dividable shores,
The primogeniture and due of birth,
Prerogative of age, crowns, sceptres, laurels,
But by degree, stand in authentic place?
Take but degree away, untune that string,
And, hark, what discord follows! [...]
[1.3.85–110]

How magnificent is the rhetoric, and how remote its tenor from modern political thought, of whatever school! Platonic in its association of the ordered hierarchy of the estates with the harmony of music, it is Ptolemaic in its identification of these two harmonies with the harmony of the spheres, while memories of the anarchy in fifteenth century England supply the emotional colouring to the picture of the deplorable results that follow for mankind and his world from the breakdown of this harmony. There is no need to insist upon the importance of the monarchy in such a scheme of things. The King or Governor is the sun in the political heavens, that is to say not merely the largest but, in those astrological days, the most potent for good or ill of all stellar bodies. Shakespeare here speaks of him as "the glorious planet Sol", and it is often overlooked that sun-symbolism for the majesty of kingship is one of Shakespeare's leading ideas. Indeed, it was the mystical conception of his position and the vital importance of preserving it unimpaired, as the sole defence against anarchy, that accounts for the semi-divine honours which their subjects accorded to Henry VIII and his great daughter Elizabeth. The point has been well brought out in an admirable general *History of England* by Professor George Trevelyan. After insisting that "the keynote of Tudor government" was "King-worship, not despotism", he continues:

Monarchs without an army at the centre or a paid bureaucracy in the countryside were not despots, for they could not compel their subjects by force. The beefeaters of the Palace could guard the barge in which a rebellious nobleman or a fallen Minister was rowed from Whitehall steps to Traitors' Gate in the Tower, because the London 'prentices never attempted a rescue on the way. But they could not coerce a population of five millions, many of whom had sword, bow or bill hanging from the cottage rafters.

The power of the Tudors, in short, was not material but metaphysical. They appealed sometimes to the love and always to the loyalty and "free awe" of their subjects. In the century that begins with Sir Thomas More and ends with Shakespeare, "the deputy elected of the Lord" walks girt with sunlike majesty. In his presence rank, genius and religion vail their pride, or lay their heads resignedly upon the block if the wrath of the Prince demands a sacrifice.

The historical and political thought, then, of Shakespeare and his contemporaries was determined by their fears of chaos and their gratitude to the royal house which had saved England from it. But what *had* been might happen again. Looking back in horror to the terrible disorders of the Wars of the Roses they asked themselves how such chaos can have come about; and they fixed upon the reign of King Richard II as the crucial turning point, finding the true cause of all that followed in the events that brought Richard to his death and his cousin Henry of Lancaster to the throne. And they were indisputably right. To the men of the late middle ages and the sixteenth century, the deposition of Richard II was as significant as the execution of Charles I was to Englishmen of the eighteenth and nineteenth centuries. Thus they viewed Richard and Henry Bolingbroke in a light quite different from that in which our historians see them to-day. Professor Trevelyan goes out of his way to compare the revolutions of 1399 and 1688. "Richard like James", he writes, "made every possible mistake at the crisis, could get no one to fight for him, and was deposed by Parliament on the express ground that he had broken the fundamental laws of the Kingdom. And Henry, like William, was called to the empty throne partly indeed by hereditary right, but yet more by Parliamentary title, for neither Henry IV nor William of Orange was the nearest heir. The result of the Revolution of 1399 was to set the power of the two Houses of Parliament on ground at once higher and firmer than ever. They had not only deposed a King – as had happened when Edward II was forced to yield the throne to his son – but this time they had chosen the successor. The Lancastrian, like the Hanoverian, Kings ruled by Parliamentary title, and under them the power and privilege of both Houses must be respected." Even more significant is the manner in which another modern historian, Sir Charles Oman, has expressed the same point of view:

Henry of Lancaster was for all intents and purposes an elective king who came to the throne under a bargain to give the realm the good government which his predecessor had denied. In one sense his position was strong, he had for the moment an immense majority of the nation at his back; but in another sense he was weaker than any of his predecessors for many a year. He had sanctioned the theory that kings can be deposed for misrule...He kept his throne only because he proved a statesman of sufficient ability to conciliate a majority of his subjects...It was a weary and often a humiliating game, for Henry had to coax and wheedle his parliament where a monarch with a strictly legitimate title could have stood upon his dignity and appealed to his divine right to govern. But the story is interesting, intensely interesting, as being the first episode of what we may call constitutional government in the modern sense.

There you have it! The weakness of Bolingbroke's title is what interests our modern historians, because weakness in the executive foreshadows the birth of constitutional and political liberty. But what is almost a virtue in Professor Oman's eyes was a crime in that of Tudor Englishmen. Henry of Lancaster was not to them the morning star of the Whig Revolution, but the man at whose door the disorders of the fifteenth century must be laid. He was in fact a usurper and his usurpation so weakened the executive that it took over eighty years of struggle to restore the nation to sanity and health, unity and order. The usurpation may be interesting to twentieth century constitutional antiquarians, but they did not have to pay for it, as those living in the fifteenth did, the fathers and grandfathers of the Elizabethans. Edward Hall, the earliest of Tudor historians, whose *Chronicle*, 1548, set the tone and to a large extent fixed the framework of his immediate successors, gives eloquent expression in the very title-page of his book to what Englishmen at that time thought about the Wars of the Roses and Henry Bolingbroke's responsibility for them. Thus it runs:

> The union of the two noble & illustre famelies of Lancastre & Yorke, beyng long in continuall discension for the croune of this noble realms, with all the actes done in both the tymes of the Princes, both of the one linage & of the other, beginnyng at the tyme of kyng Henry the fowerth, the first aucthor of this deuision, and so successiuely proceading to the reigne of the High and Prudent Prince Kyng Henry the Eight, the indubitate flower and very heire of both the saied linages.

After which Hall proceeds to an eloquent discourse upon the evils of civil strife with which his chronicle opens.

So much for the tone and general sentiment of Tudor England towards the immediate past. As for the framework of Hall's book, it is remarkable that he begins with the death of the Duke of Gloucester at King Richard's orders and the subsequent quarrel between Mowbray and Bolingbroke; in other words, at exactly the same point where Shakespeare begins his *Richard II*. Indeed, we have three elaborate accounts of the period of the Wars of the Roses, all written in the sixteenth century, viz. Hall's *Chronicle*, Shakespeare's cycle of historical plays, *Richard II* to *Richard III*, and a long poem by Samuel Daniel entitled *The Civil Wars between the two houses of Lancaster and York* – and they all begin at the same point! Furthermore, this point was selected not only by a sound historical instinct but also because it possessed a very special meaning for England at the time of Elizabeth. The political horizon was for Shakespeare and his contemporaries peculiarly uncertain. Henry VIII, building upon the foundations laid by the first of the Tudors, his father, had rehabilitated the monarchy, and restored unity and order to the nation. And he had been succeeded by three children in turn, the last of them being his most worthy heir. But when Elizabeth died, what then? Was England to relapse once more into dynastic strife? For the Tudor stock was exhausted; Elizabeth had no heirs. Writing in 1600, a lawyer enumerates no fewer than twelve different "competitors that gape for the death of that good old Princess, the now Queen". No wonder that many identified her with Richard II, and looked forward with dread to usurpation and a period of anarchy once again.

Daniel left his poem on the Civil Wars unfinished; and Shakespeare never rounded off his dramatic cycle. Why were these two great literary undertakings to remain uncompleted? The death of Elizabeth in 1603 provides at least one answer to the question. With the peaceful accession of James VI of Scotland and James I of England the problem of the succession was solved. A new dynasty was established upon the throne, a dynasty founded not upon civil war and the rise of a noble house, but upon legal right so strong that it was recognized in a foreign branch of the royal line. [...]

In any case with the death of the last of the Tudors, and the accession of a family "of undoubted title" crowned seemingly with "olives of endless age", the taste for poems and dramas on the troublous times of the fifteenth century disappeared with the political anxieties which had stimulated it. When Shakespeare desired to write history in future, he turned to Plutarch, in whose pages he found dimly reflected, as in some magic glass, a new and hitherto hardly suspected political problem, which was after his death to bring civil war of a new kind to the land. I mean of course, the conflict between the Crown and the Commons, the Governor and his people, an issue already felt in *Julius Caesar* and evident in *Coriolanus*.

But while Elizabeth lived, the older anxieties governed men's thoughts, and in their fears that her reign might be the prelude to yet another period of anarchy, they naturally bent eagerly enquiring eyes upon the events of the reign of Richard II, which had led up to the earlier time of trouble, and particularly upon the actions of the usurper Henry IV, who was, as Hall taught them, "the first aucthor of this deuision". And Shakespeare was himself especially open to such fears, since he came to the writing of his *Richard II* after first brooding upon the reigns of Henry VI and Richard III which provided substance for four plays of his nonage. In preparing them he had looked down into the abyss of chaos in England. For example, at the battle of Towton, represented in *3 Henry VI*, he gives us the grim stage-directions "Enter a Son that hath killed his father, dragging in the dead body", and "Enter a Father that hath killed his son, bringing in the body". Thus *Richard II* is as full of foreboding as it is of patriotic sentiment, and leaves one with the impression that the end of the tragedy of Richard is only the beginning of the tragedy of England.

The chief spokesman of this prophetic strain is the Bishop of Carlisle, who after proclaiming Richard as the rightful king in the parliament which is just about to depose him, denounces Bolingbroke as a traitor, and continues:

> If you do crown him, let me prophesy:
> The blood of England shall manure the ground,
> And future ages groan for this foul act;
> Peace shall go sleep with Turks and infidels,
> And in this seat of peace tumultuous wars
> Shall kin with kin and kind with kind confound;
> Disorder, horror, fear and mutiny
> Shall here inhabit, and this land be called
> The field of Golgotha and dead men's skulls.
> [4.1.127–135]

It is interesting to note that our greatest living authority on this period of history, my colleague Professor Galbraith, had expressed the belief that the lines Shakespeare puts into Carlisle's mouth may be "a poet's echo" of a speech actually delivered in parliament on that occasion. "They are", he writes, "in harmony with the stiff legalism of the age, and are confirmed by a long tradition of anti-Lancastrian disaffection..." The procedure of deposition, as well as the act itself, was a cause of the "disorder, horror, fear, and mutiny of the fifteenth century". But Carlisle is not the only prophet in the play. Old John of Gaunt himself, who upon his deathbed prophesies the downfall of his nephew Richard, condemns in advance by implication the action of his son Bolingbroke in lifting

> An angry arm against God's minister,
> [1.2.41]

and becoming the sacrilegious instrument of his deposition and death. For that Shakespeare and his audience regarded Bolingbroke as a usurper is incontestable. This is evident in the passages just quoted and from the whole tone and emphasis of *Richard II*. [...]

Those critics, therefore, such as Coleridge for example, who make him out to be in *Richard II* nothing but a deep plotter are very wide of the mark. One of the dominant conceptions of that play is the notion of the part which Fortune, a very real force in the medieval and Elizabethan universe, played in the affairs of this world; and the unaccountable action of her influence contributes much to the atmosphere of mystery which is so evident a characteristic of the play. Fortune's wheel, indeed, seems to have suggested the very shape and structure of the drama, which gives us a complete inversion. The first act opens immediately after the death of the Duke of Gloucester, when as Froissart notes Richard is "high upon the wheel", exhibiting all the hubris and tyranny expected of persons in that position, while his opponent, Bolingbroke, is shown at the lowest point of his fortunes. But from the beginning of act [2], the wheel starts turning mysteriously of itself, or rather by the action of the goddess. The will of the King seems paralysed; he becomes an almost passive agent. Bolingbroke acts, and acts forcibly; yet he too appears to be borne upwards by a power beyond his volition. Circumstance drives him on from point to point; he takes what Fortune and Fortune's puppet, Richard, throw in his path. He is an opportunist, not a schemer. This view of his character and actions emerges clearly enough from Daniel's treatment of them in the poem on the *Civil Wars* already spoken of, a poem to which, as I shall be showing on another occasion, Shakespeare was greatly indebted in the creation of his play. After discussing the question of Bolingbroke's guilt at some length, Daniel thus concludes:

> Then, Fortune, thou art guilty of his deed,
> That did his state above his hopes erect,
> And thou must bear some blame of his great sin
> That left'st him worse than when he did begin.
>
> Thou didst conspire with pride, and with the time,
> To make so easy an ascent to wrong,
> That he who had not thought so high to climb,
> (With favouring comfort still allur'd along),
> Was with occasion thrust into the crime,
> Seeing others' weakness and his part so strong:
> And, oh, in such a case who is it will
> Do good, and fear, that may live free with ill.

And if we miss much that Shakespeare intended when we regard Bolingbroke as a mere crafty villain, we miss still more if we write Richard off as the weak-willed, rather contemptible creature that Coleridge makes of him. One of the great attractions of the story of Richard of Bordeaux and Henry Bolingbroke, Duke of Lancaster, for the men of the fifteenth and sixteenth centuries was that it afforded, in its spectacle of what Hall calls the "dejecting of the one and the advancing of the other", a perfect example of the mysterious action of Fortune, under Providence. And Shakespeare's play was a mirror, not only for magistrates, but for every son of woman; for when the "dejected" king gazed (on Shakespeare's stage) into the glass, he saw the brittleness not only of his own glory but of all earthly happiness.

Yet Richard stood for much more than a man broken on Fortune's wheel. He was a king, and more even than that too. In the eyes of the later middle ages, he represented the type and exemplar of royal martyrdom, of a king not slain in battle, not defeated and killed by a foreign adversary, not even like Edward II deposed owing to weakness or tyranny in favour of his legal heir, but thrust from the throne in his may of youth, by a mere usurper, under colour of a process of law utterly illegal, and then foully murdered. By the anti-Lancastrians of his time, and France was full of them, he was almost canonized, as Charles I became later. Men dwelt upon his agony and death; compared his sufferings with those of Christ, and his judges with Pilate; and attributed his fall and capture to treachery as base as that of Judas. He became the centre of a legend, the legend of the hero and gracious monarch, betrayed into the hands of cruel and ambitious men. No fewer than four chronicles, one in Latin and three in French, embodying this legend, have come down to us from the fifteenth century; and of some versions there exist a large number of manuscript copies on the continent.

On the other hand, the followers of Henry of Lancaster had, of course, their own story, which is still to all intents that of history, though Professor Galbraith strongly suspects its validity; the story of a feckless, moody, tyrannical young man, who surrounded himself with base favourites, surrendered of his own accord, out of cowardice, and abdicated of his own free will.

The two legends are, and were intended to be, contradictory; but under the Tudor monarchy, which united the two houses of York and Lancaster and healed the breach for which Bolingbroke had originally been responsible, the legends became, so to speak, conflated. Both are found (ill-reconciled) in the pages of Holinshed, that Elizabethan tank into which the streams from various chronicle sources flowed, without mingling. Holinshed lacked the imagination to fuse the diverse, and originally contradictory, elements. Shakespeare succeeded, and his Richard is a convincing portrait, compounded from the two legends, the portrait of a king who seems to us one of the most living of his characters.

It was chance that early in his career, in 1595 to be precise, Shakespeare stumbled in the pages of Holinshed upon these twin but contrary conceptions of Richard's character, and was forced to do what he could to unify them. But it is my belief that the effort taught him a great lesson which he never forgot, and which is one of the secrets of his dramatic power. It taught him, for example, that he could challenge his audience with an unsympathetic character at the beginning of a play, and win them round to sympathize with the same character in the second half. He accomplished this with great success again in *King Lear*, a play which, as it always seems to me, possesses much closer connexions with *Richard II* than *Hamlet* does. It taught him also something without which the Prince of Denmark, as we know him, could never have come into existence, viz. the tremendous value of apparent contradictions in character for the creation of dramatic verisimilitude. It is largely because Hamlet is logically and psychologically inconsistent and, as all the critics have found, beyond the possibility of analysis, that he appears so life-like in action on the stage. King Richard II presents though in simpler form, a similar bundle of contradictions. In this case, however, Shakespeare found the contradictions in his history-book, he did not invent them. It is odd to think that the lying propaganda of Henry Bolingbroke and his partisans at the beginning of the fifteenth century may have assisted Shakespeare thus materially in the creation not only of his Richard but also of his Hamlet.

But I am concerned here to-day with politics rather than psychology, not with character-problems but with the political conceptions that lie behind Shakespeare's Lancastrian history-plays. And of that I have said enough, I hope, to show that these plays should be of particular interest to German students at this moment of that everlasting adventure which we call history.

2.2 Jean E. Howard and Phyllis Rackin, 'Richard II'

Source: *Engendering a Nation: A feminist account of Shakespeare's English histories* (London and New York: Routledge, 1997), Chapter 10, pp. 137, 141–52, 155, 157–9.

Writing in the very different context of the United States in the 1990s, feminist scholars Jean Howard and Phyllis Rackin differ fundamentally from Dover Wilson in their reading of *Richard II*. Whereas Dover Wilson interprets *Richard II* as an appeal for public order, Howard and Rackin read the play both as questioning the separation of a (masculine) public realm from a (feminine) private or domestic realm, and as an interrogation of the imperative for social order. Indeed, for Howard and Rackin, *Richard II* 'destabilizes the schematic oppositions between past and present, male and female, ... [and] English patriotism and foreign threat'. Like Dover Wilson, they locate their argument in the close analysis of selected passages from the play, and Elizabethan sources like Holinshed's *Chronicles*, but they rely on modern historians who highlight the changing role of women in the London of the 1590s. The result is an interpretation of *Richard II* that pays scrupulous attention to the representation of feminine and masculine values in the play, as well as to previously neglected female characters like the queen.

From a feminist standpoint, one of the most striking features of the second tetralogy is the restriction of women's roles. [...] In the plays of the second tetralogy, [...] female sexuality no longer threatens to disrupt legitimate authority. When Bullingbrook charges in *Richard II* that Bushy and Green "have in manner with [their] sinful hours/Made a divorce betwixt his queen and him,/Broke the possession of a royal bed" [3.1.11–13], the sexual culprits are the king and his male favorites: it is not even clear that any women are involved. The only reference to the queen's sexuality is purely metaphorical – the "unborn sorrow, ripe in fortune's womb" her feminine intuition detects [2.2.10]. The sorrow, moreover, is a fully legitimate conception: caused by a premonition of her husband's impending fall, it is implicitly designated as the offspring of her lawful marriage. The other women in the play – the Duchess of Gloucester and the Duchess of York – are too old to pose a sexual threat. The Duke and Duchess of York, in fact, make this point explicit. In [5.2] the duchess reminds her husband that her "teeming date" is "drunk up with time" [5.2.91]; and in [5.3] York opposes her attempt to plead for her son's life by reminding her how preposterous it would be if her "old dugs" should "once more a traitor rear" [5.3.88]. [...]

Here, the constriction of women's roles represents a movement into modernity, the division of labor and the cultural restrictions that accompanied the production of the household as a private place, separated from the public arenas of economic and political endeavor. To move from the first tetralogy to the second is to move backward to the time of Richard II, but it is also to move forward from a story of warring feudal families to one of the consolidation of the English nation under the power of a great king. In the first tetralogy, virtue and military power like Talbot's are inherited along with the patrilineal titles of nobility; in the second, they are the personal assets that enable the son of an enterprising upstart like Henry Bullingbrook to achieve the status of the mirror of all Christian kings and the aspiring men in the theater audience to earn their places in the commonwealth. [...]

The gendering of excessive emotion as feminine has unsettling effects on the gender position – and the authority – of Richard II, perhaps the most emotive of all Shakespeare's kings. While masculinity and femininity are never the exclusive properties of male and female persons, aspects of English culture in the late sixteenth and early seventeenth centuries made the performative and constructed nature of gender difference disturbingly visible. In the theaters, boys played women's roles and many kinds of social distinctions were indicated by a semiotics of dress and gesture. On the throne, there was a female monarch who claimed masculine authority by referring to herself as a "prince". In the streets of London, women paraded in masculine dress. An increasingly urbanized and performative culture destabilized traditional status distinctions, including the distinctions between men and women, and produced a wide variety of anxious attempts to reestablish them. For the literate, increasing concern with the need to observe masculine and feminine roles was expressed in satiric writing that made the "womanish" man and the "mannish" woman stock objects of invective. In villages, failure to abide by the codes of gendered behavior was punished by court prosecutions of scolds and witches and community shaming rituals such as charivaris.

All these efforts to enforce gender difference can be seen as responses to an emergent culture of personal achievement. If a man's place in the social hierarchy had to be achieved and secured by his own efforts, any claims to authority required that both social status and gender status had to be sustained in performance. In *Richard II*, the king's patrilineal authority is vitiated by his womanish tears and his effeminate behavior: he has no taste for foreign wars, he talks when he should act, and he wastes his kingdom's treasure by indulging in excessive luxuries. Bullingbrook, who has no hereditary right to the crown, acquires it by the successful performance of masculine virtues.

Many critics have remarked that the conflict between Richard and Bullingbrook is framed as a conflict between two models of royal authority, Richard associated with a nostalgic image of medieval royalty, grounded in heredity and expressed in ceremonial ritual, Bullingbrook with the emergence of an authority achieved by personal performance and expressed in the politically motivated theatrical self-presentation of a modern ruler. What is less frequently noted is how thoroughly the binary opposition personalized in the conflict between Bullingbrook and Richard is implicated in an early modern ideology of "masculine" and "feminine". Deborah Warner's 1995 production of the play, which starred Fiona Shaw as Richard, exploited this gendered opposition to brilliant dramatic effect. Shaw, in the words of one reviewer, "simply played Richard as a woman". Although Shakespeare does not literalize the gendered opposition between the two antagonists, his Bullingbrook, like Warner's, plays the "man" to Richard's "woman." A master of military and political strategy, Bullingbrook is shown in company with a noble father, and he alludes to the existence of an "unthrifty" son [5.3.1]; but we hear nothing of his wife or mother, and he is never represented in association with women. Richard, by contrast, has a wife but no son.

Although our own gender ideology privileges male heterosexual passion as an expression of virility, this was not yet the case in Shakespeare's time. Richard is characterized as "effeminate," but this does not mean that he is "homosexual": indeed, the terms "homosexual" and "heterosexual," along with the conceptions of gendered personal identity they denote, are post-Shakespearean inventions. Richard is effeminate because he prefers words to deeds, has no taste for battle, and is addicted to luxurious pleasures. His rapid fluctuations from overweening confidence to the depth of despair [3.3] recall early modern misogynist denunciations of feminine instability, but even his virtues are represented in feminine terms: York's sympathetic description of Richard's behavior in adversity – his "gentle sorrow" and "His face still combating with tears and smiles,/The badges of his grief and patience" [5.2.32–4] – draws on the same discourse of suffering feminine virtue as the description of Lear's Cordelia smiling and crying at once as "patience and sorrow [strove]/Who should express her goodliest" [4.3.15–16]. Bullingbrook speaks few words but raises a large army. Richard is a master of poetic eloquence, unsurpassed in what Mowbray calls "a woman's war...of...tongues" [1.1.48–9], but he surrenders to Bullingbrook without waging a single battle. His viceroy is the superannuated York, who appears "weak with age," "with signs of war about his aged neck" [2.2.83, 74]; confronted by Bullingbrook's military challenge, York immediately capitulates, declaring that he will "remain as neuter" [2.3.158].

The gendered opposition between Richard and Bullingbrook takes much of its force from the predicament of the English aristocracy at the time the play was produced. The noblemen who support Bullingbrook's rebellion are motivated by what they perceive as monarchial threats to their traditional power and authority, threats which are explicitly identified as emasculation when Ross charges that Richard's appropriation of Bullingbrook's inheritance has left him "bereft and gelded of his patrimony" [2.1.238]. As Richard Halpern points out, "the aristocracy felt emasculated by conversion from a militarized to a consuming class." This anxiety was heightened during Elizabeth's reign by the presence of a female monarch and by the queen's transformation of the medieval culture of aristocratic honor from martial service to courtly display. Richard's possession of the throne, like Elizabeth's, is authorized by the old warrant of patrilineal inheritance, but his loss of it is defined in terms of the new anxieties that Halpern describes.

Richard's father, York recalls, "Did win what he did spend, and spent not that/Which his triumphant father's hand had won" [2.1.182–3]. Richard, by contrast, has "basely yielded upon compromise/That which his noble ancestors achiev'd with blows" [2.1.254–5] and wasted the land's wealth in luxurious pleasures and courtly extravagance. Holinshed's *Chronicles*, Shakespeare's main historical source for the play, also represents Richard as indulging in unprecedented personal extravagance at the expense of the commonwealth:

> He kept the greatest port, and mainteined the most plentifull house that ever any king in England did either before his time or since . . . In his kitchen there were three hundred servitors, and everie other office was furnished after the like rate. Of ladies, chamberers, and landerers, there were above three hundred at the least. And in gorgious and costlie apparell they exceeded all measure, not one of them that kept within the bounds of his degree. Yeomen and groomes were clothed in silkes, with cloth of graine and skarlet, over sumptuous ye may be sure for their estates. And this vanitie was not onelie used in the court in those daies, but also other people abroad in the towns and countries, had their garments cut far otherwise than had beene accustomed before his daies, with imbroderies, rich furres, and goldsmiths worke, and everie daie there was devising of new fashions, to the great hinderance and decaie of the common-welth.

In Holinshed's account, as in Shakespeare's, Richard's extravagance is both a fabulous image of lost splendor and a socially disruptive innovation. Like Elizabethan pageantry, it appeals to nostalgia and to an appetite for gorgeous display, but the new-fangled "vanities" Holinshed describes also evoke the anxieties that were associated with an increasingly unstable social hierarchy. Shakespeare makes those anxieties explicit when he associates Richard's appetite for the vanity of luxurious new fashions with the figure of the "Italianated Englishman" who was a familiar object of satire in the sixteenth, but not the fourteenth, century. York explains that Richard cannot hear his venerable uncles' good advice because his ear is stopped by

> Report of fashions in proud Italy,
> Whose manners still our tardy, apish nation
> Limps after in base imitation.
> Where doth the world thrust forth a vanity –
> So it be new, there's no respect how vile –
> That is not quickly buzz'd into his ears?
> [2.1.21–6]

Like the absentee landlords of Shakespeare's own time who betrayed the old feudal traditions of obligation to enclose their property and exploit it for money to spend on lavish displays at court, Richard's taste for effeminate luxury forces him to degrade his office from king to "land-lord" [2.1.113].

Confronted by rapid cultural change, Shakespeare's contemporaries often idealized the past as a time of stable values and national glory, when social status was firmly rooted in patrilineal inheritance and expressed in chivalric virtue. In Shakespeare's representation of Richard II, however, the schematic oppositions between an idealized masculine past and a degraded effeminate present give way to expose the cultural contradictions that lay at the heart of Elizabethan nostalgia for the medieval past. In Richard's characterization – as in the case of Elizabeth herself – the polluting forces of effeminate modernity are embodied in the same person who represents the patrilineal royal authority they threaten to subvert.

Despite (or perhaps because of) its association with the cult of Elizabeth, the nostalgic ideal of a glorious English past was overwhelmingly masculine. [. . .] [This] paradox informs John of Gaunt's nostalgic projection of the England that Richard has betrayed. For although Gaunt's ideal England is a "nurse," a "teeming womb of royal kings" [2.1.51], none of its inhabitants are women. A "fortress" surrounded by a sea which serves it as a "moat," a "royal throne of kings" who are "renowned . . . for Christian service and true chivalry," the object of Gaunt's nostalgic longing is inhabited exclusively by a "happy breed of men" [2.1.40–54], and the deeds that prove its worth are their heroic battles.

Gaunt invokes an ideal past in order to rebuke a degenerate present – the degraded world of an effeminate king who wastes the land's wealth and honor on luxurious pleasures rather than augmenting them in manly wars against the French. The antithesis he constructs between a warlike, masculine historical world and a degenerate, effeminate present employs exactly the strategy that Thomas Nashe described as the virtue of the history play – the representation of a "valiant" world of English "forefathers" as a "rebuke" to "these degenerate effeminate dayes of ours." Written in the time of Elizabeth – a queen frequently compared to Richard II – Shakespeare's English histories appealed to a similar nostalgia for a masculine, historical world projected in idealized opposition to the present realities of female power and authority. In the second tetralogy, however, this gendered opposition between past and present is increasingly disrupted and deconstructed. [. . .]

In *Richard II* both forms of authority are compromised. The older model of royal authority based on patrilineal succession (which had produced a female monarch in Elizabeth I) is represented in the person of an effeminate, theatrical king, who is nonetheless the legitimate heir to the throne. The emergent masculine ideals of personal merit and performance are associated with the usurper, who is empowered by the support of the overwhelming majority of his countrymen.

Although Bullingbrook explains his unauthorized return from banishment in terms of the feudal logic of hereditary entitlement, claiming that he does so only to secure his patrilineal legacy as Duke of Lancaster, he quickly redefines it as service to the "commonwealth" [2.3.165–6]. In Shakespeare's account, as in Holinshed, Bullingbrook has the overwhelming support of the people. Describing Bullingbrook's departure for exile, Holinshed reports, "A woonder it was to see what number of people ran after him in everie towne and street where he came, before he tooke the sea, lamenting and bewailing his departure, as who would saie, that when he departed, the onelie shield, defense and comfort of the commonwealth was vaded and gone". Shakespeare's Richard reports the same event with anxious contempt: we "Observ'd his courtship to the common people," he says, "what reverence he did throw away on slaves,/Wooing poor craftsmen with the craft of smiles...Off goes his bonnet to an oyster-wench/ A brace of draymen bid God speed him well,/And had the tribute of his supple knee" [1.4.23–32]. Holinshed notes that Bullingbrook's rebellion had "the helpe and assistance (almost) of all the whole realme", and Shakespeare repeatedly alludes to the universal dissatisfaction with Richard's government and support for Bullingbrook [2.1.246–88; 3.2.112–19].

In the context of a public theater, these allusions work to empower Bullingbrook and discredit Richard. Shakespeare's descriptions of Richard's offenses against both 'the commons' and "the nobles" [2.1.246–8] and of the crowds that take up arms in support of the rebellion ("white-beards," "boys, with women's voices," "distaff-women," "both young and old" [3.2.109–15]) emphasize their inclusiveness, and they could stand equally well for a description of the heterogeneous audience in the playhouse. The theatrical milieu tended to support the emergent form of authority, in which a king, like a player, had to depend on the favorable responses of the people for whom he performed. Moreover, Richard's contempt for his humble subjects is not likely to have endeared him to their counterparts in Shakespeare's audience. [...]

In Gaunt's nostalgic projection of medieval England as a "royal throne of kings," there is a seamless union between English patriotism and loyalty to the king, but Richard's offenses set them in opposition to each other. The wars between York and Lancaster in the Henry VI plays are motivated by competing claims to genealogical authority, but the conflict in *Richard II* is framed in terms that recall the ideological conflicts in early modern England between an emergent national consciousness and the Tudor and Stuart monarchs' efforts to rationalize, defend, and extend royal authority. To Bullingbrook, as to the gardeners, England is a "commonwealth" [2.3.165]. To Richard it is simply his personal property, to be used as he desires for his own benefit. The dialogue in the early scenes is laced with patriotic sentiment, which is mobilized in opposition to Richard. Gaunt charges that the "blessed plot" England "Is now leas'd out.../Like to a tenement [i.e. land held by a tenant] or pelting [i.e. paltry] farm" [2.1.59–60]. The banishment of Mowbray and Bullingbrook elicits moving affirmations of national identity, but always with the implication that Richard is to blame for violating the bond between faithful subjects and mother England. Mowbray protests that he has deserved better at Richard's hands than to be exiled for life: "The language I have learnt these forty years,/My native English, now I must forgo.... What is thy sentence [then] but speechless death,/Which robs my tongue from breathing native breath?" [1.3.159–73]. As Richard Helgerson has observed, "a kingdom whose boundaries are determined by the language of its inhabitants is no longer a kingdom in the purely dynastic sense". The ringing couplets with which Bullingbrook departs for his own exile also invoke an emergent sense of national identity grounded in the place of his nativity:

> Then England's ground, farewell, sweet soil, adieu:
> My mother, and my nurse, that bears me yet!
> Where e'er I wander, boast of this I can,
> Though banish'd, yet a true-born Englishman.
> [1.3.269–72]

Bullingbrook defines his relationship to the land in the same terms that John of Gaunt uses when he describes "This blessed plot, this earth, this realm, this England" as "This nurse, this teeming womb of royal kings" [2.1.50–1]; but for Bullingbrook the "sweet soil" is the "mother" and "nurse" of every "true-born Englishman." To the Richard of the first two acts, it is his personal property and a source of ready cash: "We are enforc'd to farm our royal realm [i.e. sell the profits from future taxes],/ The revenue whereof shall furnish us/ For our affairs in hand" [1.4.45–7]. Moreover, even when Richard speaks lovingly of the English land, the terms he uses construct a gendered contrast that favors Bullingbrook. When Richard returns from Ireland, he "weep[s] for joy" and salutes the "dear earth...as a long-parted mother with her child" [3.2.4–8]. The rhyme words in Bullingbrook's final couplet – "boast of this I can" and "a true-born Englishman" emphasize his masculinity as well as his English-ness. Richard's language effeminizes him as a mother and infantilizes the land as his child. And unlike Bullingbrook, he does not identify the earth as English; in fact, although Richard has by far the greatest number of lines in the play, he speaks the words "England" or "English" only five times in the entire script [1.4.34; 2.1.221; 3.3.96,99; 4.1.254] and almost always perfunctorily.

Richard II destabilizes the schematic oppositions between past and present, male and female, patrilineal authority and its subversion, English patriotism and foreign threat that defined the meaning of the dramatic conflicts in the first tetralogy. It also destabilizes the binary opposition between theatrical power and historical authority, and in so doing begins the renegotiation of their relationship that will be a major project in the suceeding plays. The rhetorical impact of Richard's theatricality, like that

of Richard III, is ambivalent. On the one hand, both characters are associated by their theatricality with the feminine and with the loss of integrity in an increasingly complicated contemporary world. On the other
hand, both are empowered by their theatricality, because of its inevitable
attraction for a theater audience. What is new in *Richard II* is the association of theatrical power with legitimate royal authority.

The contest between Richard and Bullingbrook, in fact, is specifically
framed as a contention between rival actors. As early as Act 1, Richard
anxiously describes the success of Bullingbrook's theatrical self-presentation to the London citizens:

> How he did seem to dive into their hearts
> With humble and familiar courtesy,
> What reverence he did throw away on slaves,
> Wooing poor craftsmen with the craft of smiles
> And patient underbearing of his fortune,
> As 'twere to banish their affects with him.
> Off goes his bonnet to an oyster-wench,
> A brace of draymen bid God speed him well,
> And had the tribute of his supple knee,
> With "Thanks, my countrymen, my loving friends,"
> As were our England in reversion his,
> And he our subjects' next degree in hope.
>   [1.4.24–35]

Publicly acting like a king, Bullingbrook finally becomes one, and in Act 5
York explicitly compares the Londoners' enthusiastic reception of the
newly crowned Henry IV to the response of a theater audience to a
"well-graced actor," their contempt for Richard to the indifference of
playgoers to an inferior performer:

> As in a theatre the eyes of men,
> After a well-graced actor leaves the stage,
> Are idly bent on him that enters next,
> Thinking his prattle to be tedious,
> Even so, or with much more contempt, men's eyes
> Did scowl on gentle Richard.
>   [5.2.23–8]

It is significant, however, that although Bullingbrook's theatrical power is
described, it is never shown. Instead of seeing these scenes, the audience
in Shakespeare's playhouse is told about them – and told, moreover, by
characters who do not share the London crowds' enthusiasm for Bullingbrook's performance. [...]

Even in the deposition scene, where the represented action depicts
Bullingbrook's acquisition of Richard's power, Richard dominates the

stage. He deposes himself and makes long and eloquent speeches about his complicated emotional responses to the action. The other actors are restricted for the most part to single lines or even half-lines. Richard calls for a looking-glass, and it instantly appears [4.1.266]. Taking the glass and contemplating his own image, he meditates aloud for sixteen lines about his face. The instrument of feminine vanity becomes the means of theatrical empowerment, for it demands that all eyes in the playhouse, including Richard's own, will be fixed on Richard's face. Then, in a remarkable *coup de théâtre*, he dashes the glass against the floor and turns to Bullingbrook with his conclusion: "Mark, silent king, the moral of this sport,/ How soon my sorrow hath destroy'd my face" [4.1.280–1]. The silent, practical new king attempts to arrest the theatrical display with a terse rebuttal that draws on the familiar Elizabethan association between shadows and actors: "The shadow of your sorrow hath destroy'd/The shadow of your face." But Richard is much too quick-witted and voluble to be silenced by this literal-minded reply. He takes off for another twelve lines, making metaphors about shadows and ironically thanking Bullingbrook for "not only [giving him] cause to wail but [teaching him] the way/ How to lament the cause" [4.1.290–2]. In the represented historical action, Bullingbrook has taken the crown of England from Richard, but he is still compelled to play straight man to Richard's agile wit on Shakespeare's stage.

The importance of the women's roles in Act 5 is attested by the fact that both are unhistorical. York's first wife, Isabel of Castille, had died in 1393, six years earlier; but although the Duchess of York at the time of Richard's deposition and Aumerle's treachery was actually Aumerle's stepmother, Shakespeare insists on the biological connection. His duchess reproaches her husband, "Hadst thou groan'd for him/ As I have done, thou wouldst be more pitiful" [5.2.103–4]. York, in turn, rejects her desperate efforts to save her son by asking, "Thou frantic woman, what dost thou make here?/ Shall thy old dugs once more a traitor rear?" [5.3.87–8]. Richard's wife at the time of his deposition, also named Isabel, was a ten-year-old child, the daughter of the King of France, whom Richard had married when she was seven in order to secure a truce with her father. Shakespeare transforms the child into a mature woman and the dynastic marriage into a loving affective union in order to provide a retrospective ratification for Richard's patriarchal authority, now grounded in the matrimonial authority of a husband rather than the royal patrimony that Richard lost when he betrayed the legacy of his forefathers [2.1.163–85]. Neither the usurpers' insistence on sending the queen back to France nor the tearful parting between husband and wife has any basis in Holinshed, who reported that after Richard's death Henry attempted, against the will of the French, to keep the child and her dowry in England and marry her to the Prince of Wales.

Shakespeare's mature queen is nameless to the end and powerless to affect the historical action, but she provides the mystical warrant for Richard's legitimacy. Her grief, like that of the women in *Richard III*, endows her with a prophetic power that is specifically identified as feminine. She has premonitions of disaster, which she describes as an "unborn sorrow, ripe in fortune's womb" [2.2.10], and when Green brings her the news that Bullingbrook has returned to England, she calls him "the midwife to my woe" [2.2.61]. At the end of the play, Richard entrusts the queen with the task of telling his story:

> In winter's tedious nights sit by the fire
> With good old folks and let them tell [thee] tales
> Of woeful ages long ago betid:
> And ere thou bid good night, to quite their griefs,
> Tell thou the lamentable tale of me,
> And send the hearers weeping to their beds.
> For why, the senseless brands will sympathize
> The heavy accent of thy moving tongue,
> And in compassion weep the fire out,
> And some will mourn in ashes, some coal-black,
> For the deposing of a rightful king.
>
> [5.1.40–50]

Imagining his story as a nostalgic tale "of woeful ages long ago betid" told by a fire on a winter night, Richard consigns his history to the female genre of domestic oral narrative. Enjoining the queen to tell it, he depends on the "moving tongue" of a woman and the compassionate responses of her auditors to provide the posthumous ratification of his legitimacy as "a rightful king."

[. . .][T]he queen has been a focus for pathetic sentiment from the beginning. As Scott McMillin points out, she "speaks at length in only three scenes" and "in each of them she weeps – tears are her leading characteristic." It is not until the moment of their parting, however, that the sympathy she evokes is extended to Richard. In the earlier scenes where she appeared, she grieved for her husband, but always in isolation from him, and there was nothing to counter Bullingbrook's accusation that the nameless sins of Richard's courtiers had somehow "Made a divorce betwixt his queen and him,/ Broke the possession of a royal bed,/ And stain'd the beauty of a fair queen's cheeks/ With tears drawn from her eyes by your foul wrongs" [3.1.12–15]. In Act 5, by contrast, the queen's tears come from the prospect of separation from the husband who is now identified as her "true-love," and the "divorce" between them is the work of the usurpers.

In both cases, the accusation of royal divorce is a political charge, empowered by the mystification of patriarchal marriage as a paradigm of political order. Hall used it to authorize the Tudor dynasty when he entitled his history of all the kings from Henry IV to Henry VIII "The Union of the Two Noble and Illustre Famelies of Lancastre & Yorke" and explained that "the union of man and woman in the holy sacrament of matrimony" symbolized political peace and unity. Naturalizing royal authority in the image of a patriarchal family, both Elizabeth and James repeatedly likened their relationships to England to that of a husband to his wife. But the husband–sovereign analogy also worked in the opposite direction, to justify the authority of every husband by reference to the mystified image of sovereignty. At the end of *The Taming of the Shrew,* for instance, Kate rationalizes her submission by declaring that a husband is his wife's "sovereign" and comparing her duty to him to "Such duty as the subject owes the prince" [5.2.151, 159]. The troubled families in Act 5 of *Richard II*, like the imagery of troubled families that appears in both parts of *Henry IV*, imply an analogy between the failure of royal authority in Bullingbrook's kingdom and the failure of patriarchal authority in the families of ordinary subjects. Richard II makes the same connection when he accuses Bullingbrook's men: "Doubly divorc'd! Bad men, you violate/ A twofold marriage – 'twixt my crown and me,/ And then betwixt me and my married wife" [5.1.71–3]. The accusation, like the queen's wifely devotion, displaces an emergent basis for masculine authority backward in time to the Middle Ages and upward in status to the royal family when it naturalizes Richard's status as king by equating it with his status as husband. Although Richard has a clear, hereditary right to the English throne, he loses it by squandering his patrimony. He regains it in retrospect by his possession of a devoted, domesticated wife.

3 Macbeth

3.1 L. C. Knights, 'How Many Children had Lady Macbeth?'

Source: L. C. Knights, *'Hamlet' and Other Shakespearean Essays* (Cambridge: Cambridge University Press, 1979), pp. 270, 272–5, 285–91, 293–5, 298–306.

Closely associated with the Cambridge journal *Scrutiny*, L. C. Knights embraces the dual commitment to practical criticism pioneered by I. A. Richards, and to Matthew Arnold's desire to preserve for English culture 'the best that has been thought and said' in the face of burgeoning industrialism. In his major early work, *Drama and Society in the Age of Jonson*, Knights displayed a keen interest in the wider contexts of

Elizabethan and Jacobean drama, but in this essay he is concerned exclusively with the formal qualities of *Macbeth*. In his own words, 'in the era of the *Daily Mail* and the Best Seller', we need to be trained to listen or to read with an athleticism that matches that of Shakespeare's audiences. The essay, first published in 1933, has a strong polemical edge, as Knights seeks to discredit the 'character criticism' of earlier Shakespeareans like A. C. Bradley. For Knights, Shakespeare's plays are to be treated as 'dramatic poems', with a critical practice built upon meticulous attention to language, rather than unsupported speculation about character and plot. In this extract on *Macbeth*, Knights methodically assembles a case for seeing the play as 'a statement of evil', both by extensive quotation and close analysis, and by attending to the minor scenes and characters which contribute to 'the pattern of the dramatic whole'.

For some years there have been signs of a re-orientation of Shakespeare criticism. The books that I have in mind have little in common with the majority of those that have been written on Shakespeare, but they are likely to have a decisive influence upon criticism in the future. The present, therefore, is a favourable time in which to take stock of the traditional methods, and to inquire why so few of the many books that have been written are relevant to our study of Shakespeare as a poet. The inquiry involves an examination of certain critical presuppositions, and of these the most fruitful of irrelevancies is the assumption that Shakespeare was pre-eminently a great 'creator of characters'. So extensive was his knowledge of the human heart (so runs the popular opinion) that he was able to project himself into the minds of an infinite variety of men and women and present them 'real as life' before us. Of course, he was a great poet as well, but the poetry is an added grace which gives to the atmosphere of the plays a touch of 'magic' and which provides us with the thrill of single memorable lines and lyric passages. [...]

The most illustrious example is, of course, Dr. Bradley's *Shakespearean Tragedy*. The book is too well known to require much descriptive comment, but it should be observed that the Notes, in which the detective interest supersedes the critical, form a logical corollary to the main portions of the book. In the Lectures on *Macbeth* we learn that Macbeth was 'exceedingly ambitious. He must have been so by temper. The tendency must have been greatly strengthened by his marriage.' But 'it is difficult to be sure of his customary demeanour'. And Dr. Bradley seems surprised that 'This bold ambitious man of action has, within certain limits, the imagination of a poet'. These minor points are symptomatic. It is assumed throughout the book that the most profitable discussion of Shakespeare's tragedies is in terms of the characters of which they are composed. – 'The centre of the tragedy may be said with equal truth to lie in action issuing from character, or in character issuing in action. . . . What we feel strongly, as a tragedy advances to its close, is that the calamities and catastrophe follow inevitably from the deeds of men, and that the main source of these deeds is character. The dictum that, with Shakespeare, "character is destiny" is no doubt an exaggeration . . . but it is the exaggeration of a vital truth.' It is this which leads Dr. Bradley to ask us to imagine Posthumus in the place of Othello, Othello in the place of Posthumus, and to conjecture upon Hamlet's whereabouts at the time of his father's death.

The influence of the assumption is pervasive. Not only are all the books of Shakespeare criticism (with a very few exceptions) based upon it, it invades scholarship (the notes to the indispensable Arden edition may be called in evidence), and in school children are taught to think they have 'appreciated' the poet if they are able to talk about the characters – aided no doubt by the neat summaries provided by Mr. Verity which they learn so assiduously before examinations. [. . .]

A Shakespeare play is a dramatic poem. It uses action, gesture, formal grouping and symbols, and it relies upon the general conventions governing Elizabethan plays. But, we cannot too often remind ourselves, its end is to communicate a rich and controlled experience by means of words – words used in a way to which, without some training, we are no longer accustomed to respond. To stress in the conventional way character or plot or any of the other abstractions that can be made, is to impoverish the total response. 'It is in the total situation rather than in the wrigglings of individual emotion that the tragedy lies.' 'We should not look for perfect verisimilitude to life,' says Mr. Wilson Knight, 'but rather see each play as an expanded metaphor, by means of which the original vision has been projected into forms roughly correspondent with actuality, conforming thereto with greater or less exactitude according to the demands of its nature. . . . The persons, ultimately, are not human at all, but purely symbols of a poetic vision.' [. . .]

A consideration of Shakespeare's use of language demands a consideration of the reading and listening habits of his audience. Contrary to the accepted view that the majority of these were crude and unlettered, caring only for fighting and foolery, bombast and bawdry, but able to *stand* a great deal of poetry, I think there is evidence (other than the plays themselves) that very many of them had an educated interest in words, a passionate concern for the possibilities of language and the subtleties of poetry. At all events they were trained, by pamphlets, by sermons and by common conversation, to listen or to read with an athleticism which we, in the era of the *Daily Mail* and the Best Seller, have consciously to acquire or do our best to acquire. And all of them shared the speech idiom that is the basis of Shakespeare's poetry.

We are faced with this conclusion: the only profitable approach to Shakespeare is a consideration of his plays as dramatic poems, of his use of language to obtain a total complex emotional response. Yet the bulk of Shakespeare criticism is concerned with his characters, his heroines, his love of Nature or his 'philosophy' – with everything, in short, except with the words on the page, which it is the main business of the critic to examine. [...]

The habit of regarding Shakespeare's persons as 'friends for life' or, maybe, 'deceased acquaintances', is responsible for most of the vagaries that serve as Shakespeare criticism. It accounts for the artificial simplifications of the editors ('In a play one should speak like a man of business'). It accounts for the 'double time' theory for *Othello*. It accounts for Dr. Bradley's Notes. It is responsible for all the irrelevant moral and realistic canons that have been applied to Shakespeare's plays, for the sentimentalizing of his heroes (Coleridge and Goethe on Hamlet) and his heroines. And the loss is incalculable. Losing sight of the *whole* dramatic pattern of each play, we inhibit the development of that full complex response that makes our experience of a Shakespeare play so very much more than an appreciation of 'character' – that is, usually, of somebody else's 'character'. That more complete, more intimate possession can only be obtained by treating Shakespeare primarily as a poet.

Since everyone who has written about Shakespeare probably imagines that he has 'treated him primarily as a poet', some explanation is called for. How should we read Shakespeare?

We start with so many lines of verse on a printed page which we read as we should read any other poem. We have to elucidate the meaning (using Dr. Richards's fourfold definition) and to unravel ambiguities; we have to estimate the kind and quality of the imagery and determine the precise degree of evocation of particular figures; we have to allow full weight to each word, exploring its 'tentacular roots', and to determine how it controls and is controlled by the rhythmic movement of the passage in which it occurs. In short, we have to decide exactly why the lines 'are so and not otherwise'.

As we read other factors come into play. The lines have a cumulative effect. 'Plot', aspects of 'character' and recurrent 'themes' – all 'precipitates from the memory' – help to determine our reaction at a given point. There is a constant reference backwards and forwards. But the work of detailed analysis continues to the last line of the last act. If the razor-edge of sensibility is blunted at any point we cannot claim to have read what Shakespeare wrote, however often our eyes may have travelled over the page. A play of Shakespeare's is a precise particular experience, a poem – and precision and particularity are exactly what is lacking in the greater part of Shakespeare criticism, criticism that deals with *Hamlet* or *Othello* in

terms of abstractions that have nothing to do with the unique arrangement of words that constitutes these plays.

Obviously what is wanted to reinforce the case against the traditional
methods is a detailed examination of a particular play. Unfortunately
anything approaching a complete analysis is precluded by the scope of
the present essay. The following remarks on one play, *Macbeth*, are,
therefore, not offered as a final criticism of the play; they merely point to
factors that criticism must take into account if it is to have any degree of
relevance, and emphasize the kind of effect that is necessarily overlooked
when we discuss a Shakespeare play in terms of characters 'copied from
life', or of 'Shakespeare's knowledge of the human heart'. [. . .]

Macbeth is a statement of evil. I use the word 'statement' (unsatisfactory as
it is) in order to stress those qualities that are 'non-dramatic', if drama is
defined according to the canons of William Archer or Dr. Bradley. It also
happens to be poetry, which means that the apprehension of the whole
can only be obtained from a lively attention to the parts, whether they
have an immediate bearing on the main action or 'illustrate character', or
not. Two main themes, which can only be separated for the purpose of
analysis, are blended in the play – the themes of the reversal of values and
of unnatural disorder. And closely related to each is a third theme, that of
the deceitful appearance, and consequent doubt, uncertainty and confusion. All this is obscured by false assumptions about the category 'drama';
Macbeth has greater affinity with *The Waste Land* than with *The Doll's
House*.

Each theme is stated in the first act. The first scene, every word of which
will bear the closest scrutiny, strikes one dominant chord:

> Faire is foule, and foule is faire,
> Hover through the fogge and filthie ayre.
> [1.1.10–11]

It is worth remarking that 'Hurley-burley' implies more than 'the tumult
of sedition or insurrection'. Both it and 'when the Battaile's lost, and
wonne' suggest the kind of metaphysical pitch-and-toss that is about to
be played with good and evil. At the same time we hear the undertone of
uncertainty: the scene opens with a question, and the second line suggests
a region where the elements are disintegrated as they never are in nature;
thunder and lightning are disjoined, and offered as alternatives. We
should notice also that the scene expresses the same movement as the
play as a whole: the general crystallizes into the immediate particular
('Where the place?' – 'Upon the Heath.' – 'There to meet with Macbeth.')
and then dissolves again into the general presentment of hideous gloom.
All is done with the greatest speed, economy and precision.

The second scene is full of images of confusion. It is a general principle in the work of Shakespeare and many of his contemporaries that when A is made to describe X, a minor character or event, the description is not merely immediately applicable to X, it helps to determine the way in which our whole response shall develop. This is rather crudely recognized when we say that certain lines 'create the atmosphere' of the play. Shakespeare's power is seen in the way in which details of this kind develop, check, or provide a commentary upon the main interests that he has aroused. In the present scene the description

> – Doubtfull it stood,
> As two spent Swimmers, that doe cling together,
> And choake their Art –
>
> [1.2.7–9]

applies not only to the battle but to the ambiguity of Macbeth's future fortunes. The impression conveyed is not only one of violence but of unnatural violence ('to bathe in reeking wounds') and of a kind of nightmare gigantism –

> Where the Norweyan Banners flowt the Skie.
> And fanne our people cold.
>
> [1.2.49–50]

(These lines alone should be sufficient answer to those who doubt the authenticity of the scene.) When Duncan says, 'What he hath lost, Noble *Macbeth* hath wonne' [1.2.67], we hear the echo,

> So from that Spring, whence comfort seem'd to come,
> Discomfort swells,
>
> [1.2.27–8]

– and this is not the only time the Captain's words can be applied in the course of the play. Nor is it fantastic to suppose that in the account of Macdonwald Shakespeare consciously provided a parallel with the Macbeth of the later acts when 'The multiplying Villanies of Nature swarme upon him' [1.2.11–12]. After all, everybody has noticed the later parallel between Macbeth and Cawdor ('He was a Gentleman, on whom I built an absolute Trust') [1.4.13–14].

A poem works by calling into play, directing and integrating certain interests. If we really accept the suggestion, which then becomes revolutionary, that *Macbeth* is a poem, it is clear that the impulses aroused in Act 1, scenes 1 and 2, are part of the whole response, even if they are not all immediately relevant to the fortunes of the protagonist. If these scenes are 'the botching work of an interpolator', he botched to pretty good effect.

In Act 1, scene 3, confusion is succeeded by uncertainty. The Witches

> looke not like th' Inhabitants o' th' Earth,
> And yet are on't.
>
> [1.3.39–40]

Banquo asks Macbeth,

> Why doe you start, and seeme to feare
> Things that doe sound so faire?
>
> [1.3.49–50]

He addresses the Witches,

> You should be women,
> And yet your Beards forbid me to interprete
> That you are so. . . .
> . . . i' th' name of truth
> Are yet fantasticall, or that indeed
> Which outwardly ye shew?
>
> [1.3.43–4; 51–2]

When they vanish, 'what seem'd corporall' melts 'as breath into the Winde' [1.3.79–80]. The whole force of the uncertainty of the scene is gathered into Macbeth's soliloquy,

> This supernaturall solliciting
> Cannot be ill; cannot be good . . .
>
> [1.3.129–30]

which with its sickening see-saw rhythm completes the impression of 'a phantasma, or a hideous dream' [*Julius Caesar*, 2.1.65]. Macbeth's echoing of the Witches' 'Faire is foule' has often been commented upon.

In contrast to the preceding scenes, [1.4] suggests the natural order which is shortly to be violated. It stresses: natural relationships – 'children', 'servants', 'sons' and 'kinsmen'; honourable bonds and the political order – 'liege', 'thanes', 'service', 'duty', 'loyalty', 'throne', 'state' and 'honour'; and the human 'love' is linked to the natural order of organic growth by images of husbandry. Duncan says to Macbeth,

> I have begun to plant thee, and will labour
> To make thee full of growing.
>
> [1.4.28–9]

When he holds Banquo to his heart Banquo replies,

> There if I grow,
> The Harvest is your owne.
> [1.4.32–3]

Duncan's last speech is worth particular notice,

> ...in his commendations, I am fed:
> It is a Banquet to me.
> [1.4.55–6]

At this point something should be said of what is meant by 'the natural order'. In *Macbeth* this comprehends both 'wild nature' – birds, beasts and reptiles – and humankind since 'humane statute purg'd the gentle Weale'. The specifically human aspect is related to the concept of propriety and degree, –

> communities,
> Degrees in Schooles and Brother-hoods in Cities,
> Peacefull Commerce from dividable shores,
> The primogenitive, and due of byrth,
> Prerogative of Age, Crownes, Scepters, Lawrels.
> [*Troilus and Cressida*, 1.3.103–7]

In short, it represents society in harmony with nature, bound by love and friendship, and ordered by law and duty. It is one of the main axes of reference by which we take our emotional bearings in the play. [...]

A key is found in Macbeth's words spoken to the men hired to murder Banquo [3.1]. When Dr. Bradley is discussing the possibility that *Macbeth* has been abridged he remarks ('very aptly' according to the Arden editor), 'surely, anyone who wanted to cut the play down would have operated, say, on Macbeth's talk with Banquo's murderers, or on Act 3, scene 6, or on the very long dialogue of Malcolm and Macduff, instead of reducing the most exciting part of the drama'. No, the speech to the murderers is not very 'exciting' – but its function should be obvious to anyone who is not blinded by Dr. Bradley's preconceptions about 'drama'. By accepted canons it is an irrelevance; actually it stands as a symbol of the order that Macbeth wishes to restore. In the catalogue,

> Hounds, and Greyhounds, Mungrels, Spaniels, Curres,
> Showghes, Water-Rugs, and Demy-Wolves
> [3.1.94–5]

are merely 'dogs', but Macbeth names each one individually; and

> the valued file
> Distinguishes the swift, the slow, the subtle,

The House-keeper, the Hunter, every one
According to the gift, which bounteous Nature
Hath in him clos'd.

[3.1.96–100]

It is an image of order, each one in his degree. At the beginning of the scene, we remember, Macbeth had arranged 'a feast', 'a solemn supper', at which 'society' should be 'welcome'. And when alone he suggests the ancient harmonies by rejecting in idea the symbols of their contraries – 'a fruitlesse Crowne', 'a barren Scepter', and an 'unlineall' succession. But this new 'health' is 'sickly' whilst Banquo lives, and can only be made 'perfect' by his death. In an attempt to re-create an order based on murder, disorder makes fresh inroads. This is made explicit in the next scene [3.2]. Here the snake, usually represented as the most venomous of creatures, stands for the natural order which Macbeth has 'scotched' but which will 'close, and be her selfe' [3.2.16].

At this point in the play there is a characteristic confusion. At the end of [3.2] Macbeth says, 'Things bad begun, make strong themselves by ill' [3.2.56], that is, all that he can do is to ensure his physical security by a second crime, although earlier [3.1.8] he had aimed at complete 'health' by the death of Banquo and Fleance, and later he says that the murder of Fleance would have made him

perfect,
Whole as the Marble, founded as the Rocke.
[3.4.20–1]

The truth is only gradually disentangled from this illusion.

The situation is magnificently presented in the banquet scene. Here speech, action and symbolism combine. The stage direction '*Banquet prepar'd*' is the first pointer. In Shakespeare, [...] banquets are almost invariably symbols of rejoicing, friendship and concord. Significantly, the nobles sit in due order.

Macbeth. You know your owne degrees, sit downe:
    At first and last, the hearty welcome.
Lords. Thankes to your Majesty.
Macbeth. Our selfe will mingle with Society,
    And play the humble Host:
    Our Hostesse keepes her State, but in best time
    We will require her welcome.
Lady Macbeth. Pronounce it for me Sir, to all our Friends,
    For my heart speakes, they are welcome.
                    Enter first Murderer.
[3.4.1–5]

There is no need for comment. In a sense the scene marks the climax of the play. One avenue has been explored; 'Society', 'Host', 'Hostess', 'Friends' and 'Welcome' repeat a theme which henceforward is heard only faintly until it is taken up in the final orchestration, when it appears as 'Honor, Love, Obedience, Troopes of Friends'. With the disappearance of the ghost, Macbeth may be 'a man againe', but he has, irretrievably,

> displac'd the mirth,
> Broke the good meeting, with most admir'd disorder.
>   [3.4.108]

The end of the scene is in direct contrast to its beginning.

> Stand not upon the order of your going,
> But go at once
>   [3.4.118]

echoes ironically, 'You know your owne degrees, sit downe' [3.4.1]. [...]
    I have called *Macbeth* a statement of evil; but it is a statement not of a philosophy but of ordered emotion. This ordering is of course a continuous process (hence the importance of the scrupulous analysis of each line), it is not merely something that happens in the last Act corresponding to the dénouement or unravelling of the plot. All the same, the interests aroused are heightened in the last Act before they are finally 'placed', and we are given a vantage point from which the whole course of the drama may be surveyed in retrospect. There is no formula that will describe this final effect. It is no use saying that we are 'quietened', 'purged' or 'exalted' at the end of *Macbeth* or of any other tragedy. It is no use taking one step nearer the play and saying we are purged, etc., because we see the downfall of a wicked man or because we realize the justice of Macbeth's doom whilst retaining enough sympathy for him or admiration of his potential qualities to be filled with a sense of 'waste'. It is no use discussing the effect in abstract terms at all; we can only discuss it in terms of the poet's concrete realization of certain emotions and attitudes.
    At this point it is necessary to return to what I have already said about the importance of images of grace and of the holy supernatural in the play. For the last hundred years or so the critics have not only sentimentalized Macbeth – ignoring the completeness with which Shakespeare shows his final identification with evil – but they have slurred the passages in which the positive good is presented by means of religious symbols. In Act 3 the banquet scene is immediately followed by a scene in which Lennox and another Lord (both completely impersonal) discuss

the situation; the last half of their dialogue is of particular importance. The verse has none of the power of, say, Macbeth's soliloquies, but it would be a mistake to call it undistinguished; it is serenely harmonious, and its tranquillity contrasts with the turbulence of the scenes that immediately precede it and follow it, as its images of grace contrast with their 'toile and trouble'. Macduff has fled to 'the Pious Edward', 'the Holy King', who has received Malcolm 'with such grace'. Lennox prays for the aid of 'some holy Angell',

> that a swift blessing
> May soone returne to this our suffering Country,
> Under a hand accurs'd.
> [3.6.48–9]

And the 'other Lord' answers, 'Ile send my Prayers with him'. Many of the phrases are general and abstract – 'grace', 'the malevolence of Fortune', 'his high respect' – but one passage has an individual particularity that gives it prominence:

> That by the helpe of these (with him above
> To ratifie the Worke) we may againe
> Give to our Tables meate, sleepe to our Nights:
> Free from our Feasts, and Banquets bloody knives;
> Do faithful Homage, and receive free Honors,
> All which we pine for now.
> [3.6.32–7]

Food and sleep, society and the political order are here, as before, represented as supernaturally sanctioned. I have suggested that this passage is recalled for a moment in Lady Macduff's answer to the Murderer [4.2.81], and it is certainly this theme which is taken up when the Doctor enters after the Malcolm-Macduff dialogue in [4.3]; the reference to the King's Evil may be a compliment to King James, but it is not merely that. We have only to remember that the unseen Edward stands for the powers that are to prove 'the Med'cine of the sickly Weale' of Scotland to see the double meaning in

> there are a crew of wretched Soules
> That stay his Cure...
> [4.3.142–3]

Their disease 'is called the Evill'. The 'myraculous worke', the 'holy Prayers', 'the healing Benediction', Edward's 'vertue', the 'sundry Blessings...that speake him full of Grace' are reminders not only of the evil against which Malcolm is seeking support, but of the positive qualities against which the evil and disorder must be measured. Scattered notes ('Gracious England', 'Christendome', 'heaven', 'gentle Heavens') remind us of the theme until the end of the scene, when we know that Macbeth (the 'Hell-Kite', 'this Fiend of Scotland')

> Is ripe for shaking, and the Powers above
> Put on their Instruments.
>
> [4.3.240–1]

The words quoted are not mere formalities; they have a positive function, and help to determine the way in which we shall respond to the final scenes.

The description of the King's Evil [4.3.143 ff] has a particular relevance; it is directly connected with the disease metaphors of the last Act; and these are strengthened by combining within themselves the ideas of disorder and of the unnatural which run throughout the play. Lady Macbeth's sleepwalking is a 'slumbry agitation', and 'a great perturbation in Nature'. Some say Macbeth is 'mad'. We hear of his 'distemper'd cause', and of his 'pester'd senses' which

> recoyle and start,
> When all that is within him, do's condemne
> It selfe, for being there.
>
> [5.2.23–4]

In the play general impressions are pointed by reference to the individual and particular (cf. [4.3.197] where 'the general cause' is given precision by the 'Fee-griefe due to some single breast'); whilst at the same time particular impressions are reflected and magnified. Not only Macbeth and his wife but the whole land is sick. [...]

> More needs she the Divine, than the Physitian:
> God, God forgive us all.
>
> [5.1.64–5]

Macbeth asks him,

> Can'st thou not Minister to a minde diseas'd,
> Plucke from the Memory a rooted Sorrow,
> Raze out the written troubles of the Braine,
> And with some sweet Oblivious Antidote
> Cleanse the stufft bosome, of that perillous stuffe
> Which weighes upon the heart?
>
> [5.3.42–7]

There is terrible irony in his reply to the Doctor's 'Therein the Patient must minister to himselfe': 'Throw Physicke to the Dogs, Ile none of it' [5.3.47–9].

We have already noticed the association of the ideas of disease and of the unnatural in these final scenes –

> unnatural deeds
> Do breed unnatural troubles,
> [5.1.61–2]

and there is propriety in Macbeth's highly charged metaphor,

> My way of life
> Is falne into the Seare, the yellow Leafe.
> [5.3.23–4]

But the unnatural has now another part to play, in the peculiar 'reversal' that takes place at the end of *Macbeth*. Hitherto the agent of the unnatural has been Macbeth. Now it is Malcolm who commands Birnam Wood to move, it is 'the good Macduff' who reveals his unnatural birth, and the opponents of Macbeth whose 'deere causes' would 'excite the mortified man'. Hitherto Macbeth has been the deceiver, 'mocking the time with fairest show'; now Malcolm orders,

> Let every Souldier hew him downe a Bough,
> And bear't before him, thereby shall we shadow
> The numbers of our Hoast, and make discovery
> Erre in report of us.
> [5.4.4–7]

Our first reaction is to make some such remark as 'Nature becomes unnatural in order to rid itself of Macbeth'. But this is clearly inadequate; we have to translate it and define our impressions in terms of our response to the play at this point. By associating with the opponents of evil the ideas of deceit and of the unnatural, previously associated solely with Macbeth and the embodiments of evil, Shakespeare emphasizes the disorder and at the same time frees our minds from the burden of the horror. After all, the movement of Birnam Wood and Macduff's unnatural birth have a simple enough explanation. [...]

But all this disorder has now a positive tendency, towards the good which Macbeth had attempted to destroy, and which he names as 'Honor, Love, Obedience, Troopes of Friends'. At the beginning of the battle Malcolm says,

> Cosins, I hope the dayes are neere at hand
> That Chambers will be safe,
> [5.4.1–2]

and Menteith answers, 'We doubt it nothing' [5.4.3]. Siward takes up the theme of certainty as opposed to doubt:

> Thoughts speculative, their unsure hopes relate,
> But certaine issue, stroakes must arbitrate,
> Towards which, advance the warre.
>
> [5.4.19–21]

And doubt and illusion are finally dispelled:

> Now neere enough:
> Your leavy Skreenes throw downe,
> And shew like those you are.
>
> [5.6.1–2]

By now there should be no danger of our misinterpreting the greatest of Macbeth's final speeches.

> To morrow, and to morrow, and to morrow,
> Creepes in this petty pace from day to day,
> To the last syllable of Recorded time.
> And all our yesterdays, have lighted Fooles
> The way to dusty death. Out, out, breefe Candle.
> Life's but a walking Shadow, a poore Player,
> That struts and frets his houre upon the Stage,
> And then is heard no more. It is a Tale
> Told by an Ideot, full of sound and fury
> Signifying nothing.
>
> [5.5.18–27]

The theme of the false appearance is revived – with a difference. It is not only that Macbeth sees life as deceitful, but the poetry is so fine that we are almost bullied into accepting an essential ambiguity in the final statement of the play, as though Shakespeare were expressing his own 'philosophy' in the lines. But the lines are 'placed' by the tendency of the last Act (order emerging from disorder, truth emerging from behind deceit), culminating in the recognition of the Witches' equivocation ('And be these Jugling Fiends no more believ'd . . .') [5.10.19], the death of Macbeth, and the last words of Siward, Macduff and Malcolm [5.6].

This tendency has behind it the whole weight of the positive values which Shakespeare has already established, and which are evoked in Macbeth's speech –

My way of life
Is falne into the Seare, the yellow Leafe,
And that which should accompany Old-Age,
As Honor, Love, Obedience, Troopes of Friends,
I must not looke to have: but in their stead,
Curses, not lowd but deepe, Mouth-honor, breath
Which the poore heart would faine deny, and dare not.
[5.3.23–9]

Dr. Bradley claims, on the strength of this and the 'To-morrow, and to-morrow' speech, that Macbeth's 'ruin is never complete. To the end he never totally loses our sympathy. ... In the very depths a gleam of his native love of goodness, and with it a tinge of tragic grandeur, rests upon him.' But to concentrate attention thus on the *personal* implications of these lines is to obscure the fact that they have an even more important function as the keystone of the system of values that gives emotional coherence to the play. Certainly those values are likely to remain obscured if we concentrate our attention upon 'the two great terrible figures, who dwarf all the remaining characters of the drama', if we ignore the 'unexciting' or 'undramatic' scenes, or if conventional 'sympathy for the hero' is allowed to distort the pattern of the whole.

3.2 Alan Sinfield, 'Macbeth: History, Ideology, and Intellectuals'

Source: Alan Sinfield, *Faultlines. Cultural Materialism and the Politics of Dissident Reading* (Oxford: Oxford University Press, 1992), Chapter 5, pp. 95–108.

Alan Sinfield's essay on *Macbeth* contrasts in a number of significant ways with that of L. C. Knights. Published in its earliest version in Britain in the 1980s, Sinfield's essay was written under the banner of cultural materialism, a critical approach he and Jonathan Dollimore defined as follows: '[O]ur belief is that a combination of historical context, theoretical method, political commitment and textual analysis offers the strongest challenge to traditional practice' (Dollimore and Sinfield [eds], *Political Shakespeare* [Manchester University Press, 1985], p. vii). Where Knights had deferred to Arnold and Richards as intellectual guides, cultural materialists like Sinfield looked to the likes of radical critics such as Raymond Williams, Walter Benjamin, and Michel Foucault. The result is a literary criticism that self-consciously seeks not only to challenge dominant versions of how Shakespeare has been understood, but also to deliver a more wide-ranging social critique. Sinfield's essay combines an exploration of the historical context of *Macbeth*, where he compares the competing notions of kingship available in 1606, and textual analysis of routinely overlooked passages in the play, in order to pose difficult questions about the relationship between different forms of sovereignty and state violence. If A. C. Bradley treated *Macbeth* as a Victorian novel, and L. C. Knights treated it as a dramatic poem, for Sinfield the play is a privileged text to be 'creatively vandalised' (Dollimore's phrase) with an eye to uncovering radical possibilities.

It is often said that *Macbeth* is about "evil," but we might draw a more careful distinction: between the violence the state considers legitimate and that which it does not. Macbeth, we may agree, is a dreadful murderer when he kills Duncan. But when he kills Macdonwald – "a rebel" [1.2.10] – he has Duncan's approval:

> For brave Macbeth (well he deserves that name),
> Disdaining Fortune, with his brandish'd steel,
> Which smok'd with bloody execution,
> Like Valour's minion, carv'd out his passage,
> Till he fac'd the slave;
> Which ne'er shook hands, nor bade farewell to him,
> Till he unseam'd him from the nave to th' chops,
> And fix'd his head upon our battlements.
> DUNCAN. O valiant cousin! worthy gentleman!
> [1.2.16–24]

Violence is good, in this view, when it is in the service of the prevailing dispositions of power; when it disrupts them, it is evil. A claim to a monopoly of legitimate violence is fundamental in the development of the modern state; when that claim is successful, most citizens learn to regard state violence as qualitatively different from other violence, and perhaps they don't think of state violence as violence at all (consider the actions of police, army, and judiciary as opposed to those of pickets, protesters, criminals, and terrorists). *Macbeth* focuses major strategies by which the state asserted its claim at one conjuncture.

Generally in Europe in the sixteenth century, the development was from feudalism to the absolutist state. Under feudalism, the king held authority among his peers, his equals, and his power was often little more than nominal; authority was distributed also among overlapping non-national institutions such as the church, estates, assemblies, regions, and towns. In the absolutist state, power became centralized in the figure of the monarch, the exclusive source of legitimacy. The movement from one to the other was, of course, contested, not only by the aristocracy and the peasantry, whose traditional rights were threatened, but also by the gentry and urban bourgeoisie, who found new space for power and influence within more elaborate economic and governmental structures. The absolutist state, I have argued, was never fully established in England. Probably the peak of the monarch's personal power was reached by Henry VIII; the attempt of Charles I to reassert that power led to the English Civil War. In between, Elizabeth and James I, and those who believed their interests to lie in the same direction, sought to sustain royal power and to suppress dissidents. The latter category was broad; it comprised aristocrats like the Earls of Northumberland and Westmorland, who led the Northern Rising of 1569, and the Duke of Norfolk, who plotted to replace Elizabeth with Mary Queen of Scots in 1571; clergy who refused the state religion; gentry who supported them and who tried to raise awkward matters in Parliament; writers and printers who published criticism of state policy; the populace when it complained about food prices, enclosures, or anything. The exercise of state violence against such dissidents depended upon the achievement of a degree of legitimation, and hence the ideology of absolutism, which represented the English state as a pyramid, any disturbance of which would produce general disaster, and which insisted increasingly on the "divine right" of the monarch. This system was said to be "natural" and ordained by "God"; it was "good," and disruptions of it were "evil." This is what some Shakespeareans have celebrated as a just and harmonious "world picture." Compare Perry Anderson's summary: "Absolutism was essentially just this: *a redeployed and recharged apparatus of feudal domination*, designed to clamp the peasant masses back into their traditional social position." [. . .]

LAWFUL GOOD KING/USURPING TYRANT

The split between legitimacy and actual power was always a potential malfunction in the developing absolutist state. A second problem was less dramatic but more persistent. It was this: what is the difference between absolutism and tyranny? – having in mind contemporary state violence such as the Massacre of St. Bartholomew's Day in France in 1572, the arrest of more than a hundred witches and the torturing and killing of many of them in Scotland in 1590–91, and the suppression of the Irish by English armies. The immediate reference for questions of legitimate violence in relation to *Macbeth* is the Gunpowder Plot of 1605. This attempted violence against the state followed upon many years of state violence against Roman Catholics: the absolutist state sought to draw religious institutions entirely within its control, and Catholics who actively refused were subjected to fines, imprisonment, torture, and execution. Consider the sentence passed upon Jane Wiseman in 1598:

> The sentence is that the said Jane Wiseman shall be led to the prison of the Marshalsea of the Queen's Bench, and there naked, except for a linen cloth about the lower part of her body, be laid upon the ground, lying directly on her back: and a hollow shall be made under her head and her head placed in the same; and upon her body in every part let there be placed as much of stones and iron as she can bear and more; and as long as she shall live, she shall have of the worst bread and water of the prison next her; and on the day she eats, she shall not drink, and on the day she drinks she shall not eat, so living until she die.

This was for "receiving, comforting, helping, and maintaining priests," refusing to reveal, under torture, who else was doing the same thing, and refusing to plead. There is nothing abstract or theoretical about the state violence to which the present essay refers. Putting the issue succinctly in relation to Shakespeare's play, what is the difference between Macbeth's rule and that of contemporary European monarchs?

In *Basilikon Doron* (1599), King James tried to protect the absolutist state from such pertinent questions by asserting an utter distinction between "a lawful good King" and "an usurping Tyran":

> The one acknowledgeth himself ordained for his people, having received from God a burthen of government, whereof he must be countable: the other thinketh his people ordained for him, a prey to his passions and inordinate appetites, as the fruits of his magnanimity: And therefore, as their ends are directly contrary, so are their whole actions, as means whereby they press to attain to their ends.

Evidently James means to deny that the absolutist monarch has anything significant in common with someone like Macbeth. Three aspects of James's strategy in this passage are particularly revealing. First, he depends upon an utter polarization between the two kinds of ruler. Such antitheses are characteristic of the ideology of absolutism: they were called upon to tidy the uneven apparatus of feudal power into a far neater structure of the monarch versus the rest, and protestantism tended to see "spiritual" identities in similarly polarized terms. James himself explained the function of demons like this: "Since the Devil is the very contrary opposite to God, there can be no better way to know God, than by the contrary." So it is with the two kinds of rulers: the badness of one seems to guarantee the goodness of the other. Second, by defining the lawful good king against the usurping tyrant, James refuses to admit the possibility that a ruler who has *not* usurped will be tyrannical. Thus he seems to cope with potential splits between legitimacy and actual power by insisting on the unique status of the lawful good king, and to head off questions about the violence committed by such a ruler by suggesting that all his actions will be uniquely legitimate. Third, we may notice that the whole distinction, as James develops it, is cast in terms, not of the *behavior* of the lawful good king and the usurping tyrant, respectively, but of their *motives*. This seems to render vain any assessment of the actual manner of rule of the absolute monarch. On these arguments, any disturbance of the current structure of power relations is against God and the people, and consequently any violence in the interest of the status quo is acceptable. Hence the legitimate killing of Jane Wiseman. (In fact, the distinction between lawful and tyrannical rule eventually breaks down even in James's analysis, as his commitment to the state leads him to justify even tyrannical behavior by established monarchs.)

It is often assumed that *Macbeth* is engaged in the same project as King James: attempting to render coherent and persuasive the ideology of the absolutist state. The grounds for a Jamesian reading are plain enough – to the point where it is often claimed that the play was designed specially for the king. At every opportunity, Macbeth is disqualified ideologically and his opponents are ratified. An entire antithetical apparatus of nature and supernature – the concepts through which a dominant ideology most commonly seeks to establish itself – is called upon to witness against him as usurping tyrant. The whole strategy is epitomized in the account of Edward's alleged curing of "the Evil" – actually scrofula – "A most miraculous work in this good King" [4.3.146–8]. James himself knew that this was a superstitious practice, and he refused to undertake it until his advisers persuaded him that it would strengthen his claim to the throne in the public eye. As Francis Bacon observed, notions of the supernatural help to keep people acquiescent (e.g. the man in pursuit of power will do well to attribute his success "rather to divine Providence and felicity, than to his own virtue or policy"). *Macbeth* draws upon such notions more than any other play by Shakespeare. It all suggests that Macbeth is an extraordinary eruption in a good state – obscuring the thought that there might be any proneness to structural malfunctioning in the system. It suggests that Macbeth's violence is wholly bad, whereas state violence committed by legitimate monarchs is quite different.

Such maneuvers are even more necessary to a Jamesian reading of the play in respect of the deposition and killing of Macbeth. Absolutist ideology declared that even tyrannical monarchs must not be resisted, yet Macbeth could hardly be allowed to triumph. Here the play offers two moves. First, the fall of Macbeth seems to result more from (super)natural than human agency: it seems like an effect of the opposition of good and evil ("Macbeth / Is ripe for shaking, and the Powers above / Put on their instruments" [4.3.239–41]). Most cunningly, although there are material explanations for the moving of Birnam Wood and the unusual birth of Macduff, the audience is allowed to believe, at the same time, that these are (super)natural effects (thus the play works upon us almost as the Witches work upon Macbeth). Second, insofar as Macbeth's fall is accomplished by human agency, the play is careful to suggest that he is hardly in office before he is overthrown. The years of successful rule specified in the chronicles are erased, and, as Henry Paul points out, neither Macduff nor Malcolm has tendered any allegiance to Macbeth. The action rushes along, he is swept away as if he had never truly been king. *Even so*, the contradiction can hardly vanish altogether. For the Jamesian reading, it is necessary for Macbeth to be a complete usurping tyrant in order that he shall set off the lawful good king, and also, at the same time, for him not to be a ruler at all in order that he may properly be deposed and killed. Macbeth kills two people at the start of the play: a rebel and the king, and these are apparently utterly different acts of violence. That is the ideology of absolutism. Macduff also, killing Macbeth, is killing both a rebel and a king, but now the two are apparently the same person. The ultimate intractability of this kind of contradiction disturbs the Jamesian reading of the play.

Criticism has often supposed, all too easily, that the Jamesian reading of *Macbeth* is necessary on historical grounds – that other views of state ideology were impossible for Shakespeare and his contemporaries. But this was far from being so: there was a well-developed theory allowing for resistance by the nobility, and the Gunpowder Plotters were manifestly unconvinced by the king's arguments. Even more pertinent is the theory of the Scotsman George Buchanan, as we may deduce from the fact that James tried to suppress Buchanan's writings in 1584 after his assumption of personal rule; in *Basilikon Doron*, James advises his son to "use the Law upon the keepers" of "such infamous invectives". With any case so strenuously overstated and manipulative as James's, we should ask what alternative position it is trying to put down. Arguments in favor of absolutism constitute one part of *Macbeth*'s ideological field – the range of ideas and attitudes brought into play by the text; another main part may be represented by Buchanan's *De jure regni* (1579) and *History of Scotland* (1582). In Buchanan's view, sovereignty derives from and remains with the people; the king who exercises power against their will is a tyrant and should be deposed. The problem in Scotland is not unruly subjects, but unruly monarchs: "Rebellions there spring less from the people than from the rulers, when they try to reduce a kingdom which from earliest times had always been ruled by law to an absolute and lawless despotism." Buchanan's theory is the virtual antithesis of James's; it was used eventually to justify the deposition of James's son.

Buchanan's *History of Scotland* is usually reckoned to be one of the sources of *Macbeth*. It was written to illustrate his theory of sovereignty and to justify the overthrow of Mary Queen of Scots in 1567. In it the dichotomy of true, lawful king and usurping tyrant collapses, for Mary is the lawful ruler *and* the tyrant, and her deposers are usurpers *and yet* lawful also. To her are attributed many of the traits of Macbeth: she is said to hate integrity in others, to appeal to the predictions of witches, to use foreign mercenaries, to place spies in the households of opponents, and to threaten the lives of the nobility; after her surrender, she is humiliated in the streets of Edinburgh as Macbeth fears to be. It is alleged that she would not have shrunk from the murder of her son if she could have reached him. This account of Mary as arch-tyrant embarrassed James, and that is perhaps why just eight kings are shown to Macbeth by the Witches [4.1.127]. Nevertheless, it was well established in protestant propaganda and in Spenser's *Faerie Queene*, and the Gunpowder Plot would tend to revivify it. Any recollection of the alleged tyranny of Mary, the lawful ruler, prompts awareness of the contradictions in absolutist ideology, disturbing the customary interpretation of *Macbeth*. Once we are alert to this disturbance, the Jamesian reading of the play begins to leak at every joint.

One set of difficulties is associated with the theology of good, evil, and divine ordination that purports to discriminate Macbeth's violence from that legitimately deployed by the state. I write later of the distinctive attempt of Reformation Christianity to cope with the paradoxical conjunction in one deity of total power and goodness. There is also a sequence of political awkwardnesses. These are sometimes regarded as incidental, but they amount to an undertow of circumstances militating against James's binary. Duncan's status and authority are in doubt, he is imperceptive, and his state is in chaos well before Macbeth's violence against it (G. K. Hunter in the introduction to his Penguin edition [1967] registers unease at the "violence and bloodthirstiness" of Macbeth's killing of Macdonwald). Nor is Malcolm's title altogether clear, since Duncan's declaration of him as "Prince of Cumberland" [1.4.35–42] suggests what the chronicles indicate – namely that the succession was not necessarily hereditary. Macbeth seems to be elected by the thanes [2.4.29–32]. Although *Macbeth* may be read as working to justify the overthrow of the usurping tyrant, the *awkwardness* of the issue is brought to the surface by the uncertain behavior of Banquo. In the sources, he collaborates with Macbeth, but to allow that in the play would taint King James's line and blur the idea of the one monstrous eruption. Shakespeare compromises and makes Banquo do nothing at all. He fears Macbeth played "most foully for't" [3.1.3] but does not even communicate his knowledge of the Witches' prophecies. Instead, he wonders if they may "set me up in hope" [3.1.10]. If it is right for Malcolm and Macduff, eventually, to overthrow Macbeth, then it would surely be right for Banquo to take a clearer line.

Furthermore, the final position of Macduff appears quite disconcerting, once we read it with Buchanan's more realistic, political analysis in mind: Macduff at the end stands in the same relation to Malcolm as Macbeth did to Duncan in the beginning. He is now the kingmaker on whom the legitimate monarch depends, and the recurrence of the whole sequence may be anticipated (in production this might be suggested by a final meeting of Macduff and the Witches). The Jamesian reading requires that Macbeth be a distinctively "evil" eruption in a "good" system; awareness of the role of Macduff in Malcolm's state alerts us to the fundamental instability of power relations during the transition to absolutism, and consequently to the uncertain validity of the claim of the state to the legitimate use of violence. Certainly Macbeth is a murderer and an oppressive ruler, but he is one version of the absolutist ruler, not the polar opposite.

Malcolm himself raises very relevant issues in the conversation in which he tests Macduff: specifically tyrannical qualities are invoked. At one point, according to Buchanan, the Scottish lords "give the benefit of the doubt" to Mary and her husband, following the thought that "more secret faults" may be tolerated "so long as these do not involve a threat to the welfare of the state". Macduff is prepared to accept considerable threats to the welfare of Scotland:

> Boundless intemperance
> In nature is a tyranny; it hath been
> Th' untimely emptying of the happy throne,
> And fall of many kings. But fear not yet
> To take upon you what is yours: you may
> Convey your pleasures in a spacious plenty,
> And yet seem cold – the time you may so hoodwink:
> We have willing dames enough; there cannot be
> That vulture in you, to devour so many
> As will to greatness dedicate themselves,
> Finding it so inclin'd.
>
> [4.3.67–77]

Tyranny in nature means disturbance in the metaphorical kingdom of a person's nature but, in the present context, one is likely to think of the effects of the monarch's intemperance on the literal kingdom. Macduff suggests that such behavior has caused the fall not just of usurpers but of kings, occupants of "the happy throne." Despite this danger, he encourages Malcolm to "take upon you what is yours" – a sinister way of putting it, implying either Malcolm's title to the state in general or his rights over the women he wants to seduce or assault. Fortunately, the latter will not be necessary, there are "willing dames enough": Macduff is ready to mortgage both the bodies and (within the ideology invoked in the play) the souls of women to the monster envisaged as lawful good king. It will be all right, apparently, because people can be hoodwinked: Macduff allows us to see that the virtues James tries to identify with the absolutist monarch are an ideological strategy, and that the illusion of them will probably be sufficient to keep the system going.

Nor is this the worst: Malcolm claims more faults, and according to Macduff "avarice / Sticks deeper" [4.3.85–6]: Malcolm may corrupt not merely people but also property relations. Yet this too is to be condoned. Of course, Malcolm is not actually like this, but the point is that he could well be, as Macduff says many kings have been, and that would all be acceptable. And even Malcolm's eventual protestation of innocence cannot get round the fact that he has been lying. He says "my first false speaking / Was this upon myself" [4.3.131–2] and that may indeed be true, but it nevertheless indicates the circumspection that will prove useful to the lawful good king, as much as to the tyrant. In Holinshed the culminating vice claimed by Malcolm is lying, but Shakespeare replaces it with a general and rather desperate evocation of utter tyranny [4.3.92–101]; was the original self-accusation perhaps too pointed? The whole conversation takes off from the specific and incomparable tyranny of Macbeth, but in the process succeeds in suggesting that there may be considerable overlap between the qualities of the tyrant and the true king.

READING DISTURBANCE

Macbeth allows space for two quite different interpretive organizations: against a Jamesian illustration of the virtues of absolutism, we may produce a disturbance of that reading, illuminated by Buchanan. This latter makes visible the way religion is used to underpin state ideology, and undermines notions that established monarchs must not be challenged or removed and that state violence is utterly distinctive and legitimate. It is commonly assumed that the function of criticism is to resolve such questions of interpretation – to go through the text with an eye to sources, other plays, theatrical convention, historical context, and so on, deciding on which side the play comes down and explaining away contrary evidence. However, this is neither an adequate program nor an adequate account of what generally happens.

Let us suppose, to keep the argument moving along, that the Jamesian reading fits better with *Macbeth* and its Jacobean context, as we understand them at present. Two questions then offer themselves: what is the status of the disturbance of that reading, which I have produced by bringing Buchanan into view? And what are the consequences of customary critical insistence upon the Jamesian reading?

On the first question, I would make three points. First, the Buchanan disturbance *is in the play*, and inevitably so. Even if we believe that Shakespeare was trying to smooth over difficulties in absolutist ideology, to do this significantly, he must deal with the issues that resist convenient inclusion. Those issues must be brought into visibility in order to be handled, and once exposed, they are available for the reader or audience to seize and focus upon, as an alternative to the more complacent reading. Even James's writings are vulnerable to such analysis – for instance, when he brings up the awkward fact that the prophet Samuel urgently warns the people of Israel against choosing a king, because he will tyrannize over them. This prominent biblical example could hardly be ignored, so James cites it and says that Samuel was preparing the Israelites to be obedient and patient. Yet once James has brought Samuel's pronouncement into visibility, the reader is at liberty to doubt the king's tendentious interpretation of it. It is hardly possible to deny the reader this scope: even the most strenuous closure can be repudiated as inadequate.

Second, the Buchanan disturbance has been activated, in the present essay, as a consequence of the writer's skepticism about Jamesian ideological strategies and his concern with current political issues. It is conceivable that many readers of *Macbeth* will come to share this outlook. Whether this happens or not, the theoretical implication may be taken: if such a situation should come about, the terms in which *Macbeth* is customarily discussed would shift, and eventually the Buchanan disturbance would come to seem an obvious, natural way to consider the play. That is how notions of appropriate approaches to a text get established. We may observe the process, briefly, in the career of the Witches. For many members of Jacobean audiences, witches were a social and spiritual reality: they were as real as Edward the Confessor, perhaps more so. As belief in the physical manifestation of supernatural powers, and especially demonic powers, weakened, the Witches were turned into an operatic display, with new scenes, singing and dancing, fine costumes, and flying machines. [. . .] These successive accommodations of one aspect of the play to prevailing attitudes are blatant, but they illustrate the extent to which critical orthodoxy is not the mere response to the text it claims to be: it is *remaking* it within currently acceptable parameters. The Buchanan disturbance may not always remain a marginal gloss to the Jamesian reading.

Third, we may assume that the Buchanan disturbance was part of the response of some among the play's initial audiences. It is in the nature of the matter that it is impossible to assess how many people inclined towards Buchanan's analysis of royal power. That there were such may be supposed from the multifarious challenges to state authority – culminating, of course, in the Civil War. *Macbeth* was almost certainly read against James by some Jacobeans. This destroys the claim to privilege of the Jamesian reading on the ground that it is historically valid: we must envisage diverse original audiences, activating diverse implications in the text.

With these considerations about the status of the Buchanan disturbance in mind, the question about the customary insistence on the Jamesian reading appears as a question about the politics of criticism. Like other kinds of cultural production, literary criticism helps to influence the way people think about the world; that is why the present study seeks to make space for an oppositional understanding of the text and the state. It is plain that most criticism has not only reproduced but also endorsed Jamesian ideology, so discouraging scrutiny, which *Macbeth* may promote, of the legitimacy of state violence. That we are dealing with live issues is shown by the almost uncanny resemblances between the Gunpowder Plot and the bombing in 1984 by the Irish Republican Army of the Brighton hotel where leading members of the British government were staying, and in the comparable questions about state and other violence that they raise. My concluding thoughts are about the politics of the prevailing readings of *Macbeth*. I distinguish conservative and liberal positions; both tend to dignify their accounts with the honorific term *tragedy*.

The conservative position insists that the play is about "evil." Kenneth Muir offers a string of quotations to this effect: it is Shakespeare's "most profound and mature vision of evil"; "the whole play may be writ down as a wrestling of destruction with creation"; it is "a statement of evil"; "it is a picture of a special battle in a universal war"; and it "contains the decisive orientation of Shakespearean good and evil."[21] This is little more than Jamesian ideology writ large: killing Macdonwald is "good" and killing Duncan is "evil," and the hierarchical society envisaged in absolutist ideology is identified with the requirements of nature, supernature, and the "human condition." Often this view is elaborated as a sociopolitical program, allegedly expounded by Shakespeare, implicitly endorsed by the critic. So Muir writes of "an orderly and close-knit society, in contrast to the disorder consequent upon Macbeth's initial crime [i.e., killing Duncan, not Macdonwald]. The naturalness of that order, and the unnaturalness of its violation by Macbeth, is emphasized." Irving Ribner says Fleance, Banquo's son, is "symbolic of a future rooted in the acceptance of natural law, which inevitably must return to reassert God's harmonious order when evil has worked itself out."

This conservative endorsement of Jamesian ideology is not intended to ratify the modern state. Rather, like much twentieth-century literary criticism, it is backward-looking, appealing to an imagined earlier condition of society. Roger Scruton comments: "If a conservative is also a restorationist, this is because he lives close to society, and feels in himself the sickness which infects the common order. How, then, can he fail to direct his eyes towards that state of health from which things have declined?" This quotation is close to the terms in which many critics write of *Macbeth*, and their evocation of the Jamesian order allegedly restored at the end of the play constitutes a wistful gesture towards what they would regard as a happy ending for our troubled society. However, because this conservative approach is based on an inadequate analysis of political and social process, it gains no purchase on the main determinants of state power.

A liberal position hesitates to endorse any state power so directly, finding some saving virtue in Macbeth: "To the end he never totally loses our sympathy"; "we must still not lose our sympathy for the criminal." In this view there is a flaw in the state; it fails to accommodate the particular consciousness of the refined individual. Macbeth's imagination is set against the blandness of normative convention, and for all his transgressions, perhaps because of them, he transcends the laws he breaks. In John Bayley's version: "His superiority consists in a passionate sense for ordinary life, its seasons and priorities, a sense which his fellows in the play ignore in themselves or take for granted. Through the deed which tragedy requires of him he comes to know not only himself, but what life is all about." I call this view "liberal" because it is anxious about a state, absolutist or modern, that can hardly take cognizance of the individual sensibility, and it is prepared to validate to some degree the recalcitrant individual. But it will not undertake the political analysis that would press the case. Hence there is always in such criticism a reservation about Macbeth's revolt and a sense of relief that it ends in defeat: nothing could have been done anyway; it was all inevitable, written in the human condition. This retreat from the possibility of political analysis and action leaves the state virtually unquestioned, almost as fully as the conservative interpretation.

Shakespeare, notoriously, has a way of anticipating all possibilities. The idea of literary intellectuals identifying their own deepest intuitions of the universe in the experience of the "great" tragic hero who defies the limits of the human condition is surely a little absurd; we may sense delusions of grandeur. *Macbeth* includes much more likely models for its conservative and liberal critics in the characters of the two doctors. The English Doctor has just four and a half lines [4.3.142–6], in which he says that King Edward is coming and that sick people whose malady conquers the greatest efforts of medical skill await him, expecting a heavenly cure for "evil." Malcolm, the king to be, says, "I thank you, Doctor." This doctor is the equivalent of conservative intellectuals who encourage respect for mystificatory images of ideal hierarchy that have served the state in the past, and who invoke "evil," "tragedy," and "the human condition" to produce, in effect, acquiescence in state power.

The Scottish Doctor, in act 5 scenes 1 and 3, is actually invited to cure the sickness of the rulers and by implication the state: "If thou couldst, Doctor, cast / The water of my land, find her disease" [5.3.52–3]. But this doctor, like the liberal intellectual, hesitates to press an analysis. He says: "This disease is beyond my practice" [5.1.49]; "I think, but dare not speak" [5.1.69] "Therein the patient / Must minister to himself" [5.3.47–8], "Were I from Dunsinane away and clear, / Profit again should hardly draw me here" [5.3.63–4]. He wrings his hands at the evidence of state violence and protects his conscience with asides. This is like the liberal intellectual who knows there is something wrong at the heart of the system but will not envisage a radical alternative and, to ratify this attitude, discovers in Shakespeare's plays "tragedy" and "the human condition" as explanations of the supposedly inevitable defeat of the person who steps out of line.

By conventional standards, this chapter is perverse. But an oppositional criticism is bound to appear thus: its task is to work across the grain of customary assumptions and, if necessary, across the grain of the text, as it is customarily perceived. Of course, literary intellectuals don't have much influence over state violence; their therapeutic power is very limited. Nevertheless, writing, teaching, and other modes of communicating all contribute to the steady, long-term formation of opinion, to the establishment of legitimacy. This contribution King James himself did not neglect.

3.3 E. Pearlman, 'Macbeth *on Film: Politics'*

Source: *Shakespeare Survey: An Annual Survey of Shakespearian Study and Production*, 39 (1987), S. Wells (ed.), Cambridge University Press, pp. 67–74.

This third essay alerts us once again to the capacity of directors and actors to give fresh meaning to Shakespeare's plays, as it explores three film versions of *Macbeth*: by Orson Welles in 1948; by Roman Polanski in 1971; and the much looser adaptation by Akira Kurosawa in 1957 (*Throne of Blood*). Pearlman is concerned in particular to compare the different contexts in which the three films were produced, and further, to contrast their different political meanings. Pearlman's conclusion is provocative: the Welles and Polanski films 'vie with each other in fashionable and even facile pessimism', whereas the Kurosawa version 'grants his characters the power to challenge and refashion imprisoning social systems'. That such divergent meanings can be read off different versions of the same play attests to how vigorously the Shakespeare text continues to be contested.

Each of the three important directors – Welles, Polanski, and Kurosawa – who attempted to recreate *Macbeth* on the screen has had to come to terms with the play's reverence for monarchy. [...]

Although monarchy is a relic of the past, the acquisition and disposition of power is of eternal concern. Indifferent to the politics of absolutism, modern interpreters of *Macbeth* inevitably represent political ideas which are more germane to our century than to Shakespeare's. Orson

Welles unsuccessfully labours to strip *Macbeth* of its political content. He eliminates the episodes crucial to a theory of monarchy and reduces both Duncan and Malcolm to ciphers. To fill the gap, he substitutes an allegorized conflict (as his own sonorous voice pronounces in a didactic voice-over prologue) between 'agents of chaos, priests of hell and magic ...[and] christian law and order'. The film's principal iconic device opposes the spindly forked twigs of the witches – a symbol of their demonism – to the crucifixes of the newly converted Scots. The overthrow of Macbeth is achieved not so much by the march of Birnam Wood as by a moving forest of Celtic crosses. Morality-play elements are clearly embodied in Welles's pedestrian 'Holy Father' – a personage conjured up of shards stolen from four of Shakespeare's minor characters. Welles even goes so far as to invent a primitive but obtrusive ceremony in which the Father leads the multitude in abjuring 'Satan and all his works'. The priest – unfortunately a trifle malevolent and greasy for the moral weight he is asked to bear – is killed when Macbeth's pagan spear pierces his heart. In spite of such murky or inexplicable moments, Welles strives valiantly to minimize politics and emphasize religion.

In defiance of this intent, the film inadvertently generates a rudimentary political vision of its own. By concentrating so exclusively on Macbeth (a devotion which shadows Welles's own achievement as producer, director, scriptwriter, costumer and principal player), the film ruthlessly subordinates all other interests to his, and turns the play into an exploration of both dictatorship and the cult of personality. Huge Macbeth dominates the foreground of innumerable frames of this egocentric production. Other characters, petty men in comparison to Welles's colossus, are pushed into corners or confined to the margins of the frame. When Macbeth encounters the witches for the second time, the camera locates him as a speck in the middle of a distant heath (or soundstage), then tracks him with single-minded intensity until the entire frame is filled with his distorted shape. Except for the dominating presence of Macbeth, the film allows little but the anarchy of faceless masses, from whom (it is presumed) no alternative government could possibly arise.

Attempting to exclude politics, Welles engendered a film in which Shakespeare's poles of monarchy and tyranny have been replaced by a right-wing world view which can admit nothing other than dictatorship or disorder. It is no surprise that he should see the world in these terms. Welles had already demonstrated his simultaneous attraction and repulsion from the *Übermensch* in a number of films, the most familiar of which is *Citizen Kane*. He again wrestles with proto-fascism in this 1948 *Macbeth*. In it, he is both (as Macbeth) the embodiment of the wicked dictator and (as director) the creator of the civilization that bulwarks us against that horror. In his hands, *Macbeth* becomes a parable of fascism narrowly averted. Yet no more than Shakespeare can Welles imagine an alternative to absolute power, and when, at the end of the film, the camera grants us one last look at its papier-maché castle, it leaves a Scotland in which the regime of Macbeth has been overthrown, but the threat of dictatorship still looms.

[...] Orson Welles is indifferent to monarchy and fascinated by an inchoate but primitive Christianity. He is repelled by the fascism he has figured forth, but cannot find his way to a convincing moral or political alternative.

Welles's version of *Macbeth* was influenced by the bleak events of the 1930s and 40s. Roman Polanski's contact with repressive regimes has been more intimate. Displaced by the Nazis as a child, he has been in voluntary exile from Polish communism for most of his adult life. He has said that, in his *Macbeth* (1971), the superfluous brutality of the hired killers who invade Macduff's castle at Fife recalls an SS intrusion into his own home during the Second World War. If Welles creates a film in which religion is central and politics inadvertent, Polanski, whose vision is even more despairing, offers a *Macbeth* in which both Christianity and monarchy are deliberately and systematically replaced by satanism.

[...] Polanski attempts to purge *Macbeth* of its Christianity and at the same time to amplify elements of the supernatural or uncanny. The only specific Christian reference is fleeting and irrelevant – when Fife is ravaged a huge wooden structure in the shape of a cross momentarily appears in flames. The film is otherwise without Christian content. In order to salvage a dark-age setting, Polanski even falls into the anachronism of juxtaposing late medieval fortifications and armaments to neolithic religion. While Welles imagines a ceremony in which the multitude forsake pagan religion, Polanski invents a rite of coronation in which, within a ring of cardboard menhirs, Macbeth himself is lifted aloft on an improbably weightless circular stone. Such legitimate claim to kingship as Macbeth possesses seems to derive from this pseudo-druidic ceremonial. Polanski's Scots are on the whole depicted as a spiritually primitive population ripe for invasion by demons.

Stripped of Christian comfort, Scottish civilization is primarily composed of two antithetical secular elements. On the surface, the Scottish populace is depicted as healthy and prosperous. Macbeth and his wife are picture-book handsome, while Duncan looks like nothing so much as the King of Hearts. Macduff is strong and virile; Lady Macduff, in her one brief scene at Fife, a model of maternal solicitude. Seyton is a reliable soldier, the physician a responsible tradesman. Even members of the subordinate classes are healthy and attractive. When Duncan visits Macbeth's castle, Polanski lavishes a great deal of attention on preparations for the feast. Well-fed servants bustle about sweeping up and arranging the sleeping quarters. The household is apparently democratic – Lady Macbeth herself helps shake out the mattresses and strew the rushes. At the feast itself, the frame is filled with bright colours, cheerful servants, and the generous participation of musicians and singers. Unlike Welles's world, which is menacing and brooding, or Kurosawa's spare and joyless universe, Polanski's world is characterized by song, dance, and even a degree of joy. Yet there is a sinister underside to this apparently prospering community. It is permeated by the gratuitous violence for which Polanski has become notorious. The film takes as its text Macbeth's 'I am in blood / Stepped in so far, that should I wade no more, / Returning were as tedious as go o'er'; its catalogue of bloody horrors does not require rehearsal here. Polanski's Scotland, whether under the rule of Duncan or the usurper, is as brutal as it is beautiful.

To the opposition of natural prosperity and natural cruelty, the film adds a third and dominant note – the ugliness and power of the demonic. The two aged witches in the opening scene are hideous, the younger one pocked and verrucose. Their collection of enchanted objects is even fouler to the eye than Shakespeare's list of ingredients to the ear. The massed ugliness of the naked witches in their cave is an imaginative expansion of the misogyny of the original play. The world of *Macbeth* is almost perfectly Manichean. Polanski has devised a population which is natively attractive (though violent and irreligious) but prey to a powerful and supernaturally sanctioned cult.

The only gods who matter in this *Macbeth* are the demons. They control (or seem to control) the actions of men. In the strong opening moments of the film, the witches bury a number of objects on a sandy beach, most prominently a severed arm and hand with a knife in its grasp. A few moments later a bloody battle takes place on the spot – at the command of the witches, it would seem. These witches are not fantastical; they are exactly what they seem. They do not disappear 'into the air', as do Shakespeare's fiends, but into an underground cavern. Their power overwhelms both religion and monarchy. While government and other human institutions are fragile, witchcraft is perpetual. In Polanski's film, the demonic has penetrated to the core of Scottish society and displaced all other forms of power. As a result, even Macbeth's acceptance of the prophecy, a subject of troubled soliloquy in Shakespeare's play, offers only the slightest moral qualms to Polanski. Macbeth commits himself to the witches at their first meeting when he lies to Banquo and announces that the witches have simply disappeared. While Shakespeare acknowledges the witches' power, he never forgets that goodness and truth are also native to mankind. In Polanski's version of *Macbeth*, human political institutions are regularly subordinated to demonic power.

The penetration of evil into this world is revealed by one of Polanski's principal alterations of Shakespeare's text – the change in the character of Rosse. Rosse figures in the revised plot in a number of places (he is the shadowy Third Murderer, for example), and is one of the agents by which the politics of the film is defined. When he is not granted Macduff's title after aiding in the destruction of Fife, he deserts Macbeth to join the fugitives. In the film's concluding moments, it is Rosse who picks up Macbeth's fallen crown and presents it to Malcolm. This is of the greatest political significance, for when the corrupt and venal Rosse handles so important a symbolic object he contaminates it. In Shakespeare's play, the crown is divine. In Polanski's film, it is a gift to the new king by a murderer and a machiavel. Malcolm had originally been conceived of as an 'innocent lamb'; in this film, he is just another politician, tainted by both his henchmen and his own ambition.

The climax of the film is the prolonged and undignified tussle between Macbeth and Macduff. Where tradition demands a heroic duel between superb warriors, Polanski offers a brawl which borders on farce. In Polanski's version, Macbeth does not lose because he has been betrayed by the equivocation of the fiends, nor Macduff win because the prophecy is fulfilled. Macduff's victory is not inevitable, but accidental. At the point of exhaustion, he strikes a lucky blow and happens to impale his opponent. Shakespeare's confidence in the triumph of justice has been transformed into our favourite contemporary cliché – that all events are merely accidents of an indifferent universe.

The supersession of the demonic over the divine is a reiterated theme, but for those members of the audience who might possibly have missed it, Polanski provides an unequivocal and unsubtle epilogue. Donalbain, Malcolm's brother, distinguished by his jealous glare and awkward limp, heads for the lair of the witches. He will commit himself to them and attempt to displace the reigning monarch. Just as the film began with the witches, so does it end. While Shakespeare's cycle is from one legitimate king to the next, Polanski's is from demon to demon.

In Welles's *Macbeth*, the alternative to monarchy is anarchy; in Polanski's version, the alternative is diabolism. Welles's characters are prey to their basest characteristics. Polanski's version is even bleaker, and offers even less hope for a successful polity. In his world there is no reason to build political institutions, since they are all subordinated to a powerful and uncontrollable evil. It is a remarkably pessimistic view of the world, antithetical in almost all respects to Shakespeare's.

Neither Welles nor Polanski places a great deal of confidence in man's political capacity. Kurosawa's *Throne of Blood* (1957) represents politics in a far different light. At the end of his film, the question of royal succession is deliberately left unresolved, and the throne of the fallen usurper remains unclaimed. While Shakespeare offers us a pure Malcolm and Polanski a compromised one, Kurosawa breaks with tradition and precedent and brings his film to a conclusion without even bothering to instal a new monarch. Instead, he distracts our attention from the problem of succession by focusing on the fall of Washizu (Macbeth).

No viewer can forget one of the most remarkable sequences in film – that in which Washizu is assassinated by his own soliders. Isolated on the balcony from which he has been haranguing his troops, he becomes the target of innumerable arrows. A final arrow pierces his larynx and the soundtrack becomes preternaturally silent. Washizu tumbles down a flight of wooden steps, and, still attempting to draw his sword, gapes at the camera for a long moment before collapsing. The scene is very power-ful and creates a great impression of finality. But contrary to the memory of most audiences, the death of Washizu is not the last event in the film. *Throne of Blood* can be thought of as ending three times, and Washizu's death as only the first of these. The third and final conclusion is, of course, the reprise of the chant with which the film began – the lament for the ambition that leads only to death. The chorus distances the events of *Throne of Blood* by placing them somewhere in an unspecified past, and turns the inset story into a parable in which Washizu becomes the type of the ambitious man. Yet between Washizu's grotesque death and the moment the chorus begins to sing, still another 'ending' takes place on the screen. For not more than two or three seconds, the audience is returned to the perimeter of Forest Castle to catch a brief glimpse of the attacking forces who have found their way through the natural labyrinth of the forest. They have covered themselves and their battle wagons with boughs and branches and are poised for an assault. But Kurosawa withholds the satisfaction of a climactic and conclusive battle and cuts directly and precipitously to the distancing chorus. The event which resolved the earlier films, and which all versions of *Macbeth* have tradi-tionally offered – the battle and the crowning of a new monarch – is simply omitted. Kurosawa has frustrated our natural desire for closure. A battle at this moment would be out of place, for Kurosawa has re-arranged the order of events, and Washizu has already been slain. By abandoning the story just at the moment of the assault, Kurosawa does not have to decide who should succeed to the lordship of Forest Castle, and therefore sidesteps the conventional political problems raised by *Macbeth*. When he leaves Forest Castle without a master, Kurosawa forces us to think about its social and political problems in a new way. [. . .] *Throne of Blood* does not contain the seeds of a healthy polity within its ruling élite. On the contrary, Kurosawa portrays a community so defect-ive that it must be transformed root and branch before a legitimate government can be installed.

The distinguishing marks of the society of *Throne of Blood* are inequity, corruption, and frigidity of personal relationships. The gap between the feudal lords and the common people is so great that it often seems as though we are dealing as much with two species as with two classes. The members of the ruling élite rarely acknowledge the existence of the sub-ordinate classes. In the occasional instance when circumstances require communication, intercourse is stylized, formal, and stilted. When messengers bring news, as they do in the opening sequence, they prostrate themselves fearfully before the generals. At one point the Lord of Forest Castle makes a surprise visit to Washizu. There is a long shot from an elevated point of view of peasants working in a field. (This may be the sole evidence of an economic base to a society totally preoccupied by war, feuds, and dynastic squabbles.) The peasants are not seen as individuals and the camera treats them rather as objects than as people. After a few seconds, a line of horse makes its way down a path while peasants on both sides of the row humbly bow their heads. The visual statement of the distance between warriors and peasants is forcefully made. On the whole, power is the monopoly of a very few, and it is used only for the benefit of those who possess it. The society of *Throne of Blood* is also deeply corrupt. [...] Kurosawa's universe is devoid of political virtue. The present master of Forest Castle, Kunihara, has become its lord not by inheritance or election but by murdering the last occupant of the office. In one emblematic scene a group of soldiers discusses the decay of Washizu's castle. The castle is shaking, they assert, because 'the foundations have long been rotting. Even the rats have begun to leave.' The allegory tells us that not only the castle but feudalism itself is rotten. In addition to being inequitable and corrupt, the community is also without warmth. Love (or even affection), loyalty, generosity, confidence, or pleasure are rarely if ever expressed. The society is characterized instead by narrow self-interest, distrust, constant fear, and the easy recourse to violence. Relationships between individuals are remarkably sterile. In one memorable scene, when Washizu and his wife Asaji converse, they sit far apart in a conventionally bare room. Propped up on the wall behind them and separating them is an unsheathed sword – a perfect metaphor for a marriage of understated but unrelieved hostility, and an expressive symbol of the distrust which seems to characterize all human relationships. There are in fact only a handful of moments in the film in which the characters make physical contact with each other; for the most part they do not touch, and when they do, it is at such moments as Asaji's wrenching Washizu's lance from his hands. Kurosawa even contrives it so that when more than one member of the feudal élite is in the frame, the images of the persons do not overlap. On the other hand, when soldiers and servants gather, as they do for periodic choral discourse, they are disposed in more informal and intimate patterns. [...]

It is in this context that Washizu's ghastly end acquires its fine political importance. The common people, the nameless soldiers of Washizu's army, mobilize themselves to commit not a mindless act of violence but an assassination – an act of specific political rebellion. These are the people whom the film treats as the exploited and nameless victims of Japanese feudalism. They lack authority and autonomy; they have no leaders and no individuality. In fact, when Washizu is felled, Kurosawa arranges it so that an audience is conscious not of the archers but only of their arrows. It is as though the arrows appear from nowhere, and are not launched by any specific person. Yet the arrows stand for the collective mind of the masses, who, the film seems to say, have had enough of tyranny. Washizu is not killed by one arrow, or ten, or a hundred, but by thousands. The moral is obvious: the tyrant and the rotten feudalism for which he stands cannot be brought to its knees by one individual or a hundred, but can be overcome by the people acting in concert. It is nevertheless an equivocal ending. Insofar as the assassination of Washizu can be regarded as a political act, it offers some cause for optimism; to the extent that the assassination simply expresses the opportunism of the soldiers, it is dreadfully pessimistic. The death of Washizu can therefore be conceived of as mildly exhilarating and cautiously optimistic. The film can offer no improvement over tyranny, nor can it provide a successor for Washizu, but it does suggest how the first step might be taken towards a different kind of government.

Of the three films, *Throne of Blood* is the most akin to Shakespeare in the grandeur and spaciousness of its vision. While the two English-language versions of the play vie with each other in fashionable and even facile pessimism, Kurosawa grants his characters the power to challenge and refashion imprisoning social systems. *Throne of Blood* is uplifting not only for its remarkable craft, but for its confidence in human capabilities. While Kurosawa offers no easy answers, neither does he permit his film to succumb to authoritarian or demonic presences.

4 *Antony and Cleopatra*

4.1 H. Neville Davies, 'Jacobean Antony and Cleopatra'

Source: from John Drakakis (ed.), *Antony and Cleopatra*. New Casebooks. (London: Macmillan, 1994), Essay 5, pp. 126–43, 152–3.

The first version of Neville Davies's essay was published in 1985, and it represents an older form of historical scholarship, which seeks to explore the connections between the play and its immediate historical setting. Principally concerned with describing significant events and influential historical figures contemporaneous with the first staging of *Antony and Cleopatra*, Davies explains in detail parallels between James I and Augustus Caesar, and King Christian of Denmark and Antony, that might have occurred to Jacobean audiences. Davies sympathizes with James I's ideal of union, describing it as 'in essence, a noble one', but is nonetheless scrupulous in surveying the variety of strongly divergent viewpoints on Jacobean politics in 1606. Davies's version of the early Jacobean period compared to that of Sinfield (Extract 3.2) and Marcus (Extract 7.2) is ultimately an optimistic one, with peaceful consolidation seen as providing the basis for the gradual improvement of British political and economic interests. As a result, he reads the final triumph of Octavius as likely to win James's approval, despite the dramatic appeal of Antony and Cleopatra.

When the New Penguin editor of *Antony and Cleopatra* comments, in the final paragraph of his introduction, on Shakespeare's play as an imperial work, he speculates about the possibility of there having been a performance by the King's Men at the court of James I. 'James was England's, or rather "Britain's", own modern Augustus', he reminds us,

> for whom Caesar's lines in the play –
>
> > The time of universal peace is near.
> > Prove this a prosperous day, the three-nooked world
> > Shall bear the olive freely –
> >
> > [4.6.4–6]
>
> would have had special significance. James was himself an imperial, quasi-Augustan, peacemaker. So the British Augustus may have watched this Augustan tragedy.

This valedictory speculation is my starting point and prompts me to wonder how, should such a court performance ever have taken place, the king (and others) are likely to have reacted. Certainly we ought not to assume that Shakespeare's royal patron must necessarily have been embarrassed. [...] Adrian Noble's Royal Shakespeare Company (RSC) studio production recently presented a commanding and passionate Octavius, strongly played by Jonathan Hyde, a performance in which James I could readily have taken pleasure. Peter Brook's RSC main house production in 1978 gave us Jonathan Pryce's memorable Octavius – a sensible, peace-loving man who never wears armour and whose warmhearted concern for his sister's well-being was movingly demonstrated in [2.2], when he acceded to the marriage proposal. The way Pryce paused and then said with marked emotion

> A sister I bequeath you whom no brother
> Did ever love so dearly
>
> [2.2.157–8]

ruled out any question of Octavia's being sacrificed to political expediency. But perhaps Pryce went too far. Such was the evident probity of his Octavius that when Act 5 came, it was difficult to take seriously Cleopatra's savagely spoken 'He words me, girls, he words me'. Before that production, there was Keith Baxter's genial Octavius at Chichester in 1969, which seems to have set something of a fashion for sympathetic Octaviuses on the English stage. Nevertheless, the age of universal peace that Octavius inaugurates inevitably promises to be less exciting than the mélange of 'high events' and 'garboils' that it replaces. With the deaths of Antony and Cleopatra

> The odds is gone,
> And there is nothing left remarkable
> Beneath the visiting moon.
> [4.16.68–70]

And the deprivation is devastating, for without Cleopatra's voice we seem even to lack a speaker able to record the loss.

For James's contemporaries, too, a great age had recently passed with the death of Queen Elizabeth, and similarities have been observed between the behaviour of Shakespeare's lass, supposedly unparalleled, and Elizabeth that may reveal the dramatist's perception of a comparable diminishment. James, however, while honouring his predecessor, as Caesar honours the 'pair so famous' in the final speech of the play, was more attentive to the garboils than to high events. The new order he envisaged was the Augustan one of peace, and the powerful appeal of that lofty vision is not permanently impaired by Shakespeare's backward glance. There is loss at the end of the play, but the irresponsibility of Antony and of Cleopatra is hardly an example for princes. Fortunately, though, irreconcilable states like stability and excitement can co-exist in art. So it is that the lovers become united in death as they never were in life, and an audience may imagine them hand in hand 'where souls do couch on flowers', while at the court of a new Augustus their story, with all its turmoil, could live in performance when government yielded to recreation.

But no matter how James might have reacted, it is inconceivable that a dramatist late in 1606, the time when Shakespeare is usually supposed to have been writing or planning his play, could have failed to associate Caesar Augustus and the ruler whose propaganda was making just that connection. The coronation medal, for instance, minted for distribution to his new subjects, had depicted James wearing a laurel wreath, while a Latin inscription proclaimed him Caesar Augustus of Britain, Caesar the heir of the Caesars. Such versifiers as Henry Petowe and Samuel Rowlands had been quick to respond with titles like *Englands Caesar: His*

Majesties Most Royall Coronation (1603) and *Ave Caesar: God Save the King* (1603). With greater art, Samuel Daniel, in April 1603, had spoken of 'this Empire of the *North*' united by 'one Imperiall Prince' who was 'more then Emperor / Over the hearts' of his people. Although an outbreak of plague had cramped the style of the coronation itself, in March 1604 James's postponed entry into London had been celebrated with great magnificence. Both at Temple Bar and in the Strand James had been feted as successor to Augustus, so that when the Commons then declined to accept the proposal of a Welsh MP that James be styled 'emperor of Great Britain', they were rejecting a concept already gaining currency.

At Temple Bar James had passed through a triumphal arch representing the temple of Janus. On the far side and so 'within' the temple, as it were, the principal figure was Peace, a wreath of olive on her head and an olive branch in her hand. As the king approached, the Genius of the City was ready to reveal that 'this translated temple' was now consecrated to James, and over the altar an elaborate Latin inscription hailed him as *Augustus Novus*. In the Strand, Electra, in the figure of a comet suspended between two 70-foot-high pyramids, had been provided with these words by Ben Jonson to conclude the pageantry:

> Long maist thou live, and see me thus appeare
> As omenous a comet, from my spheare,
> Unto thy raigne; as that did auspicate
> So lasting glory to AUGUSTUS state.

When Francis Bacon dedicated *The Advancement of Learning* (1605) to his new sovereign, it was only politic that he too should find some way of relating James and Augustus. They are, he asserts, alike in eloquence.

Divines contributed at yet another level, the Dean of Salisbury, in a sermon of 1604, pursuing the parallel between Augustus and James with particular zeal. James's motto, *beati pacifici*, which recalls not only the Sermon on the Mount but also the fact that Christ's birth was in the days of Caesar Augustus (Luke ii:1), encapsulates and, what is more, envelops in the odour of sanctity a domestic policy of which the chief objective was the unification, or reunification, of a divided 'Britain', and a foreign policy of which the overwhelming purpose was peace. Besides being reluctant to embrace any policy that might lead to hostility abroad, James even strove, by offering his services as mediator, to resolve conflicts in which he was not directly involved. Significantly, his first major action as king of England was to end Elizabeth's long war with Spain, and in May 1604 formal peace talks opened. But enthusiasm among his new subjects for union with Scotland and peace with Spain was, at best, limited; and if Octavius' eager anticipation of the approaching time when 'the three-nooked world / Shall bear the olive freely' is at odds with the responses primarily invoked by Shakespeare's play, we may see this as reflecting the conflict, particularly acute in 1606, between James's peace policy and public feeling. Ten years later, it is true, the bishop of Winchester could refer to James as *'our* Augustus *in whose dayes our blessed* Saviour Christ Jesus *is come to a full and perfect aage'* and claim that 'Never hath there bene so *universal a Peace in* Christendome *since the time of* our Saviour Christ, *as in these his Dayes'*; but such were not the popular sentiments of 1606. A degree of historical myopia is required if the mood of a particular time is to be accurately established.

After the discovery of the Gunpowder Plot, relations with Spain deteriorated, and there was widespread grumbling about the peace. In the House of Commons on 8 March 1606, Sir Edwin Sandys spoke for many when he declared that 'the peace...had wormwood in it'. Sir Henry Neville, in a letter of June 4, tells how

> Upon *Sunday* last there were divers Merchants and Merchant's Wives at the Court, and made greivous Complaint unto the King, the one of their Servants, and the other of their Husbands, *imprisoned and put to the Gallies in* Spaine, *and of much Injustice and Oppression done there to our Nation, besides some particular Contumely to the King personally;* the like Complaint was made before to the Lords. I hear it hath *moved much,* and this I will assure you, *that the Kingdom generally wishes this Peace broken,* but Jacobus Pacificus *I believe will scarce incline to that Side.*

In fact, the merchants kept on complaining. The following February a petition was laid before the Commons and a committee duly appointed to investigate the grievances. Following the report of that committee, the strongly sympathetic Commons sought a conference with the Lords to consider drawing up a joint petition to the king 'for the redress of Spanish wrongs', but in June, when the conference eventually took place, Cecil produced a barrage of arguments to undercut and belittle the claims of the merchants while professing solicitous concern about their sufferings. Furthermore, he made it clear that matters of war and peace were *arcanum imperii,* no business of the Commons. Thus the Spanish grievances remained an emotive issue throughout the time Shakespeare was, as we think, writing *Antony and Cleopatra,* and a particular reason for deploring the royal pacifism. [...]

Contrasting James and Elizabeth, the Venetian Ambassador may have exaggerated James's unpopularity in 1607; but the essential difference is accurately observed:

> He loves quiet and repose, but has no inclination to war, nay is opposed to it, a fact that little pleases many of his subjects....He does not caress the

people nor make them that good cheer the late Queen did, whereby she won their loves; for the English adore their Sovereigns, and if the King passed through the same street a hundred times a day the people would still run to see him; they like their King to show pleasure at their devotion, as the late Queen knew well how to do; but this King manifests no taste for them but rather contempt and dislike. The result is he is despised and almost hated.

There is evidence, too, some of it in plays and poems, that by 1607 the memory of Queen Elizabeth was being revived with affection. In 1606 Thomas Dekker's *Whore of Babylon* (published 1607), which ends with the defeat of the Armada, was not the first Jacobean play to include a speaking part for the late queen, presented though she is under the name of Titania, the Faerie Queene. The play is anti-papist and significantly anti-Spanish, with Elizabeth prospering as mighty opposite to the empress of Babylon, 'Under whom is figured *Rome*'. Dekker's extravagant notion, though, that James, a 'second Phoenix', would be a successor 'of larger wing / Of stronger talent, of more dreadfull beake', a monarch who would strike terror into every opponent and 'shake all *Babilon*', is absurdly unrealistic wishful thinking that serves only to reveal the width of the gulf between popular aspiration and royal policy. Bishop Goodman was later to remember that although people were 'generally weary of an old woman's government' by the end of Elizabeth's reign, experience of James soon prompted a revival of her reputation: 'Then was her memory much magnified, – such ringing of bells, such public joy and sermons in commemoration of her, the picture of her tomb painted in many churches, and in effect more solemnity and joy in memory of her coronation than was for the coming in of King James.' It has been suggested that the dissolution of the Society of Antiquaries in 1607 was one result of James's resentment of this nostalgia. [...]

The lord mayor's pageant presented in London in the autumn of 1605 had been Anthony Munday's *The Triumphes of Re-united Britania*. The printed text is prefaced by a survey of 'British' history that besides providing an introduction to the device itself, also supplies perspectives for *King Lear* and *Antony and Cleopatra*. Munday records how Noah, who after the flood 'was sole Monarch of the World', divided the earth in three so that each of his sons would inherit a third. Britain formed part of Japhet's inheritance and was ruled by him and his descendants until Neptune's son Albion and a race of giants wrested it from them. Eventually, Brute and his Trojan followers rescued the island from these savage usurpers and gave it the name of Britain. All would then have been well had not Brute, like Noah, out of misguided love for his three sons, divided the kingdom between them: to Camber, Wales (or Cambria); to Locrine, most of England (or Loegria); to Albanact, an enlarged Scotland (or Albania). This division of the land introduced strife, and only with the accession of James, the second Brute, was the disastrous error of the first Brute repaired and the unity and peace of Britain restored. [...]

With hindsight we can recognise that despite widespread opposition at the time, James's notion of union was, in essence, a noble one. James's most thorough biographer warns us that 'to consider King James as merely a crafty politician grasping at a great prize is quite to misjudge his character. He was a man who could be fascinated by lofty ideals and sublime aspirations; and no ideal attracted him more strongly than that of unity, in the sense of universal agreement and concord.' Choice spirits such as Francis Bacon in England and Thomas Craig in Scotland appreciated the merits of these ideals in 1606, and there is no reason to think that Shakespeare must necessarily have been less perceptive. Unequivocal support of James by Shakespeare, however, is equally unlikely. The myriad-minded creator of the serpent of old Nile might reasonably be expected to have adopted a highly ambiguous attitude toward the policies and person of his unattractive sovereign.

Assessments of the historical Octavius have varied.

> *Augustus Cesar* was not such a saint
> As *Virgill* maketh him by his description

says Ariosto in Harington's translation, and assessments of Shakespeare's Octavius have varied too. British playgoers remember the ice of Corin Redgrave (RSC, 1972), as well as the warmth of Jonathan Pryce; and critics offer similarly diverse views. Robin Lee, for instance, has it that 'Shakespeare's Octavius Caesar is not at all true to what we know of history's (or even Plutarch's) Octavius. Shakespeare emphasises his qualities of self-interest, remorseless ambition for himself and his Empire, and total unconcern for individuals who stand in the way of his aims.' On the other hand, A. P. Riemer insists that commentators are wrong to regard Caesar as

> ...a ruthless megalomaniac with an almost psychological dislike of his elder partner and a jealousy of his Egyptian revels.... Caesar is a noble, well-intentioned and generally just ruler; he does virtually nothing treacherous or underhand, he does not abuse his powers, and he is much more than the Machiavellian opportunist many critics see in him. We misread Shakespeare's subtlety if we regard the presentation of this character as merely unfavourable or unsympathetic: he is, in fact, a model of political wisdom as well as of virtue; that he is unattractive, perhaps sinister, is a result of Shakespeare's mature understanding of the forces of life and history.

What is important is that the complexity of Shakespeare's portrait be acknowledged, for the ambiguity derives not from failure to achieve consistency but from Shakespeare's perceptive response to the question, What sort of a man must Caesar Augustus have been? During the crucial period of his career, when the accomplishment of his ambition was just within sight, and in the events leading up to that time, the future emperor of universal peace, later to be defied, is revealed by Shakespeare as an adept politician, an opportunist on the make, as well as a visionary whose oracular pronouncement offers the imminent realisation of one of mankind's noblest aspirations. Caesar, eagerly espousing empire and the *pax Romana*, is observed in a context that celebrates values that eclipse, if only existentially, the worth of any empire. His pre-eminence is among those who cannot condone the flaunting of a subversive transcendentalism that reduces kingdoms to clay and love that can be reckoned to beggary. And if James really did recall this Augustus, then perhaps Augustus could be glimpsed in James. Inevitably, the clever, scheming, canny, cautious Scotsman, the new Augustus whose theoretically admirable peace policy seemed in actuality less golden than the vigorous turmoil it replaced, provided Shakespeare with a sufficiently parallel life to supplement what he read in North. But to understand King James has never been simple. The ambiguities and contradictions of the 'wisest foole in Christendome' have always attracted comment: pacifist or cowardly, circumspect or devious, indolent or busy, chaste or perverted? The antitheses resist easy resolution, and this is reflected in the open verdict that one astute observer was to record: 'Some Parallel'd him to *Tiberius* for Dissimulation, yet Peace was maintained by him as in the Time of Augustus.' Such a response seems to be anticipated in the portrayal of Shakespeare's Caesar.

This is also the typical response of Shakespeare's contemporaries to the historical Octavius, commonly envisaged by them as a Jekyll-and-Hyde figure. For Montaigne he exemplified man's essential inconsistency, but for writers less drawn to sceptical uncertainties a remarkably clear distinction was frequently made between the vicious tyrant and demagogue before Actium and the ideal prince thereafter. Pedro Mexia wittily brings the two aspects together when he remarks that Octavius 'happened wisely and uprightly to governe that, which by force and cunning he had gotten', and Peter Heylyn enigmatically expresses the same idea when he claims that 'it had beene an ineffable benefit to the Commonwealth of Rome, if eyther he had never dyed, or never beene borne'. Shakespeare takes us to the point where the opposing halves of the career meet to catch the ambiguity at the juncture, for that is the key point of critical interest. The last speech of the play, thought by some to be out of character, reveals the new voice of Augustus, its style distinct from the familiar accents of Octavius. But the cleavage is earlier stressed by Octavius describing the time of universal peace as 'near' not 'here', by the irony of this reference to the coming time, and to the olive branch, following Octavius' instructions to Agrippa to 'begin the fight', and by the realisation that on that occasion the military success was to be Antony's. An avant-garde Tacitean refinement of the Jekyll-and-Hyde division delved deeper and discerned a destructive and sordid reality underlying even the appearance of imperial splendour; and that, too, invites a dramatist's irony.

As it happens, the character of James was brought sharply into focus in the summer of 1606, when his brother-in-law Christian IV of Denmark paid the first state visit to England by a foreign ruler for eighty-four years and thereby provided James's subjects with a unique opportunity to compare, or rather contrast, their monarch with one of a very different mould. Christian was everything James was not, and the distinction was not lost on bystanders. The French Ambassador reports people regretting that their king was not like Christian. The Venetian Ambassador, who observed that popular emotion had been so deeply stirred by the treatment of those English merchants sent to the Spanish galleys that 'war is openly demanded', reports:

> And so far have matters gone that at Hampton Court, where the Queen is, a letter has been picked up in which the King is urged to declare war, to leave the chase [that is, hunting, an obsessive pursuit of James's] and turn to arms, and the example of his brother-in-law, the King of Denmark, is cited, who for his prowess at the joust has won golden opinions.

One can well believe that the queen, anxious to preserve amity between her husband and her brother, 'would not allow the letter, which came into her hands, to be shown to the King'. According to gossip, Christian himself 'did use all means to persuade the King to give over his extraordinary hunting and to follow martial or more serious affairs'. That gossip may have been based on another incident reported by the Venetian Ambassador:

> A deputation of merchants recently waited on the King, complained loudly of what they had to suffer from the Spanish and begged for some redress. The King is said to have grown angry, and the King of Denmark, who was present, expressed surprise that his Majesty could submit to such injuries inflicted on his subjects.

Christian, whose instincts were so different, was an immensely attractive, impulsive, larger-than-life figure, possessed of great vitality and vigour, some eleven years younger than his forty-year-old host. If Shakespeare looked for a modern Antony to compare with the neo-Augustus, he could have found no better likeness than the king of Denmark; and as with Antony and Octavius, the two rulers were brothers-in-law, even though Anne's relationship to brother and husband was the reverse of Octavia's.

Like Antony in his prime, Christian was a military man, in his case patently spoiling for the fight with Sweden that was to ensue in the Kalmar War. The year before his English visit, Christian had seen action for the first time, albeit in a small way, when he had taken five hundred men to Brunswick to intervene, on behalf of his wife's brother Duke Heinrich Julius, in a dispute that was really none of his business. Having already done much to put Denmark's military forces into fighting shape, he was erecting a network of fortresses and fortifications. But his twin passions were artillery and the Danish fleet, and he had personal experience in all matters relating to both of them. Ships were built to his own designs, and in 1606 the navy must have been practically up to the strength of fifty or sixty large and heavily armed warships that it achieved by 1611, substantially larger than James's fleet. Christian's interest in these matters was much in evidence when he visited England, for he came with an imposing squadron of five or six warships and two pinnaces, 'all large and fine'. His flagship, the recently commissioned *Tre Kroner*, a vessel of 1500 tons sumptuously decorated 'with rich gold, and very excellent workmanship', was one of the largest, most impressive, and most heavily armed ships of the period. She carried seventy-two guns, and we are told that she attracted 'many thousands . . . to Gravesend, where she doth ride, to view her'. [. . .]

The ability to endure personal hardship and privation resolutely while on active service is a particular characteristic that Christian shares with the young Antony. Octavius pays this tribute to the soldier he remembers:

> When thou once
> Was beaten from Modena, where thou slew'st
> Hirtus and Pansa, consuls, at thy heel
> Did famine follow, whom thou fought'st against,
> Though daintily brought up, with patience more
> Than savages could suffer. Thou didst drink
> The stale of horses and the gilded puddle
> Which beasts would cough at. Thy palate then did deign
> The roughest berry on the rudest hedge.
> Yea, like the stag when snow the pasture sheets,
> The barks of trees thou browsed'st. On the Alps
> It is reported thou didst eat strange flesh,
> Which some did die to look on. And all this –
> It wounds thine honour that I speak it now –
> Was borne so like a soldier that thy cheek
> So much as lanked not.
>   [1.4.56–71]

Christian, like his predecessors, was king of Norway as well as Denmark; but he was by far the most active of the Danish kings in this other realm, visiting the country some thirty times in the course of his reign. He was, in fact, the first Danish king to take his northern responsibilities seriously; and in 1599 to the consternation of courtiers 'daintily brought up' who had to accompany him, he sailed north along the entire Norwegian coast, through Arctic waters and the regions of the midnight sun, as far as Finnmark and the island of Vardoya in the Barents Sea where Norway borders Russia. From here he made further expeditions with just two of the eight ships. [...]

Considerable mercantile, diplomatic, and cultural contact between England and Denmark around this period ensured that Christian's reputation preceded him to London. Accounts of his coronation in 1596, with its remarkable festivities, in which Thomas Sackville and the duke of Brunswick's troupe of English players had participated, must have helped to colour that reputation. Whereas James in 1603 at his English coronation only managed to endure 'the *days* brunt with *patience*, being assured he should never have such another', Christian's enthusiasm in 1596 had been boundless. Impetuously he threw himself into everything that was going on. Christian was the designer of his own crown; he led the fire-fighting team, and had himself paraded through the streets on a litter dressed as Pope Sergius VI; and then, still in papal attire, he tilted at the ring. With 150 cannon mounted on the walls of Copenhagen, and another 600 on board ship, the royal delight in the sound of artillery was made hugely evident, while Christian's personal prowess as a fighter was spectacularly demonstrated by his achievements as a tireless competitor in martial exercises. He charged at the ring or at opponents 345 times and tilted against 113 nobles, Danish and foreign. The festivities were further enlivened by shows of Oriental splendour, with nobles appearing as Turkish, Indian, and Persian women, and a fireworks display that represented the defeat of a Persian army – not quite an Alexandrian feast, perhaps, but ripening towards one.

Like Antony, Christian was extravagant, physically strong, and able to take pleasure in the company of all sorts and conditions of men, whether fellow rulers or 'knaves that smell of sweat'. Like Antony, too, he had an appetite for women that the homosexual James certainly lacked. Christian had married, in 1597, the daughter of the margrave of Brandenburg, and Anna Katrine was to bear him six children in little more than twice as many years; but his pleasure lay elsewhere. Almost immediately after his marriage, Christian openly made Kirsten Mansdatter his mistress and fathered the first of many illegitimate children. James, on the other hand, as Bishop Goodman declared, 'was never taxed with the love of any other lady' than his wife. The 'ne'er lust wearied' Christian, however, was to acquire a considerable reputation as a man of little sexual restraint, a reputation that, for instance, enabled a scurrilous exposé of the 'most secret and chamber-abominations' of the Stuart court, published during the Commonwealth, to present the Danish king as an unbridled and tyrannical womaniser.

But above all, Christian was known as a drinker. In this, he followed the settled example of his court – his father had died of drink, and his comparatively sober mother worked her way through two gallons of Rhine wine a day. In his drinking of healths, Shakespeare's Claudius is a truly royal Dane. For Christian's coronation a stock of 35,000 glasses was requisitioned from merchant vessels passing through the Sound; and as in other matters, when it came to drinking, Christian was a match for any man. He was capable of downing thirty to forty goblets of wine in an evening and, recording his excesses by means of the method Hans Christian Andersen was to adopt for relatively minor indulgences more than two centuries later, would mark his diary with a cross if he had been carried to bed incapable. A second or even a third cross was added if his condition had been paralytic. 'Now will drunkards be in request', remarked one letter-writer ominously when he heard that Christian was to visit James; and John Davies of Hereford in his *Bien Venu: Greate Britaines Welcome to Hir Greate Friends, and Deere Brethren the Danes* (1606) offered the following advice:

> Then let thy Conduits runne with rarest wines,
> That all may freely drinke all health to thee:
> And to those Kings, their Heires, and their Assignes,
> By whom thou art, or maist the better bee:
> Yet, O beware of Drunkards fowle designes,
> Take healthes, while thou from surfet maist be free;
>   'For 'tis no glorie, but a foule reproach,
>   To take (like Tuns) the wine that Shame doth broach'.

In general, James himself was 'not intemperate in his drinking' it seems. 'It is true he drank very often', says Weldon; but this 'was rather out of custom than any delight. [He] seldom drank at any one time above four spoonfulls, many times not above one or two.' There seems, however, to have been real concern in 1606 that Christian and his hard-drinking entourage would teach their English hosts to drink deep and that the state visit would degenerate into gargantuan scenes of alcoholic over-indulgence. [...]

In his preparation for the writing of *Antony and Cleopatra*, Shakespeare read in Plutarch how Sextus Pompeius, Antonius, and Octavius Caesar 'met all three together by the mount of Misena, upon a hill that runneth far into the sea, Pompey having his ships riding hard by at anchor, and Antonius and Caesar their armies upon the shore side, directly over against him'. When Pompey invites the two brother-in-law rulers to feast on his ship, a problem arises about how the guests are to reach the vessel: 'So he cast anchors enow into the sea to make his galley fast, and then built a bridge of wood to convey them to his galley from the head of Mount Misena; and there he welcomed them, and made them great cheer'. In the late summer or autumn of 1606, this would inevitably have suggested a parallel with the shipboard feast on the Medway, and Phineas Pett's remarkable bridge constructed to cope with a slightly different problem of hospitality, while the identification of James with Augustus, supported by the congruence of Christian and Antony, would only have reinforced that parallel. It hardly matters whether Shakespeare himself was an eyewitness (although the Medway festivities did include some sort of dramatic entertainment), for observers and reports must have been numerous. And it is easy to see why in his play Shakespeare should have disregarded Plutarch's ship-to-shore bridge and made no reference to the ship-to-ship Medway bridge. Any explicit link between the feasting of 1606 and that on Pompey's galley would have been unacceptable to the authorities; and besides, Shakespeare wished to emphasise the vulnerability of Pompey's guests. The several 'gables of the anchor' that Plutarch's Menas offers to cut are significantly reduced by Shakespeare to a single one.

Plutarch's feast on Pompey's galley is followed by a reciprocal feast when Antonius and Caesar play host to Pompey in their camp on shore. Shakespeare combined the two occasions but retained the shipboard setting. James's feast on the Medway was also followed the next day by a reciprocal feast, this time on the Thames, with Christian playing host. Since the people were the same and the days were consecutive, it is only reasonable to expect aspects of the one shipboard occasion to be associated or conflated with aspects of the other shipboard occasion. Plutarch gives no indication that the entertainment on Pompey's galley was drunken, and there is no clear evidence that the feasting on the Medway was either, but what happened on the Thames could certainly have prompted Shakespeare to present the scene that way. And since North's Plutarch refers to Pompey's 'admiral galley', it is easy to associate Pompey's flagship with Christian's, known by English observers simply as 'the Admiral'. [...]

Fanciful conjecture is no substitute for knowledge, and the full range of Shakespeare's sources will always elude discovery. Just how much Shakespeare's shipboard scene owes to the shipboard entertainments that marked the end of Christian's visit cannot be ascertained. But when considering Jacobean presences in Shakespeare's Roman play, it is helpful to remember two other Antony-and-Cleopatra plays of the period, one Danish and one English. Hans Thomissøn Stege's Antony-and-Cleopatra tragedy was published in Copenhagen in 1609 with a long, moralising preface. The pious author looks back to Christian's grandfather as a king of blessed memory and spells out six lessons that the play teaches a now degenerate Denmark. The first of these warns against the vice of drunken-ness, and the second inveighs against fornication. Stege does not say straight out that Christian resembles Antony, nor could he possibly say it; but there seems to be a message for a reigning monarch whose vices are obvious enough. By implication, therefore, the likeness that Stege flatteringly draws between the virtuous Octavia and Elizabeth Sophie Lindenov, to whom the play is dedicated, is not the only example that this dramatist offers of a parallel between an antique Roman and a modern Dane. The other Antony-and-Cleopatra play is Fulke Greville's. At the time of the fall of Essex, Greville destroyed his manuscript, fearful lest he be thought to have represented 'vices in the present Governours, and government'. How Elizabeth would have reacted to his untimely play we can only guess, and how Christian responded to Stege's admonitions or James to Shakespeare's opalescent fusion of ancient history and Jaco-bean observation remains beyond our knowledge. But what we can say, when it comes to Shakespeare's play, is that perplexing the dull brain to separate elements so mixed would have been fit occupation only for an ass unpolicied, and James was certainly not that.

4.2 Juliet Dusinberre, 'Squeaking Cleopatras. Gender and Performance in Antony and Cleopatra'

Source: James C. Bulman (ed.), *Shakespeare, Theory, and Performance* (London and New York: Routledge, 1996), Chapter 4, pp. 46, 53–5, 57–62, 64.

Whereas Neville Davies concentrates upon the Jacobean context of *Antony and Cleopatra*, and the characters of Octavius and Antony, Juliet Dusin-berre in this extract focuses on nineteenth- and twentieth-century perfor-mances of the play, and dramatic interpretations of the character Cleopatra. Dusinberre is concerned with how different actresses have confronted the challenge of playing Cleopatra, a role originally written for a boy actor, and further, with how generations of theatre critics have also struggled to disentangle the layers of gendered identity built into the role. She summarizes, 'the recollection of the boy [actor] confuses the issue of how Cleopatra might be played by a woman'. Of related interest are Dusinberre's comments on how energetic portrayals of Antony and Cleopatra's sexual intensity in various productions have disrupted English notions of sexual propriety. Like Howard and Rackin (Extract 2.2), Dusinberre brings a feminist commitment to bear in her reading of a Shakespeare play, but whereas the former look at gender politics at the moment of the original production, Dusinberre highlights the contested articulation of feminine identity in the performance and reception of *Antony and Cleopatra* over the last 200 years.

With a curious irony of fate, Ladbroke's, the betting and casino magnates, became the chief sponsors of Peter Hall's 1987 production of *Antony and Cleopatra* at the National Theatre with Anthony Hopkins and Judi Dench in the title roles. Shakespeare would perhaps have been the first to appreciate the appropriateness of such backing for a drama in which hero and heroine compete ceaselessly for prowess in the world of the play, in the theatre, and in the consciousness of the audience. The heart of that competition lies in the oscillating constructions of the masculine and the feminine which dominate not only the play, but the conditions of its reception in the consciousness of the audience. The play's theatrical history amply demonstrates the curious interplay between cultural assumptions – in both audience and actors – and a text which was conceived for an all-male cast in which Cleopatra would have been played by a boy. [...]

If the boy actor was a part of Shakespeare's Cleopatra not only because he had to act, but because Cleopatra herself *imagined* him, his presence has dominated the imaginations of later actresses, who echo Cleopatra's incredulity at the idea of a boy's being able to play the part. They often manifest an awareness of the boy behind the woman which never occurs in their discussions of other tragic heroines. Barbara Jefford said of her performance at the Old Vic in 1978: "I can't imagine what kind of boy played it at the time it was written – perhaps no one ever did and perhaps that is why it was hardly ever played." Janet Suzman (RSC, 1972) also doubted the capacity of the boy actor and proposed an older man in the role:

> I find it hard to think he wrote it for a boy. I think he must have written it for a man, perhaps a kind of Shakespearean Danny La Rue – there must have been some kind of prima donna in his company playing women's parts and men are notoriously good at it. It could never have been acted by a boy – Portia, Rosalind, Viola, yes – they could be breathtaking played by a stripling, a clear young spirit, but not Cleopatra.

A reviewer in *The Times* declared that "Janet Suzman, in a role created for a male actor, creates a woman who is only incidentally voluptuous." The *Financial Times* went further, claiming that of the two lovers "Cleopatra seems the stronger. Janet Suzman has given her a touch of masculinity: she is an Egyptian Elizabeth I." The *Gloucester Citizen* thought Miss Suzman "a tempestuous, gypsy tomboy Cleopatra. ... This was scarcely the highly intelligent politically shrewd Queen who ruled a vast empire with skill and cunning." Both actress and reviewers cannot rid themselves of preconceptions about how a boy could transform himself into a woman. The word "tomboy" is a staple of Cleopatra criticism: the woman usurping the boy's cultural role is somehow the equivalent to the Elizabethan boy actor's usurping the woman's part.

If anything, the recollection of the boy confuses, for both actresses and reviewers, the issue of how Cleopatra might be played by a woman. The idea of the boy stands in the way of an appreciation of the woman. When George Rylands described Vivien Leigh as Cleopatra (with Olivier in 1951) he asked: "How are we to assess Vivien Leigh's performance in the part – which is not playable by mortal woman, and was written for a boy?" Rylands, like Redgrave, had played some of Shakespeare's women and had a keen sense of their origins in the boy actor. He lamented that in modern productions "the Cleopatra of Gautier and Flaubert still exerts her spell and Shakespeare's boy player is suppressed." The actress who came nearest to an understanding of the various elements which make up Shakespeare's Cleopatra was probably Peggy Ashcroft, who ignored the boy in favor of the *Greek* Cleopatra, a being who might be the female equivalent in cunning of Ulysses in *Troilus and Cressida*. Instead of trying to perform the part with the boy haunting her imagination, Ashcroft declared: "What a relief to act Cleopatra and *cause* suffering for a change. For years in plays I have been the woman who has suffered through other men on stage." Would this perception of reversed power structures within the theatrical fiction have had any parallel in the relation between Cleopatra and the men on stage when the part was played by a boy?

Part of the answer to that question might lie in comments made by Judi Dench on Peter Hall's 1987 production for the National Theatre, in which she played opposite Anthony Hopkins. Michael Billington asserts that all later Cleopatras owed something of their success to Ashcroft, who "finally proved that Cleopatra was not the unattainable K2 it had seemed but a role that could be conquered through forethought, planning and the support of a first-rate team." Judi Dench consulted Ashcroft about the part, and the concept of a "team" may have come from the idea of the earlier Ashcroft–Redgrave partnership. Redgrave suggested that the collaborative principle was a reason for his own success as Antony, pointing to the paramount importance of Enobarbus: " 'for Enobarbus creates Antony's nobility and Cleopatra's fascination as much as the protagonists can hope to do.' " Peter Hall had required all his actors to read Granville Barker, who observes of Cleopatra: "Shakespeare's Cleopatra had to be acted by a boy, and this did everything to determine, not his view of the character, but his presenting of it. He does not shirk her sensuality, he stresses it time and again; but he has to find other ways than the one impracticable way of bringing it home to us." If the boy's presence was not palpable in the deliberately mature and middle-aged passion of Dench's and Hopkins's lovers, the idea of a team of players and of the vital importance of other players, particularly in helping to realize the sensuality of Cleopatra, recaptured the dynamic of the original theatrical conditions under which both the dramatist and his boy actors worked. Shakespeare offered the boy playing Cleopatra maximum support not only from the other apprentices who play the parts of Iras and Charmian, but from adult players – Enobarbus, Alexas, the Soothsayer, the Messenger. A review of Hall's production noted with approval that Hopkins and Dench "play the title roles as if they were not star actors."

Antony and Cleopatra both represents within the play itself, and exemplifies in its theatre history, a curious battle for supremacy between two concepts of theatre: the theatre of stars and repertory theatre. Paradoxically, the stage history of the play suggests that in performance it works the least well in the theatre of stars. This was presumably the case in Shakespeare's time. If Antony was played by Burbage, by 1609 a recognized star, his Cleopatra must have been the most accomplished of the boy actors, but he was not a star. Part of the dramatic tension of the play comes, however, from a latent drive, within the creation of Cleopatra, for a supremacy which resurrects the social condition of the apprenticed boy actor, playing the part of an Empress, possibly to his own master, Burbage himself, whom he is allowed, in theatrical terms, to supersede. Like Ashcroft, Judi Dench saw Cleopatra in terms of cunning and a will to survive: "Although Peter says that after Antony dies, the audience are longing for Cleopatra to join him, I keep finding moments when she seems to want to live." Beneath that perception lies not Peter Hall's romantic Cleopatra, but the theatrical reality of a boy apprentice revelling in the theatrical power bestowed on him in the final act of the play. Why should he die? This is the moment which, as an actor, he has been eagerly awaiting. [...]

The circulation of energy in the Elizabethan theatre is better understood in our contemporary period, with its theoretical interest in performance, than it perhaps was in the earlier star theatre, where so many Antonys felt thwarted by the role which seemed to deny them star status. Richard Findlater observes:

> Although Cleopatra's Antony is one of Shakespeare's most magnificent creations, he has been an infrequent visitor to the English stage; the role of "strumpet's fool" and "plated Mars" baffles some actors and repels many more. Garrick and Phelps failed in the part; Irving and Kean avoided it; Macready noted it, after consulting Plutarch, as "long, and I fear not effective", and found his own performance "hasty, unprepared, unfinished".

Findlater is unimpressed by the Antonys of Gielgud, Olivier, Wolfit, and Godfrey Tearle: "It is a curious record of defeat, much more surprising than the similar roll-call of routed Cleopatras. As Herbert Farjeon said,

Shakespeare 'might almost have written the part of the two lovers for the express purpose of ruining histrionic reputations'." Shakespeare has set up a dialectic in *Antony and Cleopatra* between the protagonists who compete relentlessly with each other under the charade of partnership, and the myriad supporting characters who purvey them to the audience, as Ventidius purveys Antony's success in battle. Without both elements – the ruthless competition, and the support from the other members of the cast – the play cannot ignite.

The dynamics of this competition are complicated by the presence of women actresses, because the competition becomes inseparable from extra-theatrical notions of the proper relation between men and women. The twentieth-century performance history of the play suggests that an originally ludic theatrical creation has as a consequence become *serious*. When Glenda Jackson acted Cleopatra in 1978 the production "did not forget that Cleopatra was first created for a boy actor. The Queen's sensuality was private in her relationship with Antony, although renowned throughout the world. She was an Elizabeth I in a very different and much hotter climate: powerful, but wary of her own feelings and emotions." Nevertheless Jackson's performance of Cleopatra – perhaps remembering her earlier role as Elizabeth in the 1971 television drama – stressed authority at the expense of sensuality, underplaying the Cleopatra for whom sensuality and power are both part of a theatrical performance and an entertainment, for both performer and audience. Jackson's display of power was not a game, but a cool distancing of private emotion. But Cleopatra is a constant player of games, as Elizabeth herself was. One of the reasons for the chequered fortunes of the play in the theatre is that game-playing is considered the stuff of comedy rather than of tragedy.

When Shaw decided to "improve" on Shakespeare by writing his comedy of *Caesar and Cleopatra*, he declared a Johnsonian distaste for making "sexual infatuation a tragic theme," where it can only be a comic one. Shaw's dislike of English theatre audiences centered on the inability of the English male to *play*. "The well-fed Englishman," he remarks, "cannot play... When he wants sensuality, he practises it: he does not play with voluptuous or romantic ideas. From the play of ideas – and the drama can never be anything more – he demands edification, and will not pay for anything else in that arena." In an essay written more than fifty years later in 1954, entitled "Some Notes on Stage Sexuality," Kenneth Tynan shows that the terms of Shaw's argument about play could still dominate discussion of sensuality in the English theatre: "The English, as their drama represents them, are a nation endlessly communicative about love without ever enjoying it. Full-blooded physical relationships engaged in with mutual delight are theatrically tabu." His own trenchant criticism of both Olivier and Leigh in 1951 and of Redgrave and Ashcroft in Glen Byam Shaw's Stratford production of the play two years later in 1953 reveals the preconceptions which created the taboo he identifies.

In the double bill – of Shakespeare's play and Shaw's – Olivier was widely accused of playing down to allow his wife to shine. Tynan declares of Leigh's performance in *Caesar and Cleopatra*: "She keeps a firm grip on the narrow ledge which is indisputably hers; the level on which she can be pert, sly, and spankable, and fill out a small personality." On Shakespeare's play he remarks:

> "You were a boggler ever," says Antony at one point to his idle doxy; and one can feel Miss Leigh's imagination boggling at the thought of playing Cleopatra. Taking a deep breath and resolutely focusing her periwinkle charm, she launches another of her careful readings; ably and passionlessly she picks her way among its great challenges, presenting a glibly mown lawn where her author had imagined a jungle. . . . Yet one feeling rode over these in my mind; the feeling Mr. Bennet in *Pride and Prejudice* was experiencing when he dissuaded his daughter from further pianoforte recital by murmuring that she had "delighted us long enough."

Tynan wanted Antony to be more of a hero; in the theatrical competition between the two stars he believed that Antony must win. But Olivier's own comments are revealing. He thought Vivien Leigh the finest Cleopatra he had ever seen, and he declared of his own performance as Antony:

> I'd never really thought a lot about Antony – as a person, that is. I mean, really, he's an absolute twerp, isn't he? A stupid man. But thank God Shakespeare didn't try to rectify that; if he had, there would have been no play. Not a lot between the ears has Antony. Now Cleopatra, she's the one. She has wit, style and sophistication, and if she's played well, no Antony, however brilliant, can touch her.

Olivier rightly believed that the play presents a competition in which Cleopatra vanquishes Antony. Of its sensuality he declared: "There is nothing cerebral about their love: it is pure passion, lust and enjoyment. And why not? How would you feel alone in a chamber with that lady? I don't think you'd want to discuss the *Times* crossword." How swiftly the reference to the *"Times* crossword" identifies the world described by Shaw as that of the average English playgoer, a world from which Tynan in spirit still comes.

Would Tynan's criticisms of Leigh as Cleopatra have been so scathing if he had seen Shakespeare's boy actor in the part? When he wrote about Vivien Leigh it is evident that the real body and the real actress had become inseparable in his mind from the fiction of Cleopatra and her subjection of Antony. When Tynan sees Vivien Leigh, all he can think of is, first, that British girls can't act sensuality – the point he proceeds to when he reviews Ashcroft two years later; second, that Leigh has been corrupted by Hollywood; third, that a great male actor, Olivier, has (i) made a terrible mistake in his marriage to such a pert little miss, and (ii) is allowing his marriage to ruin his career. These judgements show just as odd a confusion between life and art, the real body and the fictional body, the woman who is, and the woman who plays, as anything written of actresses from their first appearance on the Restoration stage to the present. The heart of Tynan's objection is that he doesn't want Cleopatra to win the competition with Antony, any more than he wants Leigh to win the competition with Olivier, or for Olivier, worse still, to let her do so. Olivier himself is in no doubt on the matter, saying of Antony: "It's a wonderful part. But just remember, all you future Antonys, one little word of advice: Cleopatra's got you firmly by the balls." Linda Charnes has pointed out that "in this play he [Antony] occupies a subject position almost always culturally reserved for women, and in relation to a Cleopatra who occupies a position almost always reserved for men." Would Tynan have minded Leigh's dominance as Cleopatra over Olivier as Antony, if a boy who looked like Leigh had been playing the part?

The question about the boy actor might be answered by turning to the review Tynan wrote of Redgrave and Ashcroft, which begins with some general reflections on English actresses and sensuality:

> There is only one role in *Antony and Cleopatra* that English actresses are naturally equipped to play. This is Octavia, Caesar's docile sister....The great sluts of world drama, from Clytemnestra to Anna Christie, have always puzzled our girls; and an English Cleopatra is a contradiction in terms.

Ashcroft's Cleopatra became for him a version of Lady Chatterley: "A nice intense woman, you nearly murmured; such a pity she took up with the head gamekeeper." Somewhat inconsistently, he urged Redgrave to "let up a little on lust." Antony's lust didn't fit his notion of Roman (for which read English?) manhood any more than Cleopatra fitted his idea of the English actress. Sensuality was not a fiction of sensuality, but the real thing. Wasn't Redgrave pawing Ashcroft rather more than was tasteful? Had the part been played by a boy, none of the cultural anxieties aroused by the presence on stage of a woman's body would have been set in motion.

Both these productions demonstrate the way in which the woman playing Cleopatra in the modern theatre has become the medium through which the audience produces meaning. Since the re-establishment of Shakespeare's play in preference to Dryden's – with Samuel Phelps's revival at Sadler's Wells in 1847 – the actress has become the principal signifier of the anxieties and obsessions, pleasurable and less pleasurable, which dominate the audience who watches her.

In the first successful revival of Shakespeare's play since Elizabethan times, staged just ten years after Victoria came to the throne, Isabella Glyn as Cleopatra bears – to twentieth-century eyes – an uncanny likeness to later photographs of Queen Victoria. The same actress's 1867 performance was considered "ripe in animal desire," a desire whose prohibited nature perhaps fascinated audiences the more because of the actress's curious physical resemblance to their own impeccably proper queen. The sensuality of Shakespeare's heroine blatantly contradicted notions of social respectability, thus making the theatre a site for the unleashing in the audience of repressed fantasies. From its mid-Victorian revival onwards, Shakespeare's play became a witness not only to sensuality, but to that other great symbol of male power, conspicuous consumption, linked in Herbert Tree's 1906 revival with unmistakable images of empire. Cleopatra was displayed as the goddess Isis in a curiously titillating mixture of representing "the other" to the great British public, and reminding it of past glories where another exotic title – Empress of India – represented a supreme Victorian grandeur and colonial triumph. The nostalgia which in 1606 the play conjured up for its first audiences, in recalling a Virgin Queen who had dispatched her favorites to colonize and conquer on her behalf, was capable of re-enactment in the already nostalgic Edwardian England of 1906. Similar recollections of Empire may have lain behind the connections drawn by a reviewer of Trevor Nunn's 1972 Stratford production with the magnificent Tutankhamen exhibition in London, which vast crowds queued to see almost as if it had been a theatrical production.

It seems more than coincidence that Shakespeare's play began to be revived in the nineteenth century once a woman ruler was on the throne, and has been produced more frequently in the twentieth century than ever before, when another woman – a second Elizabeth – is on the throne. The play was obviously the ideal choice for the lean post-war austerity years. 1951 marked the Festival of Britain and the celebratory partnership of Leigh and Olivier in the double Shaw/Shakespeare bill. 1953 – Coronation year – saw the triumph of Redgrave and Ashcroft at Stratford. Audiences could forget the war and their own privations in the supreme fantasies of Shakespeare's play, which celebrated a queen as they themselves were happy to do. After all, it was Elizabeth II herself who insisted, against the advice of the Government, on the Coronation's being televised in 1953, an act which brought the monarchy to the people as supreme spectacle, as Cleopatra herself is, and as Elizabeth I had herself been.

The meanings which accrue to Cleopatra under these circumstances seem less challenging to male power structures than they did when Cleopatra was played by a dispossessed male. Jonathan Dollimore has proposed that the original challenges of the play might be recaptured in performance by having the women played by men, and "all male roles would be played by women.... The woman playing Antony and the boy playing Cleopatra would subvert the very idea of sexual difference and sexual identity upon which the romantic, the moralistic, the sexist, the racist, and the decadent interpretations all at some stage rely." In 1606 the boy actor played to an audience capable of remembering a woman ruler who not only *staged* herself as powerful, but possessed *real* power. The mingling, in the single role, of contrary images of authority and subjection has not been recaptured in the modern theatre.

This is in itself surprising, since by 1972, when Janet Suzman played Cleopatra, the Women's Liberation movement had developed a consciousness in some audiences of the social conditioning of women. How was Cleopatra to be viewed in relation to the power structures of the Roman world? As oppressed or oppressor? Glenda Jackson's Empress became subsequently linked in the public mind with her own passage from actress to politician, *via* the television role of Elizabeth I. In the 1980s and 1990s, a new ruler was in evidence in Thatcher's Britain, a figure viewed as ambiguously as ever Cleopatra might have been. However, in writing about various post-Thatcher productions, H. Neville Davies talks only of Antony and Enobarbus. Without a woman ruler available to men and women outside the theatre, the production of contradictory meaning within the play becomes impoverished. Who cares about the woman ruler? She has landed us in the soup and is out of the competition. Curiously, that situation reinvents Dryden's romantic and depoliticized version of the play, simultaneously revived, alongside these productions of Shakespeare's play, at the Almeida theatre in Islington in 1991. [...]

The audience in *Antony and Cleopatra* participate in the play's awareness of its own theatricality, becoming fragmented and disparate in their reactions. Men and women watching the play are implicated in its dissolution of gender boundaries, each individual challenged by the representations of sexuality on stage, and never allowed by the dramatist to submerge that sense of separation into a comfortable group consciousness. Shakespeare himself engaged in a dialogue not only with inherited narratives, but with the political world, in which performance also, for James as for Elizabeth, encompassed the triumvirate of military, sexual, and theatrical action. The consciousness of images in the process of being made and controlled, at the center of which stood in Shakespeare's theatre the ambiguous figure of the boy actor, returns the play to its ludic and performative center, where underlings upstage their betters. The great men in the play may be world-sharers in Shakespeare's globe, but the gods in the gallery can and do forsake them, as Hercules in the end forsook Antony.

4.3 *Ania Loomba, 'Spatial Politics'*

Source: Ania Loomba, *Gender, Race, Renaissance Drama* (Delhi: Oxford University Press, 1992), pp. 124–30.

Published in 1992, this extract from Ania Loomba's book *Gender, Race, Renaissance Drama* explores concerns central to postcolonial theory in its interpretation of *Antony and Cleopatra*. In particular, Loomba seeks to explain how the character of Cleopatra is defined in relation to discourses of patriarchy and imperial domination by means of a close reading of the structure and language of the play. Loomba argues that the play's structure of 'cinematic montage' captures precisely the 'discontinuity of character, the dialectic between inner and outer, political and personal, male and female spaces'. Further, although after Cleopatra's suicide, the 'narrative of masculinity and imperialism regains control', Loomba sees Cleopatra's final defiance as undermining Octavius's triumph.

Spatial politics

[...] Three centuries of critical opinion, from Samuel Johnson onwards, has been preoccupied with 'overcoming' the heterogeneous nature of both the form and the content of Shakespeare's *Antony and Cleopatra*: the focus has variously been on its disjointed structure, mingling of tragic and comic, flux in character; its divisions between private and public, male and female, high and low life; on what Danby has called the 'dialectic' of the text. However, a correlation of these various binaries – the thematic oppositions, the broken structure, its treatment of fluid gender and racial identity – has yet to be attempted. An 'epic effect' has been noted, but in the classical sense of the word; we might more usefully employ the term in its Brechtian sense to analyse these various schisms. 'The continual hurry of the action, the variety of incidents, and the quick succession of one personage to another ... the frequent changes of scene' then emerge as contradicting the classical elevation of character or teleological progression towards catharsis, as achieving a Brechtian alienation from character to posit a radical interrogation of the imperial and sexual drama.

The geographical turbulence of the first three acts involves a redefinition of femininity and of female space: patriarchal Rome contests Egyptian Cleopatra for her geographical and sexual territory. Into the contest is woven the theme of imperial domination. Dominant notions about female identity, gender relations and imperial power are unsettled through the disorderly non-European woman. These ideas appear to be reinstated as the quick shifts of scene are abandoned in favour of a more orthodox climax at the end of the play, an apparent resolution of the dilemma. Whereas in the first three acts of the play there are twenty-three changes of scene, and shifts of location within each as well, as the play proceeds there is a change in the quality and quantity of movement: in Act 4 alone there are fifteen changes of locale, but all within Egypt. Act 5 contains only two scenes, and both are confined to the area of Cleopatra's monument. Alongside this, different characters strive to rise 'above' their earlier turbulence and assert an inner unity of being. However, this harmony is precarious; the manner of its achievement conveys the very opposite of a resolution and the various sets of oppositions noted by critics are not subscribed to but eroded by the play.

The issues of imperial expansion, political power and sexual domination are dramatically compressed into spatial and geographical shifts and metaphors. The almost cinematic movements – 'panning, tracking, and playing with the camera' – are designed to reveal the complexity of the terrain on which men and women move as well as of their inner spaces. They penetrate into different aspects of power, which is at once something concrete – land, kingdoms, wealth – and something relatively abstract – emotions, ideology, and sexuality. Theatrical space is not just an inert arena but interacts with the texts' treatment of social and psychological space.

Not only does the locale constantly shift, but in each setting we are reminded of another. In Egypt, Rome is evoked, and vice versa. While leaving for Rome, Antony tells Cleopatra: 'thou, residing here, goes yet with me, / And I, hence fleeting, here remain with thee' [1.3.104–5]. This is a common enough lovers' platitude but it serves to remind us that in addition to the purely geographical shifts of terrain, there are also those of conceptual settings; the lovers' private world is constantly contrasted to the political space. Antony identifies the former with Egypt, and in preferring it to Rome is trying to privatise love, to locate his relationship with Cleopatra in a domestic arena. But he also attempts to expand this space so that it excludes the other, threatening world of masculine politics, and crowds out other concerns:

Cleopatra. I'll set a bourn how far to be belov'd.
Antony.   Then must thou needs find out new heaven, new earth.
                                                    [1.1.16–17]
[...]

Roman patriarchy demonises Cleopatra by defining her world as private (Antony is no longer a serious general by entering it); as female (Egypt robs Antony and his soldiers of their manhood); and as barbaric (Antony is now a slave of gypsies). But both Antony and Caesar are aware that Egypt is not merely a private space and that its female, non-European nature only intensifies its challenge to imperial Rome:

Antony.	My being in Egypt, Caesar
	What was't to you?
Caesar.	No more than my residing here at Rome
	Might be to you in Egypt. Yet, if you there
	Did practice on my state, your being in Egypt
	Might be my question.

[2.2.40–4]

Objective space is always invested with political or emotional connotations; as Caesar indicates, Egypt is a place from which subversion can be practised, and as such it can never be merely a lovers' retreat. Antony too courts Cleopatra with territorial and political gifts: he will 'piece / Her opulent throne with kingdoms; all the East / ...shall call her mistress' [1.5.44–6]. Caesar complains precisely of this:

> Unto her
> He gave the establishment of Egypt; made her
> Of Lower Syria, Cyprus, Lydia,
> Absolute queen.

[3.6.8–11]

Passionate as the relationship between Antony and Cleopatra is, 'the language of desire, far from transcending the power relations which structure this society, is wholly informed by them' [argues Jonathan] Dollimore. These relations are both sexual and racial. In the beginning Antony thinks he is in control of what he regards as the opposition between politics and pleasure; therefore he assumes that he can simultaneously possess the Roman matron Octavia through the legal bonding permitted by imperial patriarchy, and the oriental seductress Cleopatra, through a sexually passionate and 'illicit' relationship:

> I will to Egypt;
> And though I make this marriage for my peace,
> I'th' East my pleasure lies.

[2.3.36–8]

He alternately views Egypt as his retreat from Roman politics and a place to consolidate his bid for power. In short, he oscillates between Cleopatra's territory and Caesar's, both literally and otherwise. As the play proceeds he is no longer in command of such a divide: his position in both Rome and Egypt becomes unstable and manifests itself as a dislocation of personality: 'I / Have lost my way for ever', 'I have fled myself', 'I have lost command' [3.11.3–4, 7, 23]. 'Authority melts from me', he cries, but like Faustus, the Duchess of Malfi, and Parolles, he invokes his lost 'essential' self: 'Have you no ears? I am / Antony yet' [3.13.92–3]. Even as

Antony complains that Caesar keeps 'harping on what I *am*, / Not what he knew I *was*' [3.13.144–5] (emphasis added), he is aware of the change in himself. Without power, without space, without Rome and without Cleopatra, Antony disintegrates.

It is important that Cleopatra's transformation into the 'whore' and 'witch' occurs precisely at this point: the language of what Antony perceives as a betrayal reduces Cleopatra's 'infinite variety' to both patriarchal and racist stereotypes. Helen Carr has pointed out that 'although the substitution of "witch" for "whore" as the primary image of the deviant woman signifies a greater degree of horror at the possibility of female sexuality, at the same time it represses the idea of a consciously sexual woman (the witch's fantasies are alien and evil intruders in her mind)'. Cleopatra, I have argued, is both: her sexuality is an aspect of her blackness and as such can only be erased later, when she herself adopts token Roman-ness. Whereas, in falling from Othello's favour, Desdemona became 'begrim'd' and morally black and false to her true self, Cleopatra as the 'foul Egyptian' only realises her 'true' position as the complete outsider. As Antony perceives that he is only nominally the site of the conflict which is actually between Cleopatra and Caesar, the latent struggle for power between him and Cleopatra escalates. The metaphors for this three-way struggle become those of the land and the sea. Whether the fight should take place on the Roman element, the land, or Cleopatra's medium, the water, is at once a matter of military strategy and a measure of Antony's emotional and political affiliations. The erosion of the absolute space of love stems from his increasing perception of his own marginality, and Cleopatra's refusal to share her space. With all worlds being lost, Antony's vacillations cease, and so do the structural shifts.

Such a movement is also dependent on the play's treatment of Cleopatra. If Cleopatra's political being threatens patriarchy it also catalyses the contradictions within her, which are inherent in the position she occupies as a sexually active non-European female ruler. Although she is unique among the independent women in Renaissance drama, for she appears to command her own spaces, these are precariously constructed: as the ruler of Egypt her space is threatened by the expansionist designs of the Roman empire, and as a woman, by the contradictions of heterosexual love. Her insecurity, her fear of invasion – not just as a ruler, but also as a woman who is threatened even (or especially) by her lover – is evident in her physical stasis, her reluctance to move from her territory. However slippery, inconstant and variable Cleopatra may be, however she may threaten the boundaries between male and female, political and private worlds, she remains geographically stationary. She resents the intrusions of Roman messengers who remind her not only of Antony's wives, first Fulvia and then Octavia, but also of the imperial threat.

Cleopatra fluctuates between establishing her emotional and her political spaces: a vacillation without end for she cannot simultaneously occupy both. She finds it much harder to locate her own territory in relation to Antony than *vis-à-vis* Caesar. She can either function within the private life of a man, or enter politics as a honorary man and chaste woman, like Elizabeth. In any case it is a double bind. As 'foul Egyptian' she will always stand outside Roman society: Antony can never fully trust her and will marry safe and obedient Roman women like Octavia to ensure his stability within that society. Her gender renders her politically unacceptable, her political status problematises her femininity, and her racial otherness troubles, doubly, both power and sexuality. To the extent that she acts as a ruler, she is perfectly comprehensible to Caesar: he even praises her for concealing her treasure from him; 'nay, blush not, Cleopatra; I approve / Your wisdom in the deed' [5.2.145–6]. But whereas he will not haggle over 'things that merchants sold' [5.2.180], he refuses to grant her autonomy even in respect of her death.

The last act appears to 'resolve' the various tensions of the play; the style now changes from montage and a mingling of comic and tragic to that of classical tragedy. It appears that Cleopatra is tamed; the wanton gypsy becomes Antony's wife, the queen is stripped to an essential femininity that attaches to all women irrespective of class: 'no more but e'en a woman, and commanded / By such poor passion as the maid that milks / And does the meanest chares' [4.16.74–6]. The variable woman is now 'marble constant'; the witch gives way to the penitent goddess as Egypt tries to do 'what's brave, / what's noble . . . after the high Roman fashion' [4.16.88–9].

Several aspects of this resolution serve to contradict its apparent implications. Firstly, Cleopatra is able to capitulate to Roman matrimony only after Antony has died, and when one aspect of her conflict has dissolved rather than being resolved. The prospect of sharing power with Antony no longer exists, and she begins to approximate Antony's own earlier expressions of absolute emotion. After his death Antony can fill her world in a way that Antony alive could never be allowed to do:

> His face was as the heav'ns, and therein stuck
> A sun and moon, which kept their course and lighted
> The little O, the earth . . .
> His legs bestrid the ocean; his rear'd arm
> Crested the world.
>
> [5.2.78–82]

The poetry has been seen as sublime. Cleopatra's words display an effort to cloak personal and political loss in the language of a transcendental, eternal romance. Given the conditions of its utterance, the poetry reveals the politics of sublimation, rather than a transcendence of politics. Antony can now comfortably be called 'husband' [5.2.278] without the risk to freedom that actual matrimony implies.

Cleopatra also lets her own fierce identification with Egypt slip for the first time. Literally, of course she still does not accept Caesar's Rome, which remains a threat:

> Shall they hoist me up,
> And show me to the shouting varletry
> Of censuring Rome? Rather a ditch in Egypt
> Be gentle grave unto me!
>
> [5.2.54–7]

But Rome was also Antony's space and as his wife she can adopt the 'Roman fashion'.

Secondly, if these moves reflect Cleopatra's contradictions, they are also strategic and constitute the unruly woman's last performances. Having lost power, it now becomes 'paltry to be Caesar' [5.2.2]; it is now time to speak of things other than power. Her suicide clouds her political defeat with mystic glamour and a show of autonomy. Her own body is the last 'space' to be wrested from Roman control. The asp will bring her 'liberty' in the absence of real territory. The maternal image of the snake at her breast tames her own earlier identification with the serpent, replacing the deadly Eastern inscrutibility with a comprehensible version of the Madonna. Of course, *both* are patriarchal constructions of women. The first demonises the alien woman while the second seeks to domesticise her.

Till the end, Cleopatra attempts to maintain some vestiges of power even as she acknowledges Caesar as 'the sole sir o'th' world' [5.2.116]. It is only when every effort has failed that she has 'immortal longings' [5.2.272]. Without power 'What should I stay – / In this vile world?' [5.2.303–5].

As Cleopatra achieves these false resolutions, the play also abandons the cinematic montage that so adequately expressed the discontinuity of character, the dialectic between inner and outer, political and personal, male and female spaces. The shifts of scene which conveyed both the vacillations of Antony and the unruly theatricality of Cleopatra give way to the elevation of the 'Roman' suicides; to the conventional 'climax' and the stock devices of formal drama, as patriarchal roles and divisions are apparently reinstated. If Cleopatra's fluid identity and play-acting demanded one kind of theatrical form, her new role as Antony's marble-constant wife employs the more classical technique. The Roman theatre takes over from the volatile Egyptian one. The closed space of the monument, the measured actions and tones, the slow, drawn-out scenes and the elevated language all tone down the fiery and unpredictable performances of the earlier Cleopatra. The narrative of masculinity and imperialism regains control but Cleopatra's final performance, which certainly exposes her own vulnerability, not only cheats Caesar but denies any final and authoritative textual closure.

Interval Two: Editing Shakespeare's Plays

Stephen Orgel, 'What Is an Editor?'

Source: *Shakespeare Studies*, XXIV (London: Associated University Presses, 1996), pp. 23–9.

Stephen Orgel is well qualified for this task of considering the problems involved in editing Shakespeare's texts, as in recent years he has edited Oxford University Press's single-volume editions of *The Tempest* and *The Winter's Tale*. In this piece, he gives a general survey of the problems which confront contemporary scholars in editing early modern texts. He points out that Renaissance writings were never fixed textual entities – like, for example, the text of a contemporary novel – since changes were made to books during the process of printing them. This means that no two copies of the 1623 first folio of Shakespeare's plays were exactly alike; each would include corrected and uncorrected pages, though these would often be in different places in the book! Orgel then clarifies his 'determination' as an editor 'to be true to the genuine obscurity ... of much of the text', and his 'stubborn refusal to emend if I can get any sense at all out of' the early texts.

Textual practice for the past twenty years has been increasingly faced with the necessity of abandoning the notion that was basic to the bibliography practiced by Greg and Bowers, that by comparing texts we can arrive at a single, authentic original, a reconstruction of the author's final manuscript. Historical study of manuscript and print culture emphasizes instead the basic instability of texts, and in some cases recognizes a fluidity that is built in – as in the case of playtexts, for example, which are designed to change as the conditions of performance change. In such cases, the printed text is simply one stage in a continuous process, with no particular authority over any of the other stages in the process. The counter-examples prove the point: Webster complaining that the actors had misrepresented his play, Jonson taking control of his texts by revising and editing them, turning them into a book. If the play is a book, it's not a play.

But even the book was a fluid text, not the final correct authorized version of the work. Renaissance printers incorporated proof corrections in the text while printing was in progress, and both corrected and uncorrected sheets were used in the final bound books. There was nothing in print technology requiring this (to us) odd system; had the printers wished to avoid it, it would only have been necessary to stop the press for the ten minutes or so it took to read through the proof sheet, make the corrections and then continue. But clearly the idea of a book embodying the final, perfected text was not a Renaissance one, and what the Renaissance practice produced was an edition in which it was unlikely that any copy of a book would be identical to any other copy. Every copy was unique. In this respect, the difference between book culture and manuscript culture so essential to the Renaissance as constructed by Father Ong and Elizabeth Eisenstein is much smaller than has been claimed. Charlton Hinman tried to get around The Truth About Renaissance Books by producing, in his Norton facsimile of the first folio, an ideal copy, which he took to be a copy in which every page was in its final, corrected state. It would have been perfectly simple for Jaggard and Blount to produce such a book; the fact that they chose not to do so, that no copy of the book exists in this state, that no reader ever read the book in this form, and most of all, that no printer had any interest in publishing such a book, are of no account in Hinman's construction of what constitutes an ideal Shakespeare folio. The text in flux, the text as process, was precisely what Renaissance printing practice preserved.

Other traditional assumptions of modern bibliography have become increasingly questionable. The idea that spelling and punctuation have no rules in the period, and are a function of the whim of the compositor, the whole concept of *accidentals*, has come under heavy scrutiny. Behind these assumptions is an unacknowledged subtext: that the printing process is transparent and what we want from the editorial process is an unmediated access to the mind of the author, and that, moreover, we can get closer to the author than the printer with a manuscript (that may or may not have been authorial) before him could; that there are elements of a text that are inessential or merely conventional, that they don't affect the meaning and we can therefore safely change them, and that all we are doing thereby is to translate them into our own equivalent conventions – that, indeed, we *have* equivalent conventions. Behind all this is a still deeper assumption, that not only the meaning of the text, but the text itself is somehow independent of its material embodiment. Historians of the book, from Stanley Morison to D. F. McKenzie, have effectively demolished this notion, but their work has had little effect on the practice of editors. As I have written in another context, the basic assumption of most editorial practice is that behind the obscure and imperfect text is a clear and perfect one and it is the editor's job not to be true to the text's obscurity and imperfection, but instead to produce some notional platonic ideal.

It is quite easy to show how problematic such assumptions are. The undeniable fact that moving around commas really does affect meaning means that commas aren't "accidentals." There is no way of modernizing "A blisse in proofe and proud and very woe," not because there is no way of knowing whether the crucial letter in "proud" is a *u* or a *v* but because for a Renaissance reader it could only be both; and this means that there is no way of detaching that particular text from its material presence and its historical moment. The rationalizing and neatening of this text, moreover, as of so much of Shakespeare, belies its genuine difficulty – elucidation is, after all, a denial of the essential reality of obscurity. But it's also difficult to see how any number of close analyses of Shakespeare's 129th sonnet are going to have any significant effect on editorial practice – we all have too much invested in our own construction of the book to abandon it to the insights of deconstruction, or even of history.

But suppose we did want to take all this into account: what would a postmodern editorial praxis look like? Jerome McGann has been one of the most incisive and articulate theorizers of post-Bowers bibliography, but his wonderful, informative, beautifully edited Byron looks, after all, very much like everyone else's Byron: it's just better. I am the first to admit that my own practice in my Oxford *Tempest* and *Winter's Tale* hasn't done much to take into account my own arguments in "What is a Text?" and "The Authentic Shakespeare," beyond a determination in the commentary to be true to the genuine obscurity, even incomprehensibility of much of the text, and a stubborn refusal to emend if I can get any sense at all out of the folio. This does leave me open to the charge of fetishizing the text, and I suppose in one sense I should be arguing that since Renaissance dramatic texts are designed to be unstable, we are in fact not being true to them by religiously preserving what happened to come from the printing house. But my basic feeling as an editor is that texts aren't ideas, they are artifacts, and I want to preserve as much as I can of their archeology.

Producing a modernized text is unquestionably not the best way of doing this, but I also want a Shakespeare accessible to the modern reader, and these two requirements are really not reconcilable. One way of attempting to take such issues into account, however, and in fact in its way a striking example of radically postmodern editorial practice, is the editorial conception embodied in the original Variorum: an unedited text with an infinite commentary, the editor acting only as referee. The impulse behind this, of course, had nothing to do with some proleptic inkling of Barthes and Derrida, but rather with an application of Bentham and Mill to literary criticism, the conviction that if all critical opinions are given an equal voice, the truth will manifest itself. I have a tremendous admiration for H. H. Furness, though the project certainly didn't produce The Truth About Shakespeare; but that's because of a flaw in the reasoning of Bentham and Mill, not in the efforts of Furness. The problem is only partly that any Truth about Shakespeare will be true at most for a generation; it's also that criticism very rarely does what we want it to do.

A brief example: when Richard Knowles's *As You Like It*, the first volume of the new Variorum, appeared, I took it up with particular interest. Curious to know what criticism had contributed to clarifying the text in the past hundred years, I started by looking up what are for me two cruxes neither of which the old Variorum had had much to say about. First, the choice of the name Ganymede for Rosalind in disguise: the new Variorum merely confirmed my impression that this is something critics haven't wanted to touch with a ten-foot pole (or perhaps a six-inch rod), and the edition was therefore on this subject nothing more than an epitome of three centuries of silence. Then I tried the most baffling moment in the play, when Rosalind, at the conclusion, appears from the woods with a figure identified in the speech headings as the god Hymen. My students always ask me who that is, and I tell them I don't know; we aren't told, and it must be significant that we aren't told – that in this most rationalized of Shakespeare's comedies, the resolution depends on a mystery; there's finally something in Rosalind's plans that we aren't let in on. So I was curious to see what Truth would emerge from the liberal democratic convictions of the new Variorum. Richard Knowles had assembled in fact a fairly modest array of opinion; there has apparently been less comment on this moment than one would have expected. Of the experts consulted, however, about two-thirds declared that the figure is some rustic who has been dressed up as Hymen for the occasion, and the rest assumed it was the god himself, and pointed to the analogous appearance of deities in wedding masques. What struck me here was that not a single one of the critics cited acknowledged that we don't know, we aren't told, saw it as a piece of dramaturgy rather than something to be explained away in the plot. The first thing that all my students, year after year, notice about that moment in the play, is, according to the Variorum, something that no critic has ever concerned herself with. Nor does Knowles, as the scrupulously neutral referee, introduce any disturbing caveat into the commentary, any sense that in these two cases, criticism has been avoiding something.

Suppose, however, we went a step beyond the Variorum, produced just an unedited text, with the materials for Doing It Yourself on some endless hypercard – all the variants, all the commentary, all the analogues and sources (these provided, of course, with no mediating principle of selection). Such a project is now, with current computer technology, perfectly feasible. Ah, but what is an unedited text? The most brilliant and radically postmodern of textual scholars, Randall McLeod, proposes that we use only facsimiles, and thereby force ourselves and our students to confront the material reality of Renaissance literature, the Renaissance text in its genuine cultural context.

Fair enough. But of course the proposal rests on the premise that the camera is a neutral observer. It is not: it turns flyspecks into punctuation marks, conceals the impression made by uninked type, will not distinguish inks (so that a handwritten correction is undetectable), knows nothing of watermarks or chainlines – in fact, reading a photographic facsimile is nothing at all like reading a Renaissance book: we are absolutely not here confronting the material object. The camera is misleading in a more serious way, too, precisely in the way that Father Ong and Elizabeth Eisenstein have misled us: every facsimile is identical to every other one, and in this respect facsimiles falsify the essential nature of the Renaissance book. When we read a Shakespeare play in facsimile, we are all reading the identical text. But Renaissance readers with different copies of a text were almost certain to be reading different texts.

I want to emphasize, moreover, that I'm not talking simply about things we think we can ignore, the small errors that were tidied up in proofreading. How is editorial practice to take into account McLeod's astounding, essential work on the text of Holinshed? Through the use of his ingenious collator he has discovered tremendous variations in the text of the book, whole sections that were removed, and their removal concealed by the adjustment of catchwords and renumbered pages. What this means is that censorship and revision were at work not at the manuscript stage, but during the actual course of printing; and that, more startlingly, it was not considered necessary for the offending material to be expunged from every copy of the book, but only from those sheets that came off the press last. Within a single edition, therefore, different copies will have differing amounts of censored and uncensored material. This is a case where a modern facsimile of a single copy of Holinshed, which is then published in an edition of a thousand and read in several hundred libraries by many thousands of students, will totally misrepresent the unstable reality of the book.

In all my examples, it will be observed that the author has little or nothing to do with the case, and it is arguable, as Foucault has shown us, that the author, in the modern sense, is an anachronistic concept in the early modern period. But just to make it clear that even this will not lead us to a usable generalization, I want to conclude with a striking counterexample discovered by my student Steven Lally in the course of editing

Thomas Phaer and Thomas Twyne's Elizabethan translation of the *Aeneid*, an immensely influential book in its own time, but one that literary history has declared of no interest whatever. For modern readers the book is undeniably not an easy read, not least because it is printed in the murkiest of black letter typefaces, but Lally became fascinated by its typography and orthography. Phaer died in 1560, having completed nine books of the translation; these were published in 1562. In 1573 all twelve books appeared, including Twyne's completion of Phaer's translation and a partial revision of Phaer's text; and in 1584 Twyne's much more elaborate revision of the work was published. Lally observed that both Twyne editions contain a number of idiosyncratic spellings, as well as an elaborate array of mysterious diacritical marks – all, be it noted, so-called *accidentals*. It didn't take long to realize that both these features of the text were entirely consistent throughout, and constituted a complete quantitative metrical system – Twyne, improving on Phaer's work, had devised a precise equivalent to Vergilian metrics, and had developed a legible notation for it. The notation was maintained, moreover, without variation, throughout both editions – it starts to break down in the editions after 1596, when the rights to the work moved to another printer. This implies the most complete and continuous authorial control over the printing of the text – a much greater degree of control than anything we believe we know about Renaissance printing-house practice would allow, and, indeed, greater than all but a very few modern writers have had over the printing of their own texts. We need cases like this to remind us that the author function is, after all, not something that was invented in the eighteenth century. Horace conceived himself to be building a monument more lasting than bronze fifteen hundred years before print culture; in the Middle Ages there were poets who were embedding their names within their poems and numbering the lines to defeat appropriation, expansion, revision: even in societies without copyright laws and notions of authorial privilege, there have always been writers who undertook to counteract the cultural vagrancy of literary texts. Foucault's argument is not about the invention of the concept of the author, it's about the extent of the cultural investment in it. Maybe its particular attraction for postmodern criticism lies in its construction of the pre-enlightenment world as a textual golden age, a world of textual free play: in some very basic way, it lets us, as editors and critics, off the hook.

5 *Hamlet*

5.1 *Jacqueline Rose, 'Hamlet – the* Mona Lisa *of Literature'*

Source: *Shakespeare and Gender. A History,* ed. D. B. Barker and I. Kamps (London: Verso, 1995), Chapter 6, pp. 104–14, 116–17.

The earliest version of this essay appeared in an influential collection of Shakespeare criticism edited by John Drakakis, *Alternative Shakespeares* (London: Methuen, 1985), and it has been anthologized many times since. Seeking to understand why 'one of the most elevated and esteemed works of our Western literary tradition should enact such a negative representation of femininity', Rose examines how writers from critic T. S. Eliot to psychoanalyst Ernest Jones have interpreted *Hamlet*. In moving between literary criticism and psychoanalysis, Rose demonstrates how women are represented in a negative light, both in *Hamlet* itself, and in influential criticism of the play. She concludes that the dominant discourses of both 'aesthetic form and sexual difference share fantasies of coherence and identity in which the woman appears repeatedly as both wager and threat'.

It does not seem to have been pointed out that T. S. Eliot's famous concept of the 'objective correlative', which has been so influential in the assessment of literature and its values, was originally put forward in 1919 in the form of a reproach against the character of a woman. The woman in question is Gertrude in Shakespeare's *Hamlet*, and the reproach Eliot makes of her is that she is not good enough aesthetically, that is, *bad* enough psychologically, which means that in relationship to the affect which she generates by her behaviour in the chief character of the drama – Hamlet himself – Gertrude is not deemed a sufficient *cause*.

The question of femininity clearly underpins this central, if not indeed *the* central, concept of Eliot's aesthetic theory, and this is confirmed by the fact that Eliot again uses an image of femininity – and by no means one of the most straightforward in its own representation or in the responses it has produced – to give us the measure of the consequent failure of the play. *Hamlet* the play, Eliot writes, is 'the Mona Lisa of literature', offering up in its essentially enigmatic and undecipherable nature something of that maimed or imperfect quality of appeal which characterizes Leonardo's famous painting. The aesthetic inadequacy of the play is caused by the figure of a woman, and the image of a woman most aptly embodies the consequences of that failure. Femininity thus becomes the stake, not only of the internal, but also of the critical drama generated by the play.

Equally important, however, is the fact that femininity has been at the heart of the psychoanalytic approach to *Hamlet*, from Ernest Jones onwards, a fact which has again been overlooked by those who have arrested their attention at the famous Oedipal saga for which his reading of the play is best known. 'Hamlet was a woman' is just one of the statements about *Hamlet* which Jones quotes as indicating the place of the 'feminine' in a drama which has paradoxically been celebrated as the birth of the modern, post-Renaissance, conception of man. In this article, I will try to focus what I see as the centrality of this question of femininity to an aesthetic theory which has crucially influenced a whole tradition of how we conceptualize literary writing, and to the psychoanalytic theory which was being elaborated at exactly the same time, at the point where they converge on the same object – Shakespeare's *Hamlet* – described by Freud as an emblem of 'the secular advance of repression in the emotional life of mankind'.

I

To start with T. S. Eliot's critique of *Hamlet*. T. S. Eliot in fact sees his reading of the play as a move away from psychological approaches to *Hamlet* which concentrate too much on the characters to the exclusion of the play itself: '*Hamlet* the play is the primary problem, and Hamlet the character only secondary'. Eliot therefore makes it clear that what he has to say exceeds the fact of the dramatic personae and strikes at the heart of aesthetic form itself. The problem with *Hamlet* is that there is something in the play which is formally or aesthetically unmanageable: 'like the *Sonnets*' (another work by Shakespeare in which a question of sexual ambivalence has always been recognized) '*Hamlet* is full of some stuff that the writer could not drag to light, contemplate, or manipulate into art'. Eliot then describes the conditions, as he sees it, of that in which *Hamlet* fails – the successful manipulation of matter into artistic form. It is here that he produces the concept of the 'objective correlative' for the first time:

> The only way of expressing emotion in the form of art is by finding an 'objective correlative'; in other words, a set of objects, a situation, a chain of events which shall be the formula of that *particular* emotion; such that when the external facts . . . are given, the emotion is immediately evoked. . . . The artistic 'inevitability' lies in this complete adequacy of the external to the emotion.

Emotion, or affect, is therefore admissible in art only if it is given an external object to which it can be seen, clearly and automatically to correspond. There must be nothing in that emotion which spills over or exceeds the objective, visible (one could say conscious) facts, no residue or trace of the primitive 'stuff' which may have been the original stimulus for the work of art. This is where *Hamlet* fails: Hamlet (the man) is dominated by an emotion which is inexpressible, because it is in *excess* of the facts as they appear. And that excess is occasioned by Gertrude, who precipitates Hamlet into despondency by her 'o'er hasty' marriage to his dead father's brother and successor, who turns out also to have been the agent of the former king's death. For Eliot, Gertrude is not an adequate equivalent for the disgust which she evokes in Hamlet, which 'envelops and exceeds her' and which, because she cannot adequately contain it, runs right across the fabric of the play. Gertrude is therefore disgusting, but not quite disgusting *enough*. Eliot is, however, clear that he is not asking for a stronger woman character on the stage, since he recognizes that it is in the nature of the problem dealt with in this play – a son's feelings towards a guilty mother – that they should be in excess of their objective cause. On this count, Gertrude's inadequacy turns around and becomes wholly appropriate: 'it is just *because* her character is so negative and insignificant that she arouses in Hamlet the feeling which she is incapable of representing'.

What is at stake behind this failing of the woman, what she fails to represent, therefore, is precisely unrepresentable – a set of unconscious emotions which, *by definition*, can have no objective outlet, and are therefore incapable of submitting to the formal constraints of art. What we get in *Hamlet* instead is 'buffoonery' – in Hamlet himself the 'buffoonery of an emotion which can find no outlet in action', for the dramatist the 'buffoonery of an emotion which he cannot express in art'. Such 'intense', 'ecstatic' (Gertrude uses the word 'ecstasy' to describe Hamlet's madness in the bedchamber scene of the play) and 'terrible' feeling is for Eliot 'doubtless a subject of study for the pathologist', and why Shakespeare attempted to express the 'inexpressibly horrible' we cannot ever know, since we should have finally 'to know something which is by hypothesis unknowable and to understand things which Shakespeare did not understand himself'.

Today we can only be struck by the extraordinary resonance of the terms which figure so negatively in Eliot's critique – buffoonery, ecstasy, the excessive and unknowable – all terms in which we have learnt to recognize (since Freud at least) something necessarily present in any act of writing (*Hamlet* included) which only suppresses them – orders them precisely into form – at a cost. Eliot's criticism of *Hamlet* can therefore be turned around. What he sees as the play's weakness becomes its source of fascination, or even strength.

In this context, the fact that it is a woman who is seen as cause of the excess and deficiency in the play, and again a woman who symbolizes its aesthetic failure, starts to look like a repetition. First, of the play itself –

Hamlet and his dead father united in the reproach they make of Gertrude for her sexual failing ('O Hamlet what a falling off was there', [1.5.47]), and *horror* as the exact response to the crime which precedes the play and precipitates its drama ('O horrible! O horrible! most horrible!', [1.5.80]). Secondly, a repetition of a more fundamental drama of psychic experience itself as described by Freud: the drama of sexual difference in which the woman is seen as the cause of just such a failure in representation, as something deficient, lacking or threatening to the system and identities which are the precondition not only of integrated artistic form but also of so-called normal adult psychic and sexual life. Located by Freud at the point where the woman is first seen to be different, this moment can then have its effects in that familiar mystification or fetishization of femininity which makes of the woman something both perfect and dangerous or obscene (obscene if *not* perfect). And perhaps no image has evoked this process more clearly than that of the *Mona Lisa* itself, which at almost exactly this historical moment (the time of Freud and Eliot alike) started to be taken as the emblem of an inscrutable feminity, cause and destination of the whole of human mystery and its desires:

> The lady smiled in regal calm: her instincts of conquest, of ferocity, all the heredity of the species, the will to seduce and to ensnare, the charm of deceit, the kindness that conceals a cruel purpose – all this appeared and disappeared by turns behind the laughing veil and buried itself in the poem of her smile. Good and wicked, cruel and compassionate, graceful and feline she laughed.

By choosing an image of a woman to embody the inexpressible and inscrutable content which he identified in Shakespeare's play. Eliot ties the enigma of femininity to the problem of interpretation itself: 'No one has solved the riddle of her smile, no one has read the meaning of her thoughts', 'a presence... expressive of what in the way of a thousand years men had come to desire'. Freud himself picks up the tone in one of his more problematic observations about femininity, when he allows that critics have recognized in the picture:

> the most perfect representation of the contrasts which dominate the erotic life of women; the contrast between reserve and seduction, and between the most devoted tenderness and a sensuality that is ruthlessly demanding – consuming men as if they were alien beings.

What other representation, we might ask, has so clearly produced a set of emotions without 'objective correlative' – that is, in excess of the facts as they appear? T. S. Eliot's reading of *Hamlet* would therefore seem to suggest that what is in fact felt as inscrutable, unmanageable or even horrible (ecstatic in both senses of the term) for an aesthetic theory which will allow into its definition only what can be controlled or managed by art is nothing other than femininity itself.

At the end of Eliot's essay, he refers to Montaigne's 'Apologie of Raymond Sebond' as a possible source for the malaise of the play. Its discourse on the contradictory, unstable and ephemeral nature of man has often been seen as the origin of Hamlet's suicide soliloquy; it also contains an extraordinary passage anticipating Freud, where Montaigne asks whether we do not live in dreaming, dream when we think and work, and whether our waking merely be a form of sleep. In relation to the woman, however, another smaller essay by Montaigne – 'Of Three Good Women' – is equally striking for the exact reversal which these three women, models of female virtue, represent *vis-à-vis* Gertrude herself in Shakespeare's play, each one choosing self-imposed death at the point where her husband is to die. The image is close to the protestations of the Player Queen in the Mousetrap scene of *Hamlet* who vows her undying love to her husband; whereupon Gertrude, recognizing perhaps in the Player Queen's claims a rebuke or foil to her own sexual laxness, comments: 'The lady doth protest too much' [3.2.210] (a familiar cliché now for the sexual 'inconstancy' of females). So what happens, indeed, to the sexuality of the woman, when the husband dies; who is there to hold its potentially dangerous excess within the bounds of a fully social constraint? This could be seen as one of the questions asked by *Hamlet* the play, and generative of its terrible effect.

Before going on to discuss psychoanalytic interpretations of *Hamlet*, it is worth stressing the extent to which Eliot's theory is shot through with sexuality in this way, and its implications for recent literary debate. Taking their cue from psychoanalysis, writers like Roland Barthes and Julia Kristeva have seen the very stability of the sign as index and precondition for that myth of linguistic cohesion and sexual identity by which we must live but under whose regimen we suffer. Literature then becomes one of the chief arenas in which this struggle is played out. Literary writing which proclaims its integrity, and literary theory which demands that integrity (objectivity/correlation) of writing, merely repeat that moment of repression when language and sexuality were first ordered into place, putting down the unconscious processes which threaten the resolution of the Oedipal drama and of narrative form alike. In this context, Eliot's critical writing, with its stress on the ethical task of writer and critic, becomes nothing less than the most accomplished (and influential) case for the interdependency and centrality of language and sexuality to the proper ordering of literary form. Much recent literary theory can be seen as an attempt to undo the ferocious effects of this particularly harsh type of literary superego – one whose political repressiveness in the case of Eliot became more and more explicit in his later allegiance to Empire, Church and State.

Eliot himself was aware of the areas of psychic danger against which he constantly brushed. He was clear that he was touching on 'perilous' issues which risk 'violating the frontier of consciousness'; and when he talks of writing as something 'pleasurable', 'exhausting', 'agitating', as a sudden 'breakdown of strong habitual barriers', the sexuality of the writing process which he seeks to order spills over into the text. And Eliot's conception of that order, what he sees as proper literary form, is finally an Oedipal drama in itself. In his other famous essay 'Tradition and the Individual Talent', which was written in the same year as the '*Hamlet*' essay, Eliot states that the way the artist can avoid his own disordered subjectivity and transmute it into form is by giving himself up to something outside himself and surrendering to the tradition that precedes and surrounds him. Only by capitulating to the world of dead poets can the artist escape his oppressive individuality and enter into historical time: 'Set [the artist] for contrast and comparison among the dead', for 'the most individual parts of his work are those in which the dead poets, his ancestors, assert their immortality most vigorously'. Thus, just as in the psychoanalytic account, the son pays his debt to the dead father, symbol of the law, in order fully to enter his history, so in Eliot's reading the artist pays his debt to the dead poets, and can become a poet only by that fact. Eliot's conception of literary tradition and form could therefore be described as a plea for appropriate mourning and for the respecting of literary rites – that mourning whose shameful inadequacy, as the French psychoanalyst Jacques Lacan pointed out in his essay on *Hamlet*, is the trigger and then constant refrain of the play: the old Hamlet cut off in the 'blossom' of his sin, Polonius interred 'hugger mugger', Ophelia buried wrongly – because of her suicide – in sacred ground.

In Eliot's reading of *Hamlet*, therefore, the sexuality of the woman seems to become the scapegoat and cause of the dearth or breakdown of Oedipal resolution which the play ceaselessly enacts, not only at the level of its theme, but also in the disjunctions and difficulties of its aesthetic form. Much has been made, of course, of the aesthetic problem of *Hamlet* by critics other than Eliot, who have pondered on its lack of integration or single-purposiveness, its apparent inability to resolve itself or come to term (it is the longest of Shakespeare's plays), much as they have pondered on all these factors in the character of Hamlet himself.

Hamlet poses a problem for Eliot, therefore, at the level of both matter and form. Femininity is the image of that problem; it seems, in fact, to be the only image through which the problem can be conceptualized or thought. The principal danger: femininity thus becomes the focus for a partly theorized recognition of the psychic and literary disintegration which can erupt at any moment into literary form. [...]

[I]n *Hamlet*, these two themes – of death and sexuality – run their course through the play, both as something which can be assimilated to social constraint and as a threat to constraint and to the social altogether. For *Hamlet* can be seen as a play which turns on mourning and marriage – the former the means whereby death is given its symbolic form and enters back into social life, the latter the means whereby sexuality is brought into the orbit of the law. When *Hamlet* opens, however, what we are given is *too much* of each (perhaps this is the excess) – too much mourning (Hamlet wears black, stands apart, and mourns beyond the natural term) and too much marriage (Gertrude passes from one husband to another too fast). As if it were the case that these two regulators of the furthest edges of social and civil life, if they become overstated, if there is too much of them, tip over into their opposite and start to look like what they are designed to hold off. Eliot's essay on *Hamlet*, and his writing on literature in general, gives us a sense of how these matters, which he recognizes in the play, underpin the space of aesthetic representation itself, and how femininity figures crucially in that conceptualization.

II

If Eliot's aesthetic theories move across into the arena of sexuality, Ernest Jones's psychoanalytic interpretation of *Hamlet* turns out also to be part of an aesthetic concern. His intention is to use psychoanalysis to establish the integrity of the literary text, that is, to uncover factors, hidden motives and desires, which will give back to rational understanding what would otherwise pass the limits of literary understanding and appreciation itself: 'The perfect work of art is one where the traits and reactions of the character prove to be harmonious, consistent and intelligible when examined in the different layers of the mind'. Jones's reading, therefore, belongs to that psychoanalytic project which restores to rationality or brings to light, placing what was formerly unconscious or unmanageable under the ego's mastery or control. It is a project which has been read directly out of Freud's much-contested statement 'Wo es war, soll Ich werden', translated by Strachey 'Where id was, there ego shall be'. Lacan, for whom the notion of such conscious mastery was only ever a fantasy (the fantasy of the ego itself), retranslates or reverses the statement: 'There where it was, so I must come to be'.

For Jones, as for Eliot, therefore, there must be no aesthetic excess, nothing which goes beyond the reaches of what can ultimately be deciphered and known. In this context, psychoanalysis acts as a key which can solve the enigma of the text, take away its surplus by offering us as readers that fully rational understanding which Shakespeare's play – Jones recognizes, like Eliot – places at risk. The chapter of Jones's book which gives the Oedipal reading of *Hamlet*, the one which tends to be included in the anthologies of Shakespeare criticism, is accordingly entitled 'The Psychoanalytic Solution'. Taking his reference from Freud's comments in *The Interpretation of Dreams* (1900), Jones sees Hamlet as a little Oedipus who cannot bring himself to kill Claudius because he stands in the place of his own desire, having murdered Hamlet's father and married his mother. The difference between Oedipus and Hamlet is that Oedipus unknowingly acts out this fantasy, whereas for Hamlet it is repressed into the unconscious, revealing itself in the form of that inhibition or inability to act which has baffled so many critics of the play. It is this repression of the Oedipal drama beneath the surface of the text which leads Freud to say of *Hamlet*, comparing it with Sophocles' drama, that it demonstrates the 'secular advance of repression in the emotional life of mankind'.

But Jones's book and the psychoanalytic engagement with *Hamlet* does not stop there, and it is finally more interesting than this Oedipal reading which, along with Jones's speculations on Hamlet's childhood and Shakespeare's own life, has most often been used to discredit it. For while it is the case that Jones's account seems to fulfil the dream of any explanatory hypothesis by providing an account of factors which would otherwise remain unaccountable, a closer look shows how this same reading infringes the interpretative and sexual boundaries which, like Eliot, it seems to be putting into place.

The relationship of psychoanalysis to *Hamlet* has in fact always been a strange and repetitive one in which Hamlet the character is constantly given the status of a truth, and becomes a pivot for psychoanalysis and its project, just as for Eliot *Hamlet* is the focal point through which he arrives at a more general problem of aesthetic form. For Freud, for instance, Hamlet is not just Oedipus, but also melancholic and hysteric, and both these readings, problematic as they are as diagnoses of literary characters, become interesting because of the way they bring us up against the limits of interpretation and sexual identity alike. The interpretative distinction between rationality and excess, between normality and abnormality, for example, starts to crumble when the melancholic is defined as a madman who also speaks the truth. Freud uses *Hamlet* with this meaning in 'Mourning and Melancholia' written in 1915:

> We only wonder why a man has to be ill before he can be accessible to a truth of this kind. For there can be no doubt that if anyone holds an opinion of himself such as this (an opinion which Hamlet holds of himself and of everyone else) he is ill, whether or not he is speaking the truth or whether he is being more or less unfair to himself.

Taken in this direction, *Hamlet* illustrates not so much a failure of identity as the precarious distinction on which this notion of identity rests. In

'Psychopathic Characters on the Stage', Freud includes *Hamlet* in that group of plays which rely for their effect on the neurotic in the spectator, inducing in her or him the neurosis watched onstage, crossing over the boundaries between onstage and offstage and breaking down the habitual barriers of the mind. A particular *type* of drama, this form is none the less effective only through its capacity to implicate us *all*: 'A person who does not lose his reason under certain conditions can have no reason to lose'. Jones makes a similar point and underscores its fullest social import when he attributes the power of *Hamlet* to the very edge of sanity on which it moves, the way that it confuses the division which 'until our generation (and even now in the juristic sphere) separated the sane and the responsible from the irresponsible insane'. T. S. Eliot also gave a version of this, but from the other side, when he described poetry in 'Tradition and the Individual Talent' as an escape from emotion and personality, and then added 'but, of course, only those who have personality and emotion can know what it means to want to escape from these things'. So instead of safely diagnosing Hamlet, his Oedipal drama, his disturbance, and subjecting them to its mastery and control, the psychoanalytic interpretation turns back on to spectator and critic, implicating the observer in those forms of irrationality and excess which Jones and Eliot, in their different ways, seek to order into place.

Calling Hamlet a hysteric, which both Freud and Jones also do, has the same effect in terms of the question of sexual difference, since it immediately raises the question of femininity and upsets the too-tidy Oedipal reading of the play. Freud had originally seen the boy's Oedipal drama as a straightforward desire for the mother and rivalry with the father, just as he first considered the little girl's Oedipal trajectory to be its simple reverse. The discovery of the girl's pre-Oedipal attachment to the mother led him to modify this too-easy picture in which unconscious sexual desires in infancy are simply the precursors in miniature of the boy's and the girl's later fitting sexual and social place. We could say that psychoanalysis can become of interest to feminism at the point where the little girl's desire for the father can no longer be safely assumed. But equally important is the effect that this upset of the original schema has on how we consider the psychic life of the boy. In a section called 'Matricide' which is normally omitted from the anthologies, Jones talks of Hamlet's desire to kill, not the father, but the mother. He takes this from Hamlet's soliloquy before he goes to his mother's bedchamber:

> Let not ever
> The soul of Nero enter this firm bosom;
> Let me be cruel, not unnatural.
> I will speak daggers to her, but use none.
> [3.2. 363–6]

and also from Gertrude's own lines 'What wilt thou do? Thou wilt not murder me? Help! Ho!' [3.4. 21–2] (the murder of Polonius is the immediate consequence of this). Thus desire spills over into its opposite, and the woman becomes guilty for the affect which she provokes.

This is still an Oedipal reading of the play, since the violence towards the mother is the effect of the desire for her (a simple passage between the two forms of excess). But the problem of desire starts to trouble the category of identification, involving Jones in a discussion of the femininity in man (not just desire *for* the woman but identification *with* her), a femininity which has been recognized by more than one critic of the play. Thus on either side of the psychoanalytic 'solution', we find something which makes of it no solution at all. And Hamlet, 'as patient as the female dove' [5.1. 271] (the image of the female dove was objected to by Knight in 1841 as a typographical error), becomes Renaissance man only to the extent that he reveals a femininity which undermines that fiction. Femininity turns out to be lying behind the Oedipal drama, indicating its impasse or impossibility of resolution, even though Freud did himself talk of its dissolution, as if it suddenly went out of existence altogether. But this observation contradicts the basic analytic premiss of the persistence of unconscious desire.

The point being not whether Hamlet suffers from an excess *of* femininity, but the way that femininity itself functions *as* excess – the excess of this particular interpretative schema (hence, presumably, its exclusion from the summaries and extracts from Jones), and as the vanishing point of the difficulties of the play. And in this, Ernest Jones outbids T. S. Eliot *vis-à-vis* the woman: 'The central mystery [of *Hamlet*] has well been called the Sphinx of modern literature'. The femininity of Hamlet is perhaps finally less important than this image of the feminine which Jones blithely projects on to the troubled and troubling aesthetic boundaries of the play. [...]

[W]hat does it mean to us that one of the most elevated and generally esteemed works of our Western literary tradition should enact such a negative representation of femininity, or even such a violent repudiation of the femininity in man? I say 'esteemed' because it is of course the case that Eliot's critique has inflated rather than reduced *Hamlet*'s status. In 'Tradition and the Individual Talent', Eliot says the poet must 'know' the mind of Europe; *Hamlet* has more than once been taken as the model for that mind. Western tradition, the mind of Europe, Hamlet himself, each one the symbol of a cultural order in which the woman is given too much and too little of a place. But it is perhaps not finally inappropriate that those who celebrate or seek to uphold that order, with no regard to the image of the woman it encodes, constantly find themselves up against a problem which they call femininity – a reminder of the precarious nature of the certainties on which that order rests.

5.2 *Terence Hawkes, 'Telmah'*

Source: *That Shakespeherian Rag. Essays on Critical Process* (London: Methuen, 1986), Chapter 5, pp. 96, 100–7, 109–12, 114–17.

Writing in Britain in the 1980s, Terence Hawkes approaches Shakespeare's most famous play by first drawing attention to the many uncertainties, revisions, and misconceptions in the text that work to disrupt a sequential progression of the plot. For Hawkes, embedded in the rational, coherent, forward-looking text of *Hamlet*, there lies a second irrational, disruptive text he chooses to call *Telmah: Hamlet* backwards. His second move in the essay is to consider a key moment in the reception of *Hamlet*, John Dover Wilson's reaction to W. W. Greg's critical review of the play published in 1917. For Greg, the inconsistencies he sees in *Hamlet* suggest that Shakespeare should no longer be seen as 'a rational playwright', a charge that horrifies Dover Wilson, and inspires a lifelong crusade to rescue the reputation of both *Hamlet* and Shakespeare. The originality of Hawkes's essay lies in his effort to try and explain the significance of Dover Wilson's extreme response to Greg. Noting that 'the discourse of literary criticism in Britain and America tends to exclude the area of politics as not overtly appropriate to itself', Hawkes explains Dover Wilson's literary criticism with reference to his attitudes to the Russian Revolution, and his role in educational reform after the First World War. Returning in conclusion to the text of *Hamlet*, he appeals in much the same way as Sinfield (see Extract 3.2) does for a politicized Shakespeare criticism that is 'not parasitic but symbiotic' in its relation to the literary text.

Looking backwards

It begins without words. A man walks out on to the stage and takes up his position, evidently as a sentry. Another man, also evidently a sentry, follows shortly after him. Approaching the first man, the second suddenly halts, seemingly apprehensive and afraid. He quickly raises the long military spear he carries, the partisan, and brings it into an offensive position. That movement – before a word is spoken – immediately pushes the action forward: it enters a different dimension. A mystery has been posited (why are the sentries nervous, why do they make elementary mistakes of military discipline?) and a story starts to unfold.

It ends without words. Two dead bodies are taken up. A troop of soldiers, among them four captains, carries them off, ceremonially and to martial music, after which we hear a 'peal of ordnance'. These sounds, music, the cannon, also forward the action. They imply a new, ordered world of correct military discipline and principled yet firm political rule that will now replace a disordered society riven by betrayal and murder.

At the beginning, it is immediately noticeable that the military are not in complete control. Fundamental errors occur. Bernardo's challenge (and the play's first line), 'Who's there?', is uttered, as Francisco immediately points out, correcting him, by the wrong sentry. The password, 'Long live the King', could hardly be less appropriate: we know that a king has recently not lived long, and that another incumbent will soon cease to live.

At the end, similar misconceptions abound. We know, from what we have seen, that the story Horatio proposes to recount to the 'yet unknowing world' –

> So shall you hear
> Of carnal, bloody, and unnatural acts,
> Of accidental judgments, casual slaughters,
> Of deaths put on by cunning and forc'd cause,
> And, in this upshot, purposes mistook
> Fall'n on th'inventors' heads
> [5.2.324–9]

– fails adequately to reflect what happened. It was not as simple, as like an 'ordinary' revenge play as that. His solemnity – 'All this can I/Truly deliver' – mocks at the subtleties, the innuendoes, the contradictions, the imperfectly realized motives and sources for action that have been exhibited to us. We are hardly surprised when Fortinbras attempts to sum up Hamlet's potential:

> he was likely, had he been put on,
> To have prov'd most royal
> [5.2.341–2]

– but his account must, surely, wring a tiny gasp of disbelief from us. Nobody, so far as we have seen (and of course Fortinbras has not seen what we have seen), was likely to have proved less royal. Fortinbras's own claim to authority is decisively undermined by this poor judgement which must strike us as fundamentally misconceived. The 'friends' to this present ground, the 'liegemen' to this latest Dane (he is of course 'wrong' even in that, being a Norwegian) may well find the future just as bleak as their mistaken predecessors.

At the beginning, the action is overshadowed by war: by the 'fair and warlike form' (the Ghost) who dominates it even in his absence. There is much talk of preparation for war.

At the end, the warlike form of Fortinbras also hangs over the action in his absence: he finally obtrudes heralded by a 'warlike noise'. Military rule, by a foreigner, is what lies in store for the Danish state. The war promised at the beginning has not taken place, but at the end the results are the same as if it had.

At the beginning a dead king's presence overhangs the action and the nervousness of the sentries evokes it. At the end another dead king's presence overhangs the action, and is evoked by those final cannons, whose sound has been associated with him throughout.

There is even a mirror reflection of phrases. At the beginning, Bernardo comments, 'How now, Horatio? You tremble and look pale' [1.1.51]. At the end, Hamlet's words echo to a larger audience: 'You that look pale and tremble at this chance' [5.2.276].

It would be wrong to make too much of 'symmetries' of this sort, and I mention them only because, once recognized, they help, however slightly, to undermine our inherited notion of *Hamlet* as a structure that runs a satisfactorily linear, sequential course from a firmly established and well-defined beginning through a clearly placed and signalled middle to a causally related and logically determined end which, planted in the beginning, develops, or grows out of it.

Like all symmetries, the ones I have pointed to suggest, not linearity, but circularity: a cyclical and recursive movement wholly at odds with the progressive, incremental ordering that our society, dominated perhaps by a pervasive metaphor of the production line, tends to think of as appropriate to art as to everything else.

If we add to this the judgement that the beginning of *Hamlet* also operates, in a quite perplexing sense, as an ending (the spear's movement forces us to look back to events that have already occurred: the Ghost presupposes a complexity of happenings that lead to its current ghostliness), and that the ending in effect constitutes a beginning (the cannons at the end make us look forward to the new order of Fortinbras, as much as back: Fortinbras's future rule is clearly presaged as the play ends), the complexity of the whole business begins to proliferate.

We can even ask, as amateurs in playhouse dynamics, and in respect of the experience of a live audience in the theatre, when does the play *effectively* begin? Is it when the first sentry walks out on to the stage? Or has the play already begun in our mind's eye as we enter the theatre, leave our house, get up on that morning, buy our ticket some days/weeks ago? In our society, in which *Hamlet* finds itself embedded in the ideology in a variety of roles, the play has, for complex social and historical reasons, always already begun. And on to its beginning we have always already imprinted a knowledge of its course of action, and its ending.

And when, then, does it effectively end? When the dialogue stops and when the soldiers carry the bodies off and the music and the explosion of the cannons is heard? Not really, for there follows applause, and then that complex of revisionary ironies, which we group together under the heading of the 'curtain call'.

This is the ultimate Pirandellian moment which any play reaches: the final moment of closure in all senses which, significantly, raises precisely the question of the nature of closing. Of course, it also nominates the one part of the play normally closed to critical discussion: nobody ever talks about it. Yet the question remains crucial. When *does* the play close? When its 'action' stops? But does not that include, at least to some degree, the curtain call (which, of course, the actors rehearse)? For at this point the actors appear before us only partly as their 'real' selves. They also remain partly, and significantly, still 'in character', retaining mannerisms, perhaps, of the personages they have been playing. Who are they, then, at this point? Hamlet is not the Prince (for he is dead), but he is certainly not the actor who played the Prince either. He does not laugh or caper about as a man might who has scored (in the soccer fashion) a success. He may smile, wanly, as befits one recently slain; he may take, ruefully, the hand of his no less 'dead' opponent Claudius; he may even embrace the long-dead Ophelia. Is not this still acting? (The actor 'playing' himself-as-actor.) Is not this part of the action? It is the part that our applause, that non-discursive aural kind of closure, creates for us. This represents the point at which we assume control, for can we not now make Hamlet go or stay for a longer or shorter time, make him smile, frown, even laugh? It is the point, in short, at which we see the 'edge' of the play before it disappears entirely.

The modern curtain call functions of course very firmly as part of the planned production, fully rehearsed in all its complicated entrances and exits. This in itself gives us a sense of the force of the modern director's feeling that he must *seal* finally and inescapably the 'interpretation' he has thrust on and through the play. Yet the curtain call cannot be thus simply nailed down any more than the play can be thus simply sealed up and made subject to the director's will, however hard he tries. In a way that makes it representative of the play at large, the curtain call slips from under the director's fingers to generate its own wider and wilder implications. Here the play's dead acquire a kind of life once more. Here, most significantly, any apparent movement of the play in one direction halts, and it begins to roll decisively in the opposite direction (if only towards the next performance, when its 'beginning' will emerge again from these smiling actors). In short, the sense of straight, purposive, linear motion forward through the play – the sense required by most 'interpretations' of it – evaporates at the moment of the curtain call, and we sense an opposing current.

In so far as that current connects decisively with elements or aspects of the play already noticed, and in so far as its force seeks to roll the play backwards, reinforcing its recursive mode, making it, as it were, move only unwillingly and haltingly forward, constantly, even as it does so, looking over its own shoulder, then I propose to recognize it and for the sake of convenience and argument to name it in relation to *Hamlet*. I call it *Telmah: Hamlet* backwards. [...]

The Mousetrap marks *Hamlet*'s most recursive moment: the point at which time runs most obviously backwards, and where the play does not just glance over its shoulder, so much as turn fully round to look squarely at the most prominent action replay of them all. More than a play-within-a-play, *The Mousetrap* offers a replay of a replay: the Ghost's revisionary account of the murder, fitted out with actions. Equally, in so far as the design of *The Mousetrap* aims decisively to generate events that will forward the action of *Hamlet*, it also firmly looks towards the future. It functions, as Hamlet himself says, 'tropically': that is, as both trope or metaphor, and as the 'tropic' or turning point of the play. For *Hamlet* to operate, the past has here to be causally fused to what lies ahead: *Hamlet*'s linear progression depends on that, and the Prince himself has made it a condition of his own future actions. The Ghost's account of the events leading up to King Hamlet's murder are here to be tested by means of asking an audience at the play to read them in a particular way.

Hamlet himself is confident: he has written part of the play and proves 'as good as a chorus' in interpreting it. Rarely can someone involved in a drama have been so convinced that, in its linear, sequential unfolding, its single, unequivocal meaning will receive ready, interpreted acknowledgement. Like the play which bears his name, the Prince seems committed, purposive, moving inexorably to a predetermined end. Like *Hamlet*, confirming its enclosing presence perhaps, the play-within-the-play begins without words. And then, suddenly, it all goes wrong. *The Mousetrap* becomes 'tropical' indeed. *Hamlet* 'turns' decisively. It turns into *Telmah*.

To the Sunderland station

The scene now shifts to a train proceeding from Leeds to Sunderland one Saturday evening in November 1917.

On that train, a man is opening his mail. Amongst his letters he finds a square envelope containing the issue of the *Modern Language Review* (XII, 4) for October 1917. Leafing through it, he finds himself attracted to a particular article and 'all unconscious of impending fate', as he puts it, begins to read.

The effect, to say the least, is odd. In fact, he later uses the term 'overwhelming' and speaks of the experience as capable of throwing 'any mind off its balance'. The man was the scholar and critic John Dover Wilson, then aged 36. The article was by W. W. Greg and it was entitled 'Hamlet's Hallucination'.

The thrust of Greg's article lies in his clear perception that something goes badly wrong with the Prince's plans right at the beginning of *The Mousetrap*. Claudius fails to make any response to that initial and vital 'action replay', the dumb-show. The 'full significance' of this, Greg argues, has never been appreciated. After all, the dumb-show presents the stark details of Claudius's supposed crime, in more or less exactly the form retailed by the Ghost. Claudius's failure to respond means, quite simply, that the Ghost has failed the test, organized by Hamlet himself, to establish its veracity.

There is no doubt, of course, that Claudius has murdered King Hamlet. The doubts are as to the mode and method of the act – and in this respect the Ghost is clearly revealed, Greg says, to fall short as an 'objective' reporter. He has not given Hamlet true information. The 'orthodox view' of the play, which requires an objective truth-bearing Ghost, with Claudius properly indicted by its testimony as the dastardly poisoning villain of the story, ignores or tries to think 'around' the dumb-show. It argues, say, that the King and Queen are in close conversation at the time and so pay no attention to what is going on. This explanation, says Greg, 'is indeed a lame one': it treats the play as 'history' not drama. Such critics enquire 'why Hamlet behaved in a ridiculous way, when the question they should have asked was why Shakespeare did – or whether he did'. He adds, remarkably for 1917, 'this tendency is particularly prominent in the work of A. C. Bradley'.

For Greg, the 'extraordinary nature' of the dumb-show needs to be grasped. If we do so, we can see how genuinely upsetting Claudius's negative response to it is. Its effect is to advance or 'upgrade' Claudius: to make him more intriguing, his actions and his motives more complex: to make him a *victim* of the Ghost's malicious reportage as much as a villain in terms of the way the play is usually seen: to confirm him, in the play's terms, as no simple moustache-twirling criminal, but Hamlet's 'mighty opposite'; an impressive figure of potentially tragic stature who calls for a degree of sympathetic attention that must inevitably pull against the response traditionally inspired by the Prince. For an orthodox Hamlet-centred interpretation of the play, Claudius's negative reaction to the dumb-show 'not merely threatens the logical structure of one of the most crucial scenes of the play, but reduces it to meaningless confusion'. As a result, Greg concludes, 'we have to choose between giving up Shakespeare as a rational playwright, and giving up our inherited beliefs regarding the story of *Hamlet*'.

Nearly seventy years later, something of the panache of Greg's argument still communicates itself to us, though its potential as light reading for a Yorkshire Saturday night and Sunday morning might perhaps be a matter for dispute. What cannot be disputed is its effect on Dover Wilson. I have described this as odd: a better phrase might be 'seriously disturbing', even 'mind-blowing'. He himself describes it as 'an intensely felt experience' which resulted in 'a state of some considerable excitement'. It filled him, he reports, with 'a sort of insanity', and cast upon him, in his own words of eighteen years later, 'a spell which changed the whole tenor of my existence, and still dominates it in part'. Give up Shakespeare as a rational playwright indeed! Give up our inherited beliefs! Having read the article 'half a dozen times before reaching Sunderland' an almost Pauline sense of mission seems to have descended upon him: 'from the first [I] realized that I had been born to answer it'.

Why such a heated response to an article in a learned journal? [...] We can begin with the fact that, in November 1917, the war was not the only source of deep-seated disturbance in the world. In fact we could point out that, on any of the Saturdays in that month, news of the impending or actual Bolshevik revolution in Russia was likely to have been competing with news from the fronts. We have Dover Wilson's own statement that 'I found it difficult to concentrate upon anything unconnected with the War' and even his comment that, spending a lot of his time in trains, 'the hours of travel were mostly occupied in reading the newspapers'.

A glance at the newspapers of November 1917 confirms that the Bolshevik action received wide coverage, and one could reasonably assume Dover Wilson's awareness of the events from that. On Saturday 3 November, *The Times* reported 'Persistent rumours in Petrograd of the imminence of armed action by the Maximalists (i.e. Bolsheviks) whose object is to seize the supreme power' (p. 6). The *coup* actually took place on Wednesday/Thursday, 7–8 November (by the Russian calendar this was October 25/26). On Friday 9 November, extensive reports appeared in *The Times*: 'Anarchy in Petrograd: Power Seized by Lenin' with editorial comment of a predictable nature: 'the most extreme party in the Soviet appears to be in power ... it is assuredly not the authentic voice of Russia'. By Saturday 10 November, what *The Times* was then calling 'The Lenin Revolution' was fully reported, together with an extensive account of what the headlines termed the 'Siege of the Winter Palace', and on both Saturday 17 November and Saturday 24 November there appeared lengthy reports headed 'Civil Strife in Petrograd' and 'Russia's Starving Armies', etc. It would have been difficult in fact for a newspaper reader to be unaware of these events.

However, it adds a dimension to the picture, and gives something of an edge to what we may presume to be the *quality* of Dover Wilson's awareness, if we take into account the nature of the mission on which he was currently engaged: his reason, that is, for being on that particular train at that particular time.

Dover Wilson's main employment then was as a school inspector of the Board of Education, stationed at Leeds. But, in common with other inspectors, he was also from time to time used in some war work: specifically, as an inspector for the Ministry of Munitions. The reason why he was travelling to Sunderland had to do with that work, and with a particular crisis concerning it. 'Some trouble', as he decorously puts it, 'had arisen with local trade-union officials' in Sunderland, and Dover Wilson had been urgently dispatched there to sort it out. [...]

Insurrection was in the air. On the first day of the Bolshevik *coup* (7 November), speaking, by chance, in the House of Lords, the Marquess of Salisbury had warned that 'The governing classes hitherto had been inclined to regard the working class as a sort of dangerous animal of enormous strength and great potential violence, which it was necessary to be very civil to, but never to trust' (*The Times*, 8 November 1917). In short, the revolutionary proposals of Greg's article on *Hamlet* must have fallen into a powder keg of a mind already in some degree prepared to be 'blown' into 'a sort of insanity' by them just as, in the wider context towards which the Leeds–Sunderland train seemed to be speeding, certain events were already shaking the world.

Before dismissing this view as one which makes far too much of a mere coincidence of dates, certain other aspects of what is really rather a complex situation should be borne in mind. First, it is Dover Wilson himself who gives all the facts, as it were compulsively, in a 'letter' entitled 'The Road to Elsinore, being an Epistle Dedicatory to Walter Wilson Greg' which prefaces his major and highly influential book *What Happens in Hamlet* [1935]. The apparently immodest, unreserved commitment to total exposition of that book's title lends its own confessional, bean-spilling air to the letter, and *vice versa*.

The literary device of the publicly printed letter has always, of course, exploited means of communication generated by its paradoxical mode. As a document whose standing is both private and public at the same time, it 'means' both by what it is seen to offer, in confidence, and by what it is seen to withhold, in public. It operates, that is to say, both directly, by intimate revelation, and indirectly by evident obfuscation and suppression. The two methods of signifying are equated and intimately involved. What such a letter says and what it does not say, its utterances and its silences, are both meaningful: each becomes an aspect of the other. In *this* letter, the overt commitment is to the whole truth. Greg is told, 'you may have guessed something of this, but you cannot know it all'. The letter will thus tell all. It will explain 'the origin and purpose of this book', take us to the final originary source of what happened before *What Happens in Hamlet* happened, and thus lead us, in effect, to the root cause of its writing. That origin is precisely, specifically and insistently dated in a spirit of 'classic realism': 'It begins some time in the November of

1917.... I reached home one Saturday evening to find an urgent telephone message awaiting me.' The related, concomitant silence, however, is no less insistent. There is absolutely no mention before or after of the Bolshevik revolution.

I think we can regard that silence as resonant, and not simply because of the interest of the revolution itself, or because of any potential connection, however oblique, between it and Dover Wilson's current journey (Sunderland lacks a Winter Palace, but things have to start somewhere). It could be seen finally as a matter of discourse. The discourse of literary criticism in Britain and America, then and now, tends to exclude the area of politics as not overtly appropriate to itself and its purposes. It would seem literally unreasonable for a literary critic to take such issues on board as, no doubt, it seems unreasonable for me to do so right now.

But in fact, the truth is that Dover Wilson had to hand, and was perfectly capable of using, another discourse designed exactly for that purpose. There is, it seems to me, great significance in respect of the way discourses operate in the fact that he makes no mention of the Bolshevik revolution. For it means that no mention is made of it, no connection drawn between it and his present highly emotional state on the part of a man who had lived within the Russian Empire (in Finland) for three years, who by his own account had become, on his return to Britain, 'a well known public lecturer' on the subject of Russia, who was currently, as he writes to Greg, making 'fitful and unsuccessful attempts to learn Russian' and who on more than one previous occasion had written coolly, seriously, and at length about exactly this possibility of revolution in Russia and its likely consequences. [...]

[T]he decided modification in Dover Wilson's views about Russia which takes place between 1906 and 1914, moving from an early commitment to Fabianism to a subsequent rejection of that in favour of Tsarism, represents a serious narrowing of options, a growing sense of urgency, and a harder and harder line. And it is thus a modification which, given the previous confidence about insights into 'national mind and character', must have lent the *actual* events of November 1917, when they occurred, the quality of a nightmare; turning them into a horror of such proportions that perhaps no overt response to them was possible. (His later embarrassment over his writings on Russia is evident in his autobiography: 'I could not prophesy', he admits, 'a portent like Lenin who arrived in 1917.')

This is what I mean when I say that the absence of any mention of the Bolshevik revolution in Dover Wilson's account of his train journey strikes me as significant. It signifies of course that the Bolshevik revolution *is* in effect being responded to, coped with, in that 'intensely felt experience', that 'spell which changed the whole tenor of my existence', and that 'sort of insanity' provoked by Greg's article on *Hamlet*.

Greg's attack, after all, is on the smooth surface of the play, seen as the product of Shakespeare the 'rational playwright', but effectively, of course, created by an 'orthodox' interpretation which seeks for unity, progression, coherence and, if possible, sequential ordering in all art, as part of a ruthless and rigorous process of domestication. There is no obvious way of placating Greg's objections to that sort of *Hamlet* for they constitute a frontal assault on what he terms the 'inherited beliefs' – that brand of literary Tsarism – which reinforce and sustain it. And the assault is certainly not Fabian in character. It is directly, violently Bolshevik.

Dover Wilson's defence took various forms. There was an immediate diagnostic response to the editor of the *Modern Language Review* by means of a postcard dispatched upon alighting from the train at Sunderland, which went so far as to nominate Greg as an unwitting agent of the arch-revolutionary himself: 'Greg's article devilish ingenious but damnably wrong', it twinkled, and offered a rejoinder, which duly appeared. There followed two major salvoes: the edition of *Hamlet* prepared by Dover Wilson for the New Cambridge Shakespeare in 1934 – a series of which, provoked into the role by Greg's article, he says, he had become general editor in 1919 – and the book *What Happens in Hamlet*, which purports to release him from thrall to the problems, by telling all. [...]

But if these salvoes represent Dover Wilson's defence against Bolshevism in its specifically displaced Shakespearian form, it is possible also to suggest that the same battle was subsequently taken up on a broader front by the same combatant. Two years later, in May 1919, a departmental committee was appointed by the president of the Board of Education to investigate what was termed 'The Teaching of English in England'. Its terms of reference were

> To inquire into the position occupied by English (Language and Literature) in the educational system of England, and to advise how its study may best be promoted in schools of all types, including Continuation Schools, and in Universities and other Institutions of Higher Education, regard being had to
>
> (1)   the requirements of a liberal education;
> (2)   the needs of business, the professions, and public services; and
> (3)   the relation of English to other studies.

The committee's chairman was Sir Henry Newbolt, and prominent amongst its members was John Dover Wilson.

Many things have been said about the Newbolt Report, as the published findings of the committee became known. The first thing to stress is that it was widely influential. It sold, in Dover Wilson's words, 'like a

best-seller', and it can be said effectively to have shaped the nature of
'English' as the academic subject we know today. Its spiritual father is
Matthew Arnold, its spiritual son F. R. Leavis. Its two central concerns –
more or less overt – are related political ones: social cohesion in the face of
potential disintegration and disaffection; and nationalism, the encourage-
ment of pride in English national culture on a broader front. The common
coin of its discourse is generated by concepts we have already encoun-
tered: notably those of 'national mind and character'. English, seen in this
light, becomes 'the only basis possible for national education', being not
merely the medium of our thought, but 'the very stuff and process of it. It
is itself the English mind.' An education based on English would thus
have a 'unifying tendency', acting as an antidote to the divisiveness, the
'bitterness and disintegration' of a class-dominated society. It would
heal one of the major causes of 'division amongst us': the 'undue
narrowness of the ground on which we meet for the true purposes of
social life' (without specifying what those might be). Recognizing that we
are 'not one nation but two', the report sees the study of English as
capable of bridging, if not closing, the 'chasm of separation', the 'mental
[sic] distances between classes'. Offering a 'bond of union between
classes' it would 'beget the right kind of national pride' [...]

To Dover Wilson – and to many others subsequently – the solution lay
quite clearly in the sort of nourishment that English literature offered: the
snap, crackle and pop of its roughage, a purgative force of considerable
political power – not because it has a direct influence on what Dover
Wilson (and others) called 'the social problem', but because of its indirect
influence on what they certainly did not call ideology, but which is clearly
signalled as such in the report's references to a general, indeed a national,
'state of mind'. If the 'state of mind' is orientated wholly towards the
'social problem', the result is an unhealthy imbalance:

> This state of mind is not a new thing in history, and even goes back as far as
> Plato. It finds a parallel in the contempt for 'poets, pipers, players, jesters
> and such-like caterpillars of the common-wealth' expressed by puritans of
> the 16th and 17th centuries, and in the hostility towards the 'culture of
> capitalism' now prevalent in Bolshevist Russia.

That hostility, that Bolshevism, is apparently best met by strengthening
the character, through massive doses of poetry administered by a solicitous education system:

> we believe that, if rightly presented, poetry will be recognized by the most
> ardent social reformers as of value, because while it contributes no specific
> solution of the social problem it endows the mind with power and sanity;
> because, in a word, it enriches personality.

Personality! The very word is like a bell. The ideological position this signals – the commitment to individualism as a long-term solution to the social problem – is a familiar one, and it remains the long-term position from which most teaching of literature is still mounted. Its political, economic and social implications are clearly spelled out in the Newbolt Report, and most clearly in those parts of the report which we know were written by Dover Wilson. The impulse generating that position, the stimulus to which it constitutes a considered response, lies in the events which took place in Russia in November 1917, and the subsequent sense of betrayal on the Allies' part in the face of the consequent German spring offensive of 1918 which nearly won the war for the Kaiser.

My point is a simple one. Dover Wilson's response to Greg's article on that train to Sunderland in 1917 offers an excellent example of the sort of interaction between literary interpretation and political and social concerns that always pertains, but normally remains covert in our culture. Confronted by what I have called a manifestation of *Telmah* – i.e. by the disruption of the normally smooth and, in terms of individual 'personality' (Hamlet's or Shakespeare's), explainable surface of a text that our society has appropriated a manifestation of great (and thus reassuring) art – he replies with a vigour and an emotionally charged nervous energy appropriate to it as what in fact it must have seemed to be: an attack or an offensive mounted against the structure of civilization as we know it – in short, an attack on our ideology. Dover Wilson's sensitivity to overt political attacks – manifested in his articles on revolutionary Russia – fuels his response to *Telmah*, which he rightly senses as potentially revolutionary in ideological terms. Today *Hamlet*, tomorrow the World! [...]

It would also be nice to conclude by turning back, now, to the play. But in a very serious sense, which I hope to have made clear, we cannot do so. There is no unitary, self-presenting play for us to turn back to, and I have no intention of turning myself inside out in pursuit of the truth. That kind of 'appeasement' of the text can be said to have its own political analogues. And indeed ... 'Dear Dr Dover Wilson' begins a missive from Birmingham dated 7 June 1936:

> I expect you will be rather surprised to get a letter from me as we have not been 'introduced'. But as we are both public characters perhaps we may dispense with formalities. ... I can't help telling you what immense pleasure I have had out of *What Happens in Hamlet*. I had asked for it as a Christmas present, and when it duly appeared I sat up several nights into the small hours reading it. ... When I had finished it, I did what I don't think I have ever done before with any book: I immediately read it all over again! And that won't be the last time of reading.

The letter was signed 'Neville Chamberlain'.

In short, I am not going to suggest that we can approach *Hamlet* by recognizing *Telmah*, or that *Telmah* is the real play, obscured by *Hamlet*. That would be to try to reconcile, to bring to peace, to appease a text whose vitality resides precisely in its plurality: in the fact that it contradicts itself and strenuously resists our attempts to resolve, to domesticate that contradiction. I am trying to suggest that its contradiction has value in that a pondering of some of the attempts that have been made to resolve it, to make the play speak coherently, within a limited set of boundaries, reveals the political, economic and social forces to which all such 'interpretation' responds and in whose name it must inevitably, if covertly, be made. I am not suggesting an 'alternative' reading of *Hamlet*, because that would be to fall into the same trap. I offer my title of *Telmah* as what it is: a sense of an ever-present potential challenge and contradiction *within* and *implied* by the text that we name *Hamlet*. In this sense, *Telmah* coexists with, is coterminous with, *Hamlet* in a way that must strike us, finally, as impossible. A thing, we are taught, cannot be both what it is and another thing. But that is precisely the principle challenged by *Telmah*. Our notion that it cannot coexist with *Hamlet* marks the limit, I suggest, of our Eurocentric view of 'sense', of 'order', of 'presence' if you like, and of 'point of view'. That Eurocentricity lies behind and validates a limited notion of 'interpretation' which will allow us to have *Hamlet* in various guises, and will also, as an alternative, allow clever and sophisticated interpreters to have, say, *Telmah*. But it will not allow us to have both, because that would explode our notion of the single and unified 'point of view' whose 'authority', as that term suggests, derives from its source, the author. [...]

6 *Twelfth Night*

6.1 C. L. Barber, 'Testing Courtesy and Humanity in Twelfth Night'

Source: *Shakespeare's Festive Comedy: A Study of Dramatic Form and its Relation to Social Custom* (Princeton, NJ: Princeton University Press, 1985), Chapter 10, pp. 240–57.

C. L. Barber's *Shakespeare's Festive Comedy* (first published 1959) is a ground-breaking study which seeks to contextualize Shakespearean comedy in terms of popular traditions of festivity; in the words of its subtitle it is 'A Study of Dramatic Form and its Relation to Social Custom'. Barber relates the comedies to the surviving evidence of Elizabethan festive ritual – so in this extract Sir Toby Belch's attack on Malvolio is compared with the conflict between the Earl of Lincoln and the Lincolnshire gentleman Talboys Dymoke, who burlesqued the Earl in a series of popular entertainments in 1601. Barber's willingness to juxtapose social history with dramatic texts and to draw on disciplines like anthropology proved highly influential on later critical movements such as new historicism. In particular, the reading of Malvolio as a comic butt whom Elizabethan audiences would have immediately recognized as an anti-festive figure has implications for how *Twelfth Night* should be performed. Is it really a near tragedy, or does it instead, as Barber suggests, release pent-up social tensions through the mockery of a self-important and antisocial figure? However, Barber's book is still very much a piece of its time. Compare his non-sexual interpretation of the relationship between Antonio and Sebastian (and the consequent repression of homoerotic elements throughout the play) with Joseph Pequigney's reading (see Extract 6.2).

...nature to her bias drew in that.

The title of *Twelfth Night* may well have come from the first occasion when it was performed, whether or not Dr. Leslie Hotson is right in arguing that its first night was the court celebration of the last of the twelve days of Christmas on January 6, 1600–1601.

The title tells us that the play is like holiday misrule – though not just like it, for it adds "or what you will." The law student John Manningham, who saw it at the Middle Temple's feast on February 2, 1602, wrote in his diary that it was "much like the Comedy of Errores, or Menechmi in Plautus, but most like and neere to that in Italian called *Inganni*." We have the now-familiar combination of festive, literary and theatrical traditions. In addition to Plautine situation and Italian comedy, Shakespeare drew on a prose romance (derived indirectly from Italian comedy), Rich's *Apolonius and Silla*. He used no written source for the part Manningham specially praised: "A good practice in it to make the Steward beleeve his Lady widdowe was in love with him. . . ."

Shakespeare can be inclusive in his use of traditions because his powers of selection and composition can arrange each element so that only those facets of it show which will serve his expressive purpose. He leaves out the dungeon in which Rich's jealous Orsino shuts up Viola, as well as Sebastian's departure leaving Olivia with child; but he does not hesitate to keep such events as the shipwreck, or Sebastian's amazing marriage to a stranger, or Orsino's threat to kill Viola. It is not the credibility of the event that is decisive, but what can be expressed through it. Thus the shipwreck is made the occasion for Viola to exhibit an undaunted, aristocratic mastery of adversity – she settles what she shall do next almost as though picking out a costume for a masquerade:

> I'll serve this duke,
> Thou shalt present me as an eunuch to him;
> It may be worth thy pains. For I can sing,
> And speak to him in several sorts of music....
> [1.2.51–4]

What matters is not the event, but what the language says as gesture, the aristocratic, free-and-easy way she settles what she will do and what the captain will do to help her. The pathetical complications which are often dwelt on in the romance are not allowed to develop far in the play; instead Viola's spritely language conveys the fun she is having in playing a man's part, with a hidden womanly perspective about it. One cannot quite say that she is playing in a masquerade, because disguising *just* for the fun of it is a different thing. But the same sort of festive pleasure in transvestism is expressed.

It is amazing how little happens in *Twelfth Night*, how much of the time people are merely talking, especially in the first half, before the farcical complications are sprung. Shakespeare is so skillful by now in rendering attitudes by the gestures of easy conversation that when it suits him he can almost do without events. In the first two acts of *Twelfth Night* he holds our interest with a bare minimum of tension while unfolding a pattern of contrasting attitudes and tones in his several persons. Yet Shakespeare's whole handling of romantic story, farce, and practical joke makes a composition which moves in the manner of his earlier festive comedies, through release to clarification.

"A most extracting frenzy"

Olivia's phrase in the last act, when she remembers Malvolio and his "madness," can summarize the way the play moves:

> A most extracting frenzy of mine own
> From my remembrance clearly banish'd his.
> [5.1.274–5]

People are caught up by delusions or misapprehensions which take them out of themselves, bringing out what they would keep hidden or did not know was there. *Madness* is a key word. The outright gull Malvolio is already "a rare turkey-cock" from "contemplation" [2.5.26] before Maria goes to work on him with her forged letter. "I do not now fool myself, to let imagination jade me" [2.5.143–4], he exclaims when he has read it, having been put "in such a dream that, when the image of it leaves him, he must run mad" [2.5.168–9]. He is too self-absorbed actually to run mad, but when he comes at Olivia, smiling and cross-gartered, she can make nothing else of it: "Why, this is very mid-summer madness"

[3.4.52]. And so the merrymakers have the chance to put him in a dark room and do everything they can to face him out of his five wits.

What they bring about as a "pastime" [3.4.123], to "gull him into a nayword, and make him a common recreation" [2.3.120–1], happens unplanned to others by disguise and mistaken identity. Sir Toby, indeed, "speaks nothing but madman" [1.5.92–3] without any particular occasion. "My masters, are you mad?" [2.3.78] Malvolio asks as he comes in to try to stop the midnight singing. Malvolio is sure that he speaks for the countess when he tells Toby that "though she harbors you as her kins-man, she's nothing allied to your disorders" [2.3.86–7]. But in fact this sober judgment shows that he is not "any more than a steward" [2.3.102–3]. For his lady, dignified though her bearing is, suddenly finds herself doing "I know not what" [1.5.278] under the spell of Viola in her page's disguise: "how now? / Even so quickly may one catch the plague?" [1.5.264–5] "Poor lady," exclaims Viola, "she were better love a dream!" [2.2.24]. In their first interview, she had told the countess, in urging the count's suit, that "what is yours to bestow is not yours to reserve" [1.5.167–8]. By the end of their encounter, Olivia says the same thing in giving way to her passion: "Fate, show thy force! Ourselves we do not owe" [1.5.280]. And soon her avowals of love come pouring out, over-coming the effort at control which shows she is a lady:

> O, what a deal of scorn looks beautiful
> In the contempt and anger of his lip!
> A murd'rous guilt shows not itself more soon
> Than love that would seem hid: love's night is noon.
> Cesario, by the roses of the spring,
> By maidhood, honour, truth, and everything,
> I love thee so....
>
> [3.1.136–42]

A little later, when she hears about Malvolio and his smile, she sum-marizes the parallel with "I am as mad as he, / If sad and merry madness equal be" [3.4.14–15].

The farcical challenge and "fight" between Viola and Sir Andrew are another species of frantic action caused by delusion. "More matter for a May morning" [3.4.127] Fabian calls it as they move from pretending to exorcise Malvolio's devil to pretending to act as solicitous seconds for Sir Andrew. When Antonio enters the fray in manly earnest, there is still another sort of comic error, based not a psychological distortion but simply on mistaken identity. This Plautine sort of confusion leads Sebas-tian to exclaim, "Are all the people mad?" [4.1.24] Just after we have seen "Malvolio the lunatic" [4.2.19–20] baffled in the dark room ("But tell me true, are you not mad indeed? or do you but counterfeit?" [4.2.104–5]), we see Sebastian struggling to understand his wonderful encounter with Olivia:

> This is the air; that is the glorious sun;
> This pearl she gave me, I do feel't and see't;
> And though 'tis wonder that enwraps me thus,
> Yet 'tis not madness.
>
> [4.3.1–4]

The open-air clarity of this little scene anticipates the approaching moment when delusions and misapprehensions are resolved by the finding of objects appropriate to passions. Shakespeare, with fine stage-craft, spins the misapprehensions out to the last moment. He puts Orsino, in his turn, through an extracting frenzy, the Duke's frustration convert-ing at last to violent impulses toward Olivia and Cesario, before he discovers in the page the woman's love he could not win from the countess.

That it should all depend on there being an indistinguishable twin brother always troubles me when I think about it, though never when I watch the play. Can it be that we enjoy the play so much simply because it is a wish-fulfillment presented so skillfully that we do not notice that our hearts are duping our heads? Certainly part of our pleasure comes from pleasing make-believe. But I think that what chance determines about particular destinies is justified, [...] by the play's realizing dynamically general distinctions and tendencies in life.

"You are betroth'd both to a maid and man"

The most fundamental distinction the play brings home to us is the difference between men and women. To say this may seem to labor the obvious; for what love story does not emphasize this difference? But the disguising of a girl as a boy in *Twelfth Night* is exploited so as to renew in a special way our sense of the difference. Just as a saturnalian reversal of social roles need not threaten the social structure, but can serve instead to consolidate it, so a temporary, playful reversal of sexual roles can renew the meaning of the normal relation. One can add that with sexual as with other relations, it is when the normal is secure that playful aberration is benign. This basic security explains why there is so little that is queazy in all Shakespeare's handling of boy actors playing women, and playing women pretending to be men. This is particularly remarkable in *Twelfth Night*, for Olivia's infatuation with Cesario-Viola is another, more fully developed case of the sort of crush Phebe had on Rosalind [in *As You Like It*]. Viola is described as distinctly feminine in her disguise, more so than Rosalind:

> ...they shall yet belie thy happy years
> That say thou art a man. Diana's lip
> Is not more smooth and rubious; thy small pipe
> Is as the maiden's organ, shrill and sound,
> And all is semblative a woman's part.
>
> [1.4.29–33]

When on her embassy Viola asks to see Olivia's face and exclaims about it, she shows a woman's way of relishing another woman's beauty – and sensing another's vanity: " 'Tis beauty truly blent...." "I see you what you are – you are too proud" [1.5.209,219]. Olivia's infatuation with feminine qualities in a youth takes her, doing "I know not what," from one stage of life out into another, from shutting out suitors in mourning for her brother's memory, to ardor for a man, Sebastian, and the clear certainty that calls out to "husband" in the confusion of the last scene.

We might wonder whether this spoiled and dominating young heiress may not have been attracted by what she could hope to dominate in Cesario's youth – but it was not the habit of Shakespeare's age to look for such implications. And besides, Sebastian is not likely to be dominated; we have seen him respond to Andrew when the ninny knight thought he was securely striking Cesario:

> *Andrew.* Now, sir, have I met you again? There's for you!
> *Sebastian.* Why, there's for thee, and there, and there!
>
> [4.1.21–3]

To see this manly reflex is delightful – almost a relief – for we have been watching poor Viola absurdly perplexed behind her disguise as Sir Toby urges her to play the man: "Dismount thy tuck, be yare in thy preparation.... Therefor on, or strip your sword naked; for meddle you must, that's certain" [3.4.199–200, 222–4]. She is driven to the point where she exclaims in an aside: "Pray God defend me! A little thing would make me tell them how much I lack of a man" [3.4.268–9]. What she lacks, Sebastian has. His entrance in the final scene is preceded by comical testimony of his prowess, Sir Andrew with a broken head and Sir Toby halting. The particular implausibility that there should be an identical man to take Viola's place with Olivia is submerged in the general, beneficent realization that there is such a thing as a man. Sebastian's comment when the confusion of identities is resolved points to the general force which has shaped particular developments:

> So comes it, lady, you have been mistook.
> But nature to her bias drew in that.
>
> [5.1.252–3]

Over against the Olivia-Cesario relation, there are Orsino-Cesario and Antonio-Sebastian. Antonio's impassioned friendship for Sebastian is one of those ardent attachments between young people of the same sex which Shakespeare frequently presents, with his positive emphasis, as exhibiting the loving and lovable qualities later expressed in love for the other sex. Orsino's fascination with Cesario is more complex. In the opening scene, his restless sensibility can find no object: "naught enters there, ... / But falls into abatement ... / Even in a minute" [1.1.11–14]. Olivia might be an adequate object; she at least is the Diana the sight of whom has, he thinks, turned him to an Acteon torn by the hounds of desires. When we next see him, and Cesario has been only three days in his court, his entering question is "Who saw Cesario, ho?" [1.4.9] and already he has unclasped to the youth "the book even of [his] secret soul" [1.4.13]. He has found an object. The delight he takes in Cesario's fresh youth and graceful responsiveness in conversation and in service, is one part of the spectrum of love for a woman, or better, it is a range of feeling that is common to love for a youth and love for a woman. For the audience, the woman who is present there, behind Cesario's disguise, is brought to mind repeatedly by the talk of love and of the differences of men and women in love. "My father had a daughter loved a man ..." [2.4.106].

> She never told her love,
> But let concealment, like a worm i' th' bud,
> Feed on her damask cheek.
>   [2.4.109–11]

This supremely feminine damsel, who "sat like patience on a monument," is not Viola. She is a sort of polarity within Viola, realized all the more fully because the other, active side of Viola does not pine in thought at all, but instead changes the subject: " ... and yet I know not. / Sir, shall we to this lady? – Ay, that's the theme" [2.4.120–1]. The effect of moving back and forth from woman to sprightly page is to convey how much the sexes differ yet how much they have in common, how everyone who is fully alive has qualities of both. Some such general recognition is obliquely suggested in Sebastian's amused summary of what happened to Olivia:

> You would have been contracted to a maid;
> Nor are you therein, by my life, deceiv'd:
> You are betroth'd both to a maid and man.
>   [5.1.254–6]

The countess marries the man in this composite, and the count marries the maid. He too has done he knows not what while nature drew him to her bias, for he has fallen in love with the maid without knowing it.

Liberty Testing Courtesy

We have seen how each of the festive comedies tends to focus on a particular kind of folly that is released along with love – witty masquerade in *Love's Labour's Lost*, delusive fantasy in *A Midsummer Night's Dream*, romance in *As You Like It*, and, in *The Merchant of Venice*, prodigality balanced against usury. *Twelfth Night* deals with the sort of folly which the title points to, the folly of misrule. But the holiday reference limits its subject too narrowly: the play exhibits the liberties which gentlemen take with decorum in the pursuit of pleasure and love, including the liberty of holiday, but not only that. Such liberty is balanced against time-serving. As Bassanio's folly of prodigality [in *The Merchant of Venice*] leads in the end to gracious fulfillment, so does Viola's folly of disguise. There is just a suggestion of the risks when she exclaims,

> Disguise, I see thou art a wickedness
> Wherein the pregnant enemy does much.
> [2.2.25–6]

As in *The Merchant of Venice* the story of a prodigal is the occasion for an exploration of the use and abuse of wealth, so here we get an exhibition of the use and abuse of social liberty.

What enables Viola to bring off her role in disguise is her perfect courtesy, in the large, humanistic meaning of that term as the Renaissance used it, the *corteziania* of Castiglione. Her mastery of courtesy goes with her being the daughter of "that Sebastian of Messalina whom I know you have heard of": gentility shows through her disguise as does the fact that she is a woman. The impact on Olivia of Cesario's quality as a gentleman is what is emphasized as the countess, recalling their conversation, discovers that she is falling in love:

> 'What is thy parentage?'
> 'Above my fortunes, yet my state is well.
> I am a gentleman.' I'll be sworn thou art.
> Thy tongue, thy face, thy limbs, actions, and spirit
> Do give thee fivefold blazon. Not too fast! soft, soft!
> Unless the master were the man.
> [1.5.259–64]

We think of manners as a mere prerequisite of living decently, like cleanliness. For the Renaissance, they could be almost the end of life, as the literature of courtesy testifies. *Twelfth Night* carries further an interest in the fashioning of a courtier which, [...] appears in several of the early comedies, especially *The Two Gentlemen of Verona*, and which in different keys Shakespeare was pursuing, about the same time as he wrote *Twelfth*

Night, in *Hamlet* and *Measure for Measure*. People in *Twelfth Night* talk of courtesy and manners constantly. But the most important expression of courtesy of course is in object lessons. It is their lack of breeding and manners which makes the comic butts ridiculous, along with their lack of the basic, free humanity which, be it virile or feminine, is at the center of courtesy and flowers through it. [...]

Mr. Van Doren observes that *Twelfth Night* has a structure like *The Merchant of Venice*. "Once again Shakespeare has built a world out of music and melancholy, and once again this world is threatened by an alien voice. The opposition of Malvolio to Orsino and his class parallels the opposition of Shylock to Antonio and his friends. The parallel is not precise, and the contrast is more subtly contrived; Shakespeare holds the balance in a more delicate hand...." One way in which this more delicate balance appears is that the contest of revellers with intruder does not lead to neglecting ironies about those who are on the side of pleasure. We are all against Malvolio, certainly, in the great moment when the whole opposition comes into focus with Toby's "Dost thou think, because thou art virtuous, there shall be no more cakes and ale?" [2.3.103–4]. The festive spirit shows up the killjoy vanity of Malvolio's decorum. The steward shows his limits when he calls misrule "this uncivil rule." But one of the revellers is Sir Andrew, who reminds us that there is no necessary salvation in being a fellow who delights "in masques and revels sometimes altogether"[1.3.94–5]. [...] To put such a leg as his into "a flame-coloured stock" only shows how meager it is. This thin creature's motive is self-improvement: he is a version of the stock type of prodigal who is gulled in trying to learn how to be gallant. As in Restoration comedy the fop confirms the values of the rake, Auguecheek serves as foil to Sir Toby. But he also marks one limit as to what revelry can do for a man: "I would I had bestowed that time in the tongues that I have in fencing, dancing and bear-baiting" [1.3.78–80]. [...]

> *Olivia.* Cousin, cousin, how have you come so early by this lethargy?
> *Toby.* Lechery? I defy lechery. There's one at the gate.
> *Olivia.* Ay, marry, what is he?
> *Toby.* Let him be the devil an he will. I care not!
>   Give me faith, say I. Well, it's all one.
>
> [1.5.108–13]

Stage drunkenness, here expressed by wit that lurches catch-as-catch-can, conveys the security of "good life" in such households as Olivia's, the old-fashioned sort that had not given up "house-keeping." Because Toby has "faith" – the faith that goes with belonging – he does not need to worry when Maria teases him about confining himself "within the modest limits of order." "Confine? I'll confine myself no finer than I am" [1.3.6–8]. In his talk as in his clothes, he has the ease of a gentleman whose place in the world is secure, so that, while he can find words like *consanguineous* at will, he can also say "Sneck up!" to Malvolio's accusation that he shows "no respect of persons, places nor time" [2.3.82–4]. Sir Toby is the sort of kinsman who would take the lead at such Christmas feasts as Sir Edward Dymoke patronized in Lincolnshire – a Talboys Dymoke. His talk is salted with holiday morals: "I am sure care's an enemy of life" [1.3.2]. "Not to be abed before midnight is to be up betimes" [2.3.1–2]. He is like Falstaff in maintaining saturnalian paradox and in playing impromptu the role of lord of misrule. But in his whole relation to the world he is fundamentally different from Prince Hal's great buffoon. Falstaff makes a career of misrule; Sir Toby uses misrule to show up a careerist.

There is little direct invocation by poetry of the values of heritage and housekeeping. [. . .] But the graciousness of community is conveyed indirectly by the value put on music and song. The Duke's famous opening lines start the play with music. His hypersensitive estheticism savors strains that have a dying fall and mixes the senses in appreciation: "like the sweet sound / That breathes upon a bank of violets" [1.1.5–6]. Toby and his friends are more at ease about "O mistress mine," but equally devoted to music in their way. (Toby makes fun of such strained appreciation as the Duke's when he concludes their praises of the clown's voice with "To hear by the nose, it is dulcet in contagion" [2.3.52–3].) Back at court, in the next scene, the significance of music in relation to community is suggested in the Duke's lines about the "old and antique song":

> Mark it, Cesario; it is old and plain.
> The spinsters and the knitters in the sun,
> And the free maids that weave their thread with bones,
> Do use to chant it. It is silly sooth,
> And dallies with the innocence of love
> Like the old age.
>
> [2.4.42–7]

The wonderful line about the free maids, which throws such firm stress on "free" by the delayed accent, and then slows up in strong, regular monosyllables, crystallizes the play's central feeling for freedom in heritage and community. It is consciously nostalgic; the old age is seen from the vantage of "these most brisk and giddy-paced times" [2.4.6].

Throughout the play a contrast is maintained between the taut, restless, elegant court, where people speak a nervous verse, and the free-wheeling household of Olivia, where, except for the intense moments in Olivia's amorous interviews with Cesario, people live in an easy-going prose. The contrast is another version of pastoral. The household is more than any one person in it. People keep interrupting each other, changing their minds, letting their talk run out into foolishness – and through it all Shakespeare expresses the day-by-day going on of a shared life:

> *Maria.* Nay, either tell me where thou hast been, or I will not open my lips so wide as a bristle may enter in way of thy excuse.
>
> [1.5.1–3]

> *Fabian.* . . . You know he brought me out o' favour with my lady about a bear-baiting here.
> *Toby.* To anger him we'll have the bear again . . .
>
> [2.5.6–8]

> *Fabian.* Why, we shall make him mad indeed.
> *Maria.* The house will be the quieter.
>
> [3.4.119–20]

Maria's character is a function of the life of "the house"; she moves within it with perfectly selfless tact. "She's a beagle truebred," says Sir Toby: her part in the housekeeping and its pleasures is a homely but valued kind of "courtiership."

All of the merrymakers show a fine sense of the relations of people, including robust Fabian, and Sir Toby, when he has need. The fool, especially, has this courtly awareness. We see in the first scene that he has to have it to live: he goes far enough in the direction of plain speaking to engage Olivia's unwilling attention, then brings off his thesis that *she* is the fool so neatly that he is forgiven. What Viola praises in the fool's function is just what we should expect in a play about courtesy and liberty:

> This fellow is wise enough to play the fool,
> And to do that well craves a kind of wit.
> He must observe their mood on whom he jests.
> The quality of persons and the time . . .
>
> [3.1.53–6]

[. . .] What Feste chiefly does is sing and beg – courtly occupations – and radiate in his songs and banter a feeling of liberty based on accepting disillusion. "What's to come is still unsure . . . Youth's a stuff will not endure" [2.3.45, 48]. [. . .] He rarely makes the expected move, but conveys by his style how well he knows what moves are expected:

> so that, conclusions to be as kisses, if your four negatives make your two affirmatives, why then, the worse for my friends and the better for my foes.
> *Duke.* Why, this is excellent.
> *Feste.* By my troth, sir, no; though it pleases you to be one of my friends.
>
> [5.1.18–21]

His feeling for people and their relations comes out most fully when he plays "Sir Topas the curate, who comes to visit Malvolio the lunatic" [4.2.19–20]. [...]

Viola, who as "nuntio" moves from tense court to relaxed household, has much in common with Feste in the way she talks, or better, uses talk; but she also commands effortlessly, when there is occasion, Shakespeare's mature poetic power:

> It gives a very echo to the seat
> Where love is throned.
> [2.4.20–1]

"Thou dost speak masterly," the Duke exclaims – as we must too. Part of her mastery is that she lets herself go only rarely, choosing occasions that are worthy. Most of the time she keeps her language reined in, often mocking it as she uses it, in Feste's fashion. Perhaps it is because he finds himself beaten at his own game that he turns on her ungraciously, as on no one else:

> *Viola.* I warrant thou art a merry fellow and car'st for nothing.
> *Clown.* Not so, sir; I do care for something; but in my conscience, sir, I do not care for you. If that be to care for nothing, sir, I would it would make you   invisible.
> [3.1.23–6]

Once when she is mocking the elaborate language of compliment, greeting Olivia with "the heavens rain odors on you," Sir Andrew overhears and is much impressed: "That youth's a rare courtier. 'Rain odors' – well" [3.1.77–9]. He plans to get her fancy words by heart. Of course, as a rare courtier, she precisely does *not* commit herself to such high-flown, Osric-style expressions. Her constant shifting of tone in response to the situation goes with her manipulation of her role in disguise, so that instead of simply listening to her speak, we watch her conduct her speech, and through it feel her secure sense of proportion and her easy, alert consciousness: "To one of your receiving," says Olivia, "enough is shown" [3.1.112–13].

Olivia says that "it was never merry world / Since lowly feigning was called compliment" [3.1.90–1]. As Sir Toby is the spokesman and guardian of that merry world, Malvolio is its antagonist. He shows his relation to festivity at once by the way he responds to Feste, and Olivia points the moral: he is "sick of self love" and tastes "with a distempered appetite." He is not "generous, guiltless, and of free disposition." Of course, nothing is more helpful, to get revelry to boil up, than somebody trying to keep the lid on – whatever his personal qualities. But the "stubborn and uncourteous parts" in Malvolio's character, to which Fabian refers in justifying the "device," are precisely those qualities which liberty shows up. Malvolio wants "to confine himself finer than he is," to paraphrase Toby in reverse: he practices behavior to his own shadow. His language is full of pompous polysyllables, of elaborate syntax deploying synonyms:

> Do ye make an alehouse of my lady's house, that ye squeak out your coziers' catches without any mitigation or remorse of voice? Is there no respect of place, persons, nor time in you?
>
> [2.3.80–3]

In "loving" his mistress, as Cesario her master, he is a kind of foil, bringing out her genuine, free impulse by the contrast he furnishes. He does not desire Olivia's person; *that* desire, even in a steward, would be sympathetically regarded, though not of course encouraged, by a Twelfth-Night mood. What he wants is "to be count Malvolio," with "a demure travel of regard – telling them I know my place, as I would they should do theirs" [2.5.48–9]. His secret wish is to violate decorum himself, then relish to the full its power over others. No wonder he has not a free disposition when he has such imaginations to keep under! When the sport betrays him into a revelation of them, part of the vengeance taken is to make him try to be festive, in yellow stockings, and crossgartered, and smiling "his face into more lines than is in the new map with the augmentation of the Indies" [3.2.67–8]. Maria's letter *tells* him to go brave, be gallant, take liberties! And when we see him "acting this in an obedient hope," [...] he is anything but free: "This does make some obstruction of the blood, this cross-gartering..." [3.4.19–20].

In his "impossible passages of grossness," he is the profane intruder trying to steal part of the initiates' feast by disguising himself as one of them – only to be caught and tormented for his profanation. As with Shylock, there is potential pathos in his bafflement, especially when Shakespeare uses to the limit the conjuring of devils out of a sane man, a device which he had employed hilariously in *The Comedy of Errors*. There is no way to settle just how much of Malvolio's pathos should be allowed to come through when he is down and out in the dark hole. Most people now agree that Charles Lamb's sympathy for the steward's enterprise and commiseration for his sorrows is a romantic and bourgeois distortion. But he is certainly pathetic, if one thinks about it, because he is so utterly cut off from everyone else by his anxious self-love. He lacks the freedom which makes Viola so perceptive, and is correspondingly oblivious:

> *Olivia.* What kind o' man is he?
> *Malvolio.* Why, of mankind.
> [1.5.133–4]

He is too busy carrying out his mistress' instructions about privacy to notice that she is bored with it, as later he is too busy doing her errand with the ring to notice that it is a love-token. He is imprisoned in his own virtues, so that there is sense as well as nonsense in the fool's "I say there is no darkness but ignorance, in which thou art more puzzled than the Egyptians in their fog" [4.2.37–9]. The dark house is, without any straining, a symbol: when Malvolio protests about Pythagoras, "I think nobly of the soul and no way approve his opinion," the clown's response is "Remain thou still in darkness." The pack of them are wanton and unreasonable in tormenting him; but his reasonableness will never let him out into "the air; ... the glorious sun" [4.3.1] which they enjoy together. To play the dark-house scene for pathos, instead of making fun out of the pathos, or at any rate out of most of the pathos, is to ignore the dry comic light which shows up Malvolio's virtuousness as a self-limiting automatism.

Malvolio has been called a satirical portrait of the Puritan spirit, and there is some truth in the notion. But he is not hostile to holiday because he is a Puritan; he is like a Puritan because he is hostile to holiday. Shakespeare even mocks, in passing, the thoughtless, fashionable antipathy to Puritans current among gallants. Sir Andrew responds to Maria's "sometimes he is a kind of Puritan," with "if I thought that, I'd beat him like a dog" [2.3.125–6]. "The devil a Puritan he is, or anything constantly," Maria observes candidly, "but a time-pleaser" [2.3.131–2]. Shakespeare's two greatest comic butts, Malvolio and Shylock, express basic human attitudes which were at work in the commercial revolution, the new values whose development R. H. Tawney described in *Religion and the Rise of Capitalism*. But both figures are conceived at a level of esthetic abstraction which makes it inappropriate to identify them with specific social groups in the mingled actualities of history: Shylock, embodying ruthless money power, is no more to be equated with actual bankers than Malvolio, who has something of the Puritan ethic, is to be thought of as a portrait of actual Puritans. Yet, seen in the perspective of literary and social history, there is a curious appropriateness in Malvolio's presence, as a kind of foreign body to be expelled by laughter, in Shakespeare's last free-and-easy festive comedy. He is a man of business, and, it is passingly suggested, a hard one; he is or would like to be a rising man, and to rise he *uses* sobriety and morality. One could moralize the spectacle by observing that, in the long run, in the 1640's, Malvolio *was* revenged on the whole pack of them.

But Shakespeare's comedy remains, long after 1640, to move audiences through release to clarification, making distinctions between false care and true freedom and realizing anew, for successive generations, powers in human nature and society which make good the risks of courtesy and liberty. And this without blinking the fact that "the rain it raineth every day." [...]

6.2 J. Pequigney, 'The Two Antonios and Same-Sex Love in Twelfth Night *and* The Merchant of Venice'

Source: *Shakespeare and Gender: A History*, ed. D. E. Barker and I. Kamps (London: Verso, 1992), Chapter 10, pp. 178–85.

Joseph Pequigney's article, 'The Two Antonios and Same-Sex Love in *Twelfth Night* and *The Merchant of Venice*', is a self-conscious intervention into the sexual politics of Shakespearean comedy. As his title indicates, Pequigney is interested in the evidence that *Twelfth Night* gives of homoeroticism. He finds this chiefly in the relationship between Sebastian and Antonio, but extrapolating from his close reading of the scenes between these characters, argues that homoerotic attraction is the psychologically latent subtext in the sexual attraction Olivia and Orsino feel for the cross-dressed Viola. Our extract concentrates on the reading of *Twelfth Night*, though it is worth noting that in his section on *The Merchant of Venice*, Pequigney argues that the relationship between Bassanio and Antonio is homosocial rather than homoerotic. Pequigney's work exemplifies a broader interest in Shakespeare studies since the 1980s in representations of sexuality, yet Pequigney goes further than most scholars (see, for example, Barber above) in viewing the Sebastian–Antonio relationship as a staging of a consummated homosexual affair.

I

The comic Antonios have more in common than a name. The earlier and more prominent one is the title character of *The Merchant of Venice*, written in 1596/97, whose friend is the suitor and winner of Portia, Bassanio. The other, created some five years later for *Twelfth Night*, is the sea captain whose companion is Viola's twin and Olivia's husband-to-be, Sebastian. Each Antonio loves his friend more than anyone or anything else, is emotionally dependent on him, proves willing to risk his very life on the friend's account, and provides him with funds, with painful consequences to himself. Neither shows romantic or other interest in a woman. The friends, however, do otherwise, both choosing wedlock and appearing with a wife or fiancée in, among other scenes, the last, where Antonio appears too, but ladyless. Of major concern here will be whether or not the striking resemblances between the Antonios include that of sexual orientation.

The Shakespeare professoriat has a long history of avoiding the topic of homosexuality, and the critics and scholars who have written on these comedies fall into three categories: those – the largest group – who have given this topic no thought; those who are doctrinaire in denying the topic pertinence; and those – a relatively small but recently growing number, many of them feminists – who ascribe homosexuality to both the Antonios. The second group always and the third ordinarily are assertive of positions that they think are self-evident and require – or admit of – no proof, so that disagreement rules in the commentary. Moreover, the critics who postulate homoerotic Antonios also maintain that the homoerotic impulses are suppressed; that the love returned by the other is non-erotic; and that the characters are finally ostracized and marginalized.

My argument will generate different answers to the above questions, and will find others germane, as how the stories of love between men are thematized in congruence [...] with the psychological/bisexual pattern that pervades *Twelfth Night*. Starting with Antonio the sea captain in *Twelfth Night* and Sebastian, I will proceed by examining: the discourse of Antonio; the treatment of the actions and characters of the two male intimates and the rendition of their shared history; scenes in which they do not appear but which serve to shed light on their behaviour; and a series of analogous love-experiences inscribed in the plot. My endeavour will be to *secure* the homoerotic character of the friendship by attempting to settle the question through textual analysis and argumentation, in the hope of removing it from current vagaries, distortions and prejudice. [...]

II

That the Antonio of *Twelfth Night* is passionately in love with his friend 'his words [that] do from such passion fly' will amply demonstrate. The openly amorous language habitual to him whenever he speaks to or about Sebastian – and rarely does his attention turn to anything else – is the foremost clue to the erotic nature of their friendship. In their first scene, when Sebastian initially proposes that they separate, Antonio says: 'If you will not murder me for my love, let me be your servant' [2.1.30–1], that is, accompany you as a 'servant', a word that can also mean 'lover'; and the love that ascribes the cruel power to slay to the beloved is romantic, smacking of Petrarchan love. Then in soliloquy at the end of the scene, despite his 'many enemies' in Illyria, Antonio resolves to go there in pursuit of Sebastian, for 'I do adore thee so,/ That danger shall seem sport, and I will go' [2.1.41–2]. Such 'adoration', especially as prompting the adorer to risk his all happily and carelessly only to be with the other, must stem from passion. Later catching up with Sebastian, Antonio explains: 'My desire, / More sharp than filed steel, did spur me forth' [3.3.4–5]. This impelling 'desire' is sensual: the very word would connote libido even apart from the intensifying metaphor of the flesh-cutting metal spur. Afterwards, under the mistaken impression that Sebastian has refused to return money given him, an offended and irate Antonio gives even fuller utterance to his idolization of the youth, with stress on his physical beauty: 'And to his image [that is, his external appearance], which methought did promise/Most venerable worth, did I devotion.' But the devotion was apparently misplaced: 'O how vile an idol proves this god', the youth deified and adored, who has 'done good feature [that is, his handsome looks] shame', for 'Virtue is beauty' and 'the beauteous evil' [that is, rascally beauties, such as this one] 'are empty trunks, o'er-flourish'd by the devil' [3.4.334–5]. Then in the last act Antonio tells of 'My love without retention or restraint', where 'without restraint' is particularly suggestive, and says: 'A witchcraft drew me hither' – that is, he was pulled into this city of enemies by erotic enchantment. The only real parallel in Shakespeare for such eroticized speech about a fair youth occurs in the sonnets.

Not his words only but also his correlated actions reflect Antonio's avid devotion to the master-mistress of *his* passion. So unacceptable is separation from Sebastian that despite the danger to himself in a hostile Illyria, Antonio follows him there and, finding him, leaves to make overnight accommodations. This second separation is followed by a second reunion at the end of the play. The companions had long since been inseparable, in fact ever since their first meeting: 'for three months ... No int'rim, not a minute's vacancy / Both day and night did [they] keep company' [5.1.90–9]. And Antonio will see to it that they 'keep company' this night also as he goes off to arrange for their dining and sleeping together at the Elephant, an inn. 'There,' he says, 'shall you have me' [3.3.42].

Before going he hands a purse to Sebastian, who asks 'Why I your purse?' He may chance upon 'some toy' he wishes to buy, Antonio replies, and 'your store [I think] is not for idle markets, sir' [3.3.44–6]. A kind and generous gesture, to be sure, but the intent behind it is less simple than the reply suggests. In the next adjacent scene, and some few lines later, Olivia, doting on Cesario, asks Maria: 'How shall I feast him? What bestow on him? / For *youth is bought more oft than begg'd or borrow'd*' [3.4.2–3]; emphasis added). This observation clearly has retrospective reference to the purse, indicating that it is given with the ulterior motive of pleasing, if not purchasing, the desired youth.

In [1.2] Viola appears for the only time dressed as a girl, and she, like her twin, is also with a sea captain. She plans to part from him too, and while she remarks his 'fair and outward character', and believes him to have a 'mind that suits' with it [1.2.46–7], their pending separation is depicted as casual and unemotional, over against the strong feelings the corresponding separation elicits in Sebastian [2.1.38–42] and *his* sea captain. These two, it is true, have been longer and closer together, but the calm parting of the unattached female and the appealing male, where attraction might have been more expected, is tellingly juxtaposed with the emotionally charged parting of the characters who are both male.

To turn now to Sebastian's part in their story: for months he has continuously remained with an adoring older man who is frankly desirous of him, who showered him with 'kindnesses' [3.4.316], and who, moreover, saved him from death at sea and nursed him back to health. It is the classic homoerotic relationship, wherein the mature lover serves as guide and mentor to the young beloved. Sebastian comes to depend on Antonio both emotionally and in practical matters: emotionally when he can scarcely hold back tears, the shedding of which he regards as effeminate ('the manners of my mother' [2.1.35]) at his proposed parting from Antonio; and practically in looking to him for advice when he is perplexed by Olivia's unaccountable conduct: 'Where's Antonio then? . . . His counsel now might do me golden service' [4.3.4–8].

For making the original decision to go off alone Sebastian gives the curious reason that he is afraid his own bad luck may rub off on his friend ('the malignancy of my fate might perhaps distemper yours' [2.1.4]). The motivation is flimsy – both dramatically (although dictated by the plot) and also in his mind – for he quickly relents when Antonio finds him and thereafter says nothing more about wanting to withdraw. Sebastian's change of heart is anticipated by the melancholy leave-taking, and is more in character than the initial decision, for everywhere else he shows himself obliging, compliant alike to the wishes of Olivia and of Antonio, as a boy who cannot say no.

When he is initially about to depart, Sebastian makes the curious admission that as a companion to Antonio he had always gone by another name, calling himself Roderigo. Why he should do so goes unexplained in both the comedy and the commentary. The alias may be demystified if it is seen as a means to hide his identity, his true name and family connections, during a drawn-out sexual liaison with a stranger in strange lands. When his twin Viola, in male disguise, correspondingly goes by an assumed name, Cesario, she gets caught up in novel, and homoerotic, sexual situations. Isn't this an intimation of something analogous happening – as it does – to Roderigo? Then, too, the given name Sebastian recalls the martyr traditionally pictured as a handsome youth – a kind of Christian Adonis – with a nearly nude body pierced by arrows. Our Sebastian is not a martyr, of course, although he once came close to death by drowning; yet like the saint, he is a young male beauty and, again like him, passive, the target of Olivia's as well as Antonio's desires.

And what will happen to the male friends after one of them is startlingly claimed by a lady for her husband? The virtually unanimous opinion of critics, in the words of one of them, is that 'Poor Antonio is left out in the cold.' Stephen Greenblatt's judgement rests on dubious textual grounds, and is connected with his sense of 'the disquieting intensity of Antonio's passion for Sebastian'. Disquieting to whom? Not to Sebastian or Antonio, nor to any other character, and not to the playwright when one looks closely at what he actually wrote. When, near the end of *Twelfth Night*, Sebastian makes his last entry, he speaks to his fiancée Olivia fondly ('sweet one') and apologetically (for hurting her kinsman), but he has far more ardent words for his comrade – whom he at first sought to quit, has since been frantically seeking, and now to his great relief finds: 'Antonio! O my dear Antonio, / How have the hours rack'd and tortur'd me, / Since I have lost thee!' [5.1. 210–12]. This, the most impassioned speech Sebastian delivers, is hardly the prelude to a rejection; and, further, with his late dramatic change of fortune, the sole reason he gives for the separation disappears. The expectation is set up that in taking a wife Sebastian will not and need not suffer the 'rack and torture' of losing his male lover. Not the rejected 'poor Antonio' of the commentary, he is instead the 'dear Antonio' here and hereafter of lucky Sebastian. Does this imply a *ménage à trois* at Olivia's house? That's anybody's guess, but a guess about nothing, for once they leave the stage the characters vanish into thin air.

From the data amassed above I gather that Sebastian has a personality endowed with a homoerotic component that has been awakened and activated under a peculiar and propitious set of circumstances. These include his continuous and clearly agreeable association, during a lengthy sojourn in the freedom of pseudonymity, with a saviour, benefactor, fervid admirer, and would-be lover. Inasmuch as he proves capable of erotically responding to man and woman, Sebastian would be bisexual, while Antonio, who is depicted with desire confined to a male object, would appear to be homosexual.

Sebastian's amorous involvement with members of both sexes falls into a broader configuration of the plot and derives substantiation from different dramatic situations. Bisexual experiences are not the exception but the rule in *Twelfth Night*, and they are vital to the course of love leading to wedlock for the three principal lovers other than Sebastian: Orsino, Olivia, and Viola.

Near the close of the play, Orsino asks Cesario for his/her hand. He proposes marriage to someone he knows and has come to love only as a male servant, seen only in masculine clothes, whose feminine name he never once utters, and whom in the scene he twice addresses as 'boy' [5.1.125,260] – even at the proposal itself – and refers to as late as his final speech as being still a 'man' [5.1.373]. Early on, despite the cross-dressing, he does perceive Viola's true gender, noting her girlish lip and voice and 'all' as 'semblative to a woman's part' [1.4.33]. The response, though, may do less to establish his heterosexual credentials than to symptomatize homoerotic proclivities, for according to Freud, 'what excited a man's love' in ancient Greece (and still may do so) 'was not the *masculine* character of a boy, but his physical resemblance to a woman as well as his feminine mental qualities', with the 'sexual object' being 'someone who combines the characters of both sexes' and 'a kind of reflection of the subject's own bisexual nature'. This theory seems clearly borne out by Orsino; and, further, his capacity to love the youth Cesario and the girl Viola is crucial to the happy ending for them both. His attraction to Olivia, where he is heterosexually straight, like the other would-be wooers Sir Andrew Aguecheek and Malvolio, is a disaster. The love for Cesario could not have changed instantaneously with the revelation of his female-ness; if it is erotic, then it would have been erotic before; what does change is that marriage suddenly becomes possible, hence the immediate proposal. This love that commences as homoerotic and conducts Orsino into nuptual heterosexuality is an unbroken curve, a bisexual continuity.

Olivia ends up engaged to marry a perfect stranger, Sebastian, and not the one she fell madly in love with and thought she had become betrothed to, who all along had been a male-impersonating girl. If she misses the telltale signs of femaleness that Orsino picks up on, that is because it is in her erotic interest to fantasize Cesario as virile, yet the feminine subtext, however ignored, remains legible. In Sebastian's last speech to her, coming just after the confusion of identity has been straightened out, he says, almost tauntingly,

> So comes it, lady, you have been mistook.
> But nature to her bias drew in that.
> You would have been contracted to a maid;
> Nor are you therein, by my life, deceiv'd:
> You are betroth'd both to a maid and man.
> [5.1.252–6]

She has been 'mistook' in two related senses: 'mistaken' in taking Cesario for a male, and 'taken amiss' in being captivated by a female [2.2.33]. But in 'that' matter of being 'mistook', nature 'drew' 'to her bias' or described a curved course (like the curve of a bowling ball that the noun denotes), and this homoerotic swerving or lesbian deviation from the heterosexual straight and narrow cannot be considered unnatural, since it is effected by nature herself. 'Would' in the third line above, indicative of a contrary-to-fact condition, may also connote 'would like [to]', a condition of wishing. That 'you are betroth'd both to a maid and man' is not a deception but precisely right: to 'both' twins, the maid who elicited your love and whom you thought you were contracting to marry, and the man who acciden-tally and unbeknownst to anyone substituted for her, and to whom you are in fact engaged. The line [5.1.256] may also bear this alternate reading: Sebastian could be referring only to himself, as a maiden man, a girl/boy, a master (to Olivia)-mistress (to Antonio).

223

Like Orsino, Olivia goes through a homoerotic phase that lasts through and beyond betrothal; both have experiences that evince their bisexuality. Nor do they ever pass beyond it, for it is the *sine qua non* of their psychological development – his away from a fruitless doting on her, hers away from fixation on a dead brother – and it has a crucial, integral, and unerasable part in both their love stories, that of Orsino with Cesario/ Viola and that of Olivia with Cesario/Sebastian.

Viola works a variation on this bisexual theme. In imitating her brother as his 'glass' [3.4.344–8], she combines both sexes: 'I am all the daughters of my father's house, / And all the brothers too' [1.4.119–20]. From the fourth scene on, however, she plays a brother rather than a daughter, being masculine in name, dress, behaviour, and the awareness of the other characters; not until the late recognition scene between the twins is she called Viola, and nobody else ever uses her real name. As Cesario she enters into a male friendship with Orsino, having man-to-'man' talks with him, mainly about women and love; and spon-taneously responding to the beauty of Olivia ('"Tis beauty truly blent' [1.5.209]), she throws herself headlong into the assignment of courting her. Partly because she is in love and knows how she would like to be wooed, she succeeds with the proud and disdainful lady, even reducing her to amorous desperation. She proves herself a better man at wooing than Orsino is, with his go-betweens, or than her brother, with the strain of passivity in his nature, could ever be. Sebastian could never have done what was necessary to win Olivia, and his only chance was for his sister to perform this masculine role for him. Her Cesario makes a lasting impression.

Sebastian turns out to be the most extreme exemplar of this recurring theme of bisexuality, for he is not only attracted to, but also able and willing sexually to enjoy, both a man and a woman – and in his case a man and a woman who are, and with obvious passion, enamoured of him. While he remains heterosexually virginal, he is unlike the virgins Viola and Olivia or Orsino in that he entertains homosexual impulses that are fully conscious and indulged. Antonio awakens those impulses, initiates him into interpersonal sexuality, and perhaps thereby prepares him to receive the sudden, surprising advances of the Illyrian lady. The reason for Antonio's portrayal as homosexual is that a liaison with him opens space for Sebastian in the diverse bisexual fictions that make up *Twelfth Night*.

These fictions have a dimension of metadrama, and nowhere else does Shakespeare more elaborately play with his theatre's convention of boys in the opposite-sex roles. In this comedy five actors play three male characters and two who are female, including the one disguised most of the time as male, that are love-related in the following pairs: a man (Orsino) and a pseudo-boy (Cesario); a cross-dressed (Viola) and another young woman (Olivia); male with female (both Sebastian with Olivia and Orsino with Viola); and two men (Sebastian and Antonio). The first two pairs are sexually ambiguous, the next two move towards heterosexual unions, and the last is homosexual. It is in this last relationship that the dramatic representation becomes most transparent to what was actually happening on the Elizabethan stage, since the lovers are both males, and so were the players who took the roles. [...]

7 *Measure for Measure*

7.1 F. R. Leavis, 'Measure for Measure'

Source: *The Common Pursuit* (London: Chatto and Windus, 1952), pp. 160–72.

One of the most influential literary critics of the twentieth century, F. R. Leavis through his editorship of the journal *Scrutiny* and numerous publications tirelessly promoted the critical analysis of Good Literature as an antidote to the encroachments of the machine age. He championed writers like John Donne, Henry James, and D. H. Lawrence, but paid only occasional attention to Shakespeare. His essay on *Measure for Measure*, however, is motivated by a characteristic desire to correct a failure of critical judgement, in this case L. C. Knights's dismissive commentary on the play. For Knights, *Measure for Measure* is flawed, too pessimistic, and poorly structured, and the character of Claudio in particular displays a self-loathing that is implausibly excessive. Leavis's response is of interest for several reasons. Firstly, as regards his critical method, he bases his contrary interpretation of the play principally on quotations from the text. Secondly, his polemical verve is much in evidence, as he accuses Knights, the author of 'How Many Children had Lady Macbeth?' (see Extract 3.1) of reverting to Bradley-style character criticism. Thirdly, in defending Shakespeare and *Measure for Measure*, his sympathies lie very much with the authority figures and the legal system, suggesting, for example, that 'if we don't see ourselves in Angelo, we have taken the play very imperfectly'.

Re-reading, both of L. C. Knights's essay and of *Measure for Measure*, has only heightened my first surprise that such an argument about what seems to me one of the very greatest of the plays, and most consummate and convincing of Shakespeare's achievements, should have come from the author of *How Many Children had Lady Macbeth?* For I cannot see that the 'discomfort' he sets out to explain is other in kind than that which, in the bad prepotent tradition, has placed *Measure for Measure* both among the 'unpleasant' ('cynical') plays and among the unconscionable compromises of the artist with the botcher, the tragic poet with the slick provider of bespoke comedy. In fact, Knights explicitly appeals to the 'admitted unsatisfactoriness' of *Measure for Measure*. The 'admitted unsatisfactoriness', I find myself with some embarrassment driven to point out [...] has to be explained in terms of that incapacity for dealing with poetic drama, that innocence about the nature of convention and the conventional possibilities of Shakespearean dramatic method and form, which we associate classically with the name of Bradley.

It is true that Knights doesn't make the usual attack on the character and proceedings of the Duke, and tell us how unadmirable he is, how indefensible, as man and ruler. Nor, in reading this critic, do we find cause for invoking the kind of inhibition that has certainly counted for a lot in establishing the 'accepted' attitude towards *Measure for Measure* – inhibition about sex: he doesn't himself actually call the play 'unpleasant' or 'cynical'. But that 'sense of uneasiness' which 'we are trying to track down' – what, when we have followed through his investigations, does it amount to? It focuses, he says, upon Claudio, or, rather, upon Claudio's offence:

> It is Claudio – who is scarcely a 'character' at all, and who stands between the two extremes – who seems to spring from feelings at war with themselves, and it is in considering the nature of his offence that one feels most perplexity.

I am moved to ask by the way what can be Knights's critical intention in judging Claudio to be 'scarcely a "character" at all'. I think it worth asking because (among other things) of his judgement elsewhere that Angelo is a 'sketch rather than a developed character-study'. True, he says this parenthetically, while remarking that Angelo is the 'admitted success of the play'; but it is an odd parenthesis to have come from the author of *How Many Children had Lady Macbeth?* It seems to me to have no point, though an unintentional significance.

But to come back to Claudio, whom Knights judges to be 'not consistently *created*': it is plain that the main critical intention would be rendered by shifting the italics to 'consistently' – he is not 'created' (*i.e.* 'scarcely a "character" ') and, what's more significant, not consistent. This inconsistency, this 'uncertainty of handling', we are invited to find localized in the half-dozen lines of Claudio's first address to Lucio – here Knights makes his most serious offer at grounding his argument in the text:

> From too much liberty, my Lucio, liberty:
> As surfeit is the father of much fast,

So every scope by the immoderate use
Turns to restraint. Our natures do pursue,
Like rats that ravin down their proper bane,
A thirsty evil, and when we drink we die.
[1.2.107–12]

What problem is presented by these lines? The only problem I can see is why anyone should make heavy weather of them. Knights finds it disconcerting that Claudio should express vehement self-condemnation and self-disgust. But Claudio has committed a serious offence, not only in the eyes of the law, but in his own eyes. No doubt he doesn't feel that the offence deserves death; nor does anyone in the play, except Angelo (it is characteristic of Isabella that she should be not quite certain about it). On the other hand, is it difficult to grant his acquiescence in the moral conventions that, barring Lucio and the professionals, everyone about him accepts? A Claudio who took an advanced twentieth-century line in these matters might have made a more interesting 'character'; but such an emancipated Claudio was no part of Shakespeare's conception of his theme. Nor, I think Knights will grant, are there any grounds for supposing that Shakespeare himself tended to feel that the prescription of premarital chastity might well be dispensed with.

No perplexity, then, should be caused by Claudio's taking conventional morality seriously; that he should do so is not in any way at odds with his being in love, or with the mutuality of the offence. And that he should be bitterly self-reproachful and self-condemnatory, and impute a heavier guilt to himself than anyone else (except Isabella and Angelo) imputes to him, is surely natural: he is not a libertine, true (though a pal of Lucio's); but, as he now sees the case, he has recklessly courted temptation, has succumbed to the uncontrollable appetite so engendered, and as a result brought death upon himself, and upon Juliet disgrace and misery. Every element of the figurative comparison will be found to be accounted for here, I think, and I can't see anything 'odd' or 'inappropriate' about the bitterness and disgust.

Further, Knights's own point should be done justice to: 'The emphasis has, too, an obvious dramatic function, for, by suggesting that the offence was indeed grave, it makes the penalty seem less fantastic; and in the theatre that is probably all one notices in the swift transition to more explicit exposition.' The complementary point I want to make is that nowhere else in the play is there anything to support Knights's diagnostic commentary. The 'uncertainty of attitude' in Shakespeare's handling of Claudio, an uncertainty manifested in a 'dislocation or confusion of feeling', depends on those six lines for its demonstration: it can't be plausibly illustrated from any other producible passage of the text. And I don't think anyone could have passed from those lines to the argument that adduces sonnet 129 and the passage from *Cymbeline*, and ends in references to *Hamlet* and *Troilus and Cressida*, who was not importing into *Measure for Measure* something that wasn't put there by Shakespeare. The importation seems to me essentially that which is provided by what I have called the bad prepotent tradition. Taking advantage of the distraction caused by the problems that propose themselves if one doesn't accept what *Measure for Measure* does offer, that tradition naturally tends to smuggle its irrelevancies into the vacancies one has created. It must be plain that the references to *Hamlet* and *Troilus and Cressida* implicitly endorse the accepted classing of *Measure for Measure* with the 'unpleasant', 'cynical' and 'pessimistic' 'problem' plays.

The strength of the *parti pris* becomes very strikingly apparent when we are told, of the Provost's sympathetic remark,

> Alas!
> He hath but as offended in a dream,
> [2.2.4]

that 'it seems to echo once more the sonnet on lust'. I am convinced it couldn't have seemed to do so to anyone who was not projecting on to the text what it gives him back. When the word 'dream', without any supporting context, can set up such repercussions, we have surely a clear case of possession by the idea or pre-determined bent. The intention of the Provost's remark is plain enough: he is merely saying that the offence (morals are morals, and we don't expect a Provost to say, or think, there has been *no* offence) can't be thought of as belonging to the world of real wrong-doing, where there is willed offending action that effects evil and is rightly held to accountability. The Provost, that is, voices a decent common-sense humanity.

Isabella takes a sterner moral line. But why this should give rise to perplexity or doubt about the attitude we ourselves are to take towards Claudio I can't see. Then I don't agree that she is not sufficiently 'placed'. Without necessarily judging that she is to be regarded with simple repulsion as an 'illustration of the frosty lack of sympathy of a self-regarding puritanism', we surely know that her attitude is not Shakespeare's, and is not meant to be ours. With the Duke it is different. His attitude, nothing could be plainer, *is* meant to be ours – his total attitude, which is the total attitude of the play. He, then, is something more complex than Isabella; but need it conduce to a 'sense of strain and mental discomfort' when, speaking as a Friar, he shows himself 'disposed to severity towards "the sin" of Claudio and Juliet'; or when, speaking both as a Friar and to Lucio, he says, 'It is too general a vice, and severity must cure it'? To impersonate a reverend friar, with the aim, essential to the plot, of being taken for a reverend friar, and talk otherwise about the given 'natural relation' – we might reasonably have found uncertainty of handling in that. As it is, the disguised Duke acts the part, so that the general confidence he wins, including Isabella's, is quite credible.

The criticism that the Duke's speech, 'Reason thus with life . . . ', 'ignores the reality of emotion' was anticipated (as Knights, by mentioning in the same footnote Claudio's 'retort to the equally "reasonable" Isabella', reminds us) by Shakespeare himself. The duly noted superiority of Claudio's speech on death to the Duke's (on which at the same time, I think, Knights is too hard) is significant, and it is, not insignificantly, in the same scene. A further implicit criticism is conveyed through Barnardine, who is not, for all the appreciative commentary of the best authorities, a mere pleasing piece of self-indulgence on Shakespeare's part: of all the attitudes concretely lived in the play, the indifference to death displayed by him comes nearest to that preached by the Friar. Those illusions and unrealities which he dismisses, and which for most of us make living undeniably positive and real, have no hold on Barnardine; for him life is indeed an after-dinner's sleep, and he, in the wisdom of drink and insensibility, has no fear at all of death. And towards him we are left in no doubt about the attitude we are to take: 'Unfit to live or die' [4.3.56], says the Duke, voicing the general contempt.

In fact, the whole context, the whole play, is an implicit criticism of that speech; the speech of which the *Arden* editor, identifying the Friar-Duke quite simply and directly with Shakespeare, says representatively, on the page now beneath my eye: 'There is a terrible and morbid pessimism in this powerful speech on "unhealthy-mindedness" that can have only escaped from a spirit in sore trouble.' Actually, no play in the whole canon is remoter from 'morbid pessimism' than *Measure for Measure*, or less properly to be associated in mood with *Hamlet* or *Troilus and Cressida*. For the attitude towards death (and life, of course) that the Friar recommends is rejected not merely by Claudio, but by its total context in the play, the varied positive aspects of which it brings out – its significance being that it does so. In particular this significance appears when we consider the speech in relation to the assortment of attitudes towards death that the play dramatizes. Barnardine is an unambiguous figure. Claudio shrinks from death because, once he sees a chance of escape, life, in spite of all the Friar may have said, asserts itself, with all the force of healthy natural impulse, as undeniably real and poignantly desirable; and also because of eschatological terrors, the significance of which is positive, since they are co-relatives of established positive attitudes (the suggestion of Dante has often been noted). Isabella can exhibit a contempt of death because of the exaltation of her faith. Angelo begs for death when he stands condemned, not merely in the eyes of others, but in his own eyes, by the criteria upon which his self-approval has been based; when, it may fairly be said, his image of himself shattered, he has already lost his life.

The death-penalty of the Romantic comedy convention that Shake-speare starts from he puts to profoundly serious use. It is a necessary instrument in the experimental demonstration upon Angelo:

> hence shall we see,
> If power change purpose, what our seemers be.
> [1.3.53–4]

The demonstration is of human nature, for Angelo is

> man, proud man,
> Drest in a little brief authority,
> Most ignorant of what he's most assured.
> His glassy essence . . .
> [2.2.120–3]

Of the nature of the issue we are reminded explicitly again and again:

> If he had been as you, and you as he,
> You would have slipped like him . . .
> [2.2.66–7]

> How would you be
> If He, which is the top of judgment, should
> But judge you as you are? O! think on that.
> [2.2.77–9]

> Go to your bosom;
> Knock there, and ask your heart what it doth know
> That's like my brother's fault; if it confess
> A natural guiltiness such as is his,
> Let it not sound a thought upon your tongue
> Against my brother's life.
> [2.2.139–44]

The generalized form in which the result of the experiment may be stated is, 'Judge not, that ye be not judged'. [. . .] But there is no need for us to create a perplexity for ourselves out of the further recognition that, even in the play of which this is the moral, Shakespeare conveys his belief that law, order, and formal justice are necessary. To talk in this connexion of the 'underlying dilemma' of the play is to suggest (in keeping with the general purpose of Knights's paper) that Shakespeare shows himself the victim of unresolved contradictions, of mental conflict or of uncertainty. But, surely, to believe that some organs and procedures of social discipline are essential to the maintenance of society needn't be incompatible with recognizing profound and salutary wisdom in 'Judge not, that ye be not judged', or with believing that it is our duty to keep ourselves alive to the human and personal actualities that underlie the 'impersonality' of justice. Complexity of attitude isn't necessarily conflict or contradiction; and, it may be added (perhaps the reminder will be found not unpardonable), some degree of complexity of attitude is involved in all social living. It is Shakespeare's great triumph in *Measure for Measure* to have achieved so inclusive and delicate a complexity, and to have shown us complexity distinguished from contradiction, conflict and uncertainty, with so sure and subtle a touch. The quality of the whole, in fact, answers to the promise of the poetic texture, to which Knights, in his preoccupation with a false trail, seems to me to have done so little justice.

To believe in the need for law and order is not to approve of any and every law; and about Shakespeare's attitude to the particular law in question there can be no doubt. We accept the law as a necessary datum, but that is not to say that we are required to accept it in any abeyance of our critical faculties. On the contrary it is an obvious challenge to judgement, and its necessity is a matter of the total challenge it subserves to our deepest sense of responsibility and our most comprehensive and delicate powers of discrimination. We have come now, of course, to the treatment of sex in *Measure for Measure*, and I find myself obliged to insist once more that complexity of attitude needn't be ambiguity, or subtlety uncertainty.

The attitude towards Claudio we have dealt with. Isabella presents a subtler case, but not, I think, one that ought to leave us in any doubt. 'What,' asks Knights, 'are we to think of Isabella? Is she the embodiment of a chaste serenity, or is she, like Angelo, an illustration of the frosty lack of sympathy of a self-regarding puritanism'? But why assume that it must be 'either or' – that she has to be merely the one or else merely the other? It is true that, as Knights remarks, *Measure for Measure* bears a relation to the Morality; but the Shakespearean use of convention permits far subtler attitudes and valuations than the Morality does. On the one hand, Isabella is clearly not a simple occasion for our feelings of critical superiority. The respect paid her on her entry by the lewd and irreverent Lucio is significant, and she convincingly establishes a presence qualified to command such respect. Her showing in the consummate interviews with Angelo must command a measure of sympathy in us. It is she who speaks the supreme enunciation of the key-theme:

> man, proud man,
> Drest in a little brief authority...

On the other hand, R. W. Chambers is certainly wrong in contending that we are to regard her with pure uncritical sympathy as representing an attitude endorsed by Shakespeare himself.

To begin with, we note that the momentary state of grace to which her influence lifts Lucio itself issues in what amounts to a criticism – a limiting and placing criticism:

> *Lucio*: I hold you as a thing ensky'd and sainted:
> By your renouncement an immortal spirit,
> And to be talked with in sincerity,
> As with a saint.
> *Isab*.: You do blaspheme the good in mocking me.
> *Lucio*: Do not believe it. Fewness and truth, 'tis thus:
> Your brother and his lover have embrac'd:
> As those that feed grow full, as blossoming time
> That from the seedness the bare fallow brings
> To teeming foison, even so her plenteous womb
> Expresseth his full tilth and husbandry.
> [1.4.33–43]

This is implicit criticism in the sense that the attitude it conveys, while endorsed dramatically by the exalted seriousness that is a tribute to Isabella, and poetically by the unmistakable power of the expression (it comes, we feel, from the centre), is something to which she, with her armoured virtue, can't attain. We note further that this advantage over her that Lucio has (for we feel it to be that, little as he has our sympathy in general) comes out again in its being he who has to incite Isabella to warmth and persistence in her intercession for Claudio. The effect of this is confirmed when, without demanding that Isabella should have yielded to Angelo's condition, we register her soliloquizing exit at the end of [Act 2, Scene 4] it is not credibly an accidental touch:

> Then, Isabel, live chaste, and, brother, die:
> More than our brother is our chastity.

The cumulative effect is such that it would need a stronger argument than R. W. Chambers's to convince us that there oughtn't to be an element of the critical in the way we take Isabella's parting discharge upon Claudio:

> *Isab*.:   Take my defiance:
> Die, perish! Might but my bending down
> Reprieve thee from thy fate, it should proceed,
> I'll pray a thousand prayers for thy death,
> No word to save thee.
> *Claud*.: Nay, hear me, Isabel.
> *Isab*.:   O! fie, fie, fie.
> Thy sin's not accidental, but a trade.
> Mercy to thee would prove itself a bawd:
> 'Tis best that thou diest quickly.
>   [Going.

Claud.:   O hear me, Isabella!
                              [3.1.144–53]

It is all in keeping that she should betray, in the exalted assertion of her chastity, a kind of sensuality of martyrdom:

> were I under the terms of death,
> The impression of keen whips I'd wear as rubies,
> And strip myself to death, as to a bed
> That longing have been sick for, ere I'd yield
> My body up to shame.
>   [2.4.100–4]

Finally, it is surely significant that the play should end upon a hint that she is to marry the Duke – a hint that, implying a high valuation along with a criticism, aptly clinches the general presentment of her.

But at this point I come sharply up against the casual and confident assumption that we must all agree in a judgement I find staggering: 'it is significant that the last two acts, showing obvious signs of haste, are little more than a drawing out and resolution of the plot.' The force of this judgement, as the last sentence of Knights's first paragraph confirms, is that the 'drawing out and resolution of the plot', being mere arbitrary theatre-craft done from the outside, in order to fit the disconcerting development of the poet's essential interests with a comedy ending that couldn't have been elicited out of their inner logic, are not, for interpretive criticism, significant at all. My own view is clean contrary: it is that the resolution of the plot of *Measure for Measure* is a consummately right and satisfying fulfilment of the essential design; marvellously adroit, with an adroitness that expresses, and derives from, the poet's sure human insight and his fineness of ethical and poetic sensibility.

But what one makes of the ending of the play depends on what one makes of the Duke; and I am embarrassed about proceeding, since the Duke has been very adequately dealt with by Wilson Knight, whose essay Knights refers to. The Duke, it is important to note, was invented by Shakespeare; in *Promos and Cassandra*, Shakespeare's source, there is no equivalent. He, his delegation of authority and his disguise (themselves familiar romantic conventions) are the means by which Shakespeare transforms a romantic comedy into a completely and profoundly serious 'criticism of life'. The more-than-Prospero of the play, it is the Duke who initiates and controls the experimental demonstration – the controlled experiment – that forms the action.

There are hints at the outset that he knows what the result will be; and it turns out that he had deputed his authority in full knowledge of Angelo's behaviour towards Mariana. [...] Subtly and flexibly as he functions, the

233

nature of the convention is, I can't help feeling, always sufficiently plain for the purposes of the moment. If he were felt as a mere character, an actor among the others, there would be some point in the kind of criticism that has been brought against him (not explicitly, I hasten to add, by Knights – though, in consistency, he seems to me committed to it). How uncondonably cruel, for example, to keep Isabella on the rack with the lie about her brother's death!

I am bound to say that the right way of taking this, and everything else that has pained and perplexed the specialists, seems to me to impose itself easily and naturally. The feeling about the Duke expressed later by Angelo –

> O my dread lord!
> I should be guiltier than my guiltiness,
> To think I can be undiscernible,
> When I perceive your grace, like power divine
> Hath look'd upon my passes,
> [5.1.358–62]

the sense of him as a kind of Providence directing the action from above, has been strongly established. The nature of the action as a controlled experiment with the Duke in charge of the controls, has asserted itself sufficiently. We know where we have to focus our critical attention and our moral sensibility: not, that is, upon the Duke, but upon the representatives of human nature that provide the subjects of the demonstration. This, we know, is to be carried to the promised upshot –

> hence shall we see,
> If power change purpose, what our seemers be,
> [1.3.53–4]

which will be, not only the exposure of Angelo, but his exposure in circumstances that develop and unfold publicly the maximum significance.

The reliance on our responding appropriately is the more patently justified and the less questionable (I confess, it seems to me irresistible) in that we can see the promise being so consummately kept. The 'resolution of the plot', ballet-like in its patterned formality and masterly in stage-craft, sets out with lucid pregnancy the full significance of the demonstration: 'man, proud man', is stripped publicly of all protective ignorance of 'his glassy essence'; the ironies of 'measure for measure' are clinched; in a supreme test upon Isabella, 'Judge not, that ye be not judged' gets an ironical enforcement; and the relative values are conclusively established – the various attitudes settle into their final placing with regard to one another and to the positives that have been concretely defined.

I don't propose to do a detailed analysis of this winding-up – that seems to me unnecessary; if you see the general nature of what is being done, the main points are obvious. I will only refer, in illustration of the economy of this masterpiece in which every touch has significance, to one point that I don't remember to have seen noted. There is (as every one knows) another invention of Shakespeare's besides the Duke – Mariana, and her treatment by Angelo. It wasn't [...] merely in order to save Isabella's chastity that Shakespeare brought in Mariana; as the winding-up scenes sufficiently insist, she plays an important part in the pattern of correspondences and responses by which, largely, the moral valuations are established. In these scenes, Angelo's treatment of her takes its place of critical correspondence in relation to Claudio's offence with Juliet; and Claudio's offence, which is capital, appears as hardly an offence at all, by any serious morality, in comparison with Angelo's piece of respectable prudence.

Finally, by way of illustrating how the moral aspect of the play is affected by an understanding of the form and convention, I must glance at that matter of Angelo's escape from death – and worse than escape ('...the pardon and marriage of Angelo not merely baffles the strong indignant claim of justice', etc.) – which has stuck in the throats of so many critics since Coleridge. One has, then, to point out as inoffensively as possible that the point of the play depends upon Angelo's not being a certified criminal-type, capable of a wickedness that marks him off from you and me. [...]

If we don't see ourselves in Angelo, we have taken the play very imperfectly. Authority, in spite of his protest, was forced upon him, and there are grounds for regarding him as the major victim of the experiment. He was placed in a position caculated to actualize his worst potentialities; and Shakespeare's moral certainly isn't that those potentialities are exceptional. It is not for nothing that Isabella reluctantly grants:

> I partly think
> A due sincerity govern'd his deeds
> Till he did look on me.
> [5.1.437–9]

If any further argument should seem necessary for holding it possible, without offending our finer susceptibilities, to let Angelo marry a good woman and be happy, it may be said in complete seriousness that he has, since his guilty self-committals, passed through virtual death; perhaps that may be allowed to make a difference. It is not merely that immediate death has appeared certain, but that his image of himself, his personality as he has lived it for himself as well as for the world, having been destroyed, he has embraced death:

> I am sorry that such sorrow I procure:
> And so deep sticks it in my penitent heart
> That I crave death more willingly than mercy:
> 'Tis my deserving, and I do entreat it.
> [5.1.468–71]

The bright idea of the recent 'Marlowe' production, the idea of injecting point, interest and modernity into the play by making him a study in neurotic abnormality, strained and twitching from his first appearance, was worse than uncalled-for. But then, if you can't accept what Shakespeare does provide, you have, in some way, to import your interest and significance.

7.2 *Leah Marcus, 'London in* Measure for Measure*'*

Source: *Puzzling Shakespeare: Local Reading and its Discontents* (Berkeley, CA: University of California Press, 1988), Chapter 4, pp. 171–82.

Written in the US in the 1980s, Leah Marcus's chapter shares with the new historicists a concern with locating Shakespeare's plays in their specific social contexts. In the extract reprinted here, Marcus explores in illuminating detail the overlap of political and religious legal systems framing the lives of the city's inhabitants, paying particular attention to how sexual relations and conduct were legislated. What this contextualization reveals is that Shakespeare's original audiences would have been divided along several lines with regard to the key conflicts in *Measure for Measure*. Where Leavis with his exclusive attention to the text of the play discovers a definitive moral and legal code, Marcus with her extensive extra-textual evidence argues that the text only partially resolves the contradictory legal *fiats* and ambiguous social *mores* of the wider society. Marcus's essay supplements those of Sinfield (Extract 3.2) and Davies (Extract 4.1) in that it provides illuminating information about the relation between Shakespeare's plays and Jacobean London, though here she offers relatively less direct discussion of the play itself.

[…] Much has been written about law in *Measure for Measure*. But law in the play is not one single thing, an absolute against which various forms of illicit "liberty" and transgression are played off. In terms of the play's meaning for London, we need to distinguish between different kinds of law: between "local" law, which is inscribed in specific places and bound within their limits, and "unlocalized" law, which operates, sometimes with apparent willfulness, across boundaries, outside the limits of place. London and its environs were a crazy quilt of different legal jurisdictions, some inextricable from topography, others more global, independent of topographical boundaries. The former would include city ordinances and customary laws. London's liberties and franchises were jealously guarded by her citizens and, in general, protected by English common law. But there was another system of law interlayered with the "local" law of the city and increasingly in competition with it during the early Jacobean period: that was the amorphous, pervasive, "unlocalized" jurisdiction associated with ecclesiastical law and the canons of the church, with royal prerogative (increasingly questioned by the advocates of common law, but buttressed by the civil law) and with the royal "dispensing power" to exempt individuals from the provisions of statute law. Common law and the liberties it guaranteed were specific to England, embedded in its particular "places" and history; civil and canon law were outgrowths of the Roman law, which was international, operating across boundaries between peoples and places.

The chief area of jurisdictional conflict in the "Vienna" of *Measure for Measure* is the matter of sexual incontinence – how it is to be defined and how it should be punished. The same matter was also a well-known battle ground between competing legal systems in the London of 1604. Twentieth-century interpreters have taken pains to establish whether, in terms of Renaissance perceptions, the play's various irregular unions would have been understood as fornication or as lawful marriage. But critical consensus on that thorny interpretive issue cannot possibly be reached if only because there *was* no single Renaissance understanding of what constituted valid marriage – at least not in England. Even in terms of the canon law, the line between illegal sexual incontinence and true marriage was very flexible in practice. The ecclesiastical courts did not always operate according to a clear-cut set of invariable principles out of medieval canonists or Justinian. And if their tolerance for exceptions was not complicated enough, there was also the problem that canon law itself had just altered. As a result of the Hampton Court Conference between James I, key bishops, and selected Puritan divines, a new canon revising the definition of lawful marriage took effect in 1604, the same year as *Measure for Measure*.

Moreover, canon law was by no means the only legal code by which contemporaries could measure the validity of marriages. What constituted "true" marriage was a more nebulous matter in the London of

1604 than it had been for decades because of new and competing initiatives on the part of Crown, church, Nonconformist divines, and agents of city government to impose consistency upon an area of human conduct which had traditionally been subject only to sporadic regulation. In *Measure for Measure*, as in London of 1604, the question of whose authority will dominate in an area of uncertainty and conflicting jurisdiction is a question which is at least as important – probably more important – than the actual punishments meted out for incontinence.

In late Elizabethan and early Jacobean England, marriage was a long, drawn-out process with a number of steps – from the first private promise of marriage *de futuro* between the two parties themselves, to a public contract and the establishment of a property settlement, to the actual church wedding (if that step was even taken at all), and, finally, to sexual consummation (if that step had not been taken already). Before the new 1604 canon took effect, the point in the process at which the couple could be said to be married was largely a matter of local custom, varying from one place to another. In some areas, particularly rural communities, sexual familiarity before the finalization of marriage was tolerated. Couples, in effect, married themselves through the mutual promise of marriage followed by copulation. If, as in the case of Claudio and Juliet in the play, they became parents before their union was publicly acknowledged, they might get hauled before the local "bawdy court" and required to do perfunctory penace before the congregation or, if they could afford it, charged a fine to commute the punishment.

If they were unlucky, however, such a couple might come to the attention of local justices of the peace, who also had jurisdiction according to a parliamentary statute of 18 Elizabeth over any case of sexual incontinence which produced a child as well as customary jurisdiction over various other sexual offenses. According to the canon law before 1604, clandestine marriage was legal but irregular; in common law, it had no legal status at all. Property settlements under the common law required proof of open, public marriage. By the provisions of the parliamentary statute, two justices of the peace acting together could determine the disposition of a bastardy case and impose "by their discretion" what seemed to them appropriate punishment of the guilty parties. It is easy to see that, given zealous officials, the statute could create a much more severe climate for sexual offenders than the church courts usually did. That, no doubt, was the intent behind the parliamentary initiative. In some areas, justices of the peace and constables actually conducted house-to-house midnight bed checks to scout out illicit sexuality. Offenders could be handed over for trial either to the ecclesiastical or to the secular courts. Some cases of sexual incontinence got bounced from the ecclesiastical to the common law courts and back again, as each legal system tried to assert its jurisdictional predominance over the other.

In addition to that possible double jeopardy, there were other quarters from which correction could come. Puritan ministers often took upon themselves the revelation and punishment of fornicators within their congregations. Their doing so was, strictly speaking, unlawful, since it preempted the jurisdiction of the ecclesiastical courts. But the divines who took such measures were usually markedly hostile toward the church courts to begin with, regarding the whole canon law system as a lamentable survival of pre-Reformation "papal filth" that made "but a jest" of vice. The public shaming Puritan divines imposed upon wayward members of the congregation might be similar to the sentence which would have been imposed by the church courts, but it would probably not involve the exacting of fines, it would be imposed in an atmosphere of greater severity toward individual transgression, and it would proceed from a competing source of spiritual jurisdiction.

Some Puritan divines were also prone (like Oliver Martext in *As You Like It*) to conduct what the official church condemned as invalid marriages outside the parish church and without banns or license. Again, part of the point of creating such unions was to circumvent the official system, which would have required "superstitious ceremonies" like the use of a wedding ring. London liberties with substantial Puritan congregations also tended to be havens for irregular marriage. The new ecclesiastical canons which took effect in 1604 were designed to stamp out such practices by specifying that marriage had to be performed by a duly licensed cleric in the parish church of one of the partners between the hours of eight in the morning and noon, after either the announcement of banns on three consecutive Sundays or festival days, or the procurement of a valid license from the bishop. Since the new regulations had been passed by convocation as early as 1584, people had had the time to become familiar with them. Even before they were formally adopted as ecclesiastical law, several ministers who had conducted irregular marriages had been censured by the church. With formal ratification, many more prosecutions were impending.

As it transpired, however, clandestine marriage between the parties themselves, without the use of a minister, remained a gray area of the ecclesiastical law. England did not go as far as Catholic Europe had after the Council of Trent, banning clandestine marriage entirely. But the continuing tolerance in practice was not specifically allowed by the canon. In 1604, with the new canons in place and new, stricter plans for forcing conformity upon resisting ministers, there was considerable uncertainty about whether clandestine marriages would have any continuing validity. Certainly they were now further from official acceptability in England than they had ever been before. The pattern of empire, by which "unlocalized" canon and civil law reached out to encompass and erase local difference, was brought closer than ever to realization in the area of marriage litigation through the canons of 1604.

In London, as we have noted, there was agitation in some reformist circles for the adoption of the Mosaic code as a basis for civil ordinance. That, if put into practice, would have brought London almost into line with the statutes of Shakespeare's "Vienna." Something very much like the Viennese ordinance was in fact put in place some forty years later, during the Interregnum. Under the Commonwealth government, a second offense of incontinence could be punished by death. In addition, church marriage was abolished and justices of the peace were empowered both to conduct marriages and to dissolve them. But such "root and branch" upheaval of the traditional system was only a theoretical model in the London of 1604. As it was, London's own customary penalties against sexual offenders – whipping, shaving the head, public carting, and jail – were far more draconian than the punishment prescribed in most other places and in the ecclesiastical courts. The City of London also claimed the "freedom" of overriding the ecclesiastical laws regulating sexuality with its own customary restraints. For example, London sometimes punished clerics for incontinence according to its own system of penalties, even though that function was in theory reserved to the ecclesiastical courts. As the crackdown against bawds and whores had made evident, reform was very much in the air in London, 1604. The city was taking on a reputation for exceptional vigor against vice. And this was happening at a time when the Crown and Anglican church were exerting their own competing effort to surmount the crazy quilt of local jurisdictions with one overarching standard governing marriage and sexuality.

If Shakespeare's "Vienna" is a jittery and confused place when it comes to questions of sexual morality, Shakespeare's London could be said to suffer from a similar insecurity. What constituted valid marriage was not some idle legal nicety: it was an issue people had to confront in the most personal terms possible unless they remained totally celibate. Amid the nervous welter of conflicting jurisdictions over the crime of sexual incontinence, contemporaries would have differed sharply in their assessment of the validity of *Measure for Measure's* clandestine marriages. Their opinions – if they were able to come to a clear-cut opinion at all – would vary according to their degree of familiarity with recent changes in secular and canon law, and according to their general ideological bent. At a time when the Anglican church itself had launched a new offensive against the problem of clandestine marriage, intolerance for the practice did not necessarily make one overbearingly "precise." Despite the range of different opinions, however, there was one area in which there would have been substantial unanimity in London, 1604. To anyone who lived from day to day amid the open jurisdictional skirmishes among competing authorities in London, the styles of legal authority played off against each other in Shakespeare's "Vienna" would have been immediately identifiable in terms of the local conflict.

Angelo, as chief governor of Vienna, is in effect the city's Lord Mayor, and as a London Lord Mayor would, he acts with the powers of a justice of the peace to defend and strengthen the city's local ordinances, in this case, the "biting" written statute that requires fornicators to be put to death. The duke initially claims that his own goal is also to restore the integrity of the statute – put teeth back into a local code which has fallen into disregard like "threatning twigs of birch" [1.3.24] long unused and therefore "More mock'd, then fear'd" [1.3.27]. But the duke's secret motive is instead to test Angelo – to probe into the workings of city government and the significance of his own delegation of authority by trying the virtue of a "precise" man whose whole demeanor and life seem dedicated to the rigor of law, specifically to civic government and to the common law. The duke praises Escalus for his knowledge of the *"Cities Institutions, and the Termes / For Common Iustice"* [1.1.10–11]. In contemporary parlance, the "Termes for Common Iustice" is a phrase specifically associating Escalus and city government with expertise in the common law. This is the realm of legal discourse within which Angelo, too, will function.

In *Measure for Measure*, Angelo and Escalus follow the basic pattern of London civic authorities or justices of the peace, conducting open, informal interrogations and, in accordance with the parliamentary statute of 18 Elizabeth but unlike any of Shakespeare's sources and analogues, working together as a pair to inquire into cases of sexual incontinence and bastardy. The obscure offense committed in Pompey's unsavory "house" against Elbow's pregnant wife at least potentially falls within the statute, since she is with child by someone, but the exact nature of the allegation Elbow wishes to make is hopelessly lost in tangles of lexical confusion. He, a constable and therefore an agent of city law and order, is an "elbow" indeed, incessantly turning the law and language back upon themselves until all possibility for stable meaning is lost. The fact that such an engine for the decomposition of system can hold public office bodes ill for public order in "Vienna." Angelo to some extent abrogates his role as a justice in dealing with Elbow's case, at least by the standard of the English parliamentary statute, in that he eventually loses patience with the constable's obscurities and leaves Escalus to deal with the matter alone. Usually he is more punctilious. In the bastardy case of Juliet and Claudio, the two justices also confer together to determine appropriate punishment and this time Angelo is the more persistent of the two in following through on the case and applying the full rigor of the law. His insistence on the exact letter of the statute makes him close kin to actual London reformers who grounded their campaigns against vice similarly in the powers of surveillance mandated by the *"Cities Institutions"* and "the Termes for Common Iustice."

Angelo, of course, proves corrupt in office, counterfeit "mettle" rather than true coin. For London theater audiences, part of the game of topicality in "Vienna" would have been the titillating pleasure of measuring the hypocrisy of Angelo against their own civic authorities. One obvious candidate for resemblance would have been Chief Justice Popham, probably the most prominent common law justice of the time, who had spearheaded the initiative against brothels about London and was called "bloody Popham" by his enemies. He was known to be so "precise" in his personal habits that he kept the Sabbath Day meticulously even when he was riding circuit for the provincial assizes. He was also widely suspected of hypocrisy. Another prime candidate might have been Sir Edward Coke, who was already known for his defense of the common law and city "liberties" and for his interest in reviving the rigor of old statutes, but who had recently entered into a scandalously irregular marriage himself despite his ostensible veneration of the law. As usual, the game of topical identification was juicy and potentially endless: other ripe candidates were available from among the ranks of pompous London authorities – aldermen, recent Lord Mayors, sheriffs, and zealous justices of the peace. The city's crackdown on vice was bound to create friction and resistance, even perhaps among those who advocated London "liberties" in theory. Other plays of the period make similar capital out of the unveiling of the secret vices of staid, bourgeois officialdom.

But the figure of the duke was just as vulnerable to the game of topical identification. His various personal likenesses to King James I do not require recapitulation here – they are obvious enough to have struck editors and readers of *Measure for Measure* since at least the eighteenth century. As we will note later on, there are several other contemporary figures whom Shakespeare's duke of Vienna could also be said to resemble. What could perhaps bear more attention at this point, however, is the remarkably Jacobean *style* of the duke's activities in the play in terms of the contemporary conflicts over law. He, like the new king of England, begins by asserting his reverence for local customs and ordinances: they are, he claims, *his* laws, "our Decrees" [1.3.27], and he commits himself to giving them more authority. As it transpires, however, the duke is not at all interested in restoring the rigor of the statute against fornication. Instead, he acts in various ways to mitigate it with flexible principles drawn from the civil law and equity. Like James I in London, he acts indirectly and through intermediaries to assert his own ultimate jurisdiction over the city's customary privilege of policing its territory within the walls.

At the end of the play, despite all the initial talk about the rigid enforcement of law, the Viennese statute punishing fornication with death is forgotten. It disappears almost unnoticed amid the splendid theatrics of the public trial before the city gates. Nobody has been executed for fornication, and no one seems likely to be. In the last act, the duke himself in effect becomes the law, the *lex loquens* or speaking law, as the Roman civil code and the speeches of James I would have it, an

independent source of legal authority which transcends the city's ordinance, coming down like universal "power divine" to reveal the defects in
a fallible local human system. The pattern was already familiar in the
London of 1604; it was to become more familiar with James's continuing
intervention in the city's affairs. In *Measure for Measure* local authority is
overriden by royal prerogative, by the principles of Roman civil law,
which fostered the idea of the monarch as the embodiment of a general,
mysterious, ultimate legal authority.

Throughout the play, the duke's style of intervention is associated, not
with the common law, but with ecclesiastical jurisdiction in a markedly
conservative form. He is garbed as a friar for most of the action, serving as
a confessor and spiritual adviser to those in need of his ministrations. He
appears and vanishes with mercurial suddenness, operating in hidden
ways outside local boundaries and limits. In several instances, his methods correlate with procedure under the Roman law. As was the practice in
the canon law courts (in marked contrast to the common law), he gathers
testimony by interrogating witnesses in private and in advance of the
trial. Given the secret way in which the relevant testimony was obtained,
at ecclesiastical trials the truth often emerged with sudden and undeniable éclat once all the evidence was revealed. Much the same effect is
achieved in the duke's public exposure of Angelo. The trial scene, with its
crowd of unruly onlookers, its attendant "clerics," and its emphasis on
shaming and public reputation, has some of the quality of a trial in the
contemporary bawdy courts, with their odd mix of the awesome and the
carnivalesque.

In the end, when the duke throws off his ecclesiastical garb to act in his
own person to confer validity on the play's irregular sexual unions, he is
assuming a prerogative like that which James I and the Anglican church
had asserted in 1604 as they tightened up the canon law governing valid
marriage by insisting upon the proper license. Within the Vienna of the
play, there are "outlaw" areas like Angelo's private garden "circum-
mur'd with Bricke" and outlying areas like Mariana's lonely grange
which appear analogous to the London suburbs, removed from the regular jurisdiction of the city. The duke's activities penetrate these places
apart, redress the anomalous situations which have been tolerated there,
and bring them under his authority, much as James I and the church were
moving in to bring the London liberties under royal and ecclesiastical
control. When the duke commands that Angelo and Mariana be immediately married, he is claiming ultimate authority over the system of ecclesiastical licensing. Ordinarily, by the 1604 canon, Angelo and Mariana
would require a license from the bishop in order to be married
"instantly," without the publication of banns. In this case, the license
emanates not from a bishop but from the ultimate ecclesiastical power
above the bishop, the *lex loquens* of the ruler.

There are also resemblances between the duke's style of justice and the English Court of Chancery. Traditionally, the chancellors of England had been clerics and the duke's disguise recalls that connection. Chancery was the final court of appeal in ecclesiastical cases involving matters of property (which often hinged upon the validity of marriage); it frequently reversed the severity of the lower common law courts, just as the duke alleviates the severity of the statute. According to one contemporary description, the chancellor "doth so *cancell* and *shut up* the *rigour* of the general *Law*, that it shall not break forth to the hurt of some one singular Case and person." By abrogating a local statute in favor of "mercy" and equity, the duke acts, in effect, as his own Lord Chancellor, overriding local justices in the name of the Roman code and the royal dispensing power. The jurisdictional morass has been cleared away; pockets of secret license have been opened up to surveillance; and the duke has publicly established for himself and for the civil and canon law the ultimate right to adjudicate "Mortallitie and Mercie in *Vienna*."

In twentieth-century editions and productions of *Measure for Measure*, the trial scene usually takes place inside the city. The First Folio itself offers no such certainty as to place. As the scene begins, the duke is approaching the city gates: "Twice haue the Trumpetes sounded. The generous, and grauest Citizens / Haue hent the gates, and very neere vpon / The Duke is entring" [4.6.13–16]. The folio stage directions which follow specify only that the "Duke, Varrius, Lords, Angelo, Esculus, Lucio" and "Citizens" enter "at seuerall doores" [5.1]. In some of the earliest editions of the play specifying the locus of the public trial which follows, the scene of the trial is described as "a public Place near the City." That added stage direction is interesting because it suggests that early editors of the play thought of Shakespeare's "Vienna" in terms of a topography very like London's: the City proper is a self-contained, walled unit surrounded by other urban areas, like the London liberties, which are not strictly part of it. What the scene enacts is the traditional public ritual by which civic authorities greet a visiting monarch. They meet the ruler with fanfare just outside the walls – the entry "at seuerall doores" suggesting that the different groups have come from different directions – to formally tender up their authority and accompany him through the gates.

In this case, however, the entry is delayed as a result of the duke's proclamation inviting petitioners to approach him publicly for the redress of grievances. The pleas of Isabella and Mariana turn the usual scene of ceremonial transfer of authority into a forum for inquiring into the conduct of the deputy. The duke establishes his superior claim to govern the city from a location just outside the wall, outside its proper jurisdiction; then, much as James I had entered London in triumph in the year 1604, he enters the gates and proceeds in state to his "Pallace,"

Measure for Measure

formally taking possession of the place he has demonstrated a transcendent right to control. That which is merely local has been made to appear small, paltry and corruptible, by comparison with an authority which partakes of the divine and the universal, which cuts through jurisdictional tangles to establish a single, centralized, yet merciful standard of law.

It is easy to see how James I would have relished the play's depiction of victory for the Roman law with which he felt such sympathy and which, in 1604, he still hoped to use as the basis of a united Britain. There are many ways in which the play seems weighted toward the "Jacobean line." The city's own authorities are an unimpressive lot: even Escalus is too shortsighted to suspect the vice of Angelo. Unless Claudio is played as an unusually repellant character, he tends to generate audience sympathy, at least by comparison with Angelo, just as his plight generates sympathy from onlookers within the play. Insofar as an audience takes the part of Claudio against Angelo and the rigor of the statute, they are being invited to side with the duke against the city – recognize the wisdom of the ruler's timely use of equity to redress a reforming zeal which has gone too far.

There were contemporaries who would have agreed with Angelo that death was not an excessive penalty for fornication, but they were the same zealots who were most vehement against the theater. They would not (it seems safe to say) have been part of the audience for *Measure for Measure*. To the extent that London theatrical audiences resented the reformers' endless campaigns against the public "enormity" of stage plays, they may have found it easy to applaud the duke's exposure of a civic leader who was overly precise. The place of the duke's highly theatrical trial just outside the jurisdiction of the city was, in London, the place of the stage itself. There is a natural topographical alliance between the theatricality of the duke and the institution which brought him to life on stage on the outskirts of London.

But for at least some members of a London audience in 1604, the play's victory over statute may have looked more like defeat. Whether or not the duke's influence is perceived as salutary depends to a marked degree on the audience's evaluation of the duke himself. For good or for ill, his *modus operandi* in the play is made to appear arbitrary, manipulative, imposed from without. In modern performances, he is often idealized as the wise exemplar of overarching authority called for by the play's "Jacobean line," a figure whose arbitrary gestures are justified as desperate counters to the rampant crimes of his surrogate. Almost as frequently in modern productions, however, the duke comes closer to Lucio's description of the "fantastical Duke of darke corners" [4.3.147] or Angelo's equally disparaging language: "In most vneuen and distracted manner, his actions show much like to madnesse, pray heauen his

245

wisedome bee not tainted" [4.4.2–4]. In modern productions, the duke can be a *deus ex machina* who descends by means of a whirligig, a shadowy trickster who delights in imposing unnecessary gyrations of misery upon his subjects merely to show his power. Like Jupiter in *Cymbeline*, he exists on a perilous boundary between the sublime and the grotesque.

In London, 1604, there may have been nearly as much potential for variability in the portrayal of the duke as there is in modern performance. Because of the heated conflicts over jurisdictional issues in the city, even relatively small alterations in the nervous balance between the duke and his antagonists could markedly have altered the political complexion of the play. Let us take one "localized" example of the problematics that contemporary performance could – perhaps fleetingly – have exploited. If a London audience saw a parallel between the duke of Vienna and James I as the promulgator of the new ecclesiastical laws regarding marriage, they could easily have been puzzled by his uncanonical behavior earlier in the play. The "bed trick" by which Mariana is substituted for Isabella to satisfy Angelo's lust was *not* lawful according to the church's new definition of marriage. The precipitous wedding ordered by the duke between Mariana and Angelo was also uncanonical unless, by some chance, they happened to be married in the parish church of one of them, or unless the duke's verbal "license" is taken to cancel out the usual rules. These are small details, perhaps: topicality thrives on what is almost too insignificant to notice. But they suggest that the duke, insofar as he is identified with James I, can be trusted to respect his beloved canon law no more than Angelo does the statute. That perception unleashes a potential for contemporary deconstruction of *Measure for Measure's* Jacobean line. Like King James, the duke acts above the law, freely overriding even his own preferred code when it suits his purpose to do so. Contemporary viewers could surmount the seeming contradiction in the duke's position by making a "leap of faith" from the law to Christian mercy, by which all legal codes are confounded. As we will note further later on, *Measure for Measure*, like *King Lear*, is associated with St. Stephen's Day, at least through its performance at court, and therefore with the holiday inversion of law and ordinary hierarchy. But to regard the duke as transcending all law would undermine the play's appeal to the ruler as an alternative and superior source of law. In *Measure for Measure*, the rule of law is overthrown by something that may be divine transcendence, but can also look like royal whim, unruly "license," a mere recapitulation of the abuse it purports to rectify. [...]

8 King Lear

8.1 Arnold Kettle, 'From Hamlet to Lear'

Source: Arnold Kettle, *Literature and Liberation: Selected Essays*, ed. G. Martin and W. R. Owens (Manchester: Manchester University Press, 1988), pp. 70–8.

This essay first appeared in the 1970s, and reacted against the dominant formalist criticism of the likes of Leavis and Knights. For Kettle, like his contemporary Raymond Williams, no literary text could be abstracted from its historical context, and he accordingly sought to explain *King Lear* in relation to the transition from feudalism to capitalism, which English Marxist historians argued was underway at the moment of the play's original production. His commitment to a Marxist historical method was aligned with a robust humanism, as he argued that 'the heroes of Renaissance drama are the men and women whose lives and struggles express the actual attempts of people at that time to extend the frontiers of human possibility'. He sums up *King Lear* as a conflict between 'those who accept the old order (Lear, Gloucester, Kent, Albany) which has to be seen as the feudal order', and 'the new people, the individualists (Goneril, Regan, Edmund, Cornwall) who have the characteristic outlook of the bourgeoisie'. In the balance of the essay, he presents evidence in support of this reading by close attention to the text of the play. Although at the time Kettle's approach to Shakespeare was shared by few, it has had a lasting influence, as a new generation of critics, including the likes of Montrose, Sinfield and Marcus, have continued to give primary attention to historical contextualization, and indeed to Marxist theory.

[...] Lear's story begins where most stories end. The old man seems to be at the finish of his reign and time. But in fact his journey has not yet begun. The opening scene is a statement – the statement of where we and Lear start from – and Shakespeare has neither the time nor the concern to make it naturalistically convincing in its every detail. Lear is there, every inch a king, disposing of his kingdom. Essentially one has to see him as a feudal king, but in saying this I refer less to the social and economic relations of feudalism than to its characteristic ideology. The point, and also its significance, becomes clear, when we remember that within Lear's kingdom there are, inside the ruling class, two tendencies or camps, which are not simply or primarily a matter of conflicting generations or social status. On the one hand are those who accept the old order (Lear, Gloucester, Kent, Albany) which has to be seen as, broadly speaking, the feudal order; on the other hand are the new people, the individualists (Goneril, Regan, Edmund, Cornwall) who have the characteristic outlook of the bourgeoisie.

These correspondences are underlined – as Professor Danby has very suggestively pointed out by the differing ways in which the people of the two camps use the word Nature, a key-word which crops up nearly fifty times in the course of the play. To Lear and those associated with him Nature is essentially a benignant traditional order, like the 'Natural Law' of the Middle Ages, in which human and divine society are at one. In Lear's language the 'offices of nature' are always linked with such concepts as

> bond of childhood,
> Effects of courtesy, dues of gratitude.
> [2.4.172–3]
> [Line references are to the conflated text
> of *King Lear* in *The Norton Shakespeare*]

Goneril and Regan become, to him, 'unnatural hags', and Gloucester, from his side, talks of 'the King falling from the bias of Nature, there's father against child'.

Such uses of the word are in direct contrast to Edmund's forthright

> Thou, Nature, art my Goddess; to thy law
> My services are bound. Wherefore should I
> Stand in the plague of custom...?
> [1.2.1–3]

Here Nature is seen as the opposite of custom, tradition, hierarchy, established order. And Professor Danby shrewdly points out that Edmund's use of Nature is precisely the use which, within half a century, the most remarkable and most consistently materialist of the early bourgeois philosophers, Thomas Hobbes, was to give the word. Hobbes, as is well known, saw the state of Nature as a state of war. Man was to him not *naturally* a social animal but had to be made one. The author of the *Leviathan* would not, of course, have approved of Edmund's worship of the Natural man; but he would have understood it and, in a wry way, appreciated its 'realism'.

In *King Lear* Shakespeare reveals, from the very start, a society in turmoil in which (in contrast to *Hamlet*) it is the representatives of the old order who feel that everything is out of joint:

> ...love cools, friendship falls off, brothers divide; in cities, mutinies; in countries discord; in palaces, treason; and the bond crack'd 'twixt son and father....We have seen the best of our time: machinations, hollowness, treachery, and all ruinous disorders, follow us disquietly to our graves.
> [1.2.99–106]

It is Gloucester speaking and the particular speech is not a deep one (Gloucester himself being a conventional and – as he comes appallingly to realise – blind old man); but it is, from his point of view and, indeed, objectively, a quite true description of the state of affairs in Lear's kingdom. [...]

Gloucester, in the speech I have just quoted, superstitiously links the social crack-up with the eclipse of the sun and moon. It is all, he insists, thoroughly unnatural. And he wanders off, scratching his head, leaving his bastard son Edmund to pour scorn in a brilliant soliloquy on his superstitious unscientific outlook: 'An admirable evasion of whoremaster man, to lay his goatish disposition on the charge of a star.' Edmund has none of his father's amiable, conservative illusions. He is intelligent, active and ruthless. His immediate personal motive is simple – 'Legitimate Edgar, I must have your land.' No beating about the bush. Edmund is emancipated. The ancient sanctities of law (he is in every sense illegitimate) and order (kingship, the property rights of fathers, primogeniture, the identity of the man-made hierarchy with a God-made one), these mean nothing to him. He is the new man of the incipient bourgeois revolution, the private enterprise man, the man who thinks he has got to be a phoenix, the individualist go-getter, the machiavel, Marlowe's aspiring hero taken to his extreme conclusion: man with the lid off.

Edgar of course is Edmund's opposite. The brothers are contrasted at every point, and it is not the crude static moral contrast of the good and the bad, even though something of this – the structure of the old Morality plays – remains in *Lear*. Edgar is the loyal son of the feudal father, pious, resourceful, kind, and above all legitimate, and when in the last act he steps forward at the third trump to defend the right, he carries on his shoulders all the glamour and the chivalry of a formalised feudal past.

Edgar defeats Edmund. Gloucester, though hideously punished for his moral laxity and political blindness, is avenged, even redeemed, gaining in his suffering, through his contact with Poor Tom, an insight which, seeing, he had lacked. His profoundest moment is when he gives Tom his purse:

> Here, take this purse, thou whom the heavens' plagues
> Have humbled to all strokes: that I am wretched
> Makes thee the happier: Heavens, deal so still!
> Let the superfluous and lust-dieted man,
> That slaves your ordinance, that will not see
> Because he does not feel, feel your power quickly;
> So distribution should undo excess,
> And each man have enough.
>
> [4.1.64–71]

It is a wonderful moment, the full significance of which lies in its echoing of some of Lear's own words which I will refer to in a moment. The power

Gloucester has not seen because he has not felt it can only, in the context, be that of common humanity, embodied in Poor Tom. Yet in the Gloucester story, even though Tom does save Gloucester and help him onwards, this outburst, moving as it is, is not really developed. It is not developed because the relation between Tom and Edgar remains ill-defined or, rather, too well-defined. Edgar simply pretends to be Tom and then becomes Edgar again. Tom is a richer character than Edgar because he includes Edgar, whereas Edgar doesn't include Tom. Edgar is not really changed by being Tom, though the play is, through the experiences of Lear and Gloucester. But the Edgar of the last act is essentially St George, the feudal hero, and he has to be, for he will become king. Only in the four final lines of the play does a doubt creep in and we are allowed to wonder whether Edgar perhaps remembers Tom.

The Lear story is deeper, more complex and more variously moving than the Gloucester story, for Lear, unlike Gloucester, is a hero.

At the beginning of the play he is not a hero at all, but a king to whom the forms of kingship and hierarchy are the basis and reality of the world. It is Cordelia who, at this stage of the story, is the heroic one, for it is she who speaks the words of aspiring humanity. When she has to define her feelings about her father she can only say

> I love your Majesty
> According to my bond; no more nor less.
> [1.1.91–2]

The words bear close scrutiny. Obviously they are not the words of a twentieth-century daughter, royal or common. Their form is essentially feudal, as the word 'bond' emphasises. Yet it becomes clear that by 'according to my bond' Cordelia is not thinking in formal feudal terms but defining as realistically and truthfully as she can a human relationship between two people, of whom one happens to be her father and a king and therefore has special claims on her. [...] Such heresy, the expression of a relationship honourable and *natural* in senses which neither party in the *Lear* world can accept, leads the child to the stake as it leads Cordelia to the gallows. And it is interesting that, near the end of the play, in a beautiful scene which shows us a Lear and a Cordelia who have come through to 'a better way', the old man uses the very Blakean image

> We two alone will sing like birds i' th' cage.
> [5.3.9]

It is also interesting that Cordelia's phrase 'no more nor less' is echoed by Lear when, the great rage dead, he comes to describe himself in the terms of his new understanding:

I am a very foolish fond old man,
Fourscore and upward, not an hour more or less;
And, to deal plainly,
I fear I am not in my perfect mind.

[4.7.61–4]

He is now, like Cordelia, dealing plainly, describing the situation realistically. He has reached the view of Nature implicit in her first statement.
I can find no better way of describing it than as the humanist view of
nature. And in the course of discovering it Lear has become a hero. His
story, put in its simplest terms, is the story of his progress from being a
king to being a man, neither more nor less. It is a story so fearful and yet
so wonderful that all human society is shaken by the terrible beauty of it
and at its supreme moments man and the universe are seen in relationships which it is scarcely possible for words other than Shakespeare's
own to describe.

When I say that *Lear* is the story of how a king becomes a man I do not
mean at all that it is an allegory or that we should use a word like
'symbolic' to describe it. For Shakespeare does not work in abstractions.
He is a supremely realistic writer who presents us all the time with actual
situations, actual relationships, and what general conclusions he offers
are always based on particular observations and insights. He is not, of
course, a *naturalistic* dramatist, attempting a 'slice of life' kind of realism,
and he uses every resource of his teeming imagination to create means of
penetrating, through words and fantasy, to the inner processes of the
situations and people he presents. The storm in *Lear* 'works' artistically
on a number of levels: the elemental storm, the social storm which shakes
the divided kingdom, the inner storm that drives Lear mad, all are inter-
connected and reinforce one another to achieve what is, I suppose, the
most extraordinary and harrowing representation of crisis in the whole of
art. But every device of art is used to produce, not some effect above or
beyond reality, but the deepest, most complex exploration of the actual
nature of reality, its texture and its implications, its movement and its
interconnectedness.

In the first three acts of *Lear* we have almost unrelieved horror and
pessimism, broken only by isolated gleams of human decency and
hope. It is one of Shakespeare's triumphs that, without compromising
for a moment on their hideousness, he does not make the opponents
of Lear crude villains. Edmund, with his gusto and energy, is in
many respects a more vital creature than the rather colourless Edgar.
Goneril and Regan have a terrible common-sense effectiveness, almost
a normality, about them. Their very baiting of their father by the reduction of the numbers of his retainers is not mere insolence: they have a
strong case and argue at least partly in the terms of a modern-sounding

contempt for the hierarchical principle. They are at once shrewd, able, shallow and morally impervious, and they are rivals because they are alike.

It is the new people with their heartless rationalisation – 'the younger rises, when the old doth fall' – who bring down Lear. And his friends, the ineffectual unseeing Gloucester and the loyal but too simple Kent, are unable to save him from the new ruthlessness. Kent's role in the play is interesting because he is of all the 'feudal' characters the most courageous and least corrupt. And he is able to shield Lear to some extent. But his ultimate failure to cope with the situation – he is unable to hold Lear within the bounds of sanity and is in fact of far less use to him than either the Fool or Poor Tom – is echoed by his own prognostications of his death in the final scene. The ultimate inadequacy of Kent despite his decent, old world virtues, is one of the expressions in the play of the impossibility of a return of the feudal past.

What we have, then, in the first three acts of *Lear* is a world in which the old order is decadent and the new people unprincipled and both, as the treatment of Cordelia shows, inhuman. Horror dominates. The terrible curse on Goneril – made by Lear in the name of Nature –

> Into her womb convey sterility!
> Dry up in her the organs of increase,
> And from her derogate body never spring
> A babe to honour her! If she must teem,
> Create her child of spleen, that it may live
> And be a thwart disnatur'd torment to her.
> [1.4.255–60]

– this curse, whose imagery overflows into the verse of scene after scene, is a measure of the depth of the horror; but not its ultimate expression. For the equal horror is Lear's own impotence. When Goneril rejects him he still can threaten vainly to 'resume the shape' of the past – to be king again. When Regan's cruelty is added to her sister's, and personal ingratitude is, so to speak, turned into a system, he is literally unable to express his emotion, though he still mutters of revenge.

> No, you unnatural hags,
> I will have such revenges on you both
> That all the world shall – I will do such things
> What they are, yet I know not, but they shall be
> The terrors of the earth.
> [2.4.273–7]

Lear has, literally, no resources of action, language or even emotion to be able to cope, within the bounds of the consciousness he has so far achieved, with the situation which faces him. From here to madness is but a short step. And the very word madness needs our thought. It can no more be taken for granted in *Lear* than in *Hamlet*. The more one examines the play the more one comes to feel that Lear's madness is not so much a breakdown as a breakthrough. It is necessary.

In the storm scene comes the first hint of resolution, the first turning-point of the play, the first breakthrough of humanity, coincident with the words 'My wits begin to turn'. For the phrase is followed by some words to the Fool:

> Come on, my boy. How dost, my boy? Art cold?
> I am cold myself. Where is this straw, my fellow?
> The art of our necessities is strange,
> That can make vile things precious. Come, your hovel.
> Poor fool and knave, I have one part in my heart
> That's sorry yet for thee.
>
> [3.2.66–71]

The words represent a change in direction: away from self-pity, pride, revenge and kingliness, towards fellow-feeling and co-operation, the minimum qualities of humanity. I do not want to present Shakespeare as some kind of 'unconscious' precursor of Engels; but I think it is very interesting that at this crisis of the play, when Lear is first beginning to feel his way towards a new freedom, Shakespeare should use the word 'necessities' and use it in a context which forbids any but a materialist significance.

It is through his madness – his incapacity to deal with reality any longer within the framework of his accepted standards of sanity – that Lear comes to a new outlook on life. The moving prayer just before his meeting with Tom is now fairly generally recognised as a crux of the whole play.

> Poor naked wretches, wheresoe'er you are,
> That bide the pelting of this pitiless storm,
> How shall your houseless heads and unfed sides,
> Your loop'd and window'd raggedness, defend you
> From seasons such as these? O! I have ta'en
> Too little care of this. Take physic, Pomp;
> Expose thyself to feel what wretches feel,
> That thou mayst shake the superflux to them,
> And show the Heavens more just.
>
> [3.4.29–37]

This speech, echoed so soon by Gloucester's words to Tom, in which precisely the same ideas are expressed and the word 'superflux' returned to, is absolutely central to the structure and meaning of the play. Lear's incapacity to deal with the inhumanity of the new people is what drives him into a solidarity, and, later, an identification, with the poor. For in his powerlessness he is forced to recognise the pervasive helplessness of the poor in the face of the power of the rich, those who have property. Thus his direct personal contact with ruling-class inhumanity leads him to question the validity of property itself and the authority and exemption from elementary human moral values it confers. In this, Lear's development is not at all unlike that of later seventeenth-century radicals like Winstanley.

[. . .] Edgar, listening to Lear's mad wanderings, remarks to the audience 'Reason in madness!' The speech he is referring to contains some of the deepest and acutest social criticism in all Shakespeare, or indeed anywhere.

> . . . A man may see how this world goes with no eyes. Look with thine ears: see how yond justice rails upon yond simple thief. Hark, in thine ear: change places and, handy-dandy, which is the justice, which is the thief? Thou hast seen a farmer's dog bark at a beggar?
>
> *Gloucester.* Ay, sir.
>
> *Lear.* And the creature run from the cur? There thou mightest behold the
> great image of authority: a dog's obey'd in office.
> Thou rascal beadle, hold thy bloody hand!
> Why dost thou lash that whore? Strip thy own back;
> Thou hotly lusts to use her in that kind
> For which thou whip'st her. The usurer hangs the cozener.
> Through tatter'd clothes small vices do appear;
> Robes and furr'd gowns hide all. Plate sin with gold,
> And the strong lance of justice hurtless breaks;
> Arm it in rags, a pigmy's straw does pierce it.
> None does offend, none, I say none; I'll able 'em:
> Take that of me, my friend, who have the power
> To seal th' accuser's lips. Get thee glass eyes,
> And, like a scurvy politician, seem
> To see the things thou dost not. Now, now, now, now!
> Pull off my boots; harder, harder; so.
>
> [4.6.146–67]

When that speech has the currency of Polonius's advice to Laertes it will seem less strange to British readers to refer to the democratic content of the bourgeois–democratic revolution and to link Shakespeare's greatness with his humanism.

If we describe Lear's, or Gloucester's, experiences as 'spiritual', that is to say, involving a change not just in fortune and circumstance but in values and quality of being, it is essential to recognise that Shakespeare links this change at every step with actual actions and social attitudes. The social emphases are not more or less casual sidethoughts but are absolutely basic to the whole conception of the play. You cannot understand it without them. The new humanity which Lear achieves is not simply a self-knowledge acquired by introspection or any kind of mystical or religious experience; it is an outlook gained through experience and action, through the necessity that has been forced upon him of exposing himself to feel that wretches feel, of facing reality in all its horror and splendour, of judging men and women by their simplest, most essential actions, and of learning who his friends are. The experience results in a turning upside-down, handy-dandy, of accepted social assumptions. The pulling off the boots at the end of the speech I have just quoted is, everyone realises, significant. Already in the hovel in the storm Lear has insistently taken off his clothes, feeling them an impediment, a mark of rank, preventing complete identification with Poor Tom. 'Off, off you lendings' he cries. The phrase is almost a summary of the play. Lear, the king, reduced by the new people of the bourgeois world to the depth of human humiliation, falls only to rise, and becomes a man. And the people who help him to achieve humanity are by no means the wise or great or powerful, but a Fool and a beggar who has gone mad. [...]

8.2 Coppélia Kahn, 'The Absent Mother in King Lear'

Source: Margaret W. Ferguson et al. (eds), *Rewriting the Renaissance: The Discourses of Sexual Difference in Early Modern Europe* (Chicago and London: Chicago University Press, 1986), Chapter 2, pp. 35–45.

Published in the United States in 1986, Coppélia Kahn's essay relies heavily upon feminist re-readings of psychoanalytic theory undertaken by Nancy Chodorow in order to explore the gender dynamics in *King Lear*. Focusing on the structure of the patriarchal family, Kahn follows Chodorow in the view that 'the mother's role rather than the father's role is the important one, as crucial to the child's individuation as to the child's sense of gender'. Locating this understanding of gender and identity formation in the context of Shakespeare's England, Kahn quotes historian Lawrence Stone's now highly contested view that between 1580 and 1640 the paternal power within the family was intensified by the political consolidation of the Tudor state and the religious shift to Puritanism. For Kahn, the contradictory consequences of this historical shift are negotiated in dramatic form in *King Lear*. After examining the pattern of bad fathers and absent mothers in the play, Kahn notes that in the conflicts between Lear and his daughters, and Gloucester and his sons, 'generational conflicts entwine with and intensify gender conflicts'. The tragic conclusion of the play attests to Shakespeare's inability to 're-imagine a world in which masculine authority *can* find mothers in its daughters'. While recent critics have been more cautious than Kahn in universalizing psychoanalytic categories, and applying them to literary texts from very different historical contexts, her reading of *King Lear* remains a powerful interpretation of the conflicts within the play.

[...] Because the family is both the first scene of individual development and the primary agent of socialization, it functions as a link between psychic and social structures and as the crucible in which gender identity is formed. From being mothered and fathered, we learn to be ourselves as men and women. The anthropologist Gayle Rubin describes psychoanalysis as "a theory of sexuality in human society...a description of the mechanisms by which the sexes are divided and deformed, or how bisexual androgynous infants are transformed into boys and girls...a feminist theory manqué." A great Shakespearean critic, C. L. Barber, calls psychoanalysis "a sociology of love and worship within the family." Freud, of course, viewed this family drama from the standpoint of a son; he conceived the development of gender as governed primarily by relationship with the father. Because Freud grounds sexual differentiation in the cultural primacy of the phallus, within the context of a family structure that mirrors the psychological organization of patriarchal society, he enables us to deconstruct the modes of feeling, the institutions, and the social codes in which much if not most of English literature is embedded.

But to use one of Freud's favorite metaphors, to excavate patriarchal sensibility in literature, we must sift through more than one layer. In the history of psychoanalysis, the discovery of the Oedipus complex precedes the discovery of pre-oedipal experience, reversing the sequence of development in the individual. Similarly, patriarchal structures loom obviously on the surface of many texts, structures of authority, control, force, logic, linearity, misogyny, male superiority. But beneath them, as in a palimpsest, we can find what I call "the maternal subtext," the imprint of mothering on the male psyche, the psychological presence of the mother whether or not mothers are literally represented as characters. In this reading of *King Lear*, I try, like an archaeologist, to uncover the hidden mother in the hero's inner world.

Now, it is interesting that there is no literal mother in *King Lear*. The earlier anonymous play that is one of Shakespeare's main sources opens with a speech by the hero lamenting the death of his "dearest Queen." But Shakespeare, who follows the play closely in many respects, refers only once in passing to this queen. In the crucial cataclysmic first scene of his play, from which all its later action evolves, we are shown only fathers and their godlike capacity to make or mar their children. Through this conspicuous omission the play articulates a patriarchal conception of the family in which children owe their existence to their fathers alone; the mother's role in procreation is eclipsed by the father's, which is used to affirm male prerogative and male power. The aristocratic patriarchal families headed by Gloucester and Lear have, actually and effectively, no mothers. The only source of love, power, and authority is the father – an awesome, demanding presence.

But what the play depicts, of course, is the failure of that presence: the failure of a father's power to command love in a patriarchal world and the emotional penalty he pays for wielding power. Lear's very insistence on paternal power, in fact, belies its shakiness; similarly, the absence of the mother points to her hidden presence, as the lines with which I began might indicate. When Lear begins to feel the loss of Cordelia, to be wounded by her sisters, and to recognize his own vulnerability, he calls his state of mind *hysteria*, "the mother," which I interpret as his repressed identification with the mother. Women and the needs and traits associated with them are supposed to stay in their element, as Lear says, "below" – denigrated, silenced, denied. In this patriarchal world, masculine identity depends on repressing the vulnerability, dependency, and capacity for feeling which are called "feminine."

Recent historical studies of the Elizabethan family, its social structure and emotional dynamics, when considered in the light of psychoanalytic theory, provide a backdrop against which Lear's family drama takes on new meaning as a tragedy of masculinity. Recently, several authors have analyzed mothering – the traditional division of roles within the family that makes the woman primarily responsible for rearing as well as bearing the children – as a social institution sustained by patriarchy, which in turn reinforces it. Notably, Nancy Chodorow offers an incisive critique of the psychoanalytic conception of how the early mother-child relationship shapes the child's sense of maleness or femaleness. She argues that the basic masculine sense of self is formed through a denial of the male's initial connection with femininity, a denial that taints the male's attitudes toward women and impairs his capacity for affiliation in general. My interpretation of *Lear* comes out of the feminist re-examination of the mothering role now being carried on in many fields, but it is particularly indebted to Nancy Chodorow's analysis.

According to her account, women as mothers produce daughters with mothering capacities and the desire to mother, which itself grows out of the mother-daughter relationship. They also produce sons whose nurturant capacities and needs are curtailed in order to prepare them to be fathers. A focus on the primacy of the mother's role in ego-formation is not in itself new. It follows upon the attempts of theorists such as Melanie Klein, Michael and Alice Balint, John Bowlby, and Margaret Mahler to cast light on that dim psychic region which Freud likened to the Minoan civilization preceding the Greek, "grey with age, and shadowy and almost impossible to revivify." Chodorow's account of the mother-child relationship, however, challenges the mainstream of psychoanalytic assumptions concerning the role of gender and family in the formation of the child's ego and sexual identity.

Because I find family relationships and gender identity central to Shakespeare's imagination, the most valuable aspect of Chodorow's work for me is its comparative perspective on the development of gender in the sexes. For both, the mother's rather than the father's role is the important one, as crucial to the child's individuation (development of a sense of self) as to the child's sense of gender. It is only for the purpose of analysis, however, that the two facets of identity can be separated. Both sexes begin to develop a sense of self in relation to a mother-woman. But a girl's sense of femaleness arises *through* her infantile union with the mother and later identification with her, while a boy's sense of maleness arises *in opposition* to those primitive forms of oneness. According to Robert Stoller, whose work supports Chodorow's argument, "Developing indissoluble links with mother's femaleness and femininity in the normal mother-infant symbiosis can only augment a girl's identity," while for a boy, "the whole process of becoming masculine . . . is endangered by the primary, profound, primal oneness with mother." A girl's gender identity is reinforced but a boy's is threatened by union and identification with the same powerful female being. Thus, as Chodorow argues, the masculine personality tends to be formed through denial of connection with femininity; certain activities must be defined as masculine and superior to the maternal world of childhood, and women's activities must, correspondingly, be denigrated. The process of differentiation is inscribed in patriarchal ideology, which polarizes male and female social roles and behavior.

The imprint of mothering on the male psyche, the psychological presence of the mother in men whether or not mothers are represented in the texts they write or in which they appear as characters, can be found throughout the literary canon. But it is Shakespeare who renders the dilemmas of manhood most compellingly and with the greatest insight, partly because he wrote at a certain historical moment. As part of a wide-ranging argument for the role of the nuclear family in shaping what he calls "affective individualism," Lawrence Stone holds that the family of Shakespeare's day saw a striking increase in the father's power over his wife and children. Stone's ambitious thesis has been strenuously criticized, but his description of the Elizabethan family itself, if not his notion of its place in the development of affective individualism, holds true.

Stone sums up the mode of the father's dominance thus:

This sixteenth-century aristocratic family was patrilinear, primogenitural, and patriarchal: patrilinear in that it was the male line whose ancestry was traced so diligently by the genealogists and heralds, and in almost all cases via the male line that titles were inherited; primogenitural in that most of the property went to the eldest son, the younger brothers being dispatched into the world with little more than a modest annuity or life interest in a small estate to keep them afloat; and patriarchal in that the husband and father lorded it over his wife and children with the quasi-absolute authority of a despot.

Patriarchy, articulated through the family, was considered the natural order of things. But like other kinds of "natural order," it was subject to historical change. According to Stone, between 1580 and 1640 two forces, one political and one religious, converged to heighten paternal power in the family. As the Tudor-Stuart state consolidated, it tried to undercut ancient baronial loyalty to the family line in order to replace it with loyalty to the crown. As part of the same campaign, the state also encouraged obedience to the *paterfamilias* in the home, according to the traditional analogy between state and family, king and father. James I stated, "Kings are compared to fathers in families: for a king is truly *parens patriae*, the politic father of his people." The state thus had a direct interest in reinforcing patriarchy in the home.

Concurrently, Puritan fundamentalism – the literal interpretation of Mosaic law in its original patriarchal context – reinforced patriarchal elements in Christian doctrine and practice as well. As the head of the household, the father took over many of the priest's functions, leading his extended family of dependents in daily prayers, questioning them as to the state of their souls, giving or withholding his blessing on their undertakings. Although Protestant divines argued for the spiritual equality of women, deplored the double standard, and exalted the married state for both sexes, at the same time they zealously advocated the subjection of wives to their husbands on the scriptural grounds that the husband "beareth the image of God." Heaven and home were both patriarchal. The Homily on the State of Matrimony, one of the sermons issued by the crown to be read in church weekly, quotes and explicates the Pauline admonition, "Let women be subject to their husbands, as to the Lord; for the husband is the head of the woman, as Christ is the head of the church." In effect, a woman's subjection to her husband's will was the measure of his patriarchal authority and thus of his manliness.

The division of parental roles in childrearing made children similarly subject to the father's will. In his study of Puritan attitudes toward authority and feeling, David Leverenz finds an emphasis on the mother's role as tender nurturer of young children, as against the father's role as disciplinarian and spiritual guide for older children. Mothers are encouraged to love their children openly in their early years but enjoined to withdraw their affections "at just about the time the father's instructional role becomes primary." Thus the breaking of the will is accomplished by the father, rather than by both parents equally. This division of duties, Leverenz holds, fostered a pervasive polarity, involving "associations of feared aspects of oneself with weakness and women, emphasis on male restraint and the male mind's governance of female emotions, the separation of 'head' from 'body', . . . a language of male anxiety, rather than of female deficiency."

A close look at the first scene in *King Lear* reveals much about lordliness and the male anxiety accompanying it. The court is gathered to watch Lear divide his kingdom and divest himself of its rule, but those purposes are actually only accessory to another that touches him more nearly: giving away his youngest daughter in marriage. While France and Burgundy wait in the wings, Cordelia, for whose hand they compete, also competes for the dowry without which she cannot marry. As Lynda Boose shows, this opening scene is a variant of the wedding ceremony, which dramatizes the bond between father and daughter even as it marks the severance of that bond. There is no part in the ritual for the bride's mother; rather, the bride's father hands her directly to her husband. Thus the ritual articulates the father's dominance both as procreator and as authority figure, to the eclipse of the mother in either capacity. At the same time, the father symbolically certifies the daughter's virginity. Thus the ceremony alludes to the incest taboo and raises a question about Lear's "darker purpose" in giving Cordelia away.

In view of the ways that Lear tries to manipulate this ritual so as to keep his hold on Cordelia at the same time that he is ostensibly giving her away, we might suppose that the emotional crisis precipitating the tragic action is Lear's frustrated incestuous desire for his daughter. For in the course of winning her dowry, Cordelia is supposed to show that she loves her father not only more than her sisters do but, as she rightly sees, more than she loves her future husband; similarly, when Lear disowns and disinherits Cordelia, he thinks he has rendered her, dowered only with his curse, unfit to marry – and thus unable to leave paternal protection. In contrast, however, I want to argue that the socially-ordained, developmentally appropriate surrender of Cordelia as daughter-wife – the renunciation of her as incestuous object – awakens a deeper emotional need in Lear: the need for Cordelia as daughter-mother.

The play's beginning, as I have said, is marked by the omnipotent presence of the father and the absence of the mother. Yet in Lear's scheme for parceling out his kingdom, we can discern a child's image of being mothered. He wants two mutually exclusive things at once: to have absolute control over those closest to him and to be absolutely dependent on them. We can recognize in this stance the outlines of a child's pre-oedipal experience of himself and his mother as an undifferentiated dual unity, in which the child perceives his mother not as a separate person but as an agency of himself, who provides for his needs. She and her breast are a part of him, at his command. In Freud's unforgettable phrase, he is "his majesty, the baby."

As man, father, and ruler, Lear has habitually suppressed any needs for love, which in his patriarchal world would normally be satisfied by a mother or mothering woman. With age and loss of vigor, and as Freud suggests in "The Theme of the Three Caskets," with the prospect of return to mother earth, Lear feels those needs again and hints at them in his desire to "crawl" like a baby "toward death." Significantly, he confesses them in these phrases the moment after he curses Cordelia for her silence, the moment in which he denies them most strongly. He says, "I lov'd her most, and thought to set my rest / On her kind nursery" [1.1.123–4].

When his other two daughters prove to be bad mothers and don't satisfy his needs for "nursery," Lear is seized by "the mother" – a searing sense of loss at the deprivation of the mother's presence. It assaults him in various ways – in the desire to weep, to mourn the enormous loss, and the equally strong desire to hold back the tears and, instead, accuse, arraign, convict, punish, and humiliate those who have made him realize his vulnerability and dependency. Thus the mother, revealed in Lear's response to his daughters' brutality toward him, makes her re-entry into the patriarchal world from which she had seemingly been excluded. The repressed mother returns specifically in Lear's wrathful projections onto the world about him of a symbiotic relationship with his daughters that recapitulates his pre-oedipal relationship with the mother. In a striking series of images in which parent-child, father-daughter, and husband-wife relationships are reversed and confounded, Lear re-enacts a childlike rage against the absent or rejecting mother as figured in his daughters.

Here I want to interject a speculation inspired by Stone's discussion of the custom of farming children out to wet nurses from birth until they were twelve to eighteen months old; at that time they were restored to the arms of their natural mother, who was by then a stranger to them. Many if not most people in the gentry or aristocracy of Shakespeare's day must have suffered the severe trauma of maternal deprivation brought on by the departure of the wet nurse. We know the effects of such a trauma from the writings of John Bowlby: a tendency to make excessive demands on others, anxiety and anger when these demands are not met, and a blocked capacity for intimacy. Lear responds to the loss of Cordelia, the "nurse" he rejects after she seems to reject him, by demanding hospitality for his hundred knights, by raging at Goneril and Regan when they refuse him courtesy and sympathy, and by rejecting human society when he stalks off to the heath. After the division of the kingdom, he re-enters the play in the fourth scene with this revealing peremptory demand: "Let me not stay a jot for dinner; go, get it ready" [1.4.8]: he wants food, from a maternal woman. I believe that Lear's madness is essentially his rage at being deprived of the maternal presence. It is tantalizing, although I can imagine no way of proving it, to view this rage as part of the social pathology of wet-nursing in the ruling classes.

The play is full of oral rage: it abounds in fantasies of biting and devouring, and more specifically, fantasies of parents eating children and children eating parents. The idea is first brought up by Lear when he denies his "propinquity and property of blood" with Cordelia; that is, he denies that he begot her, that he is her father, as he also denies paternity of Regan and Goneril later. He assures her,

> The barbarous Scythian,
> Or he that makes his generation messes
> To gorge his appetite, shall to my bosom
> Be as well neighbour'd, pitied, and reliev'd,
> As thou my sometime daughter.
> [1.1.116–20]

The savagery of the image is shocking; it indicates Lear's first step toward the primitive, infantile modes of thinking to which he surrenders in his madness. When Cordelia doesn't feed him with love, he thinks angrily of eating *her*. Lear again voices this complex conjunction of ideas about maternal nurture, maternal aggression, and aggression against the mother when he looks at Edgar's mutilated body, bleeding from its many wounds, and remarks,

> Is it fashion, that discarded fathers
> Should have thus little mercy on their flesh?
> Judicious punishment! 'twas this flesh begot
> Those pelican daughters.
> [3.4.69–73]

Lear seems to think that Edgar first transgressed against his father by "discarding" him as Regan and Goneril discarded Lear, and that Edgar's father then got back at his child, his "flesh," *in* the flesh, as Lear would like to do. But this fantasy of revenge calls forth an answering fantasy of punishment against his own flesh – a punishment he deserves for begetting children in the first place. The image of the pelican may have been suggested to Shakespeare by this passage in a contemporary text, which I will quote because it elucidates both the reciprocating spiral of aggression and revenge and the close identification between parent and child, which possesses Lear's mind:

> The Pellican loueth too much her children. For when the children be haught, and begin to waxe hoare, they smite the father and mother in the face, wherefore the mother smiteth them againe and slaieth them. And the thirde daye the mother smiteth her selfe in her side that the bloud runneth out, and sheddeth that hot bloud upon the bodies of her children. And by virtue of the bloud the birdes that were before dead, quicken againe.

The children strike their parents, the mother retaliates, then wounds herself that the children may nurse on her blood. "Is't not," Lear asks, "as this mouth should tear this hand / For lifting food to 't?" [3.4.16–17] referring to "filial ingratitude." His daughters are the mouths he fed, which now tear their father's generous hand; but at the same time, he is the needy mouth that would turn against those daughters for refusing to feed him on demand. Lear's rage at not being fed by the daughters whom, pelican-like, he has nurtured, fills the play. It is mirrored in Albany's vision of all humanity preying upon itself, like monsters of the deep [4.2.47–51], a vision inspired by the reality of Goneril turning her father out in the storm and shortly confirmed by the more gruesome reality of Regan and Cornwall tearing out another father's eyes.

Bound up with this mixture of love and hate, nurture and aggression, is Lear's deep sense of identification with his daughters as born of his flesh. When Goneril bids him return to Regan's house rather than disrupt her own, his first thought is absolute separation from her, like his banishment of Cordelia: "We'll no more meet, no more see one another." But immediately he remembers the filial bond, for him a carnal as much as a moral bond:

> But yet thou art my flesh, my blood, my daughter;
> Or rather a disease that's in my flesh,
> Which I must needs call mine: thou art a boil,
> A plague-sore, or embossed carbuncle,
> In my corrupted blood.
>   [2.4.216–20]

Gloucester echoes the same thought when he says wryly to Lear on the heath, "Our flesh and blood, my lord, is grown so vile, / That it doth hate what gets it" [3.4.133–4].

Children are products of an act that, in Elizabethan lore, was regarded as the mingling of bloods. In the metaphor of Genesis, repeated in the Anglican wedding service, man and wife become "one flesh." With regard to mother and child, however, the fleshly bond is not metaphorical but literal. Lear (like Gloucester) ignores the mother-child fleshly bond and insists that his children are, simply, *his* "flesh and blood." In the pelican image, he assimilates maternal functions to himself, as though Goneril and Regan hadn't been born of woman. Like Prospero, he alludes only once to his wife, and then in the context of adultery. When Regan says she is glad to see her father, he replies

> if thou shouldst not be glad
> I would divorce me from thy mother's tomb,
> Sepulchring an adultress.
>
> [2.4.123–4]

These lines imply, first, that Lear alone as progenitor endowed Regan with her moral nature, and second, that if that nature isn't good, she had some other father. In either case, her mother's only contribution was in the choice of a sexual partner. Thus Lear makes use of patriarchal ideology to serve his defensive needs: he denies his debt to a mother by denying that his daughters have any debt to her, either.

Lear's agonizing consciousness that he did indeed produce such monstrous children, however, persists despite this denial and leads him to project his loathing toward the procreative act onto his daughters, in a searing indictment of women's sexuality:

> The fitchew nor the soiled horse goes to 't
> With a more riotous appetite.
> Down from the waist they are centaurs,
> Though women all above:
> But to the girdle do the Gods inherit
> Beneath is all the fiend's: there's hell, there's darkness,
> There is the sulphurous pit – burning, scalding,
> Stench, consumption; fie, fie, fie! pah, pah!
>
> [4.6.119–26]

Even if he did beget these daughters, Lear implies, he's not answerable for their unkindness, because they are, after all, women – and women are tainted, rather than empowered as men are, by their sexual capacities. Thus he presses into service another aspect of patriarchal ideology, its misogyny, to separate himself from any feminine presence.

To return for a moment to the social dimensions of Lear's inner turmoil, it is important here that generational conflicts entwine with and intensify gender conflicts. Lear and his daughters, Gloucester and his sons are pitted against one another because the younger generation perceives the authority of the elder as "the oppression of aged tyranny" [1.2.47–52]. Stephen Greenblatt remarks that this period has "a deep gerontological bias," revealed in numerous claims that "by the will of God and the natural order of things, authority belonged to the old." At the same time, however, sermons, moral writings, and folk tales of the kind on which *King Lear* is based voice the fear that if parents hand over their wealth or their authority to their children, those children will turn against them. The common legal practice of drawing up maintenance agreements testifies that this fear had some basis in actual experience. In such contracts, children to whom parents deeded farm or workshop were legally bound to supply food, clothing, and shelter to their parents, even to the precise number of bushels of grain or yards of cloth. Thus the law put teeth into what was supposed to be natural kindness. Lear's contest of love in the first scene functions as a maintenance agreement in that he tries to bind his daughters, by giving them their inheritance while he is still alive, into caring for him. This generational bargain is then complicated by the demands proper to gender as well – the father's emotional demand that his daughters be his mothers and perform the tasks of nurture proper to females.

Regan and Goneril betray and disappoint Lear by not being mothers to him, but in a deeper, broader sense, they shame him by bringing out the woman in him. In the following speech, Shakespeare takes us close to the nerve and bone of Lear's shame at being reduced to an impotence he considers womanish:

> You see me here, you Gods, a poor old man,
> As full of grief as age; wretched in both!
> If it be you that stirs these daughters' hearts
> Against their father, fool me not so much
> To bear it tamely; touch me with noble anger,
> And let not women's weapons, water-drops,
> Stain my man's cheeks! No, you unnatural hags,
> I will have such revenges on you both
> That all the world shall – I will do such things,
> What they are, yet I know not, but they shall be
> The terrors of the earth. You think I'll weep;
> No, I'll not weep;
> I have full cause of weeping, but this heart
> Shall break into a hundred thousand flaws
> Or ere I'll weep.
>
> [2.4.267–81]

He calls his tears "women's weapons" not only as a way of deprecating women for using emotion to manipulate men but also because he feels deeply threatened by his own feelings. Marianne Novy has argued that Lawrence Stone, in calling attention to the "distance, manipulation, and deference" that characterized the Elizabethan family, identified "a cultural ideal of Elizabethan society...a personality type that on the one hand kept feelings of attachment and grief under strict control, but on the other was more ready to express feelings of anger." "The model," she comments, "was primarily a masculine ideal." In agreeing, I would suggest that this masculine ideal was produced by the extreme sexual division of labor within the patriarchal family, which made women at once the source and the focus of a child's earliest and most unmanageable feelings. [...]

8.3 *Alexander Leggatt, 'Grigori Kozintsev's* King Lear'

Source: *King Lear: Shakespeare in Performance* (Manchester: Manchester University Press, 1991), pp. 79–85, 89, 91–3.

In the process of analysing Russian director Grigori Kozintsev's 1970 film version of *King Lear*, Alexander Leggatt provides an instructive perspective on the challenges of translating Shakespeare's plays not only into another language and context, but also into the different medium of cinema. Drawing extensively on Kozintsev's journal record of the filming of *King Lear*, Leggatt shows how through the devices of cinema – setting, time sequencing, camera angle, dress, acting styles – Kozintsev was able to give the play a fresh meaning. The vivid and extended presence of the poor of Lear's kingdom is but one of the more striking additions in the film. Kozintsev's film version again demonstrates powerfully how directorial innovations can exploit both the instability of the text itself, and in this case the possibilities of cinema, to create a new reading of an old play.

[...]The Russian film director Grigori Kozintsev in his 1970 film was in one sense not using Shakespeare's text at all; he was using Boris Pasternak's translation into modern Russian, so that he was taking the play not just out of its language but linguistically out of its period. (The effect is unfortunately distorted in the only print I have been able to see, where the English subtitles are direct quotations from Shakespeare; they imply a closeness to the original that is quite misleading, and even viewers with no Russian can spot moments when they obviously don't reflect what the actors are saying.) Freed from the literal surface of Shakespeare's text, Kozintsev was able to find, on his own terms, a way of re-creating what he saw as its essential spirit. In his book *King Lear: The Space of Tragedy* (English translation 1977) and in other writings he describes the process in detail, allowing us to study not only the film but the thinking that lay behind it.

In Kozintsev's own words, 'The poetic texture has ... to be transformed into a visual poetry, into the dynamic organisation of film imagery'. The word 'dynamic' is particularly important for this film. On stage an actor can walk only a few steps before he is in the wings. On screen an actor can go on walking, and the camera will follow. In our collection of truisms about the difference between stage and screen, this makes the best start-ing-point for a look at Kozintsev's film, a film 'shot through with the rhythms of walking, marching, running. Everything is shaken from its place. Everything is in movement.' This picks up and expands the sense of movement we have in the play: Lear's journeys from house to house and finally into the wilderness, Gloucester's journey (as he thinks) to Dover, Cordelia's exile and return. Kozintsev open with a shot of rag-bound feet trudging along a dirt road. Lear's people, the poor of the kingdom, are on the move, through a stony waste-land. Gradually we see more and more of them, walking steadily forward through standing stones which include a rough carving with Celtic interlace design. Shot by shot, the screen image grows in scope and detail, opening out before us in a movement as steady as the movement of the people. [...] It is the rhythm, the movement of the film itself that is being established, translat-ing into screen terms, and over a broader range, Shakespeare's sense of Lear's relentless journey. Having seen the peasants we then see knights on horseback, with spears; we are moving in a different way, up the social scale. Gloucester and Kent walk down a staircase into a courtyard. Inside, Goneril and Regan are walking at a steady, dignified pace into the main hall of the castle. Cordelia runs down a flight of stairs and joins them, falling in with their pace but only after she has shown that her natural movement is swifter and freer than theirs. As in Shakespeare language is a clue to character (in Ben Jonson's words, 'Speak, that I may see thee'), here we know the characters when we see how they walk. Later we see Gloucester slowly walking a large dog as he broods in voice-over on the strange events of the day ('Kent banished ...'), and we sense a reflective melancholy beneath the sensual exterior suggested by his heavy face. When Lear wakes in Cordelia's tent, stage productions generally aim at stillness. We see him with Gloucester, then we see him run away; when we next find him he is restored and at rest, his journey apparently over. What Kozintsev emphasises is the journey: Lear is carried on a litter of reeds past a foaming river, then through fire and the sound of clashing swords. Fixing steadily on his sleeping face, the camera journeys with him, and so do we. Even his reconciliation with Cordelia takes place in the open air, by a roadside; they are still in transit. This sense of constant movement was of fundamental importance to Kozintsev. He was a great believer in walking as a way of stimulating thought: 'I conceive Shake-speare's tragedies while I am walking; I hold imaginary conversations with friends who are no longer living and with favourite authors. I argue with them and learn from them.' He recalls stories of Dostoevsky walking the streets alone, waving his arms and talking to himself.

As the camera can follow actors when they walk, it can also take us quickly into different spaces, freeing and extending the location of a scene.

We can see, for example, how characters in different rooms shut each other out. Cornwall and Regan are sitting at a table; Edmund is pouring a drink for Cornwall. Through a closed door we hear Lear arguing with Gloucester over why his relations will not see him. For a moment the king is shut out from us too. The effect is reversed when at the climax of the bargaining session – 'What need one?' – Goneril and Regan walk into the house, Oswald closes the door behind them, and Lear is left to conduct 'reason not the need' as an argument with the elements, and with himself. This time we are shut out with him. But the most powerful use of multiple space is the blinding of Gloucester. We can imagine – or perhaps we would prefer not to imagine – what the director of a popular horror film would do with this scene. Kozintsev does not try for graphic violence. We see that Cornwall puts out the first eye with his foot as Gloucester lies bound in a chair, but on the removal of the second eye we see only Cornwall's back. The real horror comes when, as Gloucester's cries ring through the house – his house – we cut to Goneril's room, where she is lacing up her boots. She pauses for a moment, then goes on lacing. Then we see Edmund, just as calmly, buckling on his sword. The moral horror of their indifference adds a new dimension to the scene. Then we are back on the move again. Mortally wounded, Cornwall staggers over to Regan. His eyes go dead and he falls at her feet. She walks past him, out of the room, then takes a zig-zag track, avoiding people, through the house till she comes to Edmund's chamber. She rips his shirt open, and the next thing we see is Cornwall's dead body, stripped to the waist, laid out on a table, with Regan bending over and planting a devouring kiss on his lips. (Penelope Gilliat observes that in this film Goneril and Regan 'snatch kisses from men as if they were eating mouths'.) As in the Phillips production, there is a dark sexuality at work in the evil characters, an appetite that will not rest till it has devoured the living and the dead.

Kozintsev opens out not only the space of the play but its range of important characters. The poor we see on the roads in the opening shots are the 'poor naked wretches' of Lear's prayer. In Shakespeare's play we never see them. They are something for Lear, Gloucester and Edgar to talk about as part of their growing knowledge of the world, but they are not an active part of the drama. Was this because Shakespeare's audience had walked past them on its way into the Globe Theatre and would walk past them again on its way out? Or because, with the economy and representative power of Shakespeare's theatre, Poor Tom can stand for them all? [...] Shakespeare's text really allows no space for the poor of Lear's kingdom on stage; but in Kozintsev's film they are a major presence. He was convinced that 'one cannot portray the life of a king without portraying the life of his subjects', and years before he made the film he imagined that Shakespeare must often have seen uprooted farm workers reduced to beggary and wandering the roads of England. When in the play Lear addresses the 'poor naked wretches' they are an idea in his mind. In Kozintsev's film they are right there with him, packed into a dark hovel where they have taken refuge from the storm, [...]

Kozinstev, whose film is made for a screen of Cinemascope width, can also open the play to the landscape and the weather. Appropriately, this is one of Shakespeare's most outdoor plays, and it was designed for a roof-less theatre. Kozintsev insisted that 'tragedy takes place not amongst landscapes but among people'; for him the world of *Lear* was as densely populated as that of Balzac; indeed, we might say that the most important feature of Kozinstev's landscape is the people. All the same, he had a film director's eye for the right symbolic location. He felt that in the studio shots he and his colleagues 'had just about achieved a mediocre quality' but as soon as they moved to the bleak, stony Kazantip promontory in the Azov sea they found 'a Shakespearean landscape, the power of reality devoid of everything specific'. Here, the real work could begin. This is the landscape through which the beggars move. The flat, desolate plain, looking like a dried-up river bed, on which the storm breaks out and Gloucester takes his final journey, was a tract of land near Narva in which all the vegetation had been killed by pollution from the State Regional Electric Power Station. [...]

In creating Lear's society Kozintsev took a generalised older period, essentially medieval but with occasional Renaissance suggestions – though his costumes are more natural and comfortable, more like some-thing from real history. [...] The castles are stone, the houses brick and half-timber; Edgar flees over a wooden stockade. [...]

The designs reflect something like Brecht's fascination with the textures of everyday life: 'wood, wool, iron, leather, fur'. Kozintsev was interested in texture, not colour, and shot his film in black and white. The background for the opening titles is the rough cloth of the beggars. [...]

[Lear's] redemption begins in earnest as he encounters the poor, the people who have nothing, and falls in with them. In Shakespeare Lear tries to dramatise his common humanity by taking his clothes off; his attendants won't let him. For them, as later for the blinded Gloucester, he is still the king. But Yarvet's Lear achieves common humanity, simply and without fuss, by walking along with its other representatives, among whom he fits in easily. As he walks he chats with Gloucester, sharing not Beckettian despair but folk wisdom. It is significant that Yarvet had originally been cast in the small role of a mad beggar and didn't believe Kozintsev was serious when he was told the director wanted him for Lear. Kozintsev wanted not an extraordinary Lear, a 'magnificent por-tent', but a Lear who could be anybody, 'like all of us, really', and whose reduction to common humanity would be not the end of his greatness but the beginning of it. [...]

Shostakovich's music gives the film some of its darkest colouring, especially in the war sequence where his wordless choir becomes 'the grief of the whole people'. But, Kozintsev added, the music also 'gives rise to faith: the evil times will pass, they cannot do otherwise if such a voice is heard'. [...]

Kozinstev's vision of the play is humane, and this is reflected in the making of the film. Whereas the actors in a film version of this play could easily be swamped by special effects, as they sometimes are on the stage, Kozintsev keeps his actors centre front. He was fascinated by the human face: 'The advantage of the cinema over the theatre is not that you can even have horses, but that you can stare closer into a man's eyes.' His search for a Lear, which did not end until perilously close to the shooting date, was a search for the right face. When he found Yuri Yarvet he wrote, 'I have at last seen the eyes on the screen: the very eyes.' Yarvet was an Estonian who spoke Russian so badly that at one point Kozintsev planned to have a Russian actor dub his lines – a plan Yarvet himself vetoed. But the shock of white hair, and above all the deep, pained eyes, framed by a network of wrinkles – these were worth any trouble; they spoke the language Kozintsev wanted to hear. He was also attracted by Yarvet's resemblance to Voltaire, 'the bitter irony, the wit of Europe'. Lear's first entrance is quirky and unexpected. Behind a closed door we hear laughter and the jingling of bells. Lear is playing a game with the Fool. When he enters there is a mask on his face. Its purpose, in theory, was to symbolise Lear's initial inhumanity. Its actual effect is that its removal throws into high relief the face of the man – a Lear we have never seen before yet somehow recognise at once, a Lear of profound and vulnerable humanity. [...]

9 *The Tempest*

9.1 *David Norbrook, ' "What Cares These Roarers for the Name of King?'': Language and Utopia in* The Tempest'

Source: K. Ryan (ed.), *Shakespeare: The Last Plays* (London: Longman, 1999), Chapter 10, pp. 246–52, 258–62.

Of all of Shakespeare's plays, in the last fifteen years *The Tempest* has attracted the most energetic and creative critical attention. Norbrook's essay (first published in 1992) is written in reaction to what he perceives to be a new historicist orthodoxy regarding the play, namely that the disruptive, radical elements in the play are ultimately contained, as mon-archical authority in the figure of Prospero regains power in the final act. A determined historicist himself, Norbrook rejects this view, detecting in the play strong traces of Renaissance utopian thought, and accordingly he sees Shakespeare less as ideologue of James I, than as European humanist in the tradition of Machiavelli and Montaigne. Focusing in this extract on the character of Prospero, Norbrook combines close reading of the text with dense historical detail to uncover connotations of the language which prevent a singular conservative interpretation of the play. The most intri-guing possibility at this stage might be to consider how Norbrook's more generous judgement of Shakespeare in Jacobean London contrasts with those of Sinfield (Extract 3.2), Davies (4.1), Marcus (7.2) and Kettle (8.1).

[...] 'Where's the Master?' That is the question that comes instinctively to King Alonso's lips as his ship is buffeted by the tempest. But the master has left the stage: the work on this ship is impersonally structured and does not need the direct presence of a figure of authority. So little respect does the boatswain have for traditional hierarchies that he refuses to answer. When Antonio repeats the question, the boatswain dismisses the king and all the courtiers with a summary 'You mar our labour... What cares these roarers for the name of king?' 'Roaring' connotes mis-rule and rebellion, roaring boys or girls. In a remarkably defiant gesture, the boundless voice of the elements and of social transgression is pitted against the name of king, the arbitrary language of power. *The Tempest* is structured around such oppositions between courtly discourse and wider linguistic contexts. Throughout the play there is a tension in Ariel between the subordination of his highly wrought fusion of music and poetry to Prospero and the desire to become 'free/As mountain winds', to liberate a purified poetry from the constraints of domination [1.2.503–4]. Utopian discourse pervades the play, most notably in Gonzalo's vision of a world where nature would produce all in common and 'Letters should not be known' [2.1.150]. But every figure on the island has some kind of vision of a society that would transcend existing codes and signs: 'Thought is free', sing Stephano and Trinculo [3.2.118].

That libertarian impulse in the play is doubtless why it appealed so strongly to Milton, who rewrote it in *Comus*, transferring Caliban's less attractive qualities to the aristocratic Comus, giving a more rigorous utopian discourse to the lady, and assigning the agency of the resolution not to the aristocrats but to the Ariel-figure and a nature goddess. Con-tinuing that utopian tradition, Shelley found in *The Tempest* a central instance of the utopian power in poetry which 'makes familiar objects be as if they were not familiar'. Ariel had for him the same utopian implications as the egalitarian spirit Queen Mab. Shelley was also alert to the claims of Caliban, as we can see from the significant parallel he draws in his preface to *Frankenstein* between Mary Wollstonecraft Shelley's novel and Shakespeare's pioneering science fiction.

Walter Cohen has recently noted Shelley's perceptive reading of the political implications of romance and has proposed a revised utopian reading of *The Tempest*. But twentieth-century criticism has tended on the whole towards the dystopian, assuming that Gonzalo's ideals are held up for ridicule. Mid-century 'neo-Christians', to use Empson's term, made a sharp distinction between modern political ideas with their sentimental utopianism and the traditional orthodoxy which held that man was a fallen Caliban and therefore needed strict hierarchical order to keep him in line. Coleridge has been a dominant influence in twentieth-century readings of Shakespeare, and Coleridge's interpretations were marked by a revulsion against the radicalism of his age. Hence while Coleridge claims, with reference to *The Tempest*, that Shakespeare 'is always the philosopher and the moralist', without political partisanship, he goes on to present him as a 'philosophical aristocrat' for whom the mob is 'an irrational animal'. With this frame of reference established, accounts of Shakespeare's impartiality had a heavy weighting. Again in the Coleridge tradition, this political conservatism was linked with a turn towards language: Shakespeare's plays were valued for their concreteness as opposed to the etiolated abstractions of Enlightenment egalitarianism. These conservative readings have been strengthened by more recent historical work linking the masque scene with court entertainments; Shakespeare's late turn to romance can be seen as marking a rejection of popular taste for an elite aristocratic genre. So dominant have courtly readings become that radical and anti-colonialist critics have tended to accept their historical premises even while contesting their political outlook. The best recent readings have indeed drawn attention to contradictions and complexities in the play which open themselves to a radical interpretation. But the general assumption is that these openings would have been unconscious effects of discourse, while Shakespeare and his audiences would have belonged to Prospero's party and seen the play as celebrating the restoration of monarchical legitimacy as a return to a transcendent natural order. Terry Eagleton sees Shakespeare as subordinating language, as signified by Ariel, to a conservative discourse of the body: the plays 'value social order and stability', and in seeking an organic unity of body and language *The Tempest* propagates a 'ridiculously sanguine ideology of Nature'.

Some recent developments in literary theory have tended to reinforce these dystopian readings. Contemporary deconstructionists, like the neo-Christians, oppose the abstract utopianism of the Enlightenment to the need for a turn towards language (there are important linking factors, as in the continuing influence of Heidegger). Language and utopia still go together for Jürgen Habermas and other theorists of universal pragmatics, for whom the 'utopian perspective of reconciliation and freedom...is built into the linguistic mechanism of the reproduction of the species'. But poststructuralists have argued that this quest for undistorted communication implies an ultimately fixed and essentialist notion of human nature, which can become repressive and mystifying, prematurely suppressing the particularities of gender and class in the name of a false universality of a subject that is held to be free of the constraints of discourse. Utopia, it can be argued, is utropia, it suppresses rhetoric and hence must fail to recognize its ineluctable basis in the materiality of language and power. In a celebrated essay, Derrida attacked Lévi-Strauss for idealizing the Brazilian Indians as a people blessed in the absence of writing. Such idealization can be seen as belonging to a humanist tradition that goes back to Rousseau's – and, one might add, Montaigne's and Gonzalo's – idealization of letterless primitives. The logocentric analysis, Derrida argues, in repressing writing represses also the materiality of discourse. A simple opposition between language and nature would in effect reinforce the ideology of the Western colonization. And it could then be argued that *The Tempest*'s utopianism is complicit in the ideology. Prospero's ideal spirits dance 'with printless foot' [5.1.34], and Ariel may represent a vision of pure thought breaking free from the material embodiment of language and time, operating between two pulsebeats [5.1.105]. Ariel's utopian vision seems pathetically illusory by the standards of Lacanian psychoanalysis, a dream of return to an androgynous state before the name of the father or king, an unmediated sucking at the place of the bee's being [5.1.88]; thus Eagleton can see him as a 'closet aesthete'.

The more it is insisted that the individual subject cannot escape the specificities of language or discourse, the more the subject may seem to be inexorably determined by existing power-structures from which it cannot escape. Foucault has reminded us of all kinds of ways in which thought is not free. While the classic utopian impulse to a transcendent critique is branded as totalitarian and essentialist, immanent critiques are often seen as inexorably contained. And indeed the play itself may seem to undermine idealist bids for an emancipated poetry. The roarers that the boatswain evokes turn out to have been controlled by Prospero with his power to work up the elements to 'roaring war' [5.1.44 cf. 1.2.205], and the rebellion of those seditious roarers Stephano, Trinculo, and Caliban will be evoked by the very power that then contains it. The roars that pervade the play are those of the tormented bodies of Prospero's enemies: 'I will plague them all,/Even to roaring' [4.1.192–3 cf. 1.2.373] and Ariel's triumphant cry of 'Hark, they roar!' [4.1.257] is underscored by Prospero's threat to return his servant to the howling agony of captivity in the tree. Music in the play may seem not so much emancipatory as deceitful and manipulative, plunging Ferdinand and Alonso into mourning and guilt which the facts do not quite merit, making the wind sing legitimism. The whimsical refrain of barking dogs to Ariel's first song turns nasty when the dog Tyrant bears down on the conspirators. Prospero commends Ariel's performance as the harpy in terms that sinisterly conflate aesthetics and violence: 'a grace it had, devouring' [3.3.84].

These newer anti-humanisms, then, may tend to confirm the dystopian perspectives of the neo-Christian anti-humanists. There is room, however, for a reading that would remain open to utopian perspectives in a way that poststructuralist methodologies cannot allow, taking account of the cogent criticisms of blandly transcendental views of the subject which recent theory has been able to make, but without surrendering some notion of the possibility of the subject as rational agent. Such a reading could lay no more claim than its adversaries to being final and exhaustive, but it would, I believe, be more genuinely historical than those which offer the play as absolutist propaganda, for it would take fuller account of the discursive and social contexts. There is no need for twentieth-century readings to be more royalist than the King's Men. A theoretical interest in language was part of the social and intellectual context of Shakespeare and his company – provided that the context is not narrowed down too specifically to courtly discourse but takes account of the immense linguistic curiosity stimulated by Renaissance humanism.

If the term 'humanism' in current discourse tends to connote an abstract resistance to the materiality of language, then Renaissance humanism was a very different phenomenon. It had made its own sharp linguistic turn, an exaltation of rhetoric against scholastic metaphysics, and thus can be seen as paralleling contemporary anti-humanisms in refusing to take for granted a fixed human essence; the attack on abstract generality gave the drama a heightened epistemological status. But Renaissance humanism also had a generalizing, philosophical impulse, an advanced sociological and historical consciousness which looked forward to the Enlightenment. While old arguments about monarchy's being part of the order of nature came to look increasingly feeble, more rationalistic theories of natural law could have a strong critical element. More's *Utopia* plays the transcendent social blueprint of the second book against the immanent critique of courtly language in the first book; More says that it would be pointless for a humanist at court to start reciting the speech in the pseudo-Senecan play *Octavia* which prophesies an egalitarian society. As Erica Sheen has shown, Seneca's plays were very much in Shakespeare's mind when he wrote the last plays. Seneca's prose writings opened up an egalitarian discourse of natural law. His plays, however, made him the very type of the compromised court intellectual, writing for a small elite, and More could still feel an affinity with this status. But by Shakespeare's time the possibilities for a politically critical drama had been transformed by the emergence of professional repertory companies which, despite their residual status as royal servants, derived their economic strength from a far wider public. Shakespeare's career reflects not just individual genius but the excitement of a whole collective institution at the possibilities of what amounted to a cultural revolution: the emergence of a literary public sphere which prepared the way for the formation of a political public sphere. That excitement, however, was certainly manifested in individuals, and recent radically anti-intentionalist readings have given too little credit to the possibility that the writer as agent could achieve a degree of independence from the prevailing structures of power and discourse.

On this account of the context, it is not surprising that *The Tempest* manifests an acute and sophisticated awareness of the relations between language and power. The play is not overtly oppositional or sensationally 'subversive'; but it subjects traditional institutions to a systematic, critical questioning. The play does not consider language and power as timeless absolutes; rather than counterposing an unmediated, presocial nature to a deterministically conceived language, it is concerned with language in specific social contexts, with the effect of political structures on linguistic possibilities. All of the play's utopian ideals, not excepting Ariel's, come up for ironic scrutiny in the course of the play, precisely because they tend to an idealism that refuses to recognize the material constraints of existing structures of power and discourse. But that awareness need not imply a pessimistic determinism. A sceptical relativism about claims to an unproblematic 'human nature' is played against a searching, universalizing quest for a more general notion of humanity. The play gives the effect at once of tremendous constriction and specificity, manifested in its rigorously classical form, and of the immense expansion through time and space characteristic of the romance mode. Critics have often counterposed romance to realism as the mode of aristocratic escapism. But *The Tempest* is a hardheaded play, rigorous in following through its own logic once the initial supernatural postulates are granted. As several critics have noted, it is not so much that the play is a romance as that it stages, and in the process distances itself from, the romance scenario of dynastic redemption that Prospero is staging. And yet the play also recognizes a certain congruence between a narrowly aristocratic romantic impulse and a broader utopian project. As Shelley, Fredric Jameson, and Raymond Williams have argued in their very different idioms, such imagination of alternatives may be an essential mode of a radical politics in resistance to a world-weary empiricism.

The magic island of Shakespeare's play is at once an instance and an allegory of the players' project of opening up new spaces for discourse. It is a place where no name, no discourse, is entirely natural; language and nature are neither simply conflated nor simply opposed to each other.

Prospero abandons the island without leaving behind a colonial force, nor does he refute Caliban's claim that 'this island's mine'. But if Caliban's matrilineal claim may seem to subvert patriarchal authority, it is itself called in question by his own recent arrival. The only figures who can be said to have some natural claim to priority, Ariel and his fellow spirits, are, precisely, not natural but supernatural, and they do not seem to think of land as something to be possessed; the spirits' history too is left open, and it is possible that Ariel has accompanied Sycorax to the island. At two points in the play the exchanges between Prospero and Ariel focus on uncertainty about what that word 'human' really means, implying that it is an open rather than a fixed category [1.2.286; 5.1.20]. Arriving on the island makes all conventional codes unfamiliar. Prospero sets up a dizzying relativization of the human by claiming that Ferdinand is a Caliban to most men and they are angels to him [1.2.483–5]. Similarly, Caliban will say that Miranda surpasses Sycorax as greatest does less; in each case, the hyperbolical comparison is at the same time undercut by the awareness that there is nothing else to compare them with – as long as she is on the island Miranda has no rival to prevent her being Prospero's 'nonpareil' [3.2.95]. Having asked Miranda a question, Ferdinand is nonetheless astonished when she answers it in his own language [1.2.432]. Miranda cannot believe that Ferdinand is 'natural' [1.2.422] and describes him as 'it' [1.2.413]. In a parallel episode Stephano is astonished that Caliban speaks his language [2.2.64], though this is not surprising to us as the play has explained that Miranda taught it to him. The Italian Trinculo scornfully observes that in England the monster would be taken for a man [2.2.29]. When the courtiers finally wake out of their trance, they 'scarce think... their words / Are natural breath' [5.1.157–9]. In a remarkable alienation-effect at the end, Miranda turns to the newly arrived courtiers – and implicitly the audience – and hails them as a 'brave new world' [5.1.186]. A world which seems to Gonzalo itself a utopia looks out at the old world and finds in it a utopia, only to be greeted with Prospero's weary ''Tis new to thee'. This repeated defamiliarization makes it very hard to see the end of the play as no more than the restoration of a natural social order. At the same time, it reminds us that when characters project an image of a new world they cannot escape the conceptual apparatus they have brought from the old. [...]

It has been tempting to allegorize him [Prospero] as a figure of Shakespeare or James I. But these readings too easily assume that the play identifies with Prospero as a natural source of authority; and that Shakespeare engages with politics only at the level of direct topical allegories. While the original audience might well have picked up some resonance with the contemporary hopes over the Palatine marriage, there is also a more generalizing sociological consciousness at work in the plays, which means that we need to pay some attention to the discourse in which

Shakespeare situates Prospero. The later Shakespeare, and Jacobeans in general, were tending to give more and more sociological specificity to Italian settings by drawing on the discourses by which Italians represented their own history. Particularly influential were Machiavelli and Guicciardini, who offered a radically sceptical analysis of political power which undercut any claim by monarchy to be natural. In the later Renaissance many republican city-states had been taken over by *signori*, rulers with little sense of communal responsibility who sought legitimacy in noble connections, in a kind of refeudalization (or what Sebastian terms 'Hereditary sloth' [2.1.219]), rather than in popular consent. Guicciardini opens his history with a lament for the monarchical harmony of late fifteenth-century Italy before the foreign invasions in the 1490s, which led eventually to Spanish absolutist hegemony. But even though Guicciardini himself favoured the Medici dynasty, he presented at length the constitutional debates about differing forms of democratic rule; and what gradually emerges is that beneath that superficial harmony there were deep-rooted republican resistances, which meant that the people were often glad to welcome foreign armies against their ruling houses. The unpopular King Alphonso of Naples, who 'knew not (with most Princes now a dayes) how to resist the furie of dominion and rule', abdicated in favour of his son Ferdinand but the people refused to allow him into the city; the precedent was to be used by supporters of the execution of Charles I. Guicciardini places the immediate blame for the foreign invasions on the ambition of Giovan Galeazzo Sforza, the *de facto* ruler of Milan who was anxious to gain legitimacy for his line, but ended up by sacrificing Milan's political autonomy altogether to his personal dynastic vanity.

What sign is there in *The Tempest* of a possible republican subtext? It may seem unduly literal-minded to imagine Shakespeare as considering the precise political status of his Italian states; but there is clear evidence that this was done by his collaborator in his last plays, John Fletcher. About 1621 Fletcher wrote with Philip Massinger a tragicomedy, *The Double Marriage*, which echoed *The Tempest*, with an exiled duke and his daughter as central characters. The play glorifies 'the noble stile of Tyrant-killers'; at the climax the hero brings in the head of the tyrannical king of Naples to cries of 'Liberty'. The political climate in 1621 had become more sharply polarized, and Shakespeare certainly does not undercut monarchical legitimacy in the same way. Nevertheless, it is worth remembering that his audience would have contained people who were far from taking an absolutist dynastic perspective for granted, and the play does permit a certain detachment from the courtly viewpoint. Prospero assures us that his people loved him [1.2.141]; but he does belong to this political world. He speaks of 'signories' [1.2.71] and he sees his power purely in personal terms, as a matter of safeguarding his dynasty: he talks familiarly of 'my

Milan' [5.1.314], while for Ferdinand 'myself am Naples' [1.2.438]. Though Prospero condemns Antonio for allowing Milan to stoop to Naples [1.2.112–16], by the end of the play he has handed the dukedom over to Naples in order to secure his line. His words as he reveals Ferdinand and Miranda to the courtiers at the end scarcely escape banality: 'a wonder to content ye / As much as me my dukedom' [5.1.172–3]. His tone is echoed by Gonzalo's breathless 'Was Milan thrust from Milan that his issue / Should become kings of Naples?' [5.1.208–9]. The union between Milan and Naples is a strikingly representative instance of the social processes by which the *signorie* sought legitimacy; the upstart Milanese has definitely made good.

The characteristic genre of such dynastic triumphs was the romance, whose aristocratic closure predominates in Prospero's world over utopian openings; Miranda and Ferdinand are standed within a very narrow courtly discourse. For Prospero, making Ferdinand do manual work is a punishment degrading him to the level of his slave. He lost his dukedom because the element of work in public life, as valorized in the republican ethos, seemed to him too degrading; he preferred a private retreat into Neoplatonic contemplation which 'but by being so retired, / O'er-prized all popular rate' [1.2.91–2]. His language and that of the courtiers generally reflects the growing class-bound stratification urged by Castiglione and courtly theorists: the rhetoric of courtly praise and dispraise rather than republican persuasion. Ferdinand observes rather clumsily that on his father's death 'I am the best of them that speak this speech': language is the king's [1.2.433]. Idealizing compliments are directed to the noble, though always with an underlying political pragmatism – Miranda is learning to let Ferdinand wrangle for a score of kingdoms and call it fair play [5.1.174]. The base are abused – Caliban is given plenty of opportunity to learn how to curse. Martines has noted that sixteenth-century political discourse in Italy reveals a growing polarity between an abstract aristocratic utopianism and a dark view of the populace as irredeemably base; as Berger has shown, such polarities are characteristic of Prospero's discourse. He reminds Caliban six times in less than seventy lines that he is a slave [1.2.311–77], and Caliban fears that his art could make Setebos a vassal [1.2.377]: Prospero extends feudal relations of service and bondage. Prospero's irascibility has come to the fore in recent productions; idealizations of Prospero require a certain suppression of the play's language. Miranda has to protest that 'My father's of a better nature, sir, / Than he appears by speech' [1.2.500–1]. These points remain relatively inconspicuous in the play, which certainly is not a satire of Prospero; nor are the elements of romance cynically dismissed as mere aristocratic fantasy. Shelley's sense of the play as utopian would have involved a recognition of the political importance of a sense of wonder, of defamiliarization, which even a narrowly class-based romance could project. As with Gonzalo, the point is not that Prospero is an evil man but that his political position entails a limited perspective.

Shakespeare's questioning of legitimacy extends even to the genre *par excellence* of the naturalization of authority, the court masque. Prospero's betrothal masque is the richest expression of his ideal society; and whereas in Gonzalo's utopia all things are in common, in Prospero's golden age there is a hierarchical structure in which the labour of the reapers is ultimately motivated by the transcendent gods and goddesses who are figures of the leisured aristocracy. As Berger has noted, however, there are signs of tension even within the masquing speeches, reflecting Prospero's tendency to oscillate between idealistic and radically pessimistic views of man. This tension in the end cannot be sustained and the masque collapses; recent criticism has rightly drawn attention to the ways in which the resolution is very different from the Stuart norm – forming an interesting parallel with *Cymbeline*, as Erica Sheen shows in her essay. The aim of the masque was to naturalize the king's name, to turn courtiers into gods and goddesses; Prospero dissolves his masque and its courtly language melts into air, leaving (according to a perhaps non-authorial stage direction) 'a strange hollow and confused noise', an undifferentiated roaring that undercuts the confident marks of social difference. The pageants are 'insubstantial'.

Prospero's 'revels' speech has given rise to a great deal of critical banality, but it is as well to be wary about taking it as a statement of Shakespeare's view of life in general; it needs to be read rather less transcendentally. The two other most celebrated comparisons of life to a play are those of Jacques in *As You Like It* and Macbeth's 'poor player' speech, and neither is unequivocally endorsed: Shakespeare seems to have been wary about generalizations about Life. Prospero is in fact in no mood to say farewell to the world; he wants his dukedom back and in a previous scene he has had Ariel, disguised as a religious spirit, tell lies about Ferdinand's death in order to facilitate his ends. In a political context, the specificities of the 'revels' speech become more evident. At the climax of the Jacobean masque, these alleged gods and goddesses would come down into the dancing area and mingle with the audience. Court masques were in many ways very substantial things, giving the necessary concrete presence to the royal name by elaborate scenery; their fabric was definitely not baseless. There were clear sacramental overtones: the substance, the body, of the king became divinely transformed. Jonson's preface to *Hymenaei* highlights this physicality with characteristic ambivalence. On the one hand the *'bodies'* are transitory and inferior in comparison to their conceptual souls; on the other hand, Jonson as a firm defender of religious and secular ceremony fiercely disputes the 'fastidious *stomachs*' of rivals like Daniel whose 'ayrie tasts' lay too little emphasis on the external body. As Jonson noted, it was the custom at the end of masques to 'deface their *carkasses*': in the spirit of *potlatch*, courtiers would tear down the scenery, the whole point being the physical concreteness of the manifestation of honour, so that its destruction was all the more potent a sign of the donor's greatness.

Prospero's speech, and the whole episode, then, highlight the ways in which his spectacle is unlike a court masque. His masque really is insubstantial, because as prince in exile he does not have any actors, musicians, and set-designers. There is something almost ludicrous in the contrivance of this spectacle for an audience of just three, even if Ferdinand dutifully declares that there are enough of them for paradise [4.1.122–4]. Prospero's situation on the island parodies the top-heavy social structure of late Renaissance despotisms, with the aristocracy syphoning off more and more wealth to expend in conspicuous courtly consumption, while representing the people as a mere grumbling margin to the transcendent centre of the court. But in Prospero's case the situation is pushed to the point of absurdity by the absence of any subjects at all apart from Caliban; and in an ideological forgetting directly parallel to Gonzalo's, Prospero's masque can last only as long as Caliban is forgotten. The political point is rubbed home when we learn that Ariel, though intending to remind Prospero about the conspiracy when he was playing the part of Ceres, had 'feared / Lest I might anger thee' [4.1.168–9]. The masque cannot reach a climax with the performers mingling with the audience, as was the rule at court, for the performers are spirits. Precisely because they really are what the courtiers pretended to be, supernatural beings, bodiless air, they cannot be taken back with Prospero to Milan. There is an ironic parallel to Stephano's exclamation: 'This will be a brave kingdom to me, where I shall have my music for nothing' [3.2.139–40]. [...]

9.2 Rob Nixon, 'African and Caribbean Appropriations of The Tempest'

Source: *Critical Inquiry*, 13 (Spring 1987), pp. 557–67, 570–4, 576–8.

Published in 1987 in the Chicago-based journal *Critical Inquiry*, Rob Nixon's essay traces in wide-ranging detail the reception of *The Tempest* in Africa and the Caribbean between 1957 and 1973. While paying due attention to colonial readings of the play by Octave Mannoni and Philip Mason, the bulk of the emphasis is on anticolonial reappropriations of the play by writers including George Lamming, Aimé Césaire, and Roberto Fernandez Retamar. Nixon explains the appeal of *The Tempest* to these writers in that it provided "a way of amplifying their calls for decolonization within the bounds of the dominant cultures". With the focus less on the text of *The Tempest* itself than on how the play has been interpreted,

Nixon quotes these writers at length in order to show that although "they reaffirmed the play's importance from outside its central tradition", they did so through a "series of insurrectional endorsements". Nixon's essay has been criticized recently for failing to problematize sufficiently the absence of feminist appropriations of the play during the same period (if Caliban can be reclaimed, what of Sycorax and Miranda?), but the essay nonetheless provides a useful overview of a rich and varied literature.

> Remember
> First to possess his books.
> (*The Tempest*)

The era from the late fifties to the early seventies was marked in Africa and the Caribbean by a rush of newly articulated anticolonial sentiment that was associated with the burgeoning of both international black consciousness and more localized nationalist movements. Between 1957 and 1973 the vast majority of African and the larger Caribbean colonies won their independence; the same period witnessed the Cuban and Algerian revolutions, the latter phase of the Kenyan "Mau Mau" revolt, the Katanga crisis in the Congo, the Trinidadian Black Power uprising and, equally important for the atmosphere of militant defiance, the civil rights movement in the United States, the student revolts of 1968, and the humbling of the United States during the Vietnam War. This period was distinguished, among Caribbean and African intellectuals, by a pervasive mood of optimistic outrage. Frequently graduates of British or French universities, they were the first generation from their regions self-assured and numerous enough to call collectively for a renunciation of Western standards as the political revolts found their cultural counterparts in insurrections against the bequeathed values of the colonial powers.

In the context of such challenges to an increasingly discredited European colonialism, a series of dissenting intellectuals chose to utilize a European text as a strategy for (in George Lamming's words) getting "out from under this ancient mausoleum of [Western] historic achievement." They seized upon *The Tempest* as a way of amplifying their calls for decolonization within the bounds of the dominant cultures. But at the same time these Caribbeans and Africans adopted the play as a founding text in an oppositional lineage which issued from a geopolitically and historically specific set of cultural ambitions. They perceived that the play could contribute to their self-definition during a period of great flux. So, through repeated, reinforcing, transgressive appropriations of *The Tempest*, a once silenced group generated its own tradition of "error" which in turn served as one component of the grander counterhegemonic nationalist and black internationalist endeavors of the period. Because that era of Caribbean and African history was marked by such extensive, open contestation of cultural values, the destiny of *The Tempest* at that time throws into uncommonly stark relief the status of value as an unstable social process rather than a static and, in literary terms, merely textual attribute.

Some Caribbean and African intellectuals anticipated that their efforts to unearth from *The Tempest* a suppressed narrative of their historical abuse and to extend that narrative in the direction of liberation would be interpreted as philistine. But Lamming, for one, wryly resisted being intimidated by any dominant consensus: "I shall reply that my mistake, lived and deeply felt by millions of men like me – proves the positive value of error." Lamming's assertion that his unorthodoxy is collectively grounded is crucial: those who defend a text's universal value can easily discount a solitary dissenting voice as uncultured or quirky, but it is more difficult to ignore entirely a cluster of allied counterjudgments, even if the group can still be stigmatized. Either way, the notion of universal value is paradoxically predicated on a limited inclusiveness, on the assumption that certain people will fail to appreciate absolute worth. As Pierre Bourdieu, Barbara Herrnstein Smith, and Tony Bennett have all shown, a dominant class or culture's power to declare certain objects or activities self-evidently valuable is an essential measure for reproducing social differentiation. But resistance to the hegemony of such hierarchies is still possible. In this context, Lamming's statement exudes the fresh confidence of the high era of decolonization, in which a "philistinism" arose that was sufficiently powerful and broadly based to generate an alternative orthodoxy responsive to indigenous interests and needs.

For Frantz Fanon, decolonization was the period when the peoples of the oppressed regions, force-fed for so long on foreign values, could stomach them no longer: "In the colonial context the settler only ends his work of breaking in the native when the latter admits loudly and intelligibly the supremacy of the white man's values. In the period of decolonization, the colonized masses mock at these very values, insult them, and vomit them up." From the late fifties onward, there was a growing resistance in African and Caribbean colonies to remote-controlled anything, from administrative structures to school curricula, and the phase of "nauseating mimicry" (in Fanon's phrase) gave way to a phase in which colonized cultures sought to define their own cultures reactively and aggressively from within. In short, decolonization was the period when "the machine [went] into reverse." This about-face entailed that indigenous cultural forms be substituted for alien ones – inevitably a hybrid process of retrieving suppressed traditions and inventing new ones. Both approaches were present in the newfound preoccupation with *The Tempest*: hints of New World culture and history were dragged to the surface, while at other moments the play was unabashedly refashioned to meet contemporary political and cultural needs.

Given the forcefulness of the reaction against the values of the colonial powers, it may appear incongruous that Caribbean and African intellectuals should have integrated a canonical European text like *The Tempest* into their struggle; it made for, in Roberto Fernández Retamar's words, "an alien elaboration." And this response may seem doubly incongruous given Shakespeare's distinctive position as a measure of the relative achievements of European and non-European civilizations. In discussions of value, Shakespeare is, of course, invariably treated as a special case, having come to serve as something like the gold standard of literature. For the English he is as much an institution and an industry as a corpus of texts: a touchstone of national identity, a lure for tourists, an exportable commodity, and one of the securest forms of cultural capital around. But the weight of Shakespeare's ascribed authority was felt differently in the colonies. What for the English and, more generally, Europeans, could be a source of pride and a confirmation of their civilization, for colonial subjects often became a chastening yardstick of their "backwardness." The exhortation to master Shakespeare was instrumental in showing up non-European "inferiority," for theirs would be the flawed mastery of those culturally remote from Shakespeare's stock. A schooled resemblance could become the basis for a more precise discrimination, for, to recall Homi Bhabha's analysis of mimicry in colonial discourse, "to be Anglicized is *emphatically* not to be English." And so, in colonial circumstances, the bard could become symptomatic and symbolic of the education of Africans and Caribbeans into a passive, subservient relationship to dominant colonial culture.

One aspect of this passive orientation toward Europe is touched on by Lamming, the Barbadian novelist who was to appropriate *The Tempest* so actively for his own ends. Discussing his schooling during the early 1940s, Lamming recalls how the teacher "followed the curriculum as it was. He did what he had to do: Jane Austen, some Shakespeare, Wells's novel *Kipps*, and so on. What happened was that they were teaching exactly whatever the Cambridge Syndicate demanded. That was the point of it. These things were directly connected. Papers were set in Cambridge and our answers were sent back there to be corrected. We had to wait three to four months. Nobody knew what was happening till they were returned." Given the resistance during decolonization to this kind of cultural dependency, those writers who took up *The Tempest* from the standpoint of the colonial subject did so in a manner that was fraught with complexity. On the one hand, they hailed Caliban and identified themselves with him; on the other, they were intolerant of received colonial definitions of Shakespeare's value. They found the European play compelling but insisted on engaging with it on their own terms. [...]

[The first] reassessment of *The Tempest* in light of the immediate circumstances leading up to decolonization [. . .] was *Psychologie de la colonisation*, written by the French social scientist, Octave Mannoni. However
much Third World intellectuals have subsequently quarreled with his
manner of mobilizing the play, Mannoni's inaugural gesture helped to
shape the trajectory of those associated appropriations which lay ahead
and, concomitantly, to bring about the reestimation of *The Tempest* in
Africa and the Caribbean. Mannoni's novel response enabled him to
evolve a theory of colonialism with Prospero and Caliban as prototypes;
conversely, his hypotheses about colonial relations, arising from his
experiences in Madagascar, made it possible for him to rethink the play.
This reciprocal process was not gratuitous but prompted by an early
stirring of African nationalism: Mannoni is insistent that his theory only
fell into place through his exposure to one of the twilight movements of
French colonialism – the Madagascan uprising of 1947–48 in which sixty
thousand Madagascans, one thousand colonial soldiers, and several hundred settlers were killed. In 1947 his ideas began to take shape, and, by the
time the revolt had been suppressed a year later, the manuscript was
complete. The occasional character of *Psychologie de la colonisation* is fore-
grounded in the introduction, which Mannoni closes by marking the
coincidence of his ideas with "a certain moment in history, a crisis in
the evolution of politics, when many things that had been hidden were
brought into the light of day; but it was only a moment, and time will
soon have passed it by." The pressing horrors of the Madagascan crisis
prompted Mannoni to find a new significance for *The Tempest*, encourag-
ing him to weave a reading of Shakespeare's poetic drama through his
reading of the incipient drama of decolonization.

Mannoni's account of the psychological climate of colonialism is
advanced through an opposition between the Prospero (or inferiority)
complex and the Caliban (or dependence) complex. On this view, Europeans in Madagascar typically displayed the need, common among people from a competitive society, to feel highly regarded by others.
However, the Prospero-type is not just any white man, but specifically
the sort whose "grave lack of sociability combined with a pathological
urge to dominate" drives him to seek out uncompetitive situations where,
among a subservient people, his power is amplified and his least skills
assume the aspect of superior magic. Whether a French settler in Africa or
Shakespeare's duke, he is loath to depart his adopted island, knowing full
well that back home his standing will shrink to mundane dimensions.
Mannoni found the Madagascans, on the other hand, to be marked by a
Caliban complex, a dependence on authority purportedly characteristic of
a people forced out of a secure "tribal" society and into the less stable,
competitively edged hierarchies of a semi-Westernized existence. According to this theory, colonialism introduced a situation where the Madagas-

can was exposed for the first time to the notion and possibility of abandonment. Crucially, the colonist failed to comprehend the Madagascan's capacity to feel "neither inferior nor superior but yet wholly dependent," an unthinkable state of mind for someone from a competitive society. So, in Mannoni's terms, the Madagascan revolt was fueled less by a desire to sunder an oppressive master-servant bond than by the people's resentment of the colonizers' failure to uphold that bond more rigorously and provide them with the security they craved. What the colonial subjects sought was the paradoxical freedom of secure dependence rather than any autonomous, self-determining freedom. This assumption clearly shaped Mannoni's skepticism about the Madagascans' desire, let alone their capacity, to achieve national independence.

Mannoni values *The Tempest* most highly for what he takes to be Shakespeare's dramatization of two cultures' mutual sense of a trust betrayed: Prospero is a fickle dissembler, Caliban an ingrate. The nodal lines here, and those that draw Mannoni's densest commentary, are spoken by Caliban in the play's second scene. They should be quoted at length, for they are taken up repeatedly by subsequent Caribbean and African appropriators of *The Tempest*.

> When thou cam'st first,
> Thou strok'st me, and made much of me, wouldst give me
> Water with berries in't, and teach me how
> To name the bigger light, and how the less,
> That burn by day and night, and then I lov'd thee
> And show'd thee all the qualities o' th' isle,
> The fresh springs, brine-pits, barren place and fertile:
> Curs'd be I that did so! All the charms
> Of Sycorax, toads, beetles, bats, light on you!
> For I am all the subjects that you have,
> Which first was mine own king; and here you sty me
> In this hard rock, whiles you do keep from me
> The rest o' th' island.
>
> [1.2.335–47]

To Mannoni, it appears evident that "Caliban does not complain of being exploited; he complains of being betrayed." He "has fallen prey to the resentment which succeeds the breakdown of dependence". This view is buttressed by an analogous interpretation of Caliban's revolt in league with Trinculo as an action launched "not to win his freedom, for he could not support freedom, but to have a new master whose 'footlicker' he can become. He is delighted at the prospect. It would be hard to find a better example of the dependence complex in its pure state."

Such statements rankled badly with Caribbean and African intellectuals who, in the fifties, for the first time sensed the imminence of large-scale decolonization in their regions. In such circumstances, the insinuation that Caliban was incapable of surviving on his own and did not even aspire to such independence in the first place caused considerable affront and helped spur Third Worlders to mount adversarial interpretations of the play which rehabilitated Caliban into a heroic figure, inspired by noble rage to oust the interloping Prospero from his island. Fanon and Aimé Césaire, two of Mannoni's most vehement critics, found the "ethno-psychologist's" disregard for economic exploitation especially jarring and accused him of reducing colonialism to an encounter between two psychological types with complementary predispositions who, for a time at least, find their needs dovetailing tidily. *Psychologie de la colonisation*, these critics charged, made Caliban out to be an eager partner in his own colonization. Mannoni, in a statement like "wherever Europeans have founded colonies of the type we are considering, it can safely be said that their coming was unconsciously expected – even desired – by the future subject peoples," seemed to discount any possibility of Europe being culpable for the exploitation of the colonies. Mannoni's critics foresaw, moreover, just how readily his paradigm could be harnessed by Europeans seeking to thwart the efforts for self-determination that were gathering impetus in the fifties. [. . .]

By the time Caribbeans and Africans took up *The Tempest*, that is, from 1959 onward, widespread national liberation seemed not only feasible but imminent, and the play was mobilized in defense of Caliban's right to the land and to cultural autonomy. "This island's mine by Sycorax my mother / Which thou tak'st from me" [1.2.334–5] are the lines that underlie much of the work that was produced by African and Caribbean intellectuals in the 1960s and early 1970s. Those same two lines introduce Caliban's extended complaint (quoted at length above), the nodal speech Mannoni had cited as evidence that Shakespeare was dramatizing a relation of dependence, not one of exploitation. But, significantly, and in keeping with his very different motives for engaging with the play, Mannoni had lopped off those two lines when working the passage into his argument. On this score, Third World responses consistently broke with Mannoni: Caliban, the decolonizer, was enraged not at being orphaned by colonial paternalism but at being insufficiently abandoned by it.

The first Caribbean writer to champion Caliban was Lamming. His nonfictional *Pleasures of Exile* can be read as an effort to redeem from the past, as well as to stimulate, an indigenous Antillean line of creativity to rival the European traditions which seemed bent on arrogating to themselves all notions of culture. Lamming's melange of a text – part essay on the cultural politics of relations between colonizer and colonized, part autobiography, and part textual criticism of, in particular, *The Tempest* and C. L. R. James' *The Black Jacobins* (1938) – was sparked by two events, one personal, the other more broadly historical. Lamming began his text in 1959, shortly after disembarking in Southampton as part of the great wave of West Indian immigrants settling in Britain in the fifties. But his circumstances differed from those of most of his compatriots, for he was immigrating as an aspirant writer. As such he was keenly aware of taking up residence in the headquarters of the English language and culture and, concomitantly, of being only ambiguously party to that language and culture, even though a dialect of English was his native tongue and even though – for such was his colonial schooling – he was more intimate with Shakespeare and the English Revolution than with the writings and history of his own region.

Lamming's reflections on the personal circumstances which occasioned *The Pleasures of Exile* are suffused with his sense of the book's historical moment. Writing on the brink of the sixties, he was highly conscious that colonial Africa and the Caribbean were entering a new phase. The political mood of the book is expectant ("Caliban's history... belongs entirely to the future"), most evidently in his account of an envious visit to Ghana, the first of the newly independent African states. That trip sharpened his anguished sense of the British West Indies' failure as yet to achieve comparable autonomy. He recalls the intensity of that feeling in his introduction to the 1984 edition: "There were no independent countries in the English-speaking Caribbean when I started to write *The Pleasures of Exile* in 1959. With the old exceptions of Ethiopia and Liberia, there was only one in Black Africa, and that was Ghana. Twenty years later almost every rock and pebble in the Caribbean had acquired this status." While looking ahead to Caribbean self-determination, Lamming was also writing self-consciously in the aftermath of an action one year back that had quickened nationalist ambitions throughout the area: "Fidel Castro and the Cuban revolution reordered our history... The Cuban revolution was a Caribbean response to that imperial menace which Prospero conceived as a civilising mission." [...]

During the era of decolonization, negritude proved to be one of the strongest components of this remedial tradition, and it was the negritudist from Martinique, Césaire, who came to renovate *The Tempest* theatrically for black cultural ends in a manner indebted to Lamming if fiercer in its defiance. These two writers' approaches coincided most explicitly in their determination to unearth an endemic lineage of cultural-cum-political activists; it is telling that within the space of two years, each man published a book resuscitating Toussaint Louverture and celebrating his example.

Césaire's *Une Tempête* (1969) exemplifies the porous boundaries between European and Afro-Caribbean cultures even within the anti-colonial endeavors of the period. As an influence on Césaire's response to Shakespeare, Lamming keeps company with Mannoni and the German critic, Janheinz Jahn. Mannoni had experience of French island colonies in both Africa and the Caribbean for, prior to his stint in Madagascar, he had served as an instructor in a Martinican school where Césaire had been his precocious student. More than twenty years later, in *Discours sur le colonialisme*, Césaire upbraided his former schoolmaster for not thinking through the implications of his colonial paradigm. And Césaire's subsequent, inevitably reactive adaptation of Shakespeare further demonstrated just how far he had diverged from Mannoni's motives for valuing *The Tempest*. [...]

Césaire has been quite explicit about his motives for reworking *The Tempest*:

> I was trying to 'de-mythify' the tale. To me Prospero is the complete totalitarian. I am always surprised when others consider him the wise man who 'forgives'. What is most obvious, even in Shakespeare's version, is the man's absolute will to power. Prospero is the man of cold reason, the man of methodical conquest – in other words, a portrait of the 'enlightened' European. And I see the whole play in such terms: the 'civilized' European world coming face to face for the first time with the world of primitivism and magic. Let's not hide the fact that in Europe the world of reason has inevitably led to various kinds of totalitarianism . . . Caliban is the man who is still close to his beginnings, whose link with the natural world has not yet been broken. Caliban can still *participate* in a world of marvels, whereas his master can merely 'create' them through his acquired knowledge. At the same time, Caliban is also a rebel – the positive hero, in a Hegelian sense. The slave is always more important than his master – for it is the slave who makes history.

Césaire's perception of Prospero as "the man of methodical conquest" and his insistence on the slave as the preeminent historical agent become the touchstones for his radically polarized adaptation of Shakespeare. Forgiveness and reconciliation give way to irreconcilable differences; the roles of Ferdinand and Miranda are whittled down to a minimum; and the play's colonial dimensions are writ large. Antonio and Alonso vie with Prospero for control over newly charted lands abroad, and Shakespeare's rightful Duke of Milan is delivered to the island not by the providence of a "happy storm" but through a confederacy rooted in imperial ambitions. Prospero is demythologized and rendered contemporary by making him altogether less white magical and a master of the technology of oppression; his far from inscrutable power is embodied in antiriot control gear and an arsenal. Violating rather than communing with life on the island, he is, in Caliban's phrase, the *"anti-Natur."*

Une Tempête self-consciously counterpoises the materialist Prospero with an animistic slave empowered by a culture that coexists empathetically with nature. Indeed, Caliban's culture of resistance is his sole weaponry, but it is more formidable than the shallow culture Shakespeare permits him, as Césaire plumbs the depths of the slave's African past to make him a more equal adversary. Caliban's defiance is expressed most strongly through the celebration of the Yoruba gods Shango and Eshu; two of his four songs of liberation fete Shango, an African figure who has survived in Caribbean voodoo and Brazilian macumba. And in a critical irruption, Eshu scatters Prospero's carefully ordered classical masque, making the imported divinities seem precious, effete, and incongruous.

Césaire's Caliban also goes beyond Shakespeare's in his refusal to subscribe to the etiquette of subjugation:

> *Caliban*: Uhuru!
> *Prospero*: Qu'est-ce que tu dis?
> *Caliban*: Je dis Uhuru!
> *Prospero*: Encore une remontée Je de ton language barbare.
> Je t'ai déjà dit que n'arrive pas ça. D'ailleurs, tu pourrais être poli, un bonjour ne te tuerait pas!

This opening exchange between Caliban and his colonial overlord sets the stage for Césaire's conviction that the culture of slaves need not be an enslaved culture. Here he is more optimistic than Lamming, who saw Caribbean cultures of resistance as ineluctably circumscribed by the colonizer's language; one thinks particularly of Lamming in Ghana, casting an envious eye over children chatting in their indigenous tongue, a language that "owed Prospero no debt of vocabulary." Even if Césaire's Caliban cannot throw off European influences entirely, his recuperation of a residual past is sufficient to secure his relative cultural autonomy. Crucially, his first utterance is "Uhuru," the Swahili term for freedom which gained international currency through the struggles for decolonization in the late fifties and sixties. And Caliban retorts to Prospero's demand for a *bonjour* by charging that he has only been instructed in the colonial tongue so he can submit to the magisterial imperatives, and by declaring that he will no longer respond to the name Caliban, a colonial invention bound anagramatically to the degrading "cannibal." Instead, the island's captive king christens himself "X" in a Black Muslim gesture that commemorates his lost name, buried beneath layers of colonial culture. The play supposes, in sum, that Caribbean colonial subjects can best fortify their revolt by reviving, wherever possible, cultural forms dating back to before that wracking sea-change which was the Middle Passage.

Césaire's remark that the slave, as maker of history, "is always more important than his master" has both a retrospective and an anticipatory force, pointing back to Louverture, Haiti, and the only triumphant slave revolt, and forward through the present to colonialism's demise. Césaire steeps his play most explicitly in the contemporary Afro-Caribbean struggles for self-determination when he stages, via Ariel and Caliban, the debate, ubiquitous in the late fifties and sixties, between the rival strategies for liberation advanced by proponents of evolutionary and revolutionary change. The mulatto Ariel shuns violence and holds that, faced with Prospero's stockpiled arsenal, they are more likely to win freedom through conciliation than refractoriness. But from Caliban's perspective Ariel is a colonial collaborator, a political and cultural sellout who, aspiring both to rid himself nonviolently of Prospero and to emulate his values, is reduced to negotiating for liberty from a position of powerlessness. The success of Caliban's uncompromising strategies is imminent at the end of the drama. When the other Europeans return to Italy, Prospero is unable to accompany them, for he is in the thrall of a psychological battle with his slave (shades of Mannoni here), shouting "Je défendrai la civilisation!" but intuiting that "le climat a changé." At the close, Caliban is chanting ecstatically, "La Liberté Ohé, La Liberté," and defying the orders of a master whose authority and sanity are teetering.

Césaire, then, radically reassessed *The Tempest* in terms of the circumstances of his region, taking the action to the brink of colonialism's demise. He valued the play because he saw its potential as a vehicle for dramatizing the evolution of colonialism in his region and for sharpening the contemporary ideological alternatives open to would-be-liberated Antilleans. Césaire sought, from an openly interested standpoint, to amend the political acoustics of Shakespeare's play, to make the action resonate with the dangers of supine cultural assimilation, a concern since his student days that was accentuated during the high period of decolonization. This renovation of the play for black cultural ends was doubly impertinent: besides treating a classic sacrilegiously, it implicitly lampooned the educational practice, so pervasive in the colonies, of distributing only bowdlerized versions of Shakespeare, of watering him down "for the natives." *Une Tempête* can thus be read as parodying this habit by indicating how the bard might have looked were he indeed made fit reading for a subject people.

Césaire's play was published in 1969. The years 1968 through 1971 saw the cresting of Caribbean and African interest in *The Tempest* as a succession of essayists, novelists, poets, and dramatists sought to integrate the play into the cultural forces pitted against colonialism. During those four years, *The Tempest* was appropriated among the Caribbeans by Césaire, Fernández Retamar (twice), Lamming (in a novelistic reworking of some of the ideas first formulated in *The Pleasures of Exile*), and the Barbadian poet Edward Braithwaite. In Africa, the play was taken up during the same period by John Pepper Clark in Nigeria, Ngugi wa Thiong'o in Kenya, and David Wallace in Zambia. Among these, Braithwaite and Fernández Retamar followed Lamming's lead, finding a topical, regional urgency for the play through articulating the Cuban revolution to Caliban's revolt. Braithwaite's poem, "Caliban," salutes the Cuban revolution against a backdrop of lamentation over the wrecked state of the Caribbean. The body of the poem, with its clipped calypso phrasing, knits together allusions to Caliban's song, " 'Ban, 'Ban, Ca-Caliban," Ferdinand's speech, "Where should this music be?" and Ariel's response, "Full fadom five." But it is Caliban the slave, not the royal Alonso, who suffers a sea-change, falling "through the water's / cries / down / down / down / where the music hides / him / down / down / down / where the si-/ lence lies." And he is revived not by Ariel's ethereal strains and, behind them, Prospero's white magic, but by the earthy music of the carnival and the intercession of black gods. [...]

The Tempest's value for African and Caribbean intellectuals faded once the plot ran out. The play lacks a sixth act which might have been enlisted for representing relations among Caliban, Ariel, and Prospero once they entered a postcolonial era, or rather (in Harry Magdoff's phrase), an era of "imperialism without colonies." Over time, Caliban's recovery of his island has proved a qualified triumph, with the autonomy of his emergent nation far more compromised than was imagined by the generation of more optimistic nationalists – politicians and writers alike – who saw independence in. Third Worlders have found it difficult to coax from the play analogies with these new circumstances wherein Prospero, having officially relinquished authority over the island, so often continues to manage it from afar. [...]

Between the late fifties and early seventies *The Tempest* was valued and competed for both by those (in the "master"-culture's terms) traditionally possessed of discrimination and those traditionally discriminated against. On the one hand, a broad evaluative agreement existed between the two sets of feuding cultures, the colonizers and the colonized both regarding the play highly. On the other hand, the two groups brought utterly different social ambitions to bear on the play. Writers and intellectuals from the colonies appropriated *The Tempest* in a way that was outlandish in the original sense of the word. They reaffirmed the play's importance from outside its central tradition not passively or obsequiously, but through what may best be described as a series of insurrectional endorsements. For in that turbulent and intensely reactive phase of Caribbean and African history, *The Tempest* came to serve as a Trojan horse, whereby cultures barred from the citadel of "universal" Western values could win entry and assail those global pretensions from within.

CRITICAL   *Part 3*
INTERVENTIONS

The study of Shakespeare has moved in many new directions in the closing decades of the twentieth century. To capture adequately the variety of recent Shakespeare scholarship and criticism is impossible. In Part Two, we tried to represent the many competing approaches to Shakespeare in relation to the nine plays, but there remains a diverse and vital tradition of critical work on Shakespeare that does not focus on specific plays, but nonetheless exerts a powerful influence. In this final section, rather than try for any kind of field coverage of this work, we limit our ambitions by returning to the three key terms in the title of the course – 'Shakespeare', 'Text', and 'Performance' – and reprint essays that address each of these terms. The essays have been selected principally because all three make some effort to survey new debates and initiatives in their respective fields.

1 Jonathan Bate, 'The National Poet'

Source: *The Genius of Shakespeare* (London: Picador, 1997), pp. 187–94, 197–204, 209.

Quite what 'Shakespeare' means in Britain at the end of the twentieth century remains a contentious question. For Jonathan Bate, as for many Shakespeare critics before him, the answer is tied up with questions of British national identity, and he turns to the beginning of the century, and to the First World War in particular, to set out the alternatives. On the one hand, there is Oxford professor Sir Walter Raleigh's patriotic Shakespeare, 'a good Tory, a believer in rank and institutions and the established order'. On the other hand, there is the Shakespeare of poet Edward Thomas, the Shakespeare who created Falstaff, and displayed sympathy for 'the common foot soldier in every age'. Although Bate rather misrepresents the arguments of more irreverent Shakespeare critics like Terence Hawkes (see Extract 5.2), and clearly tilts the balance in favour of Thomas's Shakespeare, the extract nonetheless provides vivid examples of how Shakespeare has been claimed by thinkers of very different political inclinations.

Back to basics

Imagine a country in which Shakespeare is made compulsory in the national curriculum in secondary schools and where an 'official' interpretation transforms him into the guardian of the value system of the established powers. Such a country might be England, where a set Shakespeare play is a key element of the nationally prescribed tests in English for fourteen-year-olds and where the official interpretation is heard in the mouths of government ministers.

In January 1994, the British Conservative government, in its fifteenth year of uninterrupted power, had a particularly bad month. Just as it was embracing a new leading idea of a return to 'basic' values, stories broke concerning ministerial adultery which made pious pronouncements about traditional morality look hypocritical. Then an independent auditor produced a mass of evidence that Westminster City Council, hailed by successive Conservative prime ministers as the party's 'flagship' authority in local government, had been engaged in gerrymandering, selling publicly owned housing to private individuals in return for the expectation of their votes. The day after the publication of these findings, Michael Portillo, the Chief Secretary to the Treasury, made a speech to the annual dinner of Conservative Way Forward, a grouping within the party devoted to the fostering of a strongly right-wing agenda. It was a speech which marked him out as the right's candidate for the prime ministerial succession. In it he argued that the greatest danger facing the nation was lack of respect for institutions:

> The relations which hold society together stretch from top to bottom. If Crown, Parliament, and Church are not respected, neither will be law, judges, or policemen, nor professors nor teachers nor social workers, nor bosses, managers, or foremen. Social disorder follows when respect breaks down. A society in which people hold those in authority in contempt, and don't even think much of themselves, is set upon the road to disintegration.

He then went on to support this claim by means of a substantial quotation:

> In Shakespeare's *Troilus and Cressida*, Ulysses explains how order in society depends upon a series of relationships of respect and duty from top to bottom.
>
> When degree is shaked,
> Which is the ladder to all high designs,

The enterprise is sick. How could communities,
Degrees in schools, and brotherhoods in cities,
Peaceful commerce from dividable shores,
The primogenity and due of birth,
Prerogative of age, crown, sceptres, laurels,
But by degree stand in authentic place?
Take but degree away, untune that string,
And hark what discord follows ...
Strength should be lord of imbecility.
And the rude son should strike his father dead;
Force should be right, or rather right and wrong ...
Should lose their names, and so should justice too.
                                        [1.3.101–18]

Shakespeare, it seems, was a good Tory, a believer in rank and institutions and the established order. The ellipsis in the quotation after 'right and wrong' indicates that Portillo omitted an awkward parenthesis in which Ulysses says that 'justice resides' in what seems to be a rather grey area 'between' the 'endless jar' of 'right and wrong'. Such a complication did not serve the quoter's purpose, so it was quietly suppressed. Quotation was as ever used selectively to support a particular position; for Portillo and his audience, it was comforting to see the national poet promulgating the values in which they believed and by which they sought to govern.

Shakespeare put some persuasive political rhetoric into the mouth of Ulysses in *Troilus and Cressida*, but this is not to say that Ulysses' argument is the argument of the whole play, let alone an expression of the personal political beliefs of its author. A good test of the worth of a character's opinions is their relation to that character's actions, and by this account Ulysses looks distinctly questionable. He identifies as one of the causes of the unturning of degree in the Greek camp the fact that their best soldier, Achilles, is sulking in his tent when he should be in the appropriate place for the best soldier, namely on the battlefield. But the method Ulysses then proposes by which Achilles can be restored to his proper place is itself a disruption of degree: Hector, the top Trojan warrior, has challenged the top Greek to single combat; degree should dictate that Achilles will be put forward, but Ulysses proposes the blockish Ajax instead, thus snubbing Achilles and provoking him to rejoin the army. For Ulysses, 'degree' is but rhetoric in the service of machiavellian 'policy'. Given the proximity in time of Portillo's speech to the revelations about gerrymandering by Westminster Tories, there is a certain piquancy in the fact that a few minutes after delivering his apology for 'degree', Ulysses rigs an election.

Portillo's speech was directed against those who had become 'cynical' about Britain's ancient institutions and traditional values. Ironically, there could be no better word than 'cynical' for Shakespeare's representation in *Troilus and Cressida* of traditional codes and values. It was exactly for that reason that the legitimate theatre hardly ever staged the play in the eighteenth and nineteenth century; this deeply ironic drama only came into its own in the aftermath of the First World War, when it was successful for the very reason that its cynicism about military top brass caught the public mood as the nation reflected on what General Haig and his colleagues had inflicted upon the common soldier on the Somme and at Ypres. The case of *Troilus and Cressida* demonstrates that Shakespeare has been made to speak against the Establishment as well as for it.

[. . .] Shakespeare's eighteenth-century emergence as England's genius was in part a manifestation of cultural nationalism. But the nation and the Establishment are by no means one and the same thing. This is something which the Establishment has a tendency to forget. Oddly, though, it is something which the anti-Establishment also has a tendency to forget.

At exactly the time when the British government was prescribing Shakespeare as the centre of the national secondary school curriculum in English studies, some college and university English departments began following an American lead and removing him from the centre of the higher level curriculum, so as to give space instead to those who had previously been on the margins of culture – women and blacks. In 1992, the arch-conservative newspaper *The Sunday Telegraph* was apoplectic at the news of a survey which claimed that the black American woman novelist Alice Walker had become a compulsory author in more institutions of higher education than was Shakespeare.

It was in the name of the national heritage that the Conservative government gave Shakespeare his honorific place in the school curriculum. In the late twentieth century, advanced literary theory was out of sympathy with Toryism and very uncomfortable with the idea of a national heritage. The *Sunday Telegraph* article made Shakespeare synonymous with 'our cultural inheritance' – radical theorists wanted nothing to do with that 'our'. During the 1980s literary studies became more openly politicized than they had ever been before. Demographic and cultural changes in the United States meant that there was a mounting challenge to the canons of taste which placed Dead White European Males at the centre of the literature curriculum. The idea of 'England's Heritage' became so associated with Conservative hegemony that independent-minded academics wished to detach themselves from anything tainted by association with it. Because of these developments, a new story began to be told about Shakespeare's status as National Poet, Bard of Bards, genius not of an age but for all time.

The argument goes something like this. Shakespeare's extraordinary reputation and continuing prestige are a function not of his poetic genius but of his political servility, his adaptability to Establishment values. He rose to pre-eminence in the period 1660–1830 on the back of the British Empire, the strength of the middle class and the reaction against the French Revolution. The guardians and propagators of Shakespeare's reputation in the early twentieth century – men like A. C. Bradley, Sir Walter Raleigh, John Dover Wilson, T. S. Eliot and G. Wilson Knight – were all compromised by either Romantic idealism (pretending that Shakespeare wasn't political when in fact he was) or right-wing fanaticism. By the middle of the twentieth century, Shakespeare had become an apologist for order and hierarchy as embodied in a value-structure that was best summed up by Ulysses' speech on degree. The shorthand term for this value-structure was 'The Elizabethan World Picture', and so it was that sniping at a small book so named, written in the 1940s by E. M. W. Tillyard, became the most easily recognizable badge of those whom I shall call the New Iconoclasts in Shakespeare studies.

I do not wish to nail this story as a complete lie, because I do not believe that it is one. But I do believe that it offers nothing like the whole truth and that there is a real danger of other parts of the Shakespeare story being forgotten. [...] It is my argument that, confining it to its socio-political dimension alone, the story of Shakespeare's extraordinary reputation and continuing prestige is a function not only of the impulses variously labelled by the New Iconoclasts as 'reactionary', 'hegemonic', and 'nationalistic', but also of counter-readings which could variously be labelled 'radical', 'anti- Establishment', and 'supranational'. [...]

This England

The two most influential books on Shakespeare written in the early years of the twentieth century were A. C. Bradley's *Shakespearean Tragedy* of 1904 and Walter Raleigh's *William Shakespeare* of 1907, the latter being the capstone to the best-selling series of primers, 'English Men of Letters'. In two essays which represent the New Iconoclasm in Shakespeare studies at its wittiest and most irreverent, Terence Hawkes has reconstructed and deconstructed the ideological circumstances in which these books were written. The academic careers of Bradley and Raleigh ran curiously in parallel: from Oxford to Liverpool to Glasgow and back to Oxford. Each time Bradley vacated a Chair, Raleigh stepped in to fill it. Hawkes might say that Raleigh was always there as the overtly ideological, chauvinistic shadow of Bradley's apparently supraideological idealism. I begin in the same place as Hawkes, but do so in order to reach a different destination.

In 1889, Andrew Cecil Bradley, first holder of the University of Liverpool's King Alfred Chair in English Literature, and still the first name of which many people think when 'Shakespearean Criticism' is mentioned, departed for the Regius Chair at Glasgow. He was succeeded by the twenty-eight-year-old Walter Raleigh, a man furnished with an auspicious name for the study of the 'golden' period of English literature, the age of Queen Elizabeth. When translated to Oxford early in the new century, Raleigh would gain a knighthood and complete his name, becoming Sir Walter. It was from Oxford that Raleigh had gone to Liverpool, so it is not unexpected that he said the city was drab and the people provincial.

But he was initially enthusiastic about the job. University departments of English literature were new things in the 1890s and he relished the opportunity of leading one in the investigation of a large question: 'Is Literature gossip, or philosophy, or waxworks, or homiletics?' At Oxford high tables it had been largely gossip, though in the hands of Matthew Arnold it had become homiletics. At Liverpool, Raleigh initially followed his predecessor, the Hegel-influenced Bradley, and treated it as philosophy – his inaugural lecture defined poetry as 'Life in the process of transmutation into Metaphysic', or, with nice circularity, 'Metaphysic in the process of transmutation into Life'. This high view of the subject, which had its roots in the Romantic poetics of the early nineteenth century, was still an advanced, not to say an avant-garde, one, in the 1890s. It would perhaps have surprised Raleigh that a hundred years later, the literary critical avant-garde tended towards one of his other alternatives, namely the view that the canon of English Literature is nothing more than a collection of waxworks.

The reasons for this strange reversal begin to be apparent if we turn to a letter which Raleigh wrote later in his tenure of the Liverpool Chair: 'I have just been asked to examine for the Indian Civil Service (which pleases me well) in English Literature. I have to examine on a special period, Shakespeare to Dryden. If only one could do a little towards helping to keep a crock or two away from the Service – but they are hard to recognize in writing, and often impossible to refuse marks to.' Literature has become neither philosophy nor homiletics, not even gossip, but rather a device for keeping crocks out of the Indian Civil Service. As Raleigh recognized, it was not a very satisfactory method of recruitment – the correlation between mugging up on the Bard and administering the Empire was inexact – but it was a necessary one, given that the demand for junior administrators outstripped the supply of Oxbridge men trained in the classical languages, the traditional source of recruitment for the service.

Modern historians of the discipline of English studies have seized upon this development and argued from it that the content was defined by the function: a test in 'English Literature' was invented in order to create a ruling class, so the canon of English Literature was constructed out of a body of material which propped up the value-structure of that ruling class. The primal scene of instruction becomes the colonizing Prospero oppressing the native Caliban by teaching him the English language from which his only profit is slavery and the ability to curse. Never mind that Shakespeare gave a voice to Caliban, gave him the best poetry in the play. Nor indeed that [...] identification with him has been a liberating resource for modern West Indian writers.

The New Iconoclasm regards Shakespeare as the prize waxwork in the museum of the national heritage. It has been given more ammunition by Sir Walter Raleigh than anyone else – for instance, by his 1918 British Academy lecture on 'Shakespeare and England', which fulminated against the perversion of Shakespeare on the part of German philologists. Raleigh celebrated the National Bard as the guardian of all that England was fighting for against the philistine Hun. Terence Hawkes quotes with relish a passage in which Sir Walter reconstructs Caliban as a cowering German infantryman in no man's land, Trinculo and Stephano as (somewhat unlikely) noble-hearted English Tommies:

> A small British expeditionary force, bound on an international mission, finds itself stranded in an unknown country. The force is composed of men very various in rank and profession. Two of them, whom we may call a non-commissioned officer and a private, go exploring by themselves, and take one of the natives of the place prisoner. This native is an ugly low-born creature, of great physical strength and violent criminal tendencies, a liar, and ready at any time for theft, rape, and murder. He is a child of Nature, a lover of music, slavish in his devotion to power and rank, and very easily imposed upon by authority. His captors do not fear him, and which is more, do not dislike him. They found him lying out in a kind of no man's land, drenched to the skin, so they determine to keep him as a souvenir, and to take him home with them. They nickname him, in friendly fashion, the monster, and the mooncalf, as who should say Fritz, or the Boche. But their first care is to give him a drink, and to make him swear an allegiance upon the bottle. 'Where the devil should he learn our language?' says the non-commissioned officer.

In time of war, the dominant Shakespeare will always be the Bard as Britannia ruling the waves. The routine patriotic construction had its origins in such remarkings as *Harlequin's Invasion*, David Garrick's wartime pantomime of 1759, in which the forces of King Shakespeare stave off the threat of French Harlequin to a rousing chorus of Boyce's 'Heart of Oak'. It reached a zenith in the Laurence Olivier film of *Henry V*, with its opening frame dedicating the film to the airborne and seaborne commandos who spearheaded the D-Day landings of 1944. [...]

Suppose that Raleigh [...] had been asked to put together an anthology for incorporation into the national timetable in schools. Suppose that [his] brief had been to produce a narrative of English history illustrated by suitable passages from the poets. How would Shakespeare have been represented in such an anthology? The key passages would surely have been [...]: 'This England' from *King John*, 'this England' from *Richard II*, and 'we band of brothers' from *Henry V*. It would also have been necessary to give a more conceptual sense of Shakespeare's political position, so a fourth speech would have been added. It would almost certainly have been the one that Raleigh quoted in full in his essay on the age of Elizabeth in support of his contention that Shakespeare 'believed in rank and order and subordination', for 'his speeches in favour of these things have nothing ironical about them, and are never answered by equally good speeches on the other side'. The greatest of these speeches, says Raleigh, 'is put into the mouth of Ulysses, the wisest of the Greeks' – it is the oft-cited oration on 'degree' in *Troilus and Cressida*.

What sort of commentary would Raleigh [...] have provided to accompany these passages in [his] hypothetical anthology? Something like the following, I would imagine: after the deposition of Richard II, 'The House of Lancaster had started its reign and Shakespeare was to be its retrospective Poet Laureate'; to go with Crispin's Day, 'the prince acceded to the throne as Henry V, cast off his old friends, and became a national hero – or so the genius of Shakespeare would have it'; and to go with Ulysses on degree, 'Shakespeare emphasizes to his Jacobean audience the importance of an authority which is divinely ordained and which is maintained by the hierarchical nature of society. He offers a clear warning of what would happen should the state of things be undermined.' Ulysses' speech might have been juxtaposed in the anthology with 'Let us now praise famous men' from the Book of Ecclesiasticus in the Authorized Version; this would have illustrated how 'the plays of Shakespeare and the King James Bible established the English language as the greatest glory of Western civilization'.

The anthology which represents Shakespeare by these passages and with these comments was not produced by [...] Raleigh as educational propaganda during the Great War. It was published in 1988 under the title *The Faber Book of English History in Verse*. Its editor was the Right Honourable Kenneth Baker, at that time Her Majesty's Secretary of State for Education. It was not the only substantial text which Baker oversaw in 1988. He was also responsible that year for the Great Education Reform Bill, which imposed a new National Curriculum upon English state schools. The exact content of that curriculum went through several mutations after Baker departed from the Department of Education, but his desire for Shakespeare to be one of the jewels in its crown was fulfilled to the extent that it was decreed that every fourteen-year-old in the land should be tested on a set Shakespeare play. According to a press release from the Department of Education, dated 30 June 1992, headlined

'SHAKESPEARE AND GRAMMAR TESTS FOR ALL 14 YEAR OLDS', that was what John Patten, the then minister, saw as 'real education'.

The decree had its local origins in arguments about supposedly declining standards in schools: there was a widespread perception, particularly among Tory backbenchers and their middle-class constituents, that trendy teachers had given up on 'proper' English literature in favour of the easy option of showing videos of soap operas or setting the novels of Frederick Forsyth as examination texts. The avant-garde's theory of canonical literature as waxworks added fuel to this perception.

But there was a grander design as well as the local one. The most culturally revealing political development of 1992 was the formation of a Department of National Heritage. In any other country, this would have been called a Ministry of Culture. But in Britain, the arts and related activities had to be seen to support the nation, to come under the banner of that guarantor of the nation's sense of its own greatness, its heritage. And Shakespeare is the epicentre of that heritage. Baker's mind-boggling claim that 'the plays of Shakespeare and the King James Bible established the English language as the greatest glory of Western civilization' was the ultimate justification for Shakespeare's central position in the National Curriculum. [...]

Arthur's bosom

A certain inconsistency of British Conservative government policy in the period which began with Margaret Thatcher's assumption of power in 1979 has often been remarked upon: while economic policy was driven by privatization, deregulation, and market forces, education policy was driven by nationalization (of the curriculum), regulation (of university statutes, teachers' performance, and so on), and government forces (at the expense of local education authorities). If market forces were to prevail in the reading curriculum, Frederick Forsyth would prevail over Shakespeare. Thatcher, who once confessed to her taste for *re*-reading the thrillers of Forsyth, would probably have been perfectly happy with this; but after her removal from power, the regulation of what was to be studied in schools was determined less by her laissez-faire ideology than by an old-style One Nation Toryism. Education Ministers like Kenneth Baker and John Patten really did believe that heritage – that Shakespeare – could be the glue to bind the nation together and make it feel good about itself. Michael Portillo's reading of Ulysses' speech in relation to the defence of established institutions was of a piece with their vision.

But what service did it do to Shakespeare to nationalize him in this way? What warrant was there for the interpretations propagated by Baker's anthology? The first thing that needs to be said is that the chauvinistic readings are risible simplifications of the plays, neglecting as they do the cardinal principle that dramatic speeches must be read in the context of character and action. Gaunt in *Richard II* and the Bastard who speaks the closing speech of *King John* are not disinterested apologists for England – they have agendas of their own. As I have already pointed out, the Ulysses of *Troilus and Cressida* is not so much the wisest of the Greeks as the slyest of the Greeks. Henry V's justification for being in France on Crispin's Day is distinctly questionable: as William Hazlitt put it, 'Henry, because he did not know how to govern his own kingdom, determined to make war upon his neighbours; because his own title to the crown was doubtful, he laid claim to that of France'.

That said, there is no denying that Shakespeare was interested in creating a myth of England. He was the only dramatist of the age who returned repeatedly to that foundation-text of Tudor ideology, Holinshed's *Chronicles*. But in the canon of his works as a whole, and even in the plays based on Holinshed, the England he created has a much more complex identity than that proposed by Raleigh, Gollancz, and Baker. The patriotic Bardolaters slip easily from England to Britain. Raleigh seems to have no difficulty in forgetting the years he spent as a professor in Glasgow; [...] Baker has nothing to say about the oddity of his 'National' school curriculum applying to England and Wales, but not to Scotland and Northern Ireland. For Shakespeare, on the other hand, national identity is ragged about the edges. [...] To illustrate the complexity of Shakespeare's sense of the nation, I want to show how he was used in another anthology, this time one which *was* commissioned during the First World War but which adopted a very different tone from that of the flag-waving Baker.

Published in 1915, it was called *This England: An Anthology from her Writers compiled by Edward Thomas*. It carried an unassuming prefatory note:

> This is an anthology from the work of English writers rather strictly so called. Building round a few most English poems like 'When icicles hang by the wall', – excluding professedly patriotic writing because it is generally bad and because indirect praise is sweeter and more profound, – never aiming at what a committee from Great Britain and Ireland might call complete, – I wished to make a book as full of English character and country as an egg is of meat. If I have reminded others, as I did myself continually, of some of the echoes called up by the name of England, I am satisfied.

There is nothing here of kings and queens, empire and war. Edward Thomas's idea of England was rooted in place – his anthology has a preponderance of rural writing, but also a section on London – and in home. For Thomas, England was not a set of institutions, a heritage, but 'a system of vast circumferences circling round the minute neighbouring points of home'.

The longest complete poem in the anthology is Samuel Taylor Coleridge's 'Fears in Solitude', a troubled meditation in time of war which differentiates sharply between Britain in the sense of its political institutions, which is dismissed as 'One Benefit-Club for mutual flattery', and the 'mother Isle' in the sense of a synecdochic representation of the local community and landscape which have nurtured the poet. Coleridge's poem is a reworking of Gaunt's 'this England' oration, which was itself simultaneously a panegyric of the land and a denunciation of governmental mismanagement.

In Edward Thomas's anthology, insofar as the name of England means a history, it means the defence of liberty. The collection begins with three passages from Milton's prose and part of a speech by Cromwell. Edmund Burke on tradition is represented, but is balanced by a splendid extract from Hazlitt: 'It always struck me as a singular proof of good taste, good sense and liberal thinking, in an old friend, who had Paine's *Rights of Man* and Burke's *Reflections on the French Revolution* bound up in one volume, and who said, that, both together, they made a very good book.' It was Hazlitt who said that a viewing of *Coriolanus* would save one the trouble of reading both Burke attacking the French Revolution and Paine defending it because Shakespeare gave both sides of the argument. It was also Hazlitt who, in a passage concerning Charles James Fox, gave Edward Thomas's anthology its definition of patriotism: 'his love of his country did not consist in his hatred of the rest of mankind'.

Patriotism has always been a troublesome concept, as *Chambers Dictionary* recognizes through the two-handedness with which it defines a patriot: 'one who truly, or ostentatiously and injudiciously, loves and serves his fatherland'. Coleridge in 'Fears in Solitude', Hazlitt in many of his essays, and Edward Thomas in his anthology reject ostentatious and injudicious patriotism, discovering instead a quieter and more profound love of their native land. Shakespeare is one of their paths to that discovery.

Contrary to the expectation established by his title, Thomas omitted the 'this England' speeches from *King John* and *Richard II*. The reader of *This England* first encounters Shakespeare in the form of the song of winter from *Love's Labour's Lost*, Falstaff in praise of sack, and the tale of Herne the Hunter from *The Merry Wives of Windsor*. The tone for the whole is set by the claim in the prefatory note that the 'most English' kind of writing is 'When icicles hang by the wall', a song about rural labour in which the burden is 'While greasy Joan doth keel the pot'. At the climax of the anthology is a substantial section called 'The Vital Commoners'. England is defined by its people, not its monarchs, by greasy Joan and not Queen Elizabeth. In a subtle move, Thomas includes in his final section the 'up to the mountains!' address of Belarius to Guiderius and Arviragus in *Cymbeline*, a speech in which true nobility finds itself not at court but in nature, and in which national identity is complicated because the location is Wales. Edward Thomas himself was able to negotiate between Englishness and Britain precisely because his origins were mainly Welsh; the difficulty of that negotiation is acknowledged by the prefatory note's careful rider, 'never aiming at what a committee from Great Britain and Ireland might call complete'.

The anthology does embrace the Crispin's Day oration, but the King's pep talk is not presented in isolation. In the 'Vital Commoners' section, Thomas also included Michael Williams's unanswerable argument against Harry Le Roy, 'But if the cause be not good, the king himself hath a heavy reckoning to make, when all those legs and arms and heads, chopped off in a battle, shall join together at the latter day' – the publication of this in a wartime anthology which soldiers could carry in their knapsacks was typically brave of Thomas. And on the page opposite Harry's address to his men before Agincourt, we find Falstaff's address to himself in the Boar's Head Tavern: 'Go thy ways, old Jack; die when thou wilt, if manhood, good manhood, be not forgot upon the face of the earth, then am I shotten herring. There live not three good men unhanged in England; and one of them is fat and grows old'. Thomas forces us to consider the possibility that Shakespeare gives us his ideal Patriot-Englishman not in Henry V, as Gollancz had it, but in old Jack Falstaff.

Consider what it would mean to make Falstaff into the true embodiment of England. Sir Walter Raleigh would have found the idea inconceivable. He was of the view that 'a clear stage was needed for the patriotic and warlike exploits of King Harry; here was to be no place for critics and philosophers', so 'in the name of the public safety, Falstaff must be put to death'. The sinister overtones of the Committee of Public Safety in Robespierre's Terror are wholly unintended, but revelatory of exactly what is troubling about King Harry.

By including more of Falstaff than of Harry in his anthology, Edward Thomas unobtrusively reveals his allegiance to a long tradition of liberal, dissenting Englishness. In 1817 Hazlitt's abhorrence of kings, of empire, and of war was registered by his remark that 'we never could forgive the Prince's treatment of Falstaff'. [. . .]

As prime embodiment of the Eastcheap crowd, Falstaff is Shakespeare's primary means of access to those whom Edward Thomas called 'the vital commoners' and it is in this sense that he is England. He has somehow won himself a knighthood, but he has decayed from the gentry and is back among the commoners. His language is a living vernacular prose, richer in metaphor and invention than the verse of any of the plays' noble speakers. He possesses no property, is always in debt, on the run from the law. If he has a home and a family, it is in the alehouse among his drinking companions: as Maurice Morgann put it, 'he dies where he lived, in a Tavern'.

His voice of ale and safety belongs to the common foot soldier in every age. It does not care for the rhetoric of fame with which kings and officers exhort their men. One must stress again that there is a distinction, gestured towards by Justice Shallow, between Jack Falstaff and Sir John. As a recruiting officer, Sir John sends lesser men to their deaths without even the compunction of Harry in the night before Agincourt. But in the tavern Falstaff is always Jack, and this Jack is a generic name for the vital commoners. In *Richard III*, a Jack is the opposite of a gentleman. In a pamphlet dedicated to the fishmongers and butchers of England, John Taylor the Water-poet, himself a sometime pressed man in the Elizabethan navy, saluted Jack of Newbury, Jack Drum, Jack Dog, Jack of Dover, Jack Herring, Jack Sprat, Jack Straw, Jack Cade and any number of other common-or-garden Jacks. So does Shakespeare salute Jack Falstaff. [...]

2 Gary Taylor, 'The Present Tense'

Source: *Reinventing Shakespeare. A Cultural History from the Restoration to the Present* (London: Hogarth, 1989), pp. 311–18.

The theoretical assaults in the last twenty years on the 'Shakespeare Text' have been alluded to in Interval Two on Editing Shakespeare's Plays. In this extract, Gary Taylor describes the controversy accompanying the publication in 1986 of Oxford University Press's new Collected Works of Shakespeare. Taylor notes the choice in favour of 'the more theatrical version of each play' made by the Oxford editors, and reflects on the problems involved in 'translating' the Shakespeare text into modern English. The immediate consequence of this new scholarship is that existing interpretations of the plays are rendered suspect. Taylor's snapshot impressions of the recent history of textual editing are necessarily partial and incomplete, but as one of the co-editors of the 1986 Oxford *Collected Works* (which is the copy text for *The Norton Shakespeare*), he writes with direct experience of contemporary debates.

OXFORD

October 28, 1986. Dr. Stanley Wells performs before an audience in the Sheldonian Theatre, celebrating the publication by Oxford University Press of a new text of Shakespeare's works. The Sheldonian Theatre, an edifice serving both dramatic and academic functions, is an appropriate setting for this performance, for Wells is a theatre historian as well as an editor, both a governor of the Royal Shakespeare Theatre and a Fellow of Balliol College. Like Nicholas Rowe, but in contrast to the subsequent editorial tradition initiated by Pope, Wells edits Shakespeare in the light of theatrical practice. From 1725 to 1985 editors had labored to peel away what they saw as the debasing influence of the stage, seeking to recover Shakespeare's own literary, pretheatrical text. By contrast Wells declares that "The theatre of Shakespeare's time was his most valuable collaborator"; and his edition "chooses, when possible, to print the more theatrical version of each play."

In its emphasis upon theatrical practicality the new Oxford edition reflects not only Wells' personal interests but also the new interpenetration of theatre and scholarship characteristic of his generation. Not surprisingly, one feature of the edition that Wells emphasizes in this inaugural lecture is "our treatment of stage directions":

> Editorial theorists, preoccupied by the words to be spoken, have almost totally ignored the subject of stage directions, even though they are central to a presentation of Shakespeare's, or any dramatist's, art ... What happens on stage during a play is not merely a kind of optional descant to the dialogue; it is an absolutely integral part of the author's vision.

This intensified scrutiny of stage directions affects every play. Oxford's Shakespeare calls for French prisoners to be killed onstage in *Henry V*, clarifies the spectacular staging of Prospero's masque in *The Tempest*, attends to the removal of Emilia's corpse in *Othello*, scrupulously details the arrangements for the morris dance in *The Two Noble Kinsmen*.

This fresh focus on details of implied stage action extends beyond the Oxford edition and beyond editing. Alan Dessen identifies the set of implied stage directions coded into Shakespeare's text whenever it calls for characters to enter *"from dinner"* (napkined, brushing real or imaginary crumbs from their clothes) or for women to signal that they are either *"mad"* or have been *"ravished"* (disheveled clothes and loose hair). Ann Pasternak Slater explains how *Shakespeare the Director* prescribes the movement of his actors: shaking hands, kissing, embracing, kneeling, weeping. G. K. Hunter analyzes Shakespeare's use of "diagrammatic movement" and stresses that costuming ubiquitously defines social status. John Doebler shows that the staging of the wrestling match in *As You Like It* iconographically associates Orlando with Hercules, and Huston Diehl publishes "an alphabetical compilation of every icon in every English emblem book" printed in the Renaissance. David Bevington, declaring that *Action Is Eloquence*, describes *Shakespeare's Language of Gesture*. In the late seventeenth century Rymer had been appalled by the way any actor playing Othello "rolls his eyes and gnaws his nether lip as he prepares to kill Desdemona"; for Bevington these gestures are merely "the kind of stage action that an Elizabethan audience would recognize as a conventional sign of furious distress."

A book like Bevington's reflects the new deference toward the theatre among Shakespearian scholars; but it also belongs to a larger intellectual climate manifest in events like the Toronto interdisciplinary conference on "The Language of Gesture in the Renaissance." We have become conscious of the way people communicate without words. "Body language" enters the popular lexicon in 1970, riding the title of an international best-seller; it now authenticates the babble of every talk show host and advice columnist in North America. According to political mythology, Richard Nixon lost the 1960 presidential election because he looked unshaven and haggard during a television debate; Margaret Thatcher, likewise, wins the 1979 general election after the advertising firm of Saatchi and Saatchi gives her voice lessons and a new hairdo.

Indeed, television itself, the dominant communications medium of the postwar world, continually subordinates verbal to visual signals. Even within print media, photography becomes increasingly prominent, first in magazines, then newspapers. The study of film inexorably infiltrates the curriculum of university literature departments. The 1986 volume of *Shakespeare Survey* devotes itself to "Shakespeare on Film and Television." And the finest Shakespeare films of our time – Russian director Grigori Kozintsev's *Hamlet* and *King Lear*, Japanese director Akira Kurosawa's *Throne of Blood* (based on *Macbeth*) and *Ran* (based on *King Lear*) – do not even have English sound tracks.

In such a society, semiotics, the science of signs, naturally triumphs over literary criticism. Criticism analyzes language; but language is – as we now cannot help but realize – just one set of signs. Semiotics does not confine itself to language but studies any and all signs – aural, visual, physical. Drama makes use of more semiotic systems than, say, fiction; Renaissance drama is the site of a particularly complex and influential conjunction of literary and theatrical codes. Critics now devote whole books to Shakespeare's textual silences, the points where he made performers convey pivotal choices without words or by the gestures and inflections that may accompany ambiguous words.

In its intensified attention to stage directions the new Oxford Shakespeare is a semiotician's edition, the product of a self-consciously semiotic culture. The edition does not confine its ministrations to the words Shakespeare wrote; it attends, systematically, characteristically, to all the signals conveyed by spelling, punctuation, stage directions, lineation, typography, act and scene division, line numbering. In all of these areas it alters received practice. A new sign, a crippled bracket (⌐), alerts readers to speculative stage directions; another new sign, a geometrical rose (✿), stands for an interval between acts. Even if the Oxford edition had not changed a single word of dialogue, its changes to so many other signify-ing systems would still produce what one reviewer calls "perpetual slight surprise." (That is, of course, exactly the effect achieved by a typical RSC production.)

In its emphasis upon the theatre the 1986 edition reflects the world view of its editors and their peer group. But the editors are only one part of the work force that produces this latest repackaging of Shakespeare's texts. The shape and influence of the first eighteenth-century edition was deter-mined as much by the publisher (Jacob Tonson) as by the editor (Nicholas Rowe); what was true in 1709 remains true in 1986. In fact, by 1986 an individual editor's role has, if anything, diminished. In the eighteenth century editions were identified with the name of a prominent man of letters (Rowe, Pope, Johnson); by the late twentieth, editors' names matter less than a corporate trademark. Most people now buy the Penguin or Bantam or Signet or Swan Shakespeare without knowing anything about their apparently interchangeable editors. Most purchasers of the 1986 edition could not name its general editors; they are simply buying a text published and accredited by Oxford University Press.

OUP, like the RSC, is a large nonprofit corporation based in Britain but operating internationally, with branch offices in seventeen countries. Thanks to its charitable status it pays neither taxes nor dividends; as a department of the University of Oxford it is not vulnerable to hostile corporate takeover. Its favored institutional status makes it, like the RSC, an unusually stable medium of cultural production.

Like the RSC and the Berliner Ensemble, OUP owes much of its success to its authority as the most reputable purveyor of a core product. Until the twentieth century it was sustained by its half of the legal monopoly on printings of the Authorized Version of the English Bible. But religion declines, while literacy rises; sales of the Bible decrease, sales of diction-aries increase, and the *Oxford English Dictionary* becomes the unbeatable flagship of a fleet of profitable dictionaries of every description. This gunboat authority over English usage, when combined with the com-pany's network of international bases, decisively strengthens OUP's share in another major global market, the trade in textbooks for teaching English as a second language. These profitable core products supply the capital that finances an unrivaled variety and quality of academic mono-graphs. In this way OUP becomes, in the second half of the twentieth century, the world's most important academic publisher.

Shakespeare, like God and the English language, is a valuable commer-cial property on the international culture market. OUP's new Shakespeare is marketed in every available format, in order to reach every conceivable user. Victorian readers could buy the same text either in the expensive Cambridge edition (for specialists) or the cheap Globe edition (for lay-men); but in our time the fission of the reading public demands a much greater variety of packaging. Oxford publishes its edition in two versions, one in old spelling, the other in modern spelling. The latter will be followed, within a year, by a boxed three-volume set of comedies, histories, and tragedies, intended primarily for book clubs; then will come a cheap compact text for those with small book shelves and pocketbooks, as well as other editions in a variety of formats and price ranges – including one on computer-readable floppy disk.

The financial stability of OUP and the predictable profitability of its new multibodied Shakespeare edition make possible its investment in research and development. By 1986 the Oxford Shakespeare project is employing four full-time scholars, two full-time production assistants, and half a dozen part-time proofreaders, keyboarders, and copy editors. The project consumes uncounted machine hours on the company's own mainframe computer, and draws on two other mainframes in Oxford and Munich. By comparison with the overheads of contemporary scientific or industrial research, this commitment may seem paltry; but within the insect world of literary scholarship it is colossal. Like the pharmaceutical industry, or IBM, OUP depends upon the security of its international markets to finance development of a new product.

What has long been true of scientists is becoming true of scholars and critics: we are not romantic individualists, harvesting the vineyards of solitude; we depend on hierarchic, subsidized, bureaucratized, corporate, global institutions (publishers, universities, research institutes, grant-giving agencies and foundations). We submit to the power of such institutions because their resources enable kinds of research that would otherwise be impossible.

Thus, as a consequence of OUP's investment, the text of Shakespeare that emerges from Oxford in 1986 is – as even its detractors concede – the most thoroughly researched edition of Shakespeare ever published. As such it naturally invites comparison with the Cambridge edition of 1863–66. But the old Cambridge edition had been an epic achievement of consensus and consolidation; the new Oxford edition is instead, as Stanley Wells insists, "a work of deconstruction, an attempt to see Shakespeare afresh, to cut through the accretions of the centuries." The edition is, like an RSC production, self-consciously new; it is also, like an RSC production, self-consciously transient. Wells already anticipates the day when his own edition will be "relegated to library basements," having laid down "one thin layer in the coral reef" of editorial history. (The individual dies; the corporation is eternal.)

Alongside this recognition of the transience of scholarship lies a consciousness of the mutability of language itself "One of the first tasks" Wells sets himself as general editor is "a study of the principles of modernization." He recognizes that the subject may seem trivial, even to an audience of academics. However difficult and important it might be to determine which words Shakespeare wrote, deciding how to spell them is "merely" – as another scholar has offhandedly and dismissively remarked – "a secretarial task." And indeed, although editions of Shakespeare have been modernizing his spelling for almost four centuries, the task has until now largely been left to an underclass of compositors, copy editors, secretaries, the functionaries of standardized discourse. An almost universal practice "has been attended by surprisingly little discussion" of how it should be done.

Suddenly, however, spelling has become the subject of surprisingly much discussion. In 1974 the *Riverside Shakespeare*, the most widely respected American edition, conspicuously departs from past practice by preserving "a selection of Elizabethan spelling forms that reflect, or may reflect, a distinctive contemporary pronunciation"; this policy leads to the retention of such forms as "Dolphin" (Dauphin), "fadom" (fathom), "vild" (vile), and hundreds of comparable orthographic antiques. In 1978, at a Canadian conference on editing, Randall McLeod precipitates an intellectual crisis by objecting to the way old-spelling editions standardize or modernize typographical details of the original documents; in Renaissance English, he argues, typography often determines orthography. In 1984 A. L. Rowse, a Fellow of All Souls College, Oxford, issues the first volumes of "The Contemporary Shakespeare," a series that promises to "translate" not only archaic spellings but also all obsolete and archaic words and aberrant grammatical forms.

Oxford's 1986 edition does not accept any of these models. In the first place, Oxford publishes a critical old-spelling text of the complete works alongside its modern-spelling rendition of the same "text," a juxtaposition that reveals how thoroughly modernization transforms the text. This is not simply a matter of the metamorphosis of individual meanings; it shapes the entire experience of reading. Moving from seventeenth to twentieth century spellings of Shakespeare's sonnets, Thomas M. Greene senses the degree to which modernizing systematically conceals "the different status of the word itself in a prelexicographical culture," shielding readers from "the problematic contingencies of the original," stripping away "the seclusion and the particularity of its unique inflection."

Oxford's old-spelling edition radically historicizes, in a typically postmodernist way, Shakespeare's texts; but by also publishing a modern-spelling version Oxford emphasizes, in an equally postmodernist way, the irreducible arbitrariness of text. And to many readers Oxford's modern-spelling version looks, in many of its details, as unfamiliar as its old-spelling fraternal twin. Wells, like his contemporaries, makes modernizing an urgent editorial issue. He also, like his contemporaries, abandons past practice, and his new principles transform the spelling of hundreds of words: "Ancient" Pistol becomes "Ensign" Pistol, the Forest of "Arden" becomes the Forest of "Ardenne."

Rowse professes to "translate" Shakespeare's English into contemporary equivalents, and the problems of modernizing resemble those of translation. Translating, like modernizing, is now increasingly subjected to scholarly attention. In 1974 Toshikazu Oyama founds a new journal wholly devoted to *Shakespeare Translation* worldwide. There are, for instance, some twenty different Polish verse translations of *Hamlet*, representing most periods and styles of two centuries of Polish literature; Szekspirze does not, for Polish readers or playgoers, belong to any fixed sedimentary layer of the language. When East Berlin's Deutsches Theater retrieves a clumsy 1775 translation of *A Midsummer Night's Dream*, it does so in order to alienate audiences and strip the play of its traditional lyricism. None of six East German productions of *Twelfth Night* in 1985–86 use the classic Schlegel-Tieck translation of the play, dating from the early nineteenth century; all prefer contemporary versions. A new version is no less or more authoritative than the old; both, after all, are just translations. Consequently, for foreigners Shakespeare can always speak in the present tense.

Native speakers of English are not so lucky. For them Shakespeare, even in a modern-spelling edition, remains half-fixed in a language four hundred years old, like a fly wriggling to free itself from a drop of drying paint. The fact that " 'tis" has now become archaic in English, while "it's" has become commonplace, does not affect Boris Pasternak, trying to render Shakespeare into modern Russian; but it inevitably affects every modern English reader. The commentary to any English-language edition of Shakespeare awards a disproportionate share of its attention to obsolete words, not because they were especially significant or conspicuous to the original author or audience, but simply because a modern reader needs to be told what they mean. Elizabethan English is retrospectively divided into two classes: those words which readers still understand correctly, and those which they understand not at all or in the wrong sense. The Elizabethans themselves would not have recognized this distinction. We cannot avoid it.

A modern editor, therefore, must constantly engage in one form of translation or another. Either the word is left incomprehensibly intact in the text and translated in the commentary; or the text itself is translated, either by modernizing its spelling or by substituting some other word. The *Riverside* policy reminds readers of the strangeness of Shakespeare's English by throwing nuggets of exotic orthography in their way; the Oxford policy assures readers of the familiarity of Shakespeare's English by removing the anachronistic obstacles of an alien orthography whenever possible. The difference between these policies reproduces, in miniature, the difference between old-spelling and modern-spelling editions, which has tormented Shakespeare's editors since the beginning of the twentieth century. Both strategies attempt, impossibly, to recover for a modern reader the experience of readers four centuries ago. [...]

3 Susan Bennett, 'New Ways to Play Old Texts. Discourses of the Past'

Source: *Performing Nostalgia. Shifting Shakespeare and the Contemporary Past* (London: Routledge, 1996), pp. 12–13, 17–21, 25–6, 28–35, 37.

In her study of Shakespeare in performance in the 1980s and 1990s, Susan Bennett asks whether 'there are, in fact, new ways to play old texts'. Considering among others Robert Lepage's 1992 production of *Midsummer Night's Dream* and Ariane Mnouchkine's 1981 version of *Richard II*, Bennett sees the appeal of endlessly restaging Shakespeare plays as symptomatic of a wider 'contemporary obsession with staging old texts to explore...the present itself'. Bennett attends to the impact of recent scholarship on productions of Shakespeare's plays, and also summarizes the disagreements over attempts to restore an authentic Shakespeare theatre experience through projects like the rebuilding of the Globe theatre. Given Shakespeare's capacity to be 'enlisted in the regressive discourses of the New Right', Bennett is particularly concerned to establish whether productions of Shakespeare's plays still retain an 'emancipatory potential'. At times, Bennett's own voice fades somewhat as she quotes at substantial length the views of her critical peers, but the questions she herself poses for theatre practitioners and critics about the staging of Shakespeare remain urgent and ongoing.

[...] There is at this conjuncture the dilemma around whether there are, in fact, new ways to play old texts. Theatre is, anyway, generally and rightly regarded as a conservative art form, and the devotion to Shakespeare a manifestation of that inherent conservatism. Yet the plethora of 'vandalized' Shakespeares suggest that their producers, at least, fantasize the possibility of the new. By performing (including writing) a text which in some or other way makes reference to an already existing (thereby value-laden) text, the production and reception of the 'new' text necessarily become bound to the tradition that encompasses and promotes the old. In short, is containment an inevitable effect of re-articulating the past? Or can a new text, by way of dislocating and contradicting the authority of tradition, produce a 'transgressive knowledge' which would disarticulate the terms under which tradition gains its authority? And what bodies have the capacity to re-member that which is already sedimented in them? To attest to the contingent and fractured performance of 'tradition,' there is a need to locate a canon of the 'past' and to position against it those texts apparently claiming for themselves the possibility of the 'new.' Or are we, to cite [Graham] Holderness's question, content to dismiss the millions who patronize 'the heritage' as helplessly manipulated subjects of the culture industry, one-dimensional replicants tastelessly consuming the commodified products of a reified society, to be redeemed from cultural degeneracy only by the critical potency of high culture?

It seems less than sensible to dismiss the complex interactions between the multiplicity of performances marketed at an equally diverse demography of consumption. And, equally, the nostalgic performance of the past requires much more than a cultural dupe to produce its conservative effects. [...]

The past [...] operates by way of a shifting vector of nostalgia, memory, and tradition. The cumulative effect of its historical narratives is recognized as cultural heritage. But this still almost underestimates the intensity with which the past continues to speak. In his important study *Culture and Imperialism*, Edward Said reminds us that '[m]ore important than the past itself... is its bearing upon cultural attitudes in the present'. The rest of this chapter is concerned with particular manifestations of such a bearing: how in the contemporary moment the past prevails upon both performance and criticism. After all, heritage, even if it materializes in an apparently monolithic form (such as 'Shakespeare'), 'can be inflected in a variety of different political directions'.

OPENING ON STAGE

[...] During the summer of 1992 a 'hot' theatre ticket in London was the Royal National Theatre's production of *A Midsummer Night's Dream*. This Shakespeare play was directed for the RNT by Québécois writer / composer / director / designer / actor / collaborator Robert Lepage. The British press, however, were almost uniformly caustic in their responses:

> Alas for high hopes! I ended my review of Robert Lepage's *The Dragons' Trilogy* by saying one looked forward to seeing what this French-Canadian illusionist would make of *A Midsummer Night's Dream* at the Olivier. The result turns out to be the most perverse, leaden, humourless and vilely spoken production of this magical play I have ever seen.
> (Michael Billington in the *Guardian*)

> My timing was always a little off.
> When the show-off Canadian Robert Lepage was engaged by the National Theatre to direct *A Midsummer Night's Dream*, I thought of fleeing the country. But I got my dates mixed and was back in London for this event.
> (Kenneth Hurren in the *Mail on Sunday*)

> Robert Lepage's leadenly paced, unfunny *Midsummer Night's Dream*...just opened in the Olivier.

> It's a show that will appeal principally to mud-wrestling fanatics or to chronic sufferers from *nostalgie de la boue*.
>
> (Paul Taylor in the *Independent*)

In Canada's *Globe and Mail*, however, Lepage's production is heralded as 'one that looks to be as much a touchstone for the 1990s as Peter Brook's legendary 1970 Royal Shakespeare Company staging with trapezes and acrobats was for its time'. On the one hand, it is not surprising to find Canada's national newspaper running a review which champions the success of one of the country's prodigies, especially when he is contextualized as export to the former colonizer. On the other, this more enthusiastic review marks the apparent difference between actual ticket-buying audiences and the very specific viewing public of London media critics who apparently have altogether different criteria for doing Shakespeare 'properly.'

Peter Brook's radical and innovatory productions of Shakespeare's texts were also in the summer of 1992 still very much in the spotlight. As the *Globe and Mail* review reminds us, it is now more than twenty years since Brook's *Dream* brought in a new, more physical performance style for Shakespeare (and theatre, in general) to the mainstream stage and, in the intervening period, Brook has emerged as one of the mostly highly regarded voices on both Shakespeare and theatre. At the First Drama and Education World Congress in Portugal (Porto, 20–25 July 1992), the French delegation's contribution to scholarly exchange involved a screening of video documentation of Peter Brook discussing his adaptation and direction of Shakespearean plays. He presented his ideas in French. In this instance, it seems, both Shakespeare and Brook-on-Shakespeare have been appropriated as French cultural export, a striking example of Shakespeare's impressive international currency. [...]

In any case, each of these contemporary versions of the past is in some way an event of the year and each in some way relies completely on a collective sense of the authority of that past to which their subject texts belong and which their reproductions transgress. This is not to say that any or all of these reproductions rely on an uncomplicated or naive sense of tradition. [...] Robert Lepage – in Québec and Canada at least – has attracted wildly enthusiastic media and popular attention for his part in Théâtre Repère's collaborative and visionary creations.

Perhaps itself a kind of dissident or deviant nostalgia, Lepage's process for this Royal National Theatre production of *A Midsummer Night's Dream* marks an attempt to disavow the fetish of Shakespeare's text. Lepage only introduced the text 'at the end' of the rehearsal period. First workshopped in December for an August opening, the company 'worked with people's dreams, and recurrences and drawings, so people had the impression they were playing; they were actually having fun. At the end, we read *A*

Midsummer Night's Dream' (Lepage). The British press showed a little wariness, if not hostility, to a tampering with the Bard at the hands of someone from the 'colonies' (and French-speaking Québec at that). [. . .]

What all these reworkings of the classical texts of theatrical tradition illustrate is a contemporary obsession with staging old texts to explore the possibilities of performance in the present, to explore the present itself. They belong to what Roger Bromley has called a 'genre of remembering'. They rely on willing audiences who recognize and are nostalgic for the classical text but who are attracted to the event for its innovation with and renovation of that text. That events such as Lepage's *Midsummer Night's Dream* [. . .] and Brook's analysis of his own Shakespearean interventions are seen to represent the cutting edge of high art performance in the early 1990s – and this assertion is given some weight by the quantity of attention given to Brook, Lepage [and] in the popular and scholarly presses – further suggests the fetishization of the old text as a new one. Under what conditions is the past re-presented for spectators in both global and local viewing economies? And what do we make of that past when we 'see' it?

Fredric Jameson has suggested that 'at the very moment in which we complain of the eclipse of historicity, we also universally diagnose contemporary culture as irredeemably historicist, in the bad sense of an omnipresent and indiscriminate appetite for dead styles and fashions, indeed for all the styles and fashions of a dead past' and performance is, of course, a particularly conspicuous site for such obsessions with 'a dead past.' What binds the material discussed in this book is the past, a reference point (apparently available to both readers and viewers) which enables the reception of a contemporary performance to be undertaken through recognition (if not always knowledge) of a particular historical antecedent. It would be possible, I realize, to choose almost any moment or moments from the historical past, from the very recent to the most distant, and to locate performance texts which recreate those histories in and for the present. But the performances which attach to the signifier Shakespeare add up to the most intensive and most obvious reuse of the past since Shakespeare's plays form, as Terence Hawkes has recently stated, one of the central agencies through which culture generates meaning: 'That is what they do, that is how they work, and that is what they are for. Shakespeare doesn't mean: *we* mean *by* Shakespeare'. Or more wittily (or more insolently) put, Shakespeare stands as 'the ultimate Dead White Male: the pinnacle of an oppressive, canonical hierarchy and an ally of conservative elitism, patriarchal sovereignty, and colonial imperialism' (advertisement for 'Multicultural Shakespeare,' the 1992 theme for the Annual Shakespeare Institute at the City University of New York). Such a designation signals his function at both ends of a continuum of quotation: he can be both the 'seamless cloak of univocal authoritativeness for citers to hide behind' and the claim for attention to representation 'as garment...[which] invites judgement of its cut'. [...]

Lepage's *A Midsummer's Night's Dream* [...] betokens the substantial demand for resuscitated remnants of the textual archive and these well-funded and well-attended spectacles illustrate, in performance terms, the arguments surrounding history that this chapter has already noted. They can also function as signs of contemporary social organization: 'Our society has become a recited society, in three senses: it is defined by *stories*..., by *citations* of stories, and by the interminable *recitation* of stories' (de Certeau – emphasis in original). Yet interminable (and, it might be argued, often dissonant) recitations can produce effects that escape the discipline implied in the recitation. If 'we' are bound to cite and recite, then 'we' might well explore this as a generative practice. In the context of Shakespeare, aside from recitation as performance, there is, of course, the parallel and equally intense industry of recitation produced in the form of scholarship.

If it is now something of a commonplace to argue that the Humanities are 'in crisis' [...], one of the symptoms of that crisis is recognized in the proliferation of academic discourses, in the range of readings now claiming currency in the classroom and elsewhere. And within that most proliferative discipline in the Humanities, literary criticism, nowhere is the expansion more evident – or more contested – than in the field of Shakespeare studies.

[...] [I]n the decade or so since 1980, the practice of academic criticism on Shakespeare and other Renaissance playwrights has irrevocably changed. If this assertion – or Kamps's – needs any elaboration at all, a cursory glance at the Folger Shakespeare Library journal *Shakespeare Quarterly* tells all. In the 1980 volume, articles published include 'The Structure of *King Lear*,' 'Shakespeare's *The Tempest*: The Wise Man as Hero,' 'Logic versus the Slovenly World in Shakespearean Comedy' and 'Thematic Contraries and the Dramaturgy of *Henry V*.' More recently (Fall 1991), the journal carries the following: ' "Knock me here soundly": Comic Misprision and Class Consciousness in Shakespeare,' ' "Documents in Madness": Reading Madness and Gender in Shakespeare's Tragedies and Early Modern Culture' and 'Where are the Mothers in Shakespeare? Options for Gender Representation in the English Renaissance.' These later titles reveal the interests of Cultural Materialist, feminist, and New Historicist criticism, which, if only emergent in 1980, dominated Shakespeare studies in the early 1990s. [...]

And as this body of criticism has taken account of that performance (in the broadest sense – on the stage, but also its imbrication in social practices), the positionalities of gender, class, race, and sexuality have re-entered the arena in ways that traditional humanist interpretation and collective nostalgia would seek to inhibit. Part of this energy concerns itself with Elizabethan dramatic practice, but another part insists on attending to those dramatic practices which vitalize contemporary stages.

Once again, there is a determined attention paid to the British theatre (as in the case of Alan Sinfield's 'Royal Shakespeare: theatre and the making of ideology', a useful reminder of Shakespeare's ongoing currency as an agent of royal power), but other national examples abound and almost always indicate the thoroughness of imperial 'education.' Martin Orkin, for instance, draws attention to this particular function:

> In South Africa, as often elsewhere in colonial and postcolonial worlds, Shakespeare has been primarily appropriated by most amongst the English-speaking educated members of the ruling classes as a means of evidencing their affiliations with the imperial and colonial centres. Possession and knowledge of Shakespeare texts becomes evidence of empowerment.... Shakespeare has...become for members of the educated ruling classes one signifier of 'civilisation', astoundingly that is, it should never be forgotten, in South Africa one signifier for white apartheid 'civilisation'. The web of such a use of Shakespeare spins not only through institutions of education, the media, establishment theatre, public cultural bodies, but even into the thinking of some of the country's large conglomerates of capital.

In such a 'web,' an understanding of the performance conditions (on the stage, in the classroom) emerges as the contested territory in which contemporary experiences and manifestations of power can be tested and consolidated:

> Shakespeare after all is construed within this [New Right] cultural milieu as a privileged embodiment of Western values and as a fundamental element in the substantive curriculum of Western Culture. On this view, correct interpretation of the plays is a matter of national interest.

For the 'radical' team, there has to be some cultural purchase in deconstructing the mechanisms for and of power that are both produced by and with this particular body of texts. [Jonathan] Dollimore concludes his own assessment of 'Shakespeare, cultural materialism and the new historicism' with:

> the need to disclose the effectiveness and complexity of the ideological process of containment.... [T]he very desire to disclose that process is itself oppositional and motivated by the knowledge that, formidable though it be, it is a process which is historically contingent and partial.

Others, like [Michael] Bristol, take a more equivocal stance:

317

> [I]nstitutions are actually peopled by social agents who themselves may
> have agendas that differ substantially from those initially mandated. The
> release of those potentialities would presumably be the over-arching inter-
> est of a critically motivated research program. Those interests cannot, how-
> ever, be actualized by a novel re-staging of the counter-normative script, nor
> simply by saying forbidden things about Shakespeare.

This, of course, has not stopped a great many academics and theatre
practitioners from attempting to do just that. [...]
   Two particular subcategories of this genre of criticism are of especial
interest. One is the recycling of Shakespeare to examine notions of history;
the other is the movement of Shakespearean criticism into the field of
cultural studies. In thinking about history, I want first to consider an
example in performance, Ariane Mnouchkine's version of *Richard II*
(1981), described by Dennis Kennedy as orientalist Shakespeare, which
'achieved its success through enormous cultural dislocation'. Mnouchkine ironically chose to work on Shakespeare because of his timelessness,
because his plays represented a kind of neutral textual landscape. Kennedy rightly marks the dangers of an intercultural theatrical methodology
which detaches texts from their originating enunciative terms and conditions.

> Certainly Mnouchkine managed to estrange Shakespeare for her audiences,
> to point out the wondrous otherness of the fables. There was no danger that
> a comfortable Anglocentricity would overtake the responses to these pro-
> ductions. Nonetheless, her insistent imposition of superbly foreign modes
> on the history plays tended to detach them from *any* political and historical
> meanings, Elizabethan or contemporary. *Richard II* was a dangerously poli-
> tical play in Shakespeare's time because it acts out the deposition of a king,
> an action not many monarchs like to see represented on the public stage....
> But Mnouchkine was concerned with style and substituted a powerful
> aesthetic experience for a social one.

What her production of *Richard II* in an aesthetic frame of South Asian
theatrical traditions effected, I'd suggest, is the impossibility of a responsible intercultural performance when any grammar of expression is
divorced from its historical impetus. But even an objective of aesthetic
seduction speaks of History. It speaks of a veiled set of circumstances
which give voice and movement, and which make both visible/audible.
Kennedy's characterization of audience response to *Richard II* makes this
palpable: 'Some spectators...noted with melancholy the losses in the
right's and intellectual dimensions'. If Mnouchkine insisted on an ahistor-
ical history play, then the conference organized by the British section of
the International Association of Theatre Critics to test Jan Kott's thesis,
Shakespeare Our Contemporary, some twenty-five years after its publication

in 1961, provided different anchors for historical perspective. While Kott himself rails against a trend to locate Shakespeare 'in no time and in no particular place', Michael Bogdanov picks up the discussion, contending:

> when I walk into a rehearsal with my group in *Henry IV* and *Henry V*, I look for the way in which the political circumstances were handled then, and find inspirational parallels in what is happening now. We governed disgustingly in the fourteenth century and we are still governing disgustingly today.

Bogdanov asserts, conservatively, an insistence on the continuity of H/ history, at the same time as he marks that process of conservation with its repressed texts.

Thus Bogdanov's insistence that Shakespeare is still, and must be, 'our contemporary' relies on a careful and thorough reading of the history that is staged in the source text. It is, for him, the relation between different representations of historical circumstances which inspires and produces theatre. Graham Holderness's project in *Shakespeare Recycled* is to identify the primary historiographical nature of Shakespeare's history plays, a task he develops both through readings of the individual plays and of the methodological questions which surround such readings. Furthermore, Holderness (*pace* Anne Barton) draws attention to the very flexibility of the genre of history play, accommodating as it does popular, romantic modes with historiographic inquiry. The history play enables 'varied and possibly antagonistic ideologies to interact'. Unlike History, the history play can perform the discourses of the past as fantasies, posing characters and events in the realm of 'what if?' This is clearly a productive site for the articulation of the past in/as the present, and Holderness's investigations on theatrical productions of Shakespeare's history plays 'distinguish clearly and sharply between reactionary and progressive reproduction; and between productions designed to preserve intact the Tudor ideology of national unity, and productions which revive the historical conditions of Shakespeare's theatre to make staging history a radical cultural intervention'. The practice of 'complex montage' which Holderness articulates for Shakespeare's history texts offers a usable framework for the production of historical materials (and not just Shakespeare) which will take account of the diversities of demographies and geographies. It is a framework which will stage the complexities of social formations, and not simply line them up for their place on the continuum recognized as History. This marks a need to be better able in whatever disparate and diverse communities to engage with a globally disseminated cultural product and to recognize those moments where a viewing economy might be fragmented in its response. [...]

In yet another sortie into revisions of Shakespeare, Holderness locates the power of heritage (or tradition) in the (re)emergence of reconstructions in London of the Globe and Rose Theatres. Resonant with theories already outlined here on the economically driven fetishization of the past, he outlines the motivations of the Globe Theatre reconstruction project, noting that initial difficulties with land-use permits were resolved by an appeal to historical continuity: the site selected for the construction of the replica is located close by the now partially excavated remains of the 'authentic' predecessor. But the replica Globe, even if it is to be built using authentic materials and methods, is precisely that: a replica, a souvenir of some other age and experience. And there is, as Susan Stewart determines, 'no continuous identity between these objects and their referents'. She adds:

> Restoration can be seen as a response to an unsatisfactory set of present conditions. Just as the restoration of buildings ... has as its basis the restoration of class relationships that might otherwise be in flux, so the restoration of the souvenir is a conservative idealization of the past and the distanced for the purposes of a present ideology.

Lying somewhere between a restored building (restoration of a phantom past) and a souvenir (reconstruction of a myth), the Globe Theatre project, despite its own best aims, marks the discontinuities of history. It gives performance to what we do not know, yet are obliged to invent, so as to anchor ourselves in the turbulent experience of the present. These are, perhaps, some of the most compelling performances of nostalgia.

The uncovering and subsequent battle for the protection of the remains of the Rose Theatre surface as an interesting counterpart to the project of the Globe. The Save the Rose Campaign was instituted to permit a full excavation of the site and to halt a planned office development there. Holderness offers this observation: 'The Globe and the Rose were constituted within this discourse into a series of classic binary oppositions: centre and margin, high and low priority, senior and junior partner, Shakespearean and not-really-Shakespearean, mature Shakespearean and early Shakespearean, even male and female.' What this illustrates is a determined advantage for heritage/tradition over history; of marketability over scholarship, but it also denotes the inability of both sites to recreate the past for, after all, '[t]he nostalgic is enamored of distance, not of the referent itself. Nostalgia cannot be sustained without loss'. If it were really possible to experience the original conditions of those theatres in which Shakespeare's plays were performed, it would effectively eradicate 'the desire that is nostalgia's reason for existence'. But desiring subjects we are bound to be and the parameters of such desire can be disclosed in contemporary cultural criticism engaged with the shifting citation of Shakespeare. [...]

Whether in Britain or America or elsewhere, Shakespeare, simply put, has a normative value. [...] His availability to be enlisted in the regressive discourses of the New Right is without question. What is trickier to establish is the 'considerable emancipatory potential' of that same availability which Bristol identifies. [...]

INDEX